Hotel
Investments

Issues & Perspectives

00668TXT04ENGE
PP-2286

Educational Institute Books

Hotel Investments

Issues & Perspectives

Fourth Edition

Edited by
Lori E. Raleigh, ISHC
Rachel J. Roginsky, ISHC

AMERICAN HOTEL & LODGING
EDUCATIONAL INSTITUTE

Disclaimer

This publication is designed to provide accurate and authoritative information in regard to the subject matter covered. It is sold with the understanding that the publisher is not engaged in rendering legal, accounting, or other professional service. If legal advice or other expert assistance is required, the services of a competent professional person should be sought.

— From the Declaration of Principles jointly adopted by the American Bar Association and a Committee of Publishers and Associations

The author or authors of each chapter are solely responsible for the contents of this publication. All views expressed herein are solely those of the authors and do not necessarily reflect the views of the American Hotel & Lodging Educational Institute (AHLEI) or the American Hotel & Lodging Association (AH&LA).

Nothing contained in this publication shall constitute a standard, an endorsement, or a recommendation of AHLEI or AH&LA. AHLEI and AH&LA disclaim any liability with respect to the use of any information, procedure, or product, or reliance thereon by any member of the hospitality industry.

ISBN 978-0-86612-281-8

Contents

Paul Beals, Ph.D., Visiting Professor, IMHI-ESSEC Business School (France), and
John V. Arabia, CPA, Principal, Green Street Advisors

Chad Crandell, ISHC, Co-Founder and President, Capital Hotel Management, and
Kristie Dickinson, Vice President of Portfolio Management, Capital Hotel Management

David J. Sangree, MAI, CPA, ISHC, President, Hotel & Leisure Advisors

Patty Monteson, ISHC, Co-Owner, Health Fitness Dynamics, Inc., and
Judy Singer, Ed.D, ISHC, Co-Owner, Health Fitness Dynamics, Inc.

Elaine M. McLaughlin, MPA, CDME, Instructor, Resort & Hospitality Management, Florida Gulf Coast University, and
John M. McCarthy, President, Liberty Hospitality Group

Acknowledgments

W<small>E EXTEND OUR UTMOST GRATITUDE</small> to all of the contributing authors. They have very generously contributed their time, talent, and special expertise—without remuneration—in support of this project and cause. Royalties from the book are being donated to a scholarship fund to support the advancement of education in the hospitality industry.

We also owe very special thanks to our families, friends, and colleagues, as well as to the staff at the Educational Institute, for their wonderful support of this project.

—Lori E. Raleigh
Rachel J. Roginsky

Preface

By *Jim Burba*

Jim Burba is President of Horwath Hospitality & Leisure, a leading hotel brokerage and advisory firm. Combined with its international network, Horwath is one of the world's largest hospitality practices, with more than 40 offices and 150 professionals dedicated to the hospitality industry. Burba has specialized in hospitality real estate investment since 1978, with experience that includes market and financial analysis, deal structuring, transactions, and finance. Before joining Horwath, he oversaw business development and the global consulting practice for Wimberly Allison Tong & Goo. Other prior positions include leading the business development, strategic planning, and research functions at Insignia/ESG Hotel Partners and serving as a principal at PKF International. He is also President of Burba Hotel Network (BHN). BHN organizes prominent hospitality investment conferences, including The Americas Lodging Investment Summit (ALIS), the International Hotel Investment Forum, Hotel Investment Conference Asia Pacific, and the annual Caribbean Hotel & Tourism Investment Conference. BHN was retained to assist FONATUR (Mexico's Fondo Nacional de Fomento al Turismo) in organizing Mexico's premier investment conference, Bolsa Mexicana Inversion Turistica 2005, which was held in Mexico City in September 2005.

He is a member of the International Society of Hospitality Consultants and the Industry Real Estate Financing Advisory Council (IREFAC) of the American Hotel & Lodging Association (AH&LA) and honors include the Educational Institute of AH&LA's Lamp of Knowledge Award and IREFAC's first Crystal Ball Award. Burba received his B.A. from The School of Hospitality Business at Michigan State University and his M.B.A. from UCLA. In 2005, he was appointed to the California Travel & Tourism Commission.

"The only unchangeable certainty is that nothing is certain or unchangeable."
—John F. Kennedy

IN MANY WAYS, THE BUSINESS of owning and operating hotels has not changed much in the last 30 or 40 years—the core product provides a friendly place for people to stay when they are traveling away from home for business or pleasure. Add to a hotel some food and beverage service and a gathering spot for social and business functions and it becomes the full-service hotel that populates city centers, suburbs, and resorts. It is a pretty straightforward business that has not changed much over the past several decades. Or is it?

As the industry has grown, matured, increasingly become branded, and increasingly become owned by large and often publicly traded companies, the need to sharpen competitive ownership and operating skills has increased. The successful product or operating style of the past usually is not good enough anymore. Customers and competitors are better informed and the status quo might not work.

Putting heads in beds has always been the name of the game, but our core business of providing a place to sleep is more competitive than ever. Today, we are in the midst of "bed wars" as millions of dollars are being invested in new beds. Beds have become brands of their own and can distinguish one hotel brand from another. Will this trend lead to better returns on investment for owners or is it just a permanent increase in costs?

Speaking of putting heads in beds, the Internet has fundamentally changed the relationship with customers, how they shop for lodging, and what they expect. It has emboldened customers to negotiate for better prices. Nobody expects the Internet to go away, so how can hoteliers adjust to this new reality? Who has gotten it right so far? How can a hotel's marketing effort optimize the tools provided by the Internet and e-commerce?

The skills required to operate the second largest department in a typical hotel—the food and beverage department—are numerous and profitability can vary widely between similar hotels situated next door to each other. Why the differences, and what should an owner do to optimize profits? Labor typically is the largest cost and its availability and costs are not expected to improve in the near future. How can hoteliers provide food and beverage at a level that makes economic sense, and what can be learned from the best practices of others? Does the recent trend toward outsourcing make sense?

Technology has changed the way we operate in the hotel business, from how our customers find us and what we know about them to their experiences within the guestroom. Not long ago, hotel owners were faced with agonizing decisions about retrofitting and hard-wiring hotel guestrooms for high-speed Internet access and then, before they knew it, along came wireless access. What technological innovations are next and how can hotels plan and pay for them?

The basics of marketing a hotel never change—or do they? Room pricing is under attack as the Internet has made it easy for the consumer to shop for a better deal. Pricing has become transparent and comparisons are instant, which is something quite new for hoteliers. How do hoteliers stay on the offensive in this new reality and keep from becoming a commoditized industry? Loyalty programs once thought to be a fad have become an expensive and critical part of the marketing and promotion process. Where is this trend headed?

As in any supply and demand–oriented sector, new competition emerges when the business is profitable. Hotels are no different. With the current resurgence in investment activity and the growth in new products and brands, how do we market and distinguish our existing hotels while competing with newer models?

A room with a bed still helps to define what a hotel is, but hotels increasingly are being developed as part of a mixed-use development scheme, especially at the higher quality levels. We have learned that a hotel brand can add significant value to the entire mixed-use development and hoteliers are learning how to share in these benefits. Of course, the mixed-use project has created new complexities for hoteliers with different owners, lenders, and users (office, retail, residential, and so forth) all under one roof. How has this changed the operation of the hotel? What have we learned and where is this trend headed?

Understanding the hotel ownership and operating challenges in the mixed-use development is even more complex with ownership nuances created by alternative lodging ownership structures—namely, timeshare, fractional-interest, private residence clubs, and condo hotels. While some of these ownership structures have been around in various forms for decades, many of the changes noted earlier—branding, larger companies, public companies, technology, smarter consumers, and so forth—have caused significant changes in the way these products are brought to market and operated. Best practices, to a large degree, are still evolving.

While many professionals enter the hotel ownership/investment arena with a strong pedigree in other forms of real estate, the business of hotel investment involves more than just bricks-and-mortar real estate. Hotels are also operating businesses. The operating complexities are what have driven greater returns when times are good and more modest returns when they are not. The business is more complex today than it has ever been, and while a bed is a bed and food is food, pretty much everything else related to successful ownership of a hotel continues to evolve.

Hotel Investments: Issues & Perspectives, Fourth Edition, has been designed to address many of the key factors in successful hotel investing and ownership today and is an invaluable tool for the hotel investment community. As the lodging industry has continued to mature, it has needed to change and adapt. Not every issue and future trend facing today's hotel owners can be addressed in a single textbook, and the challenges faced may have different solutions depending on the particular strengths and weaknesses of a hotel, its brand, and its management. Nonetheless, this book provides a great tool for new and existing hotel owners to get a better handle on the complex and diverse issues and opportunities in owning hotels in the twenty-first century.

Thank you to the authors, who all contributed time from their busy schedules to write the chapters and case studies in this book with no remuneration. The proceeds from the sale of this book assist the American Hotel & Lodging Educational Foundation (AH&LEF) in its continuing educational and research missions for the betterment of the industry. The authors' tremendous efforts and contributions are surpassed only by those of Lori Raleigh and Rachel Roginsky, who also wrote chapters, organized the whole team, and ensured that the project was completed with a focus and on time.

The book's release is timed to coincide with ALIS. It is through the efforts of Ms. Raleigh and Ms. Roginsky that we plan to highlight at ALIS many of the authors and their chapters or case studies in special university-like sessions. Bringing the authors' expertise directly to the hotel investment community in this way should help increase the savvy of hotel investors and assist those who have already invested in the business and those who are contemplating entry into this great and fascinating business we call the hotel industry.

Overview of the Lodging Industry

By *Randell A. Smith, ISHC*

Randell A. Smith is Chief Executive Officer and co-founder of Smith Travel Research (STR), the leading authority on current trends in occupancy, room rate, and supply/demand data for the U.S. and the North American lodging industries. Each month, STR obtains revenue data from more than 23,000 U.S. properties accounting for more than 3.2 million rooms. In addition, STR collects daily lodging performance data from more than 18,000 U.S. hotels with more than 2.3 million rooms as part of its **daySTAR** *program. Through* **daySTAR PLUS**, *STR tracks daily customer segmentation data for upscale properties in all major U.S. markets. Through its worldwide marketing alliance with Deloitte in the United Kingdom, STR provides a global perspective for all lodging trends. STR tracks market share performance for virtually every major global hotel chain and most major management companies through its various* **STAR** *programs. STR also publishes* **Lodging Review,** *a weekly newsletter endorsed by the American Hotel & Lodging Association that tracks occupancy and room rates for the United States, all 50 states, and the top 25 metropolitan markets. STR data is used as the official source of lodging information by more than 300 convention and visitors bureaus, state tourism departments, and government entities.*

Mr. Smith is a member and past co-chairman of the Industry Real Estate Financing Advisory Council (IREFAC) and the 2002 recipient of the prestigious IREFAC C. Everett Johnson Award. He is also vice-chair of the American Hotel Foundation Funding Committee. He is a charter member of the International Society of Hospitality Consultants and a former member of the board of directors. He is the recipient of the 1996 Industry Pioneer Award of the ISHC for outstanding contribution to the lodging industry. Mr. Smith is a regular keynote speaker at the major industry conferences. Prior to starting STR, Mr. Smith was Director of Research for Laventhol & Horwath and has over 25 years' experience in lodging industry research. He resides in Nashville, Tennessee, with his wife and son. Mr. Smith is an avid fisherman.

ON JUNE 1, 2005, Smith Travel Research (STR) celebrated its twentieth year of providing research to the lodging industry. We began with the creation of the Lodging Census Database, which contained detailed information about every lodging establishment in the United States. Using this database, we launched a monthly survey of industry performance in January 1987, which became known as the STAR report.

Any time a major benchmark like a twentieth anniversary is reached, it triggers reflection on the major turning points and highlights of the past two decades.

Exhibit 1   Percent Change in U.S. Room Supply and Demand: 12-Month Moving Average, 1989–May 2005

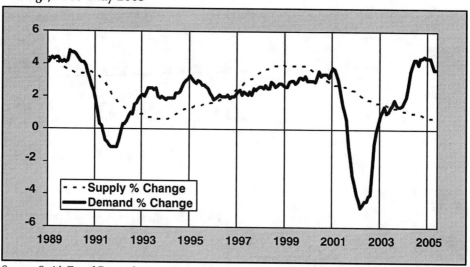

Source: Smith Travel Research.

As of Summer 2005, not only is virtually every indicator of industry performance positive, the industry is hitting record levels in a number of areas. The industry is at the sweet spot of the rebound that began during Summer 2004. Since the rebound is obvious to even the most casual observers, the focus of this chapter will not be on the short-term outlook for the industry, but on a review of the past two decades and an attempt to put current performance in the proper context.

The past 20 years have been a period of constant change with wide swings in performance caused by two recessions, wars, terrorist activity, a dot-com boom, and strong economic performance. The industry's erratic performance is illustrated in Exhibit 1, which shows the 12-month moving average of changes in room supply and room demand. Since 1989, supply growth initially slowed, then accelerated; over the past year, however, supply growth has declined to a remarkably low level. As of Summer 2005, room supply was growing at a very modest 0.6 percent over the previous 12 months. While room demand generally has grown during the past two decades, one can see in Exhibit 1 that demand is susceptible to economic recessions. During both recessions—from early 1991 to early 1993 and from early 2001 to late 2003—room demand actually declined from year-earlier levels.

Exhibit 2 illustrates that seasonally adjusted room demand has been growing at a fairly steady rate during this time period with the exception of the two recessionary periods. Room demand has grown in the long run by about two percent annually from January 1989 to April 2005, including the recessions. If you exclude the two recessions and focus on just the growth period from 1992 to March 2001, the compound annual growth rate was 2.7 percent. With room demand currently growing at a 3.7 percent rate, it is obvious the industry is rebounding sharply, but

Exhibit 2   U.S. Seasonally Adjusted Room Demand, January 1989–April 2005

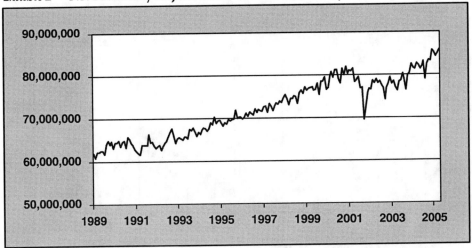

Source: Smith Travel Research.

Exhibit 3   U.S. Average Monthly Rooms Added, Closed, and Net, January 2001–March 2005

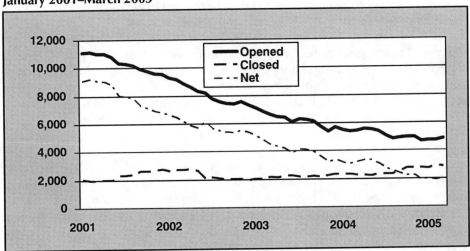

Source: Smith Travel Research.

at a historically unsustainable level. While this growth is likely to subside over the next 12 months, the industry does appear to be on the threshold of a sustained and solid rebound, particularly given the low supply growth rate.

As shown in Exhibit 3, there are several unusual issues related to the low supply growth as of mid-2005. The current cycle is unique because there are more rooms closing now than one reasonably would expect. The current unusual rate of

Exhibit 4   U.S. Percent Change in Occupancy and ADR: 12-Month Moving Average, January 1989–May 2005

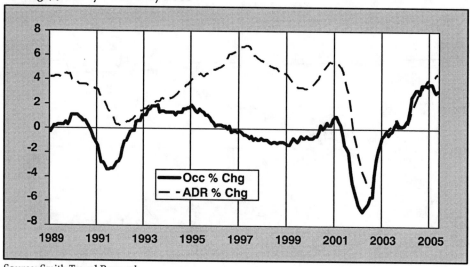

Source: Smith Travel Research.

closures has no historical precedent and can be traced to two factors. The first and more temporary factor is the large number of rooms closed in Florida because of the 2004 hurricanes. While this is significant, it also is likely that most of these rooms will open again in the foreseeable future. The second is the recent trend to convert hotels, particularly in metropolitan and resort destinations, to either condominiums or condominium hotels. This trend will result in a more permanent reduction in room supply. The net result of these factors is that the high number of room closings mitigates some of the effects of accelerating new room construction. This will result in stronger occupancies for a longer period of time than would be typical in this stage of the recovery.

This interaction of room supply and demand has caused occupancy and room rates to change in a fairly unpredictable manner. The 1991–1992 recession resulted in lower occupancy levels, but room rates never declined on a 12-month basis during this period, as illustrated in Exhibit 4. There were a few months in which room rates declined, but in general—and in spite of the downturn in occupancy—there was never any sustained drop in room rates. Coming out of that recession, both occupancy and room rates began increasing at fairly comparable levels. By mid-1993, however, room rate increases began to accelerate despite moderation in occupancy increases. This divergence of occupancy and room rate changes became particularly acute by 1997. At this time, room rates were increasing at a historically high rate of 6.8 percent, while occupancy was actually beginning to decline. This truly was a unique time when room demand and room rates were growing at record levels, but because of the strong growth in room supply, occupancy was declining and would continue to decline for the next four years.

Exhibit 5   Total U.S. Hotel Occupancy Percentage: 12-Month Moving Average, January 1989–May 2005

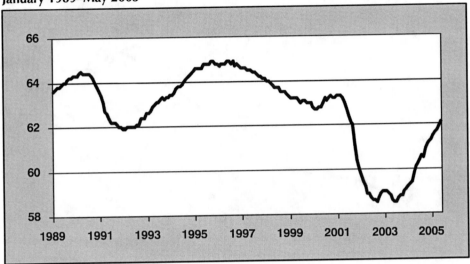

Source: Smith Travel Research.

The recession in 2001 and the impact of the September 11, 2001, terrorist attacks caused unprecedented changes for the industry. Occupancy declined as room demand fell and, for the first time in the modern lodging industry's history, room rates began to decline for an extended period. By mid-2003, however, both room rates and occupancy began to rebound at comparable levels and continued to do so until late 2004. As of mid-2005, it appears that occupancy and room rates are again diverging. With growth in room supply low but accelerating and growth in room demand high but decelerating, occupancy increases are likely to slow considerably from this point. However, there is no indication of an actual decrease in occupancy for the next two years. With demand remaining strong, it also is apparent that the industry is entering a very aggressive pricing environment.

Exhibits 5 and 6 illustrate the actual levels of occupancy and room rates during this time period. Occupancy peaked at 64.9 percent in September 1995 and May 1996, gradually declined to 63.3 percent in early 2001, and dropped rapidly during the recession to bottom out at 58.5 percent. With the current rebound, occupancy is back over 62 percent and, at the rate it is improving, should reach 20-year highs by the fall of 2006. On a long-term basis, room rates have increased about 2.9 percent annually, but with a 4.4 percent increase during the peak years. Room rates peaked at an industry-high average of $86.36 in June 2001 and, after a decline associated with the latest recession, are back to hitting record levels on nominal terms. One should be aware that after accounting for inflation during the last four years, real room rates are still below the previous record. With nominal rates currently increasing by nearly five percent annually, real rates should hit record levels within the next year.

Exhibit 6   Average Daily Rate for U.S. Hotels: 12-Month Moving Average, January 1989–May 2005

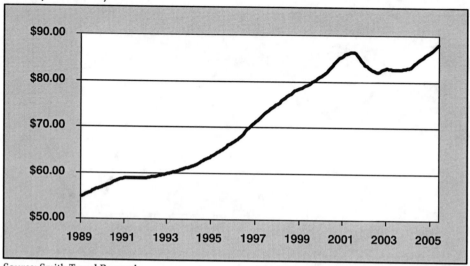

Source: Smith Travel Research.

All of these various changes culminate in the impact on revenue per available room (RevPAR). For the entire period from 1989 to February 2001, RevPAR grew by a fairly stable four to six percent with the brief exception of the 1991–1992 recession, as shown in Exhibit 7. With significant declines in both occupancy and room rates, RevPAR fell sharply during the last recession, dropping 10.2 percent from year-earlier levels by June 2002. With the current rebound underway, RevPAR increased by a very impressive 8.1 percent in February 2005, a record change in this key measure for the industry. RevPAR increases will continue to moderate from this point, but RevPAR should continue to increase at or slightly above the long-term trend for the next two years.

Historical trends for the industry as a whole are not always indicative of segment performance. In fact, virtually every segment and market within the industry has experienced similar but varying trends. It is useful to look at all of the various segments of the industry for a complete understanding of current trends. To highlight this issue, the following is a detailed analysis of trends in the location segments.

Analysis by Location Type

STR classifies hotels by a variety of parameters, including physical location. In 2005, STR updated and modified these location types to provide the lodging community with additional insight into segment performance.

Previous codes kept up well with the changing markets, but STR decided to examine the "highway" designation a little more closely. It became clear that there

Exhibit 7   Percent Change in RevPar for U.S. Hotels: 12-Month Moving Average, January 1989–May 2005

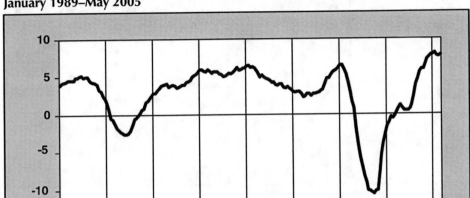

Source: Smith Travel Research.

was a need for a location code that classified hotels located outside the major markets but not located near highways. A number of hotels were reclassified as either "interstate" or "small metro/town" (SMT). The exact definitions are as follows:

- *Urban.* Properties located in urbanized metropolitan areas with more than 150,000 citizens. Size can vary depending on market orientation.

- *Suburban.* Properties located in suburbs of urbanized areas. Distance from city center varies based on population and market orientation.

- *Airport.* Properties in close proximity of international airports that primarily serve demand related to airport traffic. Distance from airports varies.

- *Interstate.* Properties in close proximity of major interstate highways whose primary source of business is interstate travel. Interstate properties located in suburban areas retain the suburban classification.

- *Resort.* Properties located in resort areas where the primary source of business is leisure destination travel.

- *Small Metro/Town.* Metropolitan or small-town areas with less than 150,000 people. Size can vary depending on market orientation. Suburban locations do not exist in proximity to these areas.

Locations are based on ZIP codes. STR spent considerable time ensuring that each ZIP code with hotels is characterized by the location code that best describes the hotel population. Of the approximately 42,000 ZIP codes in the United States, only 10,277 have hotels located in them. To establish performance by location type, STR averaged the performance of all hotels in the designated ZIP codes.

Exhibit 8   U.S. Rooms and Revenue by Location Type

Location Code	Properties	Rooms	Percent of Total Rooms	2004 Rooms Revenue	Percent of Total Rooms Revenue	RevPAR 2004
Urban	4,720	713,417	15.8 %	$19,736,768,680	22.9 %	$75.99
Suburban	15,986	1,575,628	35.0 %	$26,301,982,753	30.5 %	$46.10
Airport	1,927	275,003	6.1 %	$ 5,280,102,673	6.1 %	$52.80
Interstate	6,773	451,900	10.0 %	$ 5,262,034,567	6.1 %	$32.27
Resort	4,369	618,696	13.7 %	$17,784,322,614	20.7 %	$78.99
Small Metro / Town	15,430	872,927	19.4 %	$11,735,089,894	13.6 %	$37.91
Total	49,205	4,507,571	100.0 %	$86,100,301,181	100.0 %	$52.88

Source: Smith Travel Research.

It should be noted that the way hotels are distributed by location is not equally reflected in the generation of room revenues. Urban and resort hotels, which combine to make up only 29.5 percent of rooms, together account for 43.6 percent of all room revenue generated in 2004. The ratio of rooms and room revenue by location type is detailed in Exhibit 8.

The following sections will describe recent trends in the six location types and examine a few pertinent issues in depth. Please note that STR defines "weekdays" as Sunday through Thursday nights and "weekends" as Friday and Saturday nights.

Hotels in Urban Locations

The 4,720 urban hotels generate 23 percent of all room revenue in the United States, although only roughly 16 percent of all hotel rooms are located in urban areas. This disparity speaks to the importance of urban hotels to the U.S. lodging industry. In 2004, almost 170 million urban hotel rooms were sold, which translates to an occupancy of 65.4 percent. This represents a 4.6 percent increase from 2003, when urban hotels achieved an occupancy of 62.5 percent. Not surprisingly, hoteliers capitalized on the higher demand by increasing their room rates, raising them by 5.5 percent to $116.28 at year-end 2004.

Urban hotels traditionally are more attractive to business travelers and STR estimates that their ongoing demand, as observed in 2004, will continue in 2005. This trend, paired with a very moderate supply growth of only 1.1 percent, bodes well for rate growth at a level above inflation in 2005 and beyond.

Despite these strong indicators, urban hotels still are not performing at the levels experienced in 2000. At that time, urban hotel occupancy was reported at 68.2 percent with a rate of $119.91. It is worth mentioning, however, that there were roughly 37,800 fewer rooms in 2000 than at the end of 2004.

In June of 2000, urban hotels experienced their highest occupancy of the recent past at over 75 percent. Furthermore, urban hotels broke the 70 percent occupancy mark in eight months in 2000. In 2004, however, June and July were the only

Exhibit 9 Percent Change in Occupancy and ADR for U.S. Hotels: 12-Month Moving Average, January 1999–April 2005

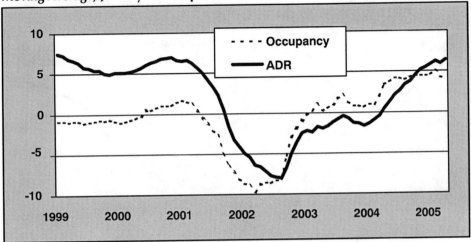

Source: Smith Travel Research.

months in which occupancy broke the 70 percent barrier. It stands to reason that growing room rates to the levels seen in 2000 will likely take a while longer because of the newly opened rooms.

Since urban hotels are associated with business travel, which traditionally takes place midweek, we also examined the weekday performance of urban hotels. Over the last three years and through the beginning of 2005, Friday and Saturday night occupancies (67.9 percent and 71.8 percent) were higher than those of Wednesdays (66.1 percent), but room rates were consistently higher on Tuesdays and Wednesdays. The seeming anomaly of increased weekend occupancy stems from the development of weekend-only vacations that allow urban hotels to market their vicinity to cultural venues and to attract leisure visitors. The rebounding economy and increasing corporate travel budgets allow hotel managers to charge business travelers higher rates and these travelers will pay that premium because of their location preference.

Exhibit 9 details the performance of urban hotels and shows the 12-month moving average for changes in both room rate and occupancy.

Hotels in Suburban Locations

Hotels in suburban locations represent roughly one in three hotels in the United States and generated 30 percent of all room revenue in 2004. In that year, 351 million suburban hotels rooms were sold, occupancy was 61.6 percent, and the average rate was $74.84. This occupancy was 3.7 percent higher than the 59.4 percent reported in 2003 and the rate increased 3.3 percent from $72.48. The increase in rooms sold and room rate translated into an increase of total room revenue of a little less than $2 billion from 2003.

Exhibit 10   Percent Change in Occupancy and ADR for U.S. Suburban Properties: 12-Month Moving Average, January 1999–April 2005

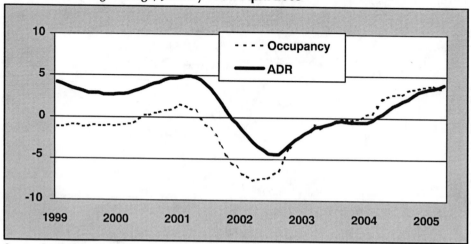

Source: Smith Travel Research.

New room supply growth has been slowing steadily in this segment. Growth rates were as follows over the last three years: 2.3 percent (2002), 1.5 percent (2003), and 1.0 percent (2004). Operators of existing hotels in suburban locations will benefit from this trend as it allows them to capture the increased demand with little new competition.

Compared with performance in the year 2000, suburban hotels still lag in both rate and occupancy. In 2000, STR observed an occupancy of 64.7 percent and a rate of $75.27. Total room revenue that year reached $25.8 billion, with three months (June, July, and August) breaking the 70 percent occupancy mark. No month in 2004 reached this occupancy level. The highest occupancy month in 2000 was June with 72.8 percent, while the highest for 2004 was July with 69.7 percent. The inability of occupancy to rebound fully may have been partially a function of the additional 1,000 hotels and 40 million annual room nights that were added in the previous three years.

Examining the average day-of-week performance over the last three years, the lowest occupancy and rate day is Sunday with 45.2 percent and $70.49. The highest average occupancy was achieved on Saturdays (66.6 percent) and the highest rate on Tuesdays ($76.33). Exhibit 10 details the performance of hotels in suburban locations and shows the monthly percent change for both room rates and occupancy.

Hotels in Airport Locations

In 2004, the number of room nights offered by properties located near airports topped 100 million, 66.6 million of which were sold. The resulting occupancy was 66.6 percent at year-end and the achieved rate was $79.25. Room rates increased 3.6 percent from $76.48 in 2003 and occupancy increased 5.9 percent from 62.9 percent. Total room revenue generated was $5.3 billion, which increased 10.4 percent from

Exhibit 11   Percent Change in Occupancy and ADR for U.S. Airport Properties: 12-Month Moving Average, January 1999–April 2005

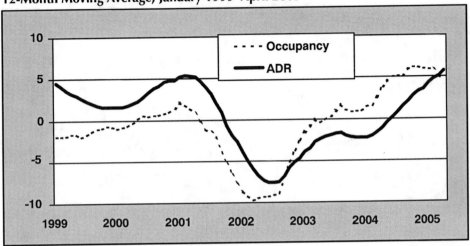

Source: Smith Travel Research.

2003. This revenue represents roughly 6 percent of total room revenue for the industry and is equal to the airport hotels' share of existing rooms in the United States. The growth rate of 0.5 percent (17 hotels) in 2004 is the lowest it has been in eight years. This low supply growth coupled with a demand increase of 6.5 percent should set the stage for good performance in 2005.

Airport hotels have not yet been able to reach the peaks achieved in 2000 when occupancy was 69.3 percent and room rate was reported at $84.28. The tragic events of September 11 hit these hotels particularly hard and December 2001 showed an especially poor occupancy of 48.6 percent and a rate of $71.81—the lowest recorded in the last five years. Eight months in 2000 showed an occupancy of over 70 percent, whereas only three months in 2004 hit this level. The highest occupancy month in 2000 was June with 75.9 percent; the highest recorded occupancy in 2004 was July with 72.2 percent.

Airport hotels traditionally are busiest on Tuesdays and Wednesdays and average occupancies for these days over the last three years were 69.2 percent and 70.5 percent, respectively. Room rates on those two days also are highest for the week, with $84.48 on Tuesdays and $84.09 on Wednesdays. Even with these strong performances on Tuesdays and Wednesdays, weekends consistently outperform weekdays because of poor performance on Mondays. In 2004, the average occupancy in airport hotels on weekends was 67.1 percent, as opposed to a weekday occupancy of 66.4 percent. However, room rates on the weekends averaged $72.00, more than 12 percent lower than the weekday rates of $82.20.

Exhibit 11 details the performance of hotels in airport locations and shows the monthly percent change for both room rates and occupancy.

Come Fly with Me: Deplanements and Room Demand. In December 2004, STR launched its new Airport Statistics Reports for the 455 airports in the United States.

Exhibit 12   Percent Change in Deplanement and Room Demand in the Top 25 U.S. Markets

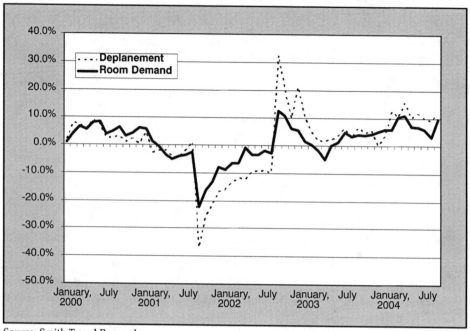

Source: Smith Travel Research.

These reports help to establish for the first time meaningful connections between airport deplanements and room demand in major cities. Reports cover all airports from Hartsfield-Jackson International in Atlanta with 12.5 million deplanements in 2003 to Lebanon Municipal Airport in New Hampshire with 5,784 passengers arriving that year. Airport data comes from the Federal Aviation Administration (FAA) and lodging demand data comes from STR. Unfortunately, the FAA's data is not as timely as STR's, so reports currently cover only the period through September 2004. Nonetheless, since we are able to examine a period of 69 months, starting in January 1999, we believe that our findings are a good indicator of trends and of potential future behavior.

This discussion will focus on the 25 largest lodging markets (excluding Las Vegas) and the relationships between airport traffic, hotel demand growth rates, and the ratio of hotel room demand per deplaned passenger. For cities that are served by multiple major airports, we summed deplanement numbers for all airports (e.g., Washington D.C.'s deplanement number comprises figures for Dulles and Reagan Airports).

Percent Change Comparison: Deplanement vs. Room Demand. Exhibit 12 plots changes in hotel room demand and deplanement numbers over time. Not surprisingly, the room demand change follows the deplanement change closely, with deplanement serving as a leading indicator. The number of deplanements

Exhibit 13   Percent Change in Deplanement and Room Demand in the Top 25 U.S. Markets: 12-Month Moving Average, January 2001–July 2004

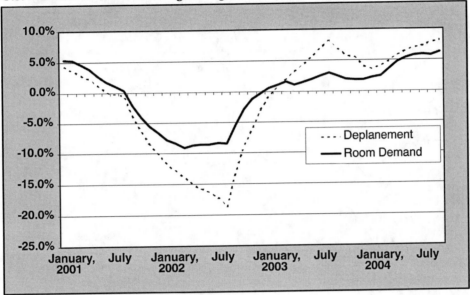

Source: Smith Travel Research.

decreased by 2.7 percent in February and the room demand change followed, going down 0.5 percent in March of 2001. After the tragic events of September 11, airplane traffic for the rest of the month came to a virtual standstill and total deplanement numbers dropped 37 percent to 11.8 million, while rooms sold decreased by a smaller 22.4 percent to 22 million. A year later, the return of the traveling public resulted in strong percentage gains in deplanements, up 32.6 percent or 3.8 million passengers, but room demand was up only 12.5 percent (or 2.8 million stays). For the most recent data available, airline deplanements were trending upward and were higher than lodging demand; September 2004 deplanement growth was 11.7 percent and room demand growth was 9.8 percent.

Using the same data set, Exhibit 13 is a 12-month moving average chart that shows a comparable general trend in demand behavior without the monthly fluctuations. Swings in room demand are not as pronounced as changes in deplanement. After March 2003, deplanement growth outperformed room sales and since then demand changes trended upward and passenger traffic rates showed slightly higher growth rates than room demand.

Ratio of Room Demand to Visitor Deplanement. Total deplanement numbers on their own may not be a good indicator of the number of travelers needing overnight accommodations because a large number of passengers flying into an airport are returning to their homes. For discussion purposes, we will assume that the ratio of returning passengers to visiting passengers (from here on referred to as "visitors" for short) is 1:1.

Exhibit 14   Top 25 U.S. Markets: Demand to Visitor Deplanement Ratio

Market	Airport Code(s)	Demand to Visitor Deplanement Ratio (69-Month Moving Average)
New York, NY	JFK, EWR, LGA	1.60
Seattle, WA	SEA	1.72
Denver, CO	DEN	1.82
Minneapolis–St. Paul, MN	MSP	2.21
Detroit, MI	DTW	2.25
Dallas, TX	DFW, DAL	2.25
Boston, MA	BOS	2.27
Chicago, IL	ORD, MDW	2.29
Phoenix, AZ	PHX	2.34
San Francisco/San Mateo, CA	SFO	2.57
Tampa/St. Petersburg, FL	TPA	2.79
Philadelphia, PA	PHL	2.85
St. Louis, MO	STL	2.94
Oahu Island, HI	HNL	2.94
Los Angeles/Long Beach, CA	LAX	2.95
Atlanta, GA	ATL	2.98
San Diego, CA	SAN	3.71
Miami/Hialeah, FL	MIA	3.75
New Orleans, LA	MSY	3.86
Houston, TX	IAH	4.02
Nashville, TN	BNA	4.16
Washington, DC	IAD, DCA	4.41
Orlando, FL	MCO	4.61
Anaheim/Santa Ana, CA	SNA	6.53
Norfolk/Virginia Beach, VA	ORF	10.65
Total		**2.80**

Source: Smith Travel Research.

STR established a ratio of rooms sold to visitors by market for the top 25 markets. The overall average for these markets was 2.8 rooms for every visitor, or roughly 28 rooms sold for every ten visitors flying into the market. As seen in Exhibit 14, this ratio fluctuates from 1.6 rooms per visitor in New York City to 10.6 rooms per visitor in Norfolk, Virginia. We hypothesize that visitors to New York City find accommodations outside the city's hotel market, which decreases the ratio. The high ratio in Norfolk may be explained not only by the fact that it is a drive-to market, but also that military personnel are using civilian hotels but military aircraft to reach the area. The higher ratios in Orlando, Anaheim, and Norfolk may be explained by vacation travelers staying multiple nights in these destination markets.

In the top 25 markets, roughly half (13 markets) have a ratio of between two and three rooms sold per visitor. The majority of these cities are served by a single airport, so even if our assumed 1:1 ratio of visitors to returning passengers does not hold, it seems that there is a quantifiable pattern of deplanement numbers to room demand. This implies that the majority of guests reach their destination through other modes of transport, be it railway, bus, or car. Given these assumptions, STR estimates that roughly two out of three rooms are sold to people not using an airplane to reach the hotel market.

While a relationship between air travel and hotel demand seems obvious, the magnitude of this relationship had not been proven prior to the new STR airport reports. General managers and revenue managers can now gather better insight into the reaction the local lodging market has to the fluctuations in air traffic. Airports clearly can make a compelling case for the influence they have on the local economy and the hotel industry in particular.

Hotels in Interstate Locations

The roughly 450,000 hotel rooms in interstate locations make up 10 percent of the total U.S. room supply, but their $5.2 billion in room revenue in 2004 accounts for only 6.1 percent of the national total. Interstate hotels achieved an occupancy of 55.8 percent and a room rate of $57.78 in 2004. Both measures improved marginally from 2003 with occupancy up two percent in 2004 and room rates up three percent. Total room revenue increased six percent. New annual room supply was a moderate 1.4 million room nights, which was only 0.9 percent higher than in 2003. This growth was the lowest in the last four years and has been steadily declining since 2000.

The performance of interstate hotels in 2004 compared with peak performance in 2000 was different from that of hotels in the previously discussed location types. Occupancy in 2000 was 55.5 percent and room rate was $52.86 so, unlike some of the other location types in 2004, interstate hotels were able to surpass their previous highs. The increase in room rate since the year 2000 was about 8.5 percent, which roughly equates to the cumulative rate of inflation over the last four years. The rate and occupancy increases occurred despite additional room supply of 8.5 million room nights over the last four years.

In 2000, the best performance was in July with 67.7 percent occupancy and $56.90 room rate. Only three months broke the 60 percent occupancy mark (June, July, and August) that year. Intuitively, this pattern makes sense with summer vacation travelers utilizing hotels near highways and interstates. The highest occupancy and rate levels for 2004 were reached in July, at 68.4 percent and $61.93, respectively. But in this year, four months broke the 60 percent mark, with September 2004 showing better results than September 2000.

Weekends outperformed weekdays by a wide margin. Weekend occupancy in 2004 was 64.6 percent and 52.3 percent on weekdays. Room rates were $61.04 on weekends and $56.16 on weekdays. Not surprisingly, the highest average occupancy and rate levels over the last three years were achieved on Friday and Saturdays. This implies that interstate hotels benefit from leisure travel and should be

Exhibit 15   Percent Change in Occupancy and ADR for U.S. Interstate Properties: 12-Month Moving Average, January 1999–April 2005

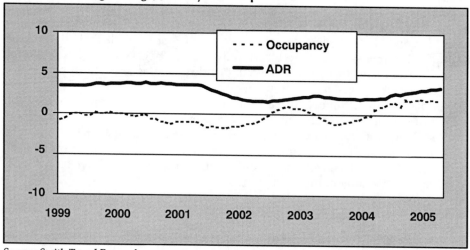

Source: Smith Travel Research.

sensitive to such outside shocks to the leisure travel market as decreases in disposable income.

Exhibit 15 details the performance of hotels in interstate locations and shows the monthly percent change for both room rates and occupancy.

Hotels in the Midscale with Food and Beverage Category. Over the last couple of years, the number of hotels categorized as midscale with food and beverage has been declining. STR tracked over 4,700 hotels in this category in 1999, but only about 4,500 hotels fit the criteria at the beginning of 2005. This translates into a loss of roughly 60,000 rooms or 22 million room nights per year. At the same time, year-end occupancy declined from 60.2 percent in 1999 to 57.1 percent in 2004, a loss of roughly 20 million room nights. It is worth debating what came first—the decline in travelers or the repositioning of hotels in this category to upscale or midscale without food and beverage. In any case, the idea of a midpriced hotel with a restaurant seems to have lost its appeal and now operators and owners are trying to reestablish their position amidst different market forces.

When the interstate system was developed in the 1950s, such chains as Holiday Inn provided a one-stop shop for travelers as they explored the United States in their newly purchased vehicles. The hotels provided overnight quarters, food and beverage service, a pool, and other amenities to provide travelers appropriate accommodations. As price and brand competition increased, costs had to be cut and hotel managers were narrowing their focus with regard to the services they could profitably provide. Chain restaurants clustered around the midscale properties now provide the dining experience desired by travelers and former hotel restaurant space makes way for such income-generating opportunities as business centers.

Examining midscale hotels with food and beverage at interstate locations shows that their performance has been a little better than average compared with other interstate location hotels. The 742 hotels achieved an occupancy of 54.9 percent in 2004 at a rate of $63.72. Total room revenue at midscale hotels with food and beverage was $952 million, an increase of 4.6 percent from 2003. Compared to performance in 2000, rate has recovered, but occupancy has not. Room rate in 2000 was recorded at $59.65, with an occupancy of 55.8 percent.

Hotels in Resort Locations

Hotels in resort areas make up only 13.7 percent of all rooms in the nation, but contribute a disproportionate 20.7 percent to total room revenue. The 2004 year-end occupancy of resort hotels was 65.9 percent, up 4.7 percent from 2003. Resorts posted a room rate of $119.67, which increased 3.6 percent from 2003. Overall, room revenue grew 8.6 percent to just under $17.8 billion. Few rooms were added as the supply growth rate stayed at a moderate 0.2 percent or 340,000 room nights. Supply growth for hotels in this category has been decreasing for the last five years from a high of 1.9 percent in 2000 to the current level.

As of 2004, occupancy had not yet returned to pre–September 11 levels. In 2000, hotels in resort locations reported an occupancy of 67.3 percent based on 218 million room nights available and 146.7 million room nights sold. In 2004, there were seven million more room nights available (225.4 million), but only two million more rooms (148.6 million) were sold. The room rate achieved in 2000 was $113.24 and although the 2004 rate was reported at $119.67, this equates to an increase of only 5.6 percent over five years—hardly an impressive performance. Total room revenue in 2000 was $16.6 billion, but increased to $17.8 billion in 2004.

Examining the monthly performance, six months in 2000 broke the 70 percent occupancy barrier and the months of December and January had occupancies below 60 percent. In 2004, only four months reached occupancies over 70 percent, and in July of 2004 the occupancy was the highest recorded in the last five years at 76.4 percent.

Not surprisingly, resort properties recorded a higher occupancy on weekends in 2004 than on weekdays, 71.9 percent versus 60.5 percent. What may be surprising, though, is the parity of room rates in these two time periods. Room rates for 2004 were $133.08 on weekdays and $135.00 on weekends, which is a difference of only 1.4 percent. Hoteliers were able to translate their rate premium from the weekend to the weekdays, demonstrating their ability to manage their yield exceptionally well, despite lower occupancies.

Exhibit 16 details the performance of hotels in resort locations and shows the 12-month moving average of both room rate and occupancy.

To Spa or Not to Spa—That Is the Question. STR examined hotels located in resort locations to determine the impact of offering spa services on occupancy and rate. STR routinely requests amenity information from lodging establishments for a variety of purposes and has identified 136 resorts with spas out of the 4,369 total resort hotels in our census database. Interestingly, the occupancies of

Exhibit 16   Percent Change in Occupancy and ADR for U.S. Resort Properties: 12-Month Moving Average, January 1999–April 2005

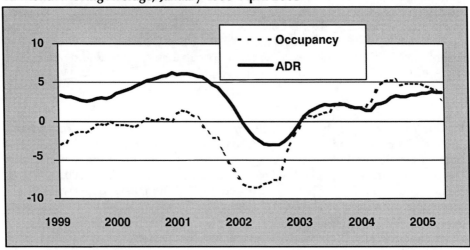

Source: Smith Travel Research.

resort hotels with and without spas are virtually identical (66.2 percent and 66.0 percent, respectively), but there is a clear difference in achieved rate. The room rate for resort hotels without a spa is $127.71, whereas resort hotels with spas generated a rate of $222.90—almost 75 percent higher. Resorts with spas increased their room demand by roughly 13 million room nights, up 10.7 percent from 2003, while revenue rose 12.9 percent to $2.5 billion. Resort hotels without spas had more modest increases in demand and revenue, with demand up 5.5 percent and revenue up 9.1 percent.

Historically, resort hotels with spas have always outperformed resorts without spas. In 2000, occupancy for resorts with spas reached a high of 71.8 percent, as opposed to 67.2 percent for those without. That year, the room rate for resorts with spas reached $177.75, which is $70 more than it was for non-spa resorts. And while the occupancy of resorts with spas bottomed out post–September 11 at 63.2 percent in 2002, their counterparts only reached 61.9 percent occupancy that year.

The observation of resorts with spas charging higher rates than their fellow resort hotels also holds true when focusing on luxury and upper upscale resort hotels. Luxury resorts without a spa outperform those having a spa by 420 occupancy basis points, 70.8 percent vs. 66.6 percent, but the spa rate premium is $82. Luxury and upper upscale resort hotels with spas achieved a rate of $271.15, which yielded a RevPAR of $192.03. Resort locations with spas saw double-digit revenue growth of 18.9 percent in 2004 and 13.9 percent in 2003. This compares to revenue growth for resort hotels without spas of 8.3 percent in 2004 and 3.0 percent in 2003.

The presence of a spa, of course, is not the only reason for a rate premium and we do not mean to imply causality. Still, there is a correlation of the two facts. It does stand to reason that resort hotels with larger product offerings that appeal to the current demand for spas should benefit as they can provide their guests a more varied experience.

Hotels in Small Metro/Town Locations

With the update of the STR location codes, a new grouping called "small metro/ town" (SMT) was created. This code was necessary because there had previously been no good way to determine the performance of hotels located outside major metropolitan suburbs, but not located on major highways. This new location type adequately portrays the geographic and performance makeup of the hotels located in these outlying areas.

STR identified more than 15,000 hotels with more than 870,000 rooms located in areas it designates as SMT. Although these hotels made up almost 20 percent of the total room supply, they generated less than 14 percent of total room revenue in 2004. SMT hotels had the lowest occupancy of all location types at only 55.2 percent in 2004. Their room rate of $68.64 was 3.1 percent higher than in 2003. In 2004, SMT hotels had over 309 million room nights available and over 170 million room nights were sold. The $11.7 billion in room revenue generated in 2004 was 6.1 percent higher than in 2003.

Supply growth in 2004 was limited as only 1.2 percent of rooms or 150 hotels were added. Since demand increased 2.9 percent over 2003, existing hoteliers benefited from the low increase in new rooms and were able to increase their occupancy. Overall, roughly 1,000 hotels with 19 million more room nights were added over the last five years.

Compared to the peak year, occupancy has recovered well and is almost back to the 2000 level of 55.8 percent. In contrast to hotels in other locations, the 2000 room rate of $63.79 was not a high point in the recent past. In fact, the room rate for SMT hotels increased steadily over the last four years and reached $64.71 in 2001, $65.44 in 2002, and $66.58 in 2003. Although these increases often are below the rate of inflation, it nonetheless is a good sign for hoteliers in these tertiary markets that were able to benefit from the increase in travelers while supply growth stayed low.

The days with the highest occupancy and rate over the last two years were the weekends. On average, Fridays had occupancies of 62.3 percent with a rate of $70.82 and Saturdays achieved an occupancy of 65.5 percent and a rate of $75.52. In contrast, Wednesday occupancy was only 56.2 percent at a rate of $64.55. The combined weekend occupancy was 64.0 percent in 2004 and has fluctuated around this point over the last five years. Weekday occupancy dropped from a high of 53.4 percent in 2000 to a low of 50.5 percent in 2003 and recovered to 51.7 percent in 2004. Rates increased steadily for both weekends and weekdays and the year-end room rate of $61.96 on weekdays and $67.49 on weekends in 2000 was the lowest in the last five years. In 2005, the weekday room rate was $66.24 and the weekend rate was $73.46.

Exhibit 17 details the performance of hotels in SMT locations and shows the 12-month moving average for both room rate and occupancy.

Exhibit 17   Percent Change in Occupancy and ADR for U.S. Small Metro/Town Properties: 12-Month Moving Average, January 1999–April 2005

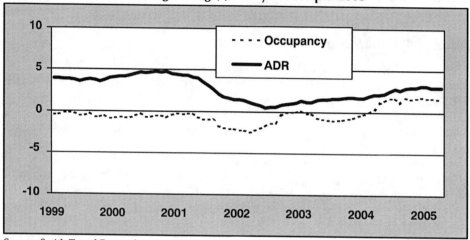

Source: Smith Travel Research.

Exhibit 18   U.S. ADR by Hotel Opening Date

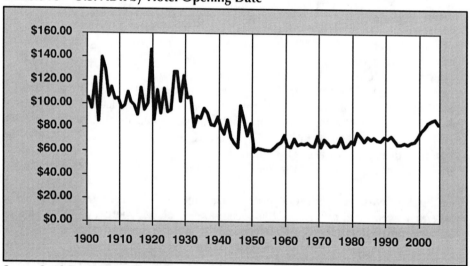

Source: Smith Travel Research.

Age Matters: Hotel Performance Based on Property Age

To examine the influence of property age on hotel performance, STR grouped hotels by the year they reported as their opening (back to 1900) and compared their full-year 2004 room rates, as shown in Exhibit 18. Three observations stand out.

Exhibit 19 U.S. Property Count by Hotel Opening Date

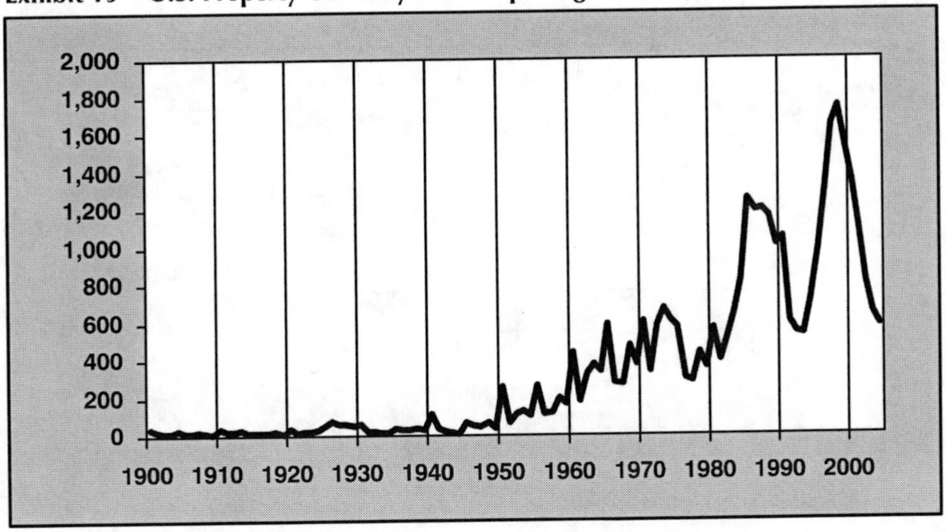

Source: Smith Travel Research.

First, while we might intuitively expect that older hotels should not be able to charge as much as newer hotels, Exhibit 18 shows that older hotels actually seem to outperform newer hotels. This anomaly can be explained by the fact that the number of hotels that opened between the years 1900 and 1930 is relatively small and the hotels that are still in operation are either luxury or upper upscale hotels or high-end independent hotels. Hotels with few rooms and few amenities that were open in the early part of the twentieth century probably were closed a long time ago. The surviving hotels tend to be landmark trophy buildings that command a rate premium precisely because of their age and history.

Second, there is a pronounced drop in rate for hotels opened around 1952 and the rate seems to move in a much narrower band for hotels opened after that point in time. To explain this drop, STR examined the number of hotels that opened in each year and grouped them by year (see Exhibit 19). At the exact point when the room rate dropped in 1952, there was a pronounced increase in the number of new hotels. The early 1950s saw two phenomena that could explain this increase in hotels. The newly expanded federal highway system allowed Americans to travel longer distances much faster and with this newfound freedom came the need for roadside lodging. This call was answered by Holiday Inn and other brands and the expansion of affordable midscale hotels along the highway system contributed to the drop in rate. The majority of newly built hotels since the 1950s were what is now classified by STR as "midscale with/without F&B."

Third, there is a pronounced increase in rate for hotels built after 2003 and then a drop in rate for hotels under one year of age. The first observation can be explained through the increase in hotels that are classified as "upper upscale" and "upscale" in the last several years. Although their total number has not changed historically, the extremely low growth rates of hotels overall gave the newly

Exhibit 20 Total Estimated U.S. Revenue and Profitability, 1992–2004

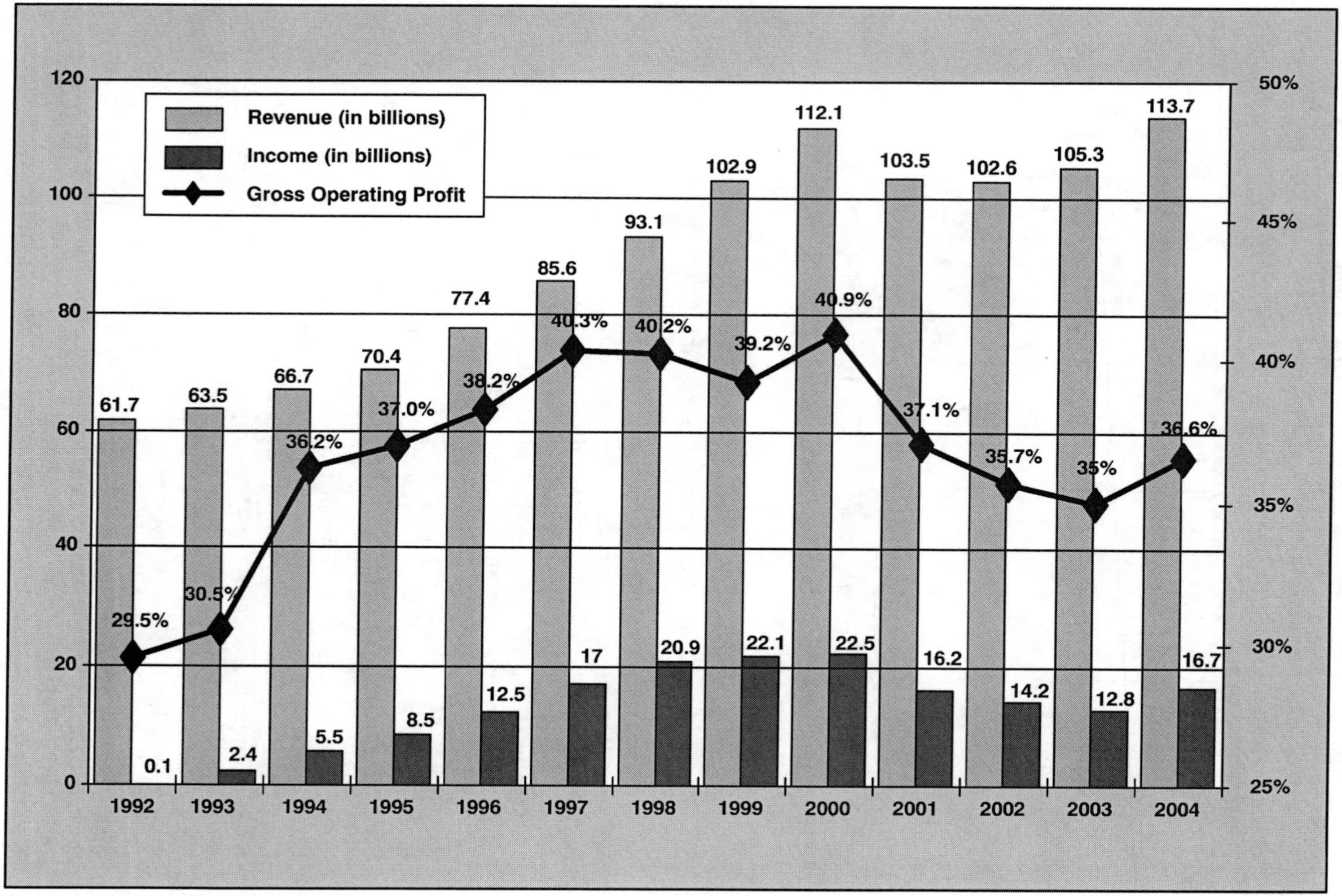

Legend:
- Revenue (in billions)
- Income (in billions)
- Gross Operating Profit

Year	Revenue (in billions)	Income (in billions)	Gross Operating Profit
1992	61.7	0.1	29.5%
1993	63.5	2.4	30.5%
1994	66.7	5.5	36.2%
1995	70.4	8.5	37.0%
1996	77.4	12.5	38.2%
1997	85.6	17	40.3%
1998	93.1	20.9	40.2%
1999	102.9	22.1	39.2%
2000	112.1	22.5	40.9%
2001	103.5	16.2	37.1%
2002	102.6	14.2	35.7%
2003	105.3	12.8	35%
2004	113.7	16.7	36.6%

Source: Smith Travel Research.

opened higher-end hotels more weight, which pushed the rate upward. For hotels open less than one year, an explanation for the drop in rate may be that these hotels are still in the beginning stages of their life cycle and have not yet stabilized their rates.

Conclusion

In 2004, total revenue for the industry reached $113.7 billion while gross operating income rebounded to $16.7 billion, as shown in Exhibit 20. This is in sharp contrast to the recession of the early 1990s when the industry lost over $5 billion in 1991 and profit grew at a very modest pace for the next several years. During the recent recession, the industry remained profitable even with occupancy and room rates declining sharply. Given that the industry is in much better financial health than in the previous recession, we are confident that higher revenue will result in higher profit as the industry moves through the rebound.

As of Summer 2005, the lodging industry is poised for an extended recovery. All indicators point to higher occupancy, room rates, and revenue. However, there are a number of issues that could affect all of the positive scenarios and cause the industry considerable difficulty. Leading the list is some type of terrorist attack within the United States. The September 11 attacks involved the airlines, and therefore the travel industry overall. If a future attack also involves the travel industry, it could be equally damaging. If another component of the U.S. economy is targeted in the future, the impact on lodging may be diffused. The cost of operating a hotel is also of concern at this point with insurance, energy, and labor leading the list. Competitive pressure to improve room contents is leading to "amenity creep" on a large scale. Internet access, flat-screen televisions, and better beds and showers are all escalating the costs of ongoing maintenance.

Ongoing problems within the airline industry seem to actually be helping the lodging industry. The difficulties that airlines face at this time seem insurmountable, but one of the immediate effects is lower air fares. This is helping to offset the general hassle associated with air travel and has spurred record numbers of new travelers.

It is interesting to note that as we enter this new phase, a number of the industry's leading companies have chosen new CEOs from outside the industry. Clearly, there is a belief that the industry needs to consider different approaches to growth than what has been attempted in the past. Given the new Internet landscape and the demands from a constantly changing customer, perhaps new ideas coming from a different direction will be the catalyst for a new extended period of growth.

2

The Relationship Between the U.S. Economy and the Lodging Industry

By *Bjorn Hanson, Ph.D.*

Bjorn Hanson is the Global Hospitality Industry Partner for PricewaterhouseCoopers. He is well known for his consulting and econometric and statistical research. He holds Certified Real Estate Counselor (CRE), Certified Fraud Examiner (CFE) and Food Service Consultants International (FSCI) professional designations.

    Dr. Hanson is an author and frequent speaker who has been quoted in almost every major business periodical and industry journal including: Financial Times, Time, Newsweek, Forbes, Fortune, U.S. News & World Report, The Wall Street Journal (US, European and Asian editions), Barron's, and The New York Times and has appeared numerous times on CBS, NBC, CNN, CNNfn, CNBC, FOXfn, WCBS, PBS and other television and radio systems. He has served as International President of the Cornell Society of Hotelmen and was the Cornell Hotelier of the Year in 1994. He has served as a Visiting Assistant Professor at Cornell and in addition to having been an adjunct faculty member at NYU for 16 years, he is the Chair of the Executive Board for New York University's Center for Hospitality, Tourism and Sports Management and The Cornell Center for Hospitality Research Advisory Board.

    Dr. Hanson holds a bachelor's from Cornell University, School of Hotel Administration, an MBA from Fordham University, and a Ph.D. from New York University.

THE LODGING INDUSTRY has seen dramatic RevPAR improvement in 2004 and 2005. According to Smith Travel Research, RevPAR increased 7.8 percent in 2004 and PricewaterhouseCoopers forecasts a 7.8 percent increase for 2005. Based on Price-waterhouseCoopers's long–term lodging history (dating back to 1922), these are the largest increases since 1984.

    There have been many changes in recent years in the way the U.S. lodging industry has been affected by the economy, sources of capital, loan delinquency rates, the demographics of demand, including inbound and outbound international travel, and the effect of the Internet. This chapter presents more information on these subjects and concludes with the PricewaterhouseCoopers forecast as of September 2005.

Exhibit 1   Percent Change in Lodging Demand and U.S. GDP

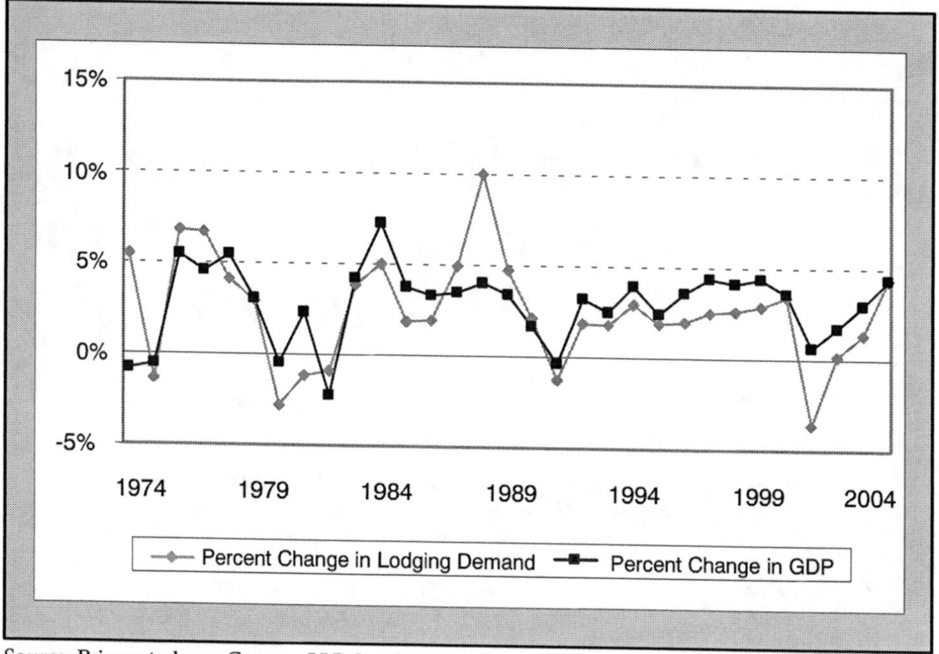

Source: PricewaterhouseCoopers LLP, Smith Travel Research, and Macroeconomic Advisors.

Relationship Between the U.S. Economy and the Lodging Industry

Because lodging industry performance relies on consumer and business travel expenditures, the overall U.S. economy's performance has a direct effect on lodging demand. The key economic determinant of lodging demand is real gross domestic product (GDP). The GDP of the United States is defined as the annual total market value of all goods and services produced within the United States. As shown in Exhibit 1, the pattern of lodging demand closely follows that of GDP.

An expanding economy supports increases in corporate profits, employment and wages, and consumer confidence and generates increased spending on business and leisure travel. During an economic slowdown or recession, with profit and consumers' disposable income in decline or uncertain, businesses and consumers may view travel as a discretionary expenditure that can be reduced.

Evolution of the Lodging Industry's Response to Economic Changes

The relationship of the U.S. lodging industry and the U.S. economy can be expressed in terms of elasticity. Elasticity is the responsiveness of one variable, such as lodging demand, to changes in another, such as real GDP.

From 1967 to 1991, the elasticity of lodging demand to real GDP was 1.2 (see Exhibit 2). Therefore, a 10 percent increase in real GDP was associated with a 12

Exhibit 2 Demand Elasticity and Correlation to Real GDP

Time Period	Elasticity	Correlation
1967–1991	1.2	0.89
1991–2000	0.7	0.93
2002	0.2	0.29
2003	0.5	0.83
2004 estimate	1.04	

Source: PricewaterhouseCoopers LLP.

percent increase in lodging demand. The relationship has changed since 1991, with demand becoming less responsive to changes in economic conditions. The elasticity of lodging demand relative to GDP has decreased only 0.7 from 1991 to 2000. Therefore, a 10 percent increase in GDP was associated with a 7 percent increase in lodging demand. The elasticity fell even further in 2002 and 2003, but Exhibit 2 shows that the 2004 estimate had climbed back to 1.04.

PricewaterhouseCoopers research has shown that an important factor in this elasticity change was the growth of the technology and information sectors (especially software, Internet, and related businesses) of the economy. These sectors grew more rapidly than the rest of the economy and contributed a larger portion of the GDP, but they tended to generate less lodging demand than the rest of the economy.

The productivity growth of the U.S. workforce and of the overall economy has accelerated, averaging between two and four percent during the past five years. This increased productivity has increased GDP, but the increase has not translated to lodging demand.

Recent Changes in the Relationship of Lodging Demand to GDP

After September 11, 2001, travel safety concerns also contributed a change in the relationship between real GDP growth and lodging demand. Lodging demand per unit of GDP has been lower since 2001. Exhibit 3 shows real GDP and lodging demand since 1987, with both series indexed to 1987 as a base year. Through 1996, lodging demand growth closely followed changes in the economy. While real GDP began to grow slightly faster than lodging demand in the mid-1990s, the most significant change in the relationship between real GDP and lodging demand occurred after 2001. During 2002 and 2003, the economic recovery did not result in past levels of gains for lodging demand because of consumers' concerns about the Iraq war and traveling.

The outlook is for demand elasticity in 2005 to again exceed the level of the last 10 years reflecting a recovery of business travel as the economy strengthens, businesses increase capital and other investments, and travel policies become less restrictive. By 2006 and 2007, demand elasticity will return to 1991–2000 levels, indicating some return toward the long-term relationship shown in earlier years,

Exhibit 3   Real GDP and Lodging Demand

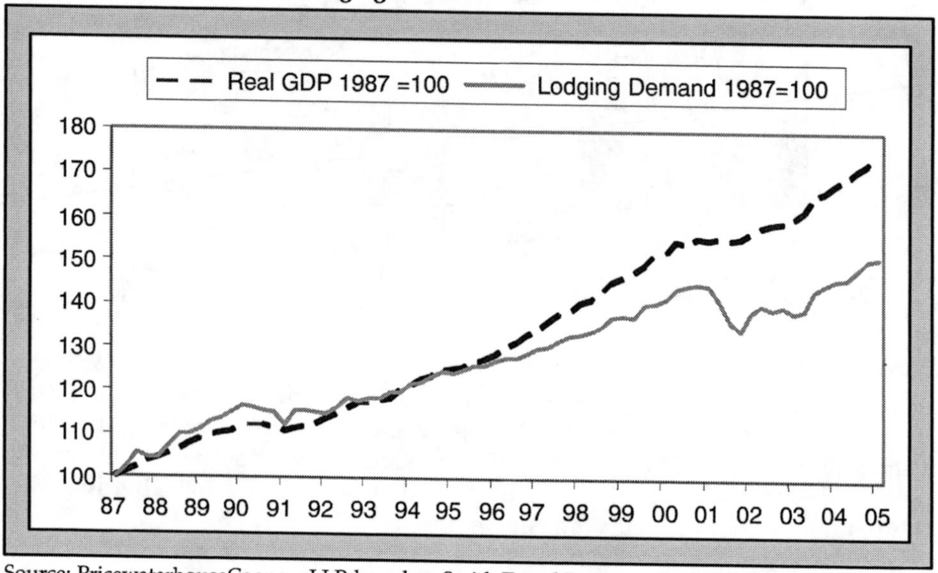

Source: PricewaterhouseCoopers LLP, based on Smith Travel Research data; U.S. Bureau of Economic Analysis.

but reflecting a structural change in the relationship of the level of demand relative to economic output.

Cycles in the U.S. Lodging Industry

Increasing lodging demand, as measured by occupied room nights, marks periods of industry expansion, and contractions in lodging demand mark periods of industry downturn. A demand *peak*, which marks both the end of an expansion and the start of a downturn, is the point of maximum lodging demand for a given cycle. A demand *trough*, which marks both the start of an expansion and the end of a downturn, is the point of minimum lodging demand for a given cycle. A complete cycle includes an expansion and a contraction.

During the last eight lodging cycles (including the 2000–2001 contraction and the ongoing expansion), lodging demand expansion periods averaged 61.6 months, while demand contraction periods averaged 13.4 months (see Exhibit 4). The average lodging demand cycle had a duration of 75 months. The next cycle will occur when demand peaks.

Lodging cycles are diverse in shape, size, and duration. Exhibit 5 illustrates the following:

- Duration of the downturn—the number of quarters from peak to trough

- Severity of the downturn—the magnitude of the decline from the peak, which is the starting point of each line

Exhibit 4   Contractions and Expansions in the U.S. Lodging Industry

U.S. Recessions	Months in Contraction			Months in Expansion		
	U.S. Economy	Rooms Sold	Real Room Receipts	U.S. Economy	Rooms Sold	Real Room Receipts
Aug-57 to Apr-58	8	14	13	24	26	29
Apr-60 to Feb-61	10	14	11	106	91	91
Dec-69 to Nov-70	11	24	24	36	42	42
Nov-73 to Mar-75	16	9	9	58	53	53
Jan-80 to Jul-80	6	7	7	12	10	10
Jul-81 to Nov-82	16	14	17	92	93	90
Jul-90 to Mar-91	8	13	13	120	116	116
Mar-01 to Nov-01	8	12	12			
Average	**10.4**	**13.4**	**13.3**	**64.0**	**61.6**	**61.6**

Source: PricewaterhouseCoopers LLP and U.S. Bureau of Economic Research.

Exhibit 5   Lodging Cycles

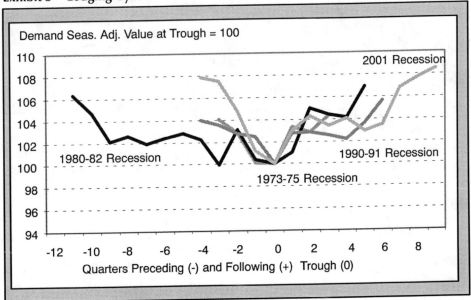

Source: PricewaterhouseCoopers LLP and Smith Travel Research.

- Duration of the recovery—from the trough to the point where the next peak is reached

The 2001 downturn is notable for the severity and duration of the decline compared with previous downturns. In 2001, demand declined at more than twice

Exhibit 6   Peaks and Troughs of the U.S. Lodging Industry Cycle

Peaks				
U.S. Economy	**Rooms Demand**	**Lead or Lag (-)**	**Real Room Receipts**	**Lead or Lag (-)**
Aug-57	Jan-57	7 mos.	Feb-57	6 mos.
Apr-60	May-60	-1 mos.	Aug-60	-4 mos.
Dec-69	Feb-69	10 mos.	Feb-69	10 mos.
Nov-73	Aug-74	-9 mos.	Aug-74	-9 mos.
Jan-80	Oct-79	3 mos.	Oct-79	3 mos.
Jul-81	Mar-81	4 mos.	Mar-81	4 mos.
Jul-90	Feb-90	5 mos.	Feb-90	5 mos.
Mar-01	Sep-00	6 mos.	Sep-00	6 mos.
Average		**3.1 mos.**		**2.6 mos.**
Troughs				
U.S. Economy	**Rooms Demand**	**Lead or Lag (-)**	**Real Room Receipts**	**Lead or Lag (-)**
Apr-58	Mar-58	1 mos.	Mar-58	1 mos.
Feb-61	Jul-61	-5 mos.	Jul-61	-5 mos.
Nov-70	Feb-71	-3 mos.	Feb-71	-3 mos.
Mar-75	May-75	-2 mos.	May-75	-2 mos.
Jul-80	May-80	2 mos.	May-80	2 mos.
Nov-82	May-82	6 mos.	Aug-82	3 mos.
Mar-91	Mar-91	0 mos.	Mar-91	0 mos.
Nov-01	Sep-01	2 mos.	Sep-01	2 mos.
Average		**0.1 mos.**		**-0.3 mos.**

Source: PricewaterhouseCoopers LLP and U.S. Bureau of Economic Research.

the rate of any other downturn of the last four lodging cycles. Further, the length of time needed to recover demand to the level of the next peak was significantly longer than in other lodging cycles.

Relationship Between Lodging Cycles and U.S. Business Cycles

While the lodging cycle in general moves closely with the overall economy, it does not exactly match the peaks and troughs of the U.S. business cycles. The two main differences are the timing and the duration of the expansion and contractions.

Timing. Exhibit 6 shows that the timing of the lodging cycle does not exactly correspond with the U.S. business cycle. Lodging downturns tend to precede U.S. recessions. During the past eight business cycles, lodging demand and real revenue peaked an average of three months before the U.S. economy.

Lodging downturns tend to precede national recessions because of relatively short lead times traditionally involved in arranging many trips. As already explained, a slowdown in economic activity causes both corporations and individuals to reduce travel expenditures.

The timing of lodging recoveries relative to U.S. recoveries is less predictable. In three of the four most recent cycles, lodging recoveries began before the U.S. business recoveries, but in the preceding three cycles, lodging recoveries lagged behind U.S. recoveries. A positive number in the lead or lag column next to room demand in Exhibit 6 means that room demand peaked or troughed ahead of the respective U.S. cycle.

Duration. The duration of the U.S. lodging cycle does not necessarily correspond with the national business cycle. Contractions in the lodging industry tend to be longer than economic downturns, while expansions tend to be shorter. Contractions in the lodging industry, as measured by room nights sold and real room receipts, lasted an average of 13.4 and 13.3 months respectively, while economic recessions persisted an average of only 10.4 months (see Exhibit 4). Lodging industry expansions last an average of 61.6 months compared to 64.0 months for the overall economy.

The lodging industry experiences longer periods of contraction than the U.S. economy. Because lodging expansions end earlier than U.S. expansions, as they did during the last four cycles, lodging contractions are not necessarily shorter than the respective U.S. contractions (see Exhibit 6). While businesses and individuals respond quickly to economic declines, they are not as quick to increase spending on lodging, as businesses continue to maintain restrictions on travel costs in periods of uncertainty and concerns about job and economic security encourage consumers to limit discretionary spending.

Cycles in Lodging Construction

Lodging construction and, therefore, room supply growth also experience regular cycles. The factor that most strongly correlates with hotel construction is real average daily rate (ADR). Two additional factors that affect new construction are interest rates or the cost of capital and the level of existing supply relative to existing and expected room demand.

As we look to the future, if trends and history are a guide, contractions will shorten and expansions will be longer. This is good news and reflects investors, lenders, and others making better decisions because of more widespread availability of industry data.

Lodging Consolidation, Capital Markets, and Lodging Performance

The term lodging consolidation refers to the process of combining one or more lodging entities into larger businesses, whether by acquisition or merger.

Lodging mergers and acquisitions (M&A) peaked in 1998, when 25 transactions valued at $32.9 billion were completed (see Exhibit 7). Consolidation has decelerated significantly since 1998, coinciding with a decline in the availability of public capital. By 1999, lodging M&A activity decreased to just 12 consolidations valued at $6.8 billion and M&A activity in 2001 was $440 million. Since 1998, the 45

Exhibit 7   Lodging Merger and Acquisition Activity in Billions

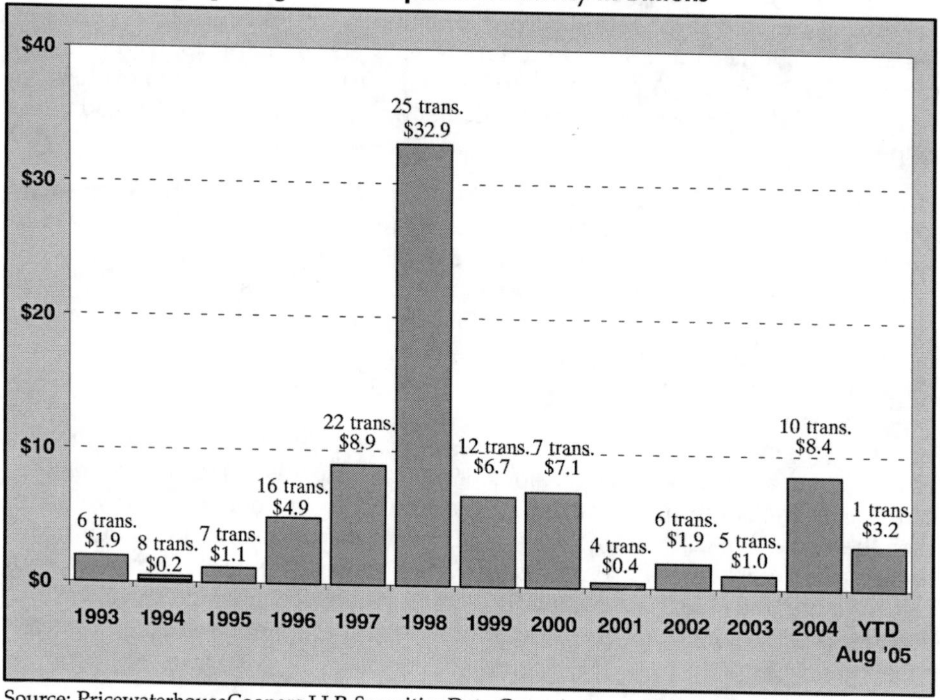

Source: PricewaterhouseCoopers LLP, Securities Data Commission, and Thomson Financial.

M&A transactions in the lodging industry have totaled $18.2 billion in value—approximately 55 percent of the value of the transactions completed in 1998.

The lodging industry's M&A activity has come in three forms: mergers, stock purchases, and cash purchases. During a stock purchase, the purchasing company offers shares of its stock as payment to the owners of the company being acquired. In a cash purchase, the purchaser offers cash as payment.

Companies merge for cost savings and potential strategic benefits. An example is Hilton's $3.6 billion acquisition of Promus in November 1999, which provided the opportunity for the merged entity to expand and diversify its portfolio both geographically and by service and price levels. At the same time, the merger helped reduce costs attributed to operating two (or more) reservations, information, purchasing, corporate, and other systems.

The merged entity is able to benefit from increased market share and name recognition. For example, Accor's $1.1 billion acquisition of Red Roof Inns in August 1999 positioned Accor in the U.S. economy hotel sector, with more than 10 percent of sector supply. The Blackstone Group acquired Extended StayAmerica in May 2004 for $3.1 billion and positioned itself as the leading owner in the U.S. extended stay market.

In 2004, M&A activity in the lodging sector reached a six-year high with 10 transactions valued at $8.4 billion and as of August 2005, activity had reached $3.4 billion.

Exhibit 8   Lodging Company Public Debt and Equity Issued

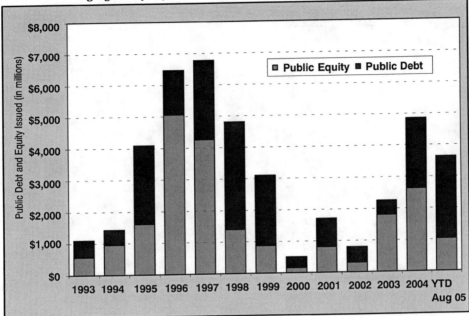

Source: PricewaterhouseCoopers LLP, Securities Data Commission, and Thomson Financial.

Capital Markets

The capital or financing for new hotels comes from a variety of sources. Capital is generated primarily from public or private equity, institutional debt, public bonds, or a combination of these.

Since 1993, public markets have generated a total of $39.5 billion in capital through the issuance of public debt and equity (see Exhibit 8). From 1993 to 1997, market activity steadily accelerated with a peak of $6.8 billion in 1997. From 1997 to 2000, capital market activity declined and, in 2000, only $500 million in public lodging debt and equity was issued.

Delinquency Rates

The delinquency rate is the ratio of the dollar amount of delinquent loans to the dollar amount of all outstanding loans. Loan delinquency rates provide a measure of the intensity of financial stress experienced in the industry.

During the recent business cycle, lodging delinquency rates peaked in March and April 2002 and 2003 at 5.5 percent, well below the 16.2 percent reached during the 1990–1991 recession. In addition, the industry has experienced substantial improvement in operating leverage with significant reductions in costs, as it reduced expenses on food and beverage operations (which typically achieve departmental profits of 0 percent to almost 30 percent, depending on the purpose

Exhibit 9   CMBS Delinquency Rates

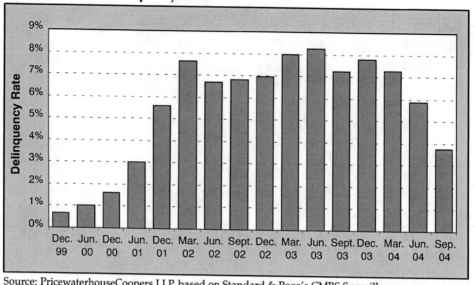

Source: PricewaterhouseCoopers LLP, based on Standard & Poor's CMBS Surveillance.

and style of the operation—fine dining in New York is among the least profitable and banquet is among the most profitable), use of technology (scheduling systems or reducing the number of accounting employees), reductions in selected services (turndown service offered only upon request), and revenue enhancement through charging more for services or adding new charges.

Commercial mortgage-backed securities (CMBS) and the American Council of Life Insurers (ACLI) account for 22 and 13 percent of total property-level debt in the lodging industry, respectively. For CMBS, the delinquency rate of 3.75 percent in September 2004 was less than half the rate in June 2003 (see Exhibit 9). Delinquency rates for ACLI lodging mortgage loans peaked in 2001 at less than one percent and well below the 16 percent peak reached during the 1990–1991 recession (see Exhibit 10). As of the first quarter of 2005, the CMBS delinquency rate stood at 2.9 percent.[1]

The outlook is for delinquency rates to continue to decline, stabilizing at about 3 percent and 2 percent for 2005 and 2006.

Lodging Performance

Since the early 1990s, the lodging industry has developed and matured significantly. Some of the changes include:

- Lower interest expenses as a percent of revenues.

- Fewer employees per 100 occupied rooms.

- Lower breakeven occupancies.

Exhibit 10   Delinquency Rates on ACLI Lodging Morgage Loans

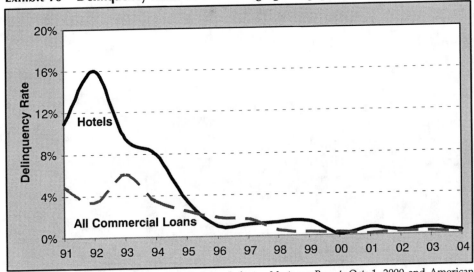

Source: PricewaterhouseCoopers LLP, *Lodging Industry Mortgage Report*, Oct. 1, 2000 and American Council of Life Insurers, *Mortgage Loan Portfolio Profile*.

Exhibit 11   Interest Expense as a Percentage of Total Revenues

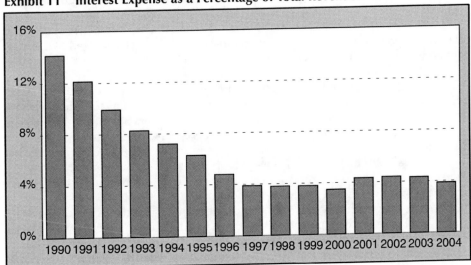

Source: PricewaterhouseCoopers LLP and Smith Travel Research.

Low interest rates by historical comparisons and lower financial leverage have benefited the industry with interest expenses accounting for only 3.9 percent of revenue in 2004, compared to the peak of 14.2 percent in 1990 (see Exhibit 11).

Efforts to reduce expenses and increase efficiency, including the growth of limited services lodging, have resulted in fewer employees per 100 occupied

Exhibit 12   Number of Employees per 100 Occupied Rooms

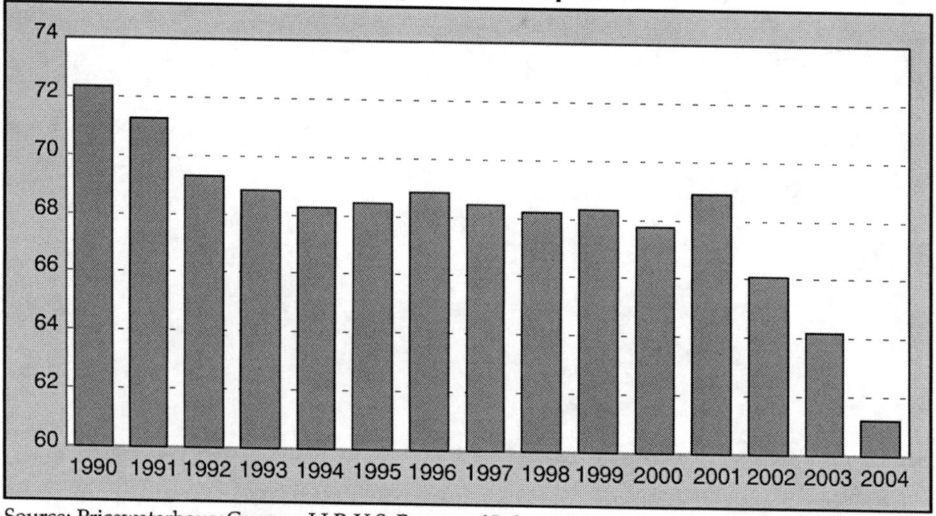

Source: PricewaterhouseCoopers LLP, U.S. Bureau of Labor Statistics, and Smith Travel Research.

rooms. In 1990, there were 72.3 employees per 100 occupied rooms (see Exhibit 12). By 2004, there were just 61.2 employees per 100 occupied rooms.

From 1990 to 2000, the midscale without food and beverage (F&B) segment and the upscale segment—with limited F&B departments and fewer F&B employees—both grew at faster rates than other chain scale segments in terms of total room inventory. Room inventory in those two segments increased by 151 percent between 1990 and 2000, while the rest of the U.S. lodging industry expanded by only 11 percent.[2]

Hotel companies continue to pursue productivity enhancements. Emphasis is being placed on introducing new ways of substituting capital for labor without diminishing customer service. For example, Sheraton offers Sheraton Speed Check that allows guests to check in and out on their own, duplicate room keys, print out messages received at the front desk, and e-mail guest folios at any time during their stay—all of which reduce front-desk operation costs. Similarly, Holiday Inn currently offers electronic food and beverage menus—"E-Menus"—that reduce staffing requirements and expedite meal orders.

Because the industry has improved operating efficiency, breakeven occupancy levels are ten occupancy points lower in 2004 than in the early 1990s (see Exhibit 13). In 1990, the average hotel would have required an occupancy rate of 65.1 percent to break even. By 2004, the average hotel required an occupancy of 53 percent to break even.

Changing Demographics and the Future of Lodging Demand

Long-term trends in lodging demand will be affected substantially by changing U.S. demographics. The Baby Boom generation, born between 1946 and 1964, and

Exhibit 13   Lodging Industry Breakeven Occupancy

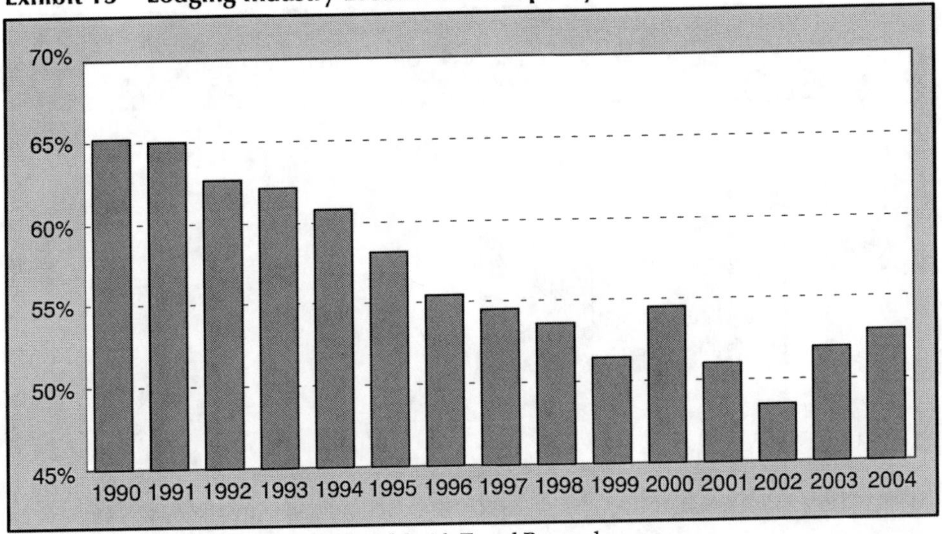

Source: PricewaterhouseCoopers LLP and Smith Travel Research.

Generation X, born between 1965 and 1980, are emerging as forces with important implications for the lodging industry.

It has long been anticipated that as Baby Boomers matured, they would increase their lodging consumption. The results, as have been observed during the past four years, have exceeded most expectations. Demand generated per capita is 5.2 annual room nights.

What most demographers and industry analysts did *not* anticipate is the amount of travel and lodging spending by Generation Xers. In 2004, Generation X's per capita lodging demand exceeded that of the Baby Boomers for both business and leisure travel (see Exhibit 14). In addition, Generation X's total lodging demand is growing faster than Baby Boomers' demand (see Exhibit 15).

While Baby Boomers continue to spend more per trip per capita on business travel, Generation X is now spending more per capita on leisure trips (see Exhibit 16). In addition, when business and leisure travel are combined, Generation X outspends Baby Boomers per trip per capita. Because Generation X has a median income of more than $10,000 less than Baby Boomers, Generation X spends proportionately more income on travel (see Exhibit 17).

The Short-Term Outlook for the U.S. Lodging Industry

Based on the latest PricewaterhouseCoopers lodging industry outlook through 2007, the lodging industry is expected to experience substantial gains as the overall economy is forecast to continue advancing at a measured noninflationary pace. As consumer expenditures on travel and lodging are still below historical averages, the potential for the lodging sector is even more positive. At the same time, such new leisure product offerings as fractional ownership and condo-hotels provide an array of alternatives for consumers and lodging industry expansions.

Exhibit 14   Lodging Demand per Capita

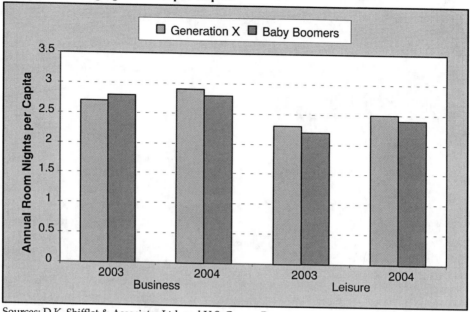

Sources: D.K. Shifflet & Associates Ltd. and U.S. Census Bureau

Exhibit 15   Generation X and Baby Boomer Lodging Demand

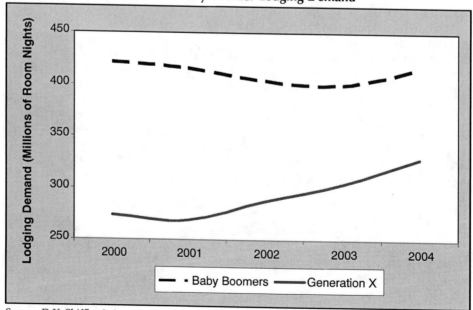

Source: D.K. Shifflet & Associates Ltd.

Exhibit 16   Travel Spending

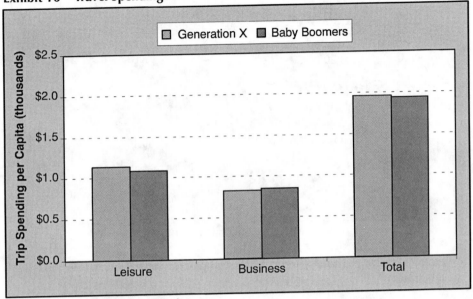

Source: D.K. Shifflet & Associates Ltd.

Exhibit 17   Generation X and Baby Boomer Statistics

Baby Boomers

Birth Years, Ages	1946–1964, 41–59
2004 Population	80,357,000
Median Income	$56,200

Generation X

Birth Years, Ages	1965–1980, 25–40
2004 Population	61,893,000
Median Income	$45,330

Source: PricewaterhouseCoopers LLP, based on data from D.K. Shifflet & Associates Ltd. and the U.S. Census Bureau.

International arrival trends have significant implications for lodging demand. While in 2000 international arrivals accounted for approximately 13 percent of total lodging demand, by 2004 they accounted for 9.9 percent and are forecast to account for 10.6 percent in 2005. Exchange rate trends are expected to continue to favor both foreign and domestic travel to the United States because of the relatively low value of the dollar, providing further support to the lodging industry.

The Internet will continue to affect the lodging industry. The number of people using the Internet for travel research increased from 3 million to more than

Exhibit 18   PricewaterhouseCoopers Forecast Comparison

2002 Occupancy	
PwC Forecast December 13, 2001	59.6%
Actual 2002 (STR)	58.9%
2003 Occupancy	
PwC Forecast December 12, 2002 (Iraq war)	59.6%
Actual 2003 (STR)	59.1%
2004 Occupancy	
PwC Forecast December 11, 2003	61.2%
Actual 2004 (STR)	61.3%

Source: PricewaterhouseCoopers LLP and Smith Travel Research.

Exhibit 19   PricewaterhouseCoopers U.S. Lodging Industry Forecast for 2005 through 2007

	2001	2002	2003	2004	Forecast 2005	2006	2007
Average Daily Rooms Sold	-3.4%	0.4%	1.4%	4.4%	3.5%	3.1%	3.2%
End-of-Year Supply	1.9	1.5	0.9	0.4	1.2	1.4	1.6
Occupancy Level (%)	59.7	59.0	59.2	61.3	63.0	64.1	65.2
Average Daily Rate	-1.4	-1.5	0.1	4.0	5.0	4.3	4.4
Revenue per Available Room	-7.0	-2.7	0.4	7.8	7.8	6.2	6.1

Source: PricewaterhouseCoopers LLP.

50 million between 1996 and 1999.[3] According to PricewaterhouseCoopers, an estimated 18 percent of all hotel bookings in 2004 were made over the Internet and Internet bookings are expected to reach 23 percent by 2006. In 2005 PricewaterhouseCoopers estimated that the Internet will result in the generation of 60,000 incremental room nights and $1.787 billion in incremental industry revenues.

Through 2005, 2006, and possibly into 2007, the capital markets are likely to view the lodging industry favorably as RevPAR increases faster than inflation and industry profits are projected to reach new record levels beginning in 2006 (see Exhibit 18).

Industry Forecasts

Exhibit 19 presents the PricewaterhouseCoopers U.S. Lodging Industry Forecast for 2005 through 2007.

Some may find it interesting to compare PricewaterhouseCoopers forecasts with actual performance figures, especially during many of the most challenging

Exhibit 20   Industry Profit

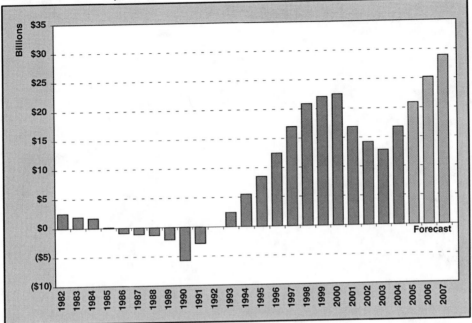

Source: PricewaterhouseCoopers LLP.

years ever for forecasting. Exhibit 20 presents PricewaterhouseCoopers occupancy forecasts issued in December for the following year compared to the actual occupancy based on Smith Travel Research. No other firm or organization has a comparable record of forecast accuracy.

The outlook for 2005 is for occupancy growth to continue, but slow down, and for rate to increase by the largest margin since 1998 before beginning to slow. But even with slowing occupancy and rate growth in 2006, RevPAR will grow at impressive rates of 7.8 percent in 2005, 6.2 percent in 2006, and 6.1 percent in 2007.

These RevPAR increases combined with operation and capital changes since 2001, which have changed the operating leverage of the lodging industry, will result in record property level profits of $25.2 billion in 2006.

Endnotes

1. Based on Standard & Poor's and ACLI data.

2. Smith Travel Research.

3. Travel Industry Association of America, *Travelers' Use of the Internet*, 2004.

3

Hotel Development Costs

By *Jan A. deRoos, Ph.D.,* and *Elaine Sahlins*

Jan A. deRoos, on the faculty of the School of Hotel Administration at Cornell University since 1988, has devoted his career to hospitality real estate with a focus on the valuation, financing, development, and operation of lodging, timeshare, and restaurant assets. He holds B.S., M.S., and Ph.D. degrees from Cornell University, all with majors in Hotel Administration. Areas of teaching expertise span the entire range of hospitality real estate topics, property valuation, hospitality asset management, feasibility studies, hotel/resort planning and design, hotel/resort development and construction, and timeshare/vacation ownership. Prof. deRoos' current research is focused on two themes: investment returns to lodging properties and supply/demand dynamics of lodging markets. Prior to his teaching career at Cornell, Prof. deRoos worked extensively in the hospitality industry. Industry experience includes work for the Sheraton Corporation in engineering operations and work with Remington Hotel Corporation as Director of Engineering, and later as Senior Project Manager, responsible for the construction of new properties and renovation of existing hotels. During this period, Prof. deRoos was responsible for the construction of Marriott Hotels, Hilton Hotels, and Hampton Inns.

Elaine Sahlins is Senior Vice President at HVS International's San Francisco office and co-director of the HVS Gaming Services division. She has an A.B. from Barnard College, Columbia University, and an M.P.S. degree from Cornell University's School of Hotel Administration. Her professional experience includes hotel and gaming appraisal review and management at Bank of America and hotel and resort acquisitions analysis with VMS Partners.

THE COST OF HOTEL CONSTRUCTION is a hot topic. Hotel operating performance has rebounded in many markets over the past two years and developers are looking at new hotel projects with renewed interest. Meanwhile, the cost of construction materials has soared. This chapter addresses the surge in hotel development and the impact of construction costs on investment returns.

New hotel development is cyclical. What drives the construction of new hotel rooms? Expectations of strong demand and higher room rates, which yield higher operating incomes and better project feasibility. Other factors that drive hotel

43

development are new hotel products that capture niche demand in established markets, areas undergoing new economic development or redevelopment, the development cost of new construction compared to acquisition pricing, and the ready availability of capital at reasonable rates—all of which provide attractive rates of return on new hotel construction.

In recent months, many of these factors have converged, resulting in renewed interest in new hotel construction. The price of construction materials also has escalated in the past 12 to 18 months. The hot topic for developers and economists is whether construction costs have been reset to a permanently higher benchmark. We present data that indicate this is the case. There is no reason to believe that labor costs will drop or that labor productivity will increase substantially, so any price decreases must come through decreases in the prices of building materials. Given the emerging global market for commodities and continued growth in Asia, material price declines are unlikely to happen. According to Gardiner & Theobald, an international project and cost management firm:

> After years of hype, the reality of the huge Chinese economy started to have a global effect in 2004; China became the main driver of international construction cost trends, replacing a role previously played by the U.S. and Western Europe. China's economic engine helped reverse years of deflation for construction costs in neighbouring Asian markets and its huge appetite for raw materials sparked worldwide inflation for a broad range of construction materials. The U.S. market, where construction costs rose at a double-digit pace, was the hardest hit but inflation also posted large gains in many other countries.[1]

Higher Construction Costs

Higher prices for construction materials are now an international concern; supply and demand trends are forcing prices upward. Whereas hotel development traditionally competed with domestic housing and other commercial construction, the construction industry in the 21st century is an international marketplace competing for materials and capital. Construction-industry cost statistics point to the surge of new building in Asia, particularly in China, as having a major impact on material pricing. The rising demand for steel and lumber is an international challenge. Also fueling construction-cost escalation is the higher price of gas, a major cost component for large infrastructure projects and for transporting raw construction materials. Construction equipment, much of which is manufactured in the United States, is selling robustly abroad, spurring higher equipment prices domestically. All these forces are surfacing at a time when material and equipment inventories purposely were controlled by suppliers in anticipation of slower construction trends in a weakened post–September 11 economic environment.

Describing the increased cost of construction materials in 2004 and the first quarter of 2005 requires superlatives: extraordinary and unexpected. The more than 30 percent increase in steel and more than 15 percent increase in lumber significantly affected many hotel projects, although lower increases in labor costs and other materials moderated overall development costs. In 2004, industry surveys and developer interviews indicate overall development costs were typically 5

Exhibit 1   Rooms in the Hotel Development Pipeline as of December 2004

	Existing Supply	Recently Opened	In Construction	Final Planning	Planning	Total	Pre-Planning
Chain Scale							
Luxury	75,760	1,510	2,383	200	2,276	4,859	1,520
Upper Upscale	526,336	6,004	16,990	1,953	20,902	39,845	7,595
Upscale	372,523	12,830	21,767	2,230	12,903	36,900	4,989
Midscale w/ F&B	584,145	2,809	4,318	214	4,698	9,230	1,657
Midscale w/o F&B	618,848	19,459	21,927	2,446	13,485	37,858	3,302
Economy	773,875	5,344	2,705	284	982	3,971	869
Unaffiliated	1,550,920	7,289	21,126	5,778	114,084	140,988	76,359
Total	4,502,407	55,245	91,216	13,105	169,330	273,651	96,291

Source: Smith Travel Research.

percent to 8 percent higher than in 2003. *Engineering News-Record (ENR)* indicates that the overall increase for 2005 is anticipated to be somewhat lower than in 2004.

New Hotel Pipeline

Even with the surge in construction costs, new hotel development has accelerated significantly. Smith Travel Research reports more than 270,000 rooms in the development pipeline. The acceleration notwithstanding, with an existing inventory of more than 4.5 million hotel rooms nationwide, the overall growth in rooms is regarded as modest. The relatively low ratio of supply growth comes when national demand for hotel rooms is rebounding. In some urban markets, the conversion of hotels to residential uses has reduced the inventory of guestrooms. Hotel investors remain optimistic that the proposed supply increase over the next few years will not have a significant effect on the current market's recovery.

Given the difficulty and expense of developing hotels in major urban areas, it is no surprise that the majority of the hotel development pipeline consists of limited- and focused-service hotels planned for suburban and lower-density markets. Some of this new supply is replacing lodging stock that is now 30 to 40 years old. Newer select- and focused-service hotel products are anticipated to garner more than their market share and, with their new construction and appealing room product, negatively affect the performance of older properties.

As of December 2004, Smith Travel Research estimated the inventory of existing hotel rooms to be approximately 4.5 million nationally. Exhibit 1 sets forth new hotel supply changes for the next three years.

If all the pipeline supply comes on-line, hotel supply is anticipated to increase by approximately 6 percent. On a national basis, the relative number of new rooms is not expected to significantly affect national occupancy levels, barring a softening in demand growth, though individual properties and markets will likely be affected.

With the modest increases in supply and the strong rebounding in market performance in many markets, developers increasingly are investigating new hotel projects. Higher construction costs have not dampened the planning of new hotels, but will they over the next few years? While the upward cost trend could be expected to temper the ability to build new rooms, the timing of the cost increases fortuitously coincides with a robust hotel market recovery. In 2004, construction costs increased by 7 to 8 percent, while RevPAR increased by 7.8 percent, a positive trend for hotel feasibility. Construction costs are not expected to increase as dramatically over the next few years; however, experts from PricewaterhouseCoopers forecast that RevPAR will continue to improve by roughly 6 to 8 percent per year in 2005, 2006, and 2007.

With increases in RevPAR, many hotels will experience exponential increases on net operating income. In the most recent recession, hotel management trimmed operating expenses. The positive leverage resulting from managing expenses leads to strong income flow-through from room revenue growth. With higher RevPAR, hotels become more profitable; the higher profitability supports new construction. A RevPAR growth rate that exceeds the increases in construction costs bodes well for the future feasible development of additional hotel supply.

Renovation and Refurbishment Issues

Construction costs also affect existing properties. Maintaining a brand-compliant product requires ongoing expenditures. Conversion expenses, which are not tracked in the Development Cost Survey, continue to be a substantial portion of hotel capital expenditures. Flat-screen televisions, new casegoods to replace now-obsolete armoires, new bedding, wireless Internet connectivity, and more upscale design motifs that used to be the signatures of upscale and luxury properties are now sought after at all price points. Because of the changing trends, the rebounding hotel market, and the low cost of capital, annual property capital plans are more extensive. As the cost of acquiring and maintaining existing hotels escalates, hotel investors become more motivated to build new product.

HVS International Hotel Development Cost Survey

HVS International has tracked hotel construction costs throughout the United States since 1976. Each year, HVS International researches development costs from its database of actual hotel construction budgets, industry reports, and uniform franchise offering circulars. These sources provide the basis for its range of per-room component costs. New-project construction cost data collected each year may increase the range and/or affect the mean and median of the construction cost components. These development cost ranges are then adjusted each year based on data reflecting the trend in each component cost category.

Hotel Development Cost Survey data are set forth for six hotel product types: budget/economy hotels, extended-stay hotels, midscale hotels without food and beverage, midscale hotels with food and beverage, full-service hotels, and luxury hotels. The following section addresses issues for each of these products based on current development trends. Because of their similar development processes, full-service and luxury hotels are discussed jointly.

Budget/Economy Hotels

Due to the predominance of low-rise, wood-framed design, the construction cost of budget/economy hotels tends to be the most stable of all the surveyed products. Constructed on less valuable land in secondary and tertiary locations, development of these hotels requires less time and money than other products. Notable component increases in development costs for budget/economy hotels have been in soft costs and furniture, fixtures, and equipment (FF&E) expenditures. Design and amenity creep has now permeated the lower-rated segments of the hotel market as travelers at all price points have higher expectations.

Extended-Stay Hotels

Extended-stay hotels continue to be a desirable development product for hotel investors. The wide range of rate price points and brands for extended-stay hotels results in a large per-room range of development costs. As with midscale products, the pipeline for extended-stay hotels is expanding with sites in lower-density areas where the product can feasibly be developed.

Midscale Hotels without F&B

Going forward, the pipeline for midscale hotels without food and beverage has the largest percentage increase in the number of rooms. Some of the planned product will take the place of an aging motel inventory in highway and tertiary locations. Another segment of new rooms is planned for secondary locations in high-density urban and suburban areas. Many of these hotels have wood-framed construction with less complex design than extended-stay hotels. Construction costs for this segment did not increase as much as for more elaborately designed full-service and extended-stay hotels.

Midscale Hotels with F&B

The midscale hotel with food and beverage is a highly desirable hotel product for developers. With lower construction costs and higher operating leverage, such midscale hotels with food and beverage as Courtyard by Marriott, Hilton Garden Inn, and Indigo are an important product type for new development. With lower per-room development costs than full-service hotels and competitive room rates when opened, these products that traditionally were designed for suburban sites are now planned for urban and lower-density sites as alternatives to the aging full-service and midscale hotel stock. Increases in development costs for midscale hotels with food and beverage reflect changes in material pricing and development of these products in markets with higher barriers to entry.

Full-Service and Luxury Hotels

Mixed-use projects, particularly with a residential component, are now mainstays of hotel development. Many upscale and luxury hotels in urban and resort settings are now including an ownership component to the development. Ownership structures range from conventional timeshare weeks to fractional ownerships, wholly-owned condominiums, and hotel-condominiums. These components provide strong capital structures that increase the feasibility of upscale and luxury full-service hotels.

Full-service and luxury hotel properties traditionally have been the hardest to develop feasibly. Their high quality finishes, large room sizes, and extensive public spaces require profitable operations to support construction. As a result of the high barriers to entry for larger hotel properties, the current investment market for existing full-service hotels in urban and suburban markets is robust. Until purchase prices exceed the high development costs of full-service hotels without a mixed-use component, the trend of mixed-used development that combines residential ownership and hotel components is expected to continue.

Survey Results

As reflected in the HVS International Hotel Development Cost Survey, construction costs surged in 2004 and continue to do so at a more moderate pace in 2005. Escalating costs will affect development projects currently under construction and those planned for the next few years. Some project managers are stockpiling raw materials inventories to avoid further increases in material costs.

Exhibits 2 and 3 set forth the overall results of the most current HVS International Hotel Development Cost Survey. Due to the wide variety of development projects and their diverse geographic locations, per-room development cost ranges for property-type categories overlap. Additional differences in site characteristics, density, height, construction materials, building and zoning codes, local labor markets, and other construction costs account for the wide range of per-room costs in each category. For example, extended-stay and limited-service hotels may be more expensive (on a per-room basis) to develop in downtown urban areas than full-service hotels in suburban or tertiary cities.

Even with all the varying circumstances that affect hotel development across the different segments, it is interesting to note that the allocation of costs among the five different components tracked by HVS International results in consistent contribution ratios to total development cost. With the exception of the luxury and resort development category, all the hotel categories show consistent trends in their distributions of costs.

It is important to note that there is no uniform system of allocation for hotel development budgets. Hotel development costs are accounted for in numerous line items and categories. Individual accounting for specific projects can be affected by tax implications, underwriting requirements, and investment structures. For example, in a development project, FF&E installation and construction finish work can overlap. Accounting for these items is not always the same from one project to another.

Exhibit 2   2005 Hotel Development Cost Survey Per-Room Averages

	Land	Building and Site Improvements	Soft Costs	FF&E	Pre-Opening and Working Capital	Total
Budget/Economy Hotels						
Average	$14,205	$40,796	$4,205	$8,308	$3,047	$61,761
Median	13,560	37,100	2,238	8,300	2,796	50,004
Allocation	16%	67%	5%	16%	7%	
Midscale Hotels w/o F&B						
Average	16,514	63,743	11,816	9,774	4,098	97,313
Median	13,916	56,309	8,513	9,498	2,748	81,539
Allocation	15%	68%	10%	11%	5%	
Extended-Stay Hotels						
Average	15,330	74,600	12,252	13,084	3,317	128,814
Median	13,675	65,419	10,623	13,500	2,381	103,239
Allocation	13%	64%	10%	12%	2%	
Midscale Hotels w/ F&B						
Average	17,142	70,382	13,898	12,659	3,754	112,271
Median	12,553	58,097	10,876	11,887	2,993	96,165
Allocation	14%	64%	11%	13%	3%	
Full-Service Hotels						
Average	19,933	110,850	24,541	22,706	6,941	205,640
Median	15,728	100,719	15,423	18,527	5,763	154,408
Allocation	12%	64%	11%	13%	4%	
Luxury Hotels and Resorts						
Average	103,177	320,421	115,016	55,575	21,436	608,631
Median	105,422	277,878	98,914	59,284	19,362	547,321
Allocation	16%	53%	17%	12%	4%	

Source: HVS International.

In addition, users of the HVS International Development Cost Survey should consider the per-room amount in the individual cost categories only as a general guide for that category. The totals for low and high ranges in each cost category do not add up to the high and low range of the sum of the categories. None of the data used in the survey showed a project that was either all at the low range of costs or all at the high range of costs. A property that has a high land cost may have lower construction costs and higher soft costs. The total costs shown in Exhibit 2 are from

Exhibit 3   Hotel Development Cost Survey Per-Room Range of Costs for 2004

	Land	Building and Site Improvements	Soft Costs	FF&E	Pre-Opening and Working Capital	Total
Budget/Economy Hotels	$ 4,100–$ 25,400	$ 22,000–$ 69,300	$ 600–$ 12,200	$ 4,100–$ 15,300	$ 1,300–$ 6,400	$ 32,700–$ 109,100
Midscale Hotel w/o F&B	4,100– 33,100	37,900– 132,900	2,000– 36,600	5,000– 20,200	800– 22,300	51,100– 190,100
Extended Stay Hotels	2,400– 44,500	43,400– 138,800	2,000– 42,500	3,200– 20,400	600– 10,700	57,300– 198,800
Midscale Hotels w/ F&B	3,600– 53,300	38,400– 163,300	3,100– 41,700	6,000– 30,600	1,000– 17,000	57,300– 237,000
Full-Service Hotels	3,500– 93,100	50,800– 233,600	2,100– 72,900	7,600– 40,400	1,700– 29,300	77,100– 339,700
Luxury Hotels and Resorts	12,900– 231,800	157,700– 1,123,100	24,300– 222,300	31,100– 104,600	9,700– 45,100	343,500– 1,406,500

Source: HVS International.

per-room budgets for hotel development projects and are not sums of the individual components.

All material used by HVS International for the Development Cost Survey is provided on a confidential basis and is believed to be reliable. Data from individual sources are not disclosed.

Construction Cost Index Data

RSMeans (a product line of Reed Construction Data) and *ENR* provide a historical cost record useful for benchmarking and for identifying specific areas within building costs that are driving price increases. The RSMeans data provides detailed information on the component costs of a building, while the *ENR* data breaks overall costs down into materials costs and labor costs.

Means Square Foot Costs Data

Specifically, the *Means Square Foot Costs* publication provides an annual estimate of the construction costs for four different types of lodging properties.[2] By tracking the costs to construct the same prototype building over time, differences can be tracked and attributed directly to changes in the costs of construction. The categories are as follows:

- *Motel, One Story*—The tracked prototype is a one-story building, with a nine-foot story height, 8,000 square feet, and approximately 25 rooms.

- *Motel, Two to Three Story*—The tracked prototype is a three-story building, with a nine-foot story height, 49,000 square feet, and approximately 125 rooms.

- *Hotel, Four to Seven Story*—The tracked prototype is a six-story building, with a 10-foot story height, 135,000 square feet, and approximately 300 rooms.

- *Hotel, Eight to Twenty-four Story*—The tracked prototype is a 15-story building, with a 10-foot story height, 450,000 square feet, and approximately 700 rooms.

Exhibit 4 contains the overall costs per square foot for the past 10 years for each prototype. It is followed by a detailed breakdown of costs and percentage changes from year to year in Exhibits 5–12. The prices shown are national averages for the United States at the beginning of the year.

Note that the Means data present building construction costs only. The data presented do not include the costs of land, soft costs, FF&E, and pre-opening costs. Unlike the survey data presented in Exhibits 2 and 3, the data in Exhibit 4 is based on a hypothetical prototype that does not change over time and can be used to measure changes in individual cost components in a controlled fashion.

Exhibits 5–12 reveal what generally is acknowledged within the industry: after a period of relatively stable development costs from 1997 through 2004, construction costs jumped dramatically in 2004 at more than double the inflation rate for motels and roughly four times as fast as inflation for hotels.

In the case of motels, the superstructure is built of wood, which has seen large but not dramatic price increases. In addition, there were large increases in the price of electrical systems, driven by large increases in the price of copper and aluminum.

The price increases were most dramatic in mid-rise and high-rise buildings, built from masonry, concrete, and steel. All of these basic commodities have seen price increases due to demand growth–driven economic strength in East Asia (particularly China) and the United States. Demand was further stimulated by natural disasters in 2004, including the damaging hurricane season in the United States and the Indian Ocean tsunami. Building superstructure costs increased dramatically in 2005 and significant increases were seen in the costs of plumbing systems, heating, ventilating, and air conditioning systems, and electrical systems.

Engineering News-Record

ENR produces a series of monthly construction cost indexes as part of its weekly reporting.[3] Exhibit 13 summarizes the rolling 12-month change in construction prices in the United States, starting in January 2003 and ending in August 2005. The dashed line shows the percentage change in the overall construction cost index, which is a weighted average of the building cost, and the two labor indexes—skilled wages and common (unskilled) wages. The building cost index shows the percentage change in the prices of building materials. Again, there is a story in the figures, with construction costs rising dramatically in March 2004, driven by a rapid increase in building material prices. These price increases are a marked change from the experience prior to March 2004; indeed, the data show that material price increases were lagging labor rate increases for much of 2003.

Labor rates, on the other hand, have exhibited a relatively constant annual rate of increase of about 4 percent over the 32-month period.

An additional note is that construction costs are moderating back to an annual rate of about 4 percent as building cost increases appear to be diminishing back to an annual rate that equals the overall labor rate changes.

Endnotes

1. Gardiner & Theobald, Levett & Bailey, and Rider Hunt, "Global Inflation on the Move," available online at http://www.gardiner.com/NewsSystem/newsstory.asp?id=286.

2. *Means Square Foot Costs* (Kingston, Mass.: RS Means Co.), 1996–2005.

3. *Engineering News-Record* (New York: McGraw-Hill), 2003–2005.

Exhibit 4 Hotel Construction Cost Per Square Foot

Motel—One-story building, nine-foot story height, 8,000 square feet of floor area [25 room property]

	1996	1997	1998	1999	2000	2001	2002	2003	2004	2005
Total Construction Cost	$84.80	$87.81	$87.89	$89.71	$92.70	$94.76	$97.58	$103.15	$102.44	$109.03

Motel—Three-story building, nine-foot story height, 49,000 square feet of floor area [125 room property]

	1996	1997	1998	1999	2000	2001	2002	2003	2004	2005
Total Construction Cost						$111.13	$114.88	$118.69	$120.47	$127.49

Hotel—Six-story building, 10-foot story height, 135,000 square feet of floor area [300 room property]

	1996	1997	1998	1999	2000	2001	2002	2003	2004	2005
Total Construction Cost	$92.26	$95.08	$95.49	$96.80	$98.58	$101.10	$103.15	$106.37	$108.62	$119.57

Hotel—15-story building, 10-foot story height, 450,000 square feet of floor area [700 room property]

	1996	1997	1998	1999	2000	2001	2002	2003	2004	2005
Total Construction Cost	$88.22	$89.91	$91.64	$93.72	$95.32	$96.05	$98.09	$101.10	$103.72	$114.35

Source: *Means Square Foot Costs* (Kingston, Mass.: RSMeans, 1996–2005).

Exhibit 5   Construction Costs Per Square Foot for the One-Story Motel Prototype

	1996	1997	1998	1999	2000	2001	2002	2003	2004	2005
Substructure	$ 8.98	$ 9.39	$ 9.38	$ 9.70	$ 9.99	$ 10.17	$ 10.78	$ 12.96	$ 10.59	$ 11.34
Shell	$ 18.10	$ 19.33	$ 18.61	$ 19.18	$ 20.31	$ 20.24	$ 20.45	$ 21.14	$ 21.61	$ 22.99
Superstructure	$ 4.25	$ 4.35	$ 4.33	$ 4.43	$ 4.94	$ 4.88	$ 4.90	$ 5.08	$ 5.02	$ 5.64
Exterior Closure	$ 11.58	$ 12.68	$ 11.93	$ 12.34	$ 12.86	$ 12.78	$ 12.89	$ 13.32	$ 13.80	$ 14.45
Roofing	$ 2.27	$ 2.30	$ 2.35	$ 2.41	$ 2.51	$ 2.58	$ 2.66	$ 2.74	$ 2.79	$ 2.90
Interior Construction	$ 16.20	$ 16.52	$ 17.00	$ 17.28	$ 17.81	$ 18.46	$ 18.46	$ 18.98	$ 19.47	$ 20.63
Services	$ 20.12	$ 20.41	$ 20.72	$ 20.91	$ 21.20	$ 21.98	$ 23.27	$ 24.04	$ 24.92	$ 26.56
Conveying	$ -									
Plumbing	$ 10.24	$ 10.42	$ 10.60	$ 10.58	$ 10.59	$ 10.80	$ 11.50	$ 12.16	$ 12.57	$ 13.38
HVAC	$ 3.02	$ 3.03	$ 3.09	$ 3.14	$ 3.22	$ 3.24	$ 3.59	$ 3.41	$ 3.50	$ 3.52
Fire Protection	$ 2.01	$ 2.04	$ 2.09	$ 2.08	$ 2.13	$ 2.27	$ 2.34	$ 2.37	$ 2.54	$ 2.68
Electrical	$ 4.85	$ 4.92	$ 4.94	$ 5.11	$ 5.26	$ 5.67	$ 5.84	$ 6.10	$ 6.31	$ 6.98
Subtotal Building	$ 63.40	$ 65.65	$ 65.71	$ 67.07	$ 69.31	$ 70.85	$ 72.96	$ 77.12	$ 76.59	$ 81.52
Contractor Fees	$ 15.85	$ 16.41	$ 16.43	$ 16.77	$ 17.33	$ 17.71	$ 18.24	$ 19.28	$ 19.15	$ 20.38
Architect Fees	$ 5.55	$ 5.74	$ 5.75	$ 5.87	$ 6.06	$ 6.20	$ 6.38	$ 6.75	$ 6.70	$ 7.13
Total Construction Cost	$ 84.80	$ 87.81	$ 87.89	$ 89.71	$ 92.70	$ 94.76	$ 97.58	$ 103.15	$ 102.44	$ 109.03

Source: *Means Square Foot Costs* (Kingston, Mass.: RSMeans, 1996–2005).

Exhibit 6   Construction Cost Indexes for the One-Story Motel Prototype

	1996	1997	1998	1999	2000	2001	2002	2003	2004	2005
					Percentage Change from Prior Year					
Substructure		4.6%	-0.1%	3.4%	3.0%	1.8%	6.0%	20.2%	-18.3%	7.1%
Shell		6.8%	-3.7%	3.1%	5.9%	-0.3%	1.0%	3.4%	2.2%	6.4%
Superstructure		2.4%	-0.5%	2.3%	11.5%	-1.2%	0.4%	3.7%	-1.2%	12.4%
Exterior Closure		9.5%	-5.9%	3.4%	4.2%	-0.6%	0.9%	3.3%	3.6%	4.7%
Roofing		1.3%	2.2%	2.6%	4.1%	2.8%	3.1%	3.0%	1.8%	3.9%
Interior Construction		2.0%	2.9%	1.6%	3.1%	3.6%	0.0%	2.8%	2.6%	6.0%
Services		1.4%	1.5%	0.9%	1.4%	3.7%	5.9%	3.3%	3.7%	6.6%
Conveying										
Plumbing		1.8%	1.7%	-0.2%	0.1%	2.0%	6.5%	5.7%	3.4%	6.4%
HVAC		0.3%	2.0%	1.6%	2.5%	0.6%	10.8%	-5.0%	2.6%	0.6%
Fire Protection		1.5%	2.5%	-0.5%	2.4%	6.6%	3.1%	1.3%	7.2%	5.5%
Electrical		1.4%	0.4%	3.4%	2.9%	7.8%	3.0%	4.5%	3.4%	10.6%
Subtotal Building		3.5%	0.1%	2.1%	3.3%	2.2%	3.0%	5.7%	-0.7%	6.4%
Contractor Fees		3.5%	0.1%	2.1%	3.3%	2.2%	3.0%	5.7%	-0.7%	6.4%
Architect Fees		3.5%	0.1%	2.1%	3.3%	2.2%	3.0%	5.7%	-0.7%	6.4%
Total Building Cost		3.5%	0.1%	2.1%	3.3%	2.2%	3.0%	5.7%	-0.7%	6.4%

Source: *Means Square Foot Costs* (Kingston, Mass.: RSMeans, 1996–2005).

Exhibit 7   Construction Costs Per Square Foot for the Three-Story Motel Prototype

	1996	1997	1998	1999	2000	2001	2002	2003	2004	2005
Substructure						$ 3.05	$ 3.14	$ 3.76	$ 3.03	$ 3.25
Shell						$ 20.79	$ 17.19	$ 17.42	$ 17.99	$ 18.81
Superstructure						$ 11.06	$ 7.33	$ 7.34	$ 7.51	$ 7.86
Exterior Closure						$ 8.32	$ 8.44	$ 8.63	$ 8.99	$ 9.41
Roofing						$ 1.41	$ 1.42	$ 1.45	$ 1.49	$ 1.54
Interior Construction						$ 28.73	$ 33.02	$ 34.31	$ 35.20	$ 37.06
Services						$ 31.30	$ 33.35	$ 34.09	$ 34.70	$ 37.10
Conveying						$ 2.62	$ 2.70	$ 2.73	$ 2.87	$ 3.04
Plumbing						$ 15.74	$ 16.88	$ 17.59	$ 17.57	$ 18.95
HVAC						$ 5.04	$ 5.60	$ 5.31	$ 5.45	$ 5.47
Fire Protection						$ 1.21	$ 1.26	$ 1.28	$ 1.39	$ 1.45
Electrical						$ 6.69	$ 6.91	$ 7.18	$ 7.42	$ 8.19
Subtotal Building						$ 83.87	$ 86.70	$ 89.58	$ 90.92	$ 96.22
Contractor Fees						$ 20.97	$ 21.68	$ 22.40	$ 22.73	$ 24.06
Architect Fees						$ 6.29	$ 6.50	$ 6.72	$ 6.82	$ 7.22
Total Construction Cost						$111.13	$114.88	$118.69	$120.47	$127.49

Note: Data for 1996–2000 are not shown due to a change in the RSMeans prototype.

Source: *Means Square Foot Costs* (Kingston, Mass.: RSMeans, 2001–2005).

Exhibit 8 Construction Cost Indexes for the Three-Story Motel Prototype

Percentage Change from Prior Year

	1996	1997	1998	1999	2000	2001	2002	2003	2004	2005
Substructure							3.0%	19.7%	-19.4%	7.3%
Shell							-17.3%	1.3%	3.3%	4.6%
Superstructure							-33.7%	0.1%	2.3%	4.7%
Exterior Closure							1.4%	2.3%	4.2%	4.7%
Roofing							0.7%	2.1%	2.8%	3.4%
Interior Construction							14.9%	3.9%	2.6%	5.3%
Services							6.5%	2.2%	1.8%	6.9%
Conveying							3.1%	1.1%	5.1%	5.9%
Plumbing							7.2%	4.2%	-0.1%	7.9%
HVAC							11.1%	-5.2%	2.6%	0.4%
Fire Protection							4.1%	1.6%	8.6%	4.3%
Electrical							3.3%	3.9%	3.3%	10.4%
Subtotal Building							3.4%	3.3%	1.5%	5.8%
Contractor Fees							3.4%	3.3%	1.5%	5.8%
Architect Fees							3.4%	3.3%	1.5%	5.8%
Total Building Cost							3.4%	3.3%	1.5%	5.8%

Note: Data for 1996–2001 are not shown due to a change in the RSMeans prototype.

Source: *Means Square Foot Costs* (Kingston, Mass.: RSMeans, 2002–2005).

Exhibit 9 Construction Costs Per Square Foot for the Six-Story Hotel Prototype

	1996	1997	1998	1999	2000	2001	2002	2003	2004	2005
Substructure	$ 1.71	$ 1.79	$ 1.78	$ 1.84	$ 1.91	$ 1.95	$ 2.01	$ 2.29	$ 1.98	$ 2.13
Shell	$ 16.39	$ 17.68	$ 17.45	$ 17.98	$ 18.28	$ 19.66	$ 19.51	$ 19.76	$ 20.25	$ 23.59
Superstructure	$ 8.85	$ 9.48	$ 9.69	$ 9.98	$ 10.10	$ 11.24	$ 10.97	$ 10.92	$ 11.13	$ 14.11
Exterior Closure	$ 6.98	$ 7.61	$ 7.15	$ 7.37	$ 7.54	$ 7.77	$ 7.89	$ 8.17	$ 8.43	$ 8.78
Roofing	$ 0.56	$ 0.59	$ 0.61	$ 0.63	$ 0.64	$ 0.65	$ 0.65	$ 0.67	$ 0.69	$ 0.70
Interior Construction	$ 17.65	$ 18.08	$ 18.22	$ 18.88	$ 19.41	$ 19.22	$ 19.60	$ 20.27	$ 20.86	$ 22.10
Services	$ 33.88	$ 34.21	$ 34.62	$ 34.36	$ 34.80	$ 35.47	$ 36.73	$ 37.96	$ 38.89	$ 42.42
Conveying	$ 3.93	$ 3.56	$ 3.63	$ 3.76	$ 3.87	$ 3.89	$ 3.99	$ 4.04	$ 4.19	$ 4.39
Plumbing	$ 10.26	$ 10.63	$ 10.87	$ 10.63	$ 10.48	$ 10.57	$ 11.19	$ 11.71	$ 11.94	$ 13.00
HVAC	$ 10.96	$ 11.10	$ 10.97	$ 10.71	$ 10.93	$ 11.20	$ 11.38	$ 11.61	$ 11.82	$ 13.10
Fire Protection	$ 1.36	$ 1.39	$ 1.42	$ 1.41	$ 1.46	$ 1.48	$ 1.57	$ 1.64	$ 1.72	$ 1.79
Electrical	$ 7.37	$ 7.53	$ 7.73	$ 7.85	$ 8.06	$ 8.33	$ 8.60	$ 8.96	$ 9.22	$ 10.14
Subtotal Building	$ 69.63	$ 71.76	$ 72.07	$ 73.06	$ 74.40	$ 76.30	$ 77.85	$ 80.28	$ 81.98	$ 90.24
Contractor Fees	$ 17.41	$ 17.94	$ 18.02	$ 18.27	$ 18.60	$ 19.08	$ 19.46	$ 20.07	$ 20.50	$ 22.56
Architect Fees	$ 5.22	$ 5.38	$ 5.41	$ 5.48	$ 5.58	$ 5.72	$ 5.84	$ 6.02	$ 6.15	$ 6.77
Total Construction Cost	$ 92.26	$ 95.08	$ 95.49	$ 96.80	$ 98.58	$ 101.10	$ 103.15	$ 106.37	$ 108.62	$ 119.57

Source: *Means Square Foot Costs* (Kingston, Mass.: RSMeans, 1996–2005).

Exhibit 10 Construction Cost Indexes for the Six-Story Hotel Prototype

	1996	1997	1998	1999	2000	2001	2002	2003	2004	2005
					Percentage Change from Prior Year					
Substructure		4.7%	-0.6%	3.4%	3.8%	2.1%	3.1%	13.9%	-13.5%	7.6%
Shell		7.9%	-1.3%	3.0%	1.7%	7.5%	-0.8%	1.3%	2.5%	16.5%
Superstructure		7.1%	2.2%	3.0%	1.2%	11.3%	-2.4%	-0.5%	1.9%	26.8%
Exterior Closure		9.0%	-6.0%	3.1%	2.3%	3.1%	1.5%	3.5%	3.2%	4.2%
Roofing		5.4%	3.4%	3.3%	1.6%	1.6%	0.0%	3.1%	3.0%	1.4%
Interior Construction		2.4%	0.8%	3.6%	2.8%	-1.0%	2.0%	3.4%	2.9%	5.9%
Services		1.0%	1.2%	-0.8%	1.3%	1.9%	3.6%	3.3%	2.4%	9.1%
Conveying		-9.4%	2.0%	3.6%	2.9%	0.5%	2.6%	1.3%	3.7%	4.8%
Plumbing		3.6%	2.3%	-2.2%	-1.4%	0.9%	5.9%	4.6%	2.0%	8.9%
HVAC		1.3%	-1.2%	-2.4%	2.1%	2.5%	1.6%	2.0%	1.8%	10.8%
Fire Protection		2.2%	2.2%	-0.7%	3.5%	1.4%	6.1%	4.5%	4.9%	4.1%
Electrical		2.2%	2.7%	1.6%	2.7%	3.3%	3.2%	4.2%	2.9%	10.0%
Subtotal Building		3.1%	0.4%	1.4%	1.8%	2.6%	2.0%	3.1%	2.1%	10.1%
Contractor Fees		3.1%	0.4%	1.4%	1.8%	2.6%	2.0%	3.1%	2.1%	10.1%
Architect Fees		3.1%	0.4%	1.4%	1.8%	2.6%	2.0%	3.1%	2.1%	10.1%
Total Building Cost		3.1%	0.4%	1.4%	1.8%	2.6%	2.0%	3.1%	2.1%	10.1%

Source: *Means Square Foot Costs* (Kingston, Mass.: RSMeans, 1996–2005).

Exhibit 11   Construction Costs Per Square Foot for the 15-Story Hotel Prototype

	1996	1997	1998	1999	2000	2001	2002	2003	2004	2005
Substructure	$ 1.02	$ 1.09	$ 1.07	$ 1.12	$ 1.15	$ 1.18	$ 1.23	$ 1.26	$ 1.24	$ 1.34
Shell	$ 13.75	$ 14.45	$ 14.89	$ 15.41	$ 15.71	$ 17.15	$ 16.58	$ 16.64	$ 17.08	$ 20.30
Superstructure	$ 9.71	$ 10.36	$ 10.74	$ 10.99	$ 11.12	$ 12.43	$ 11.67	$ 11.61	$ 11.85	$ 14.88
Exterior Closure	$ 3.82	$ 3.86	$ 3.92	$ 4.17	$ 4.34	$ 4.47	$ 4.66	$ 4.78	$ 4.97	$ 5.14
Roofing	$ 0.22	$ 0.23	$ 0.23	$ 0.25	$ 0.25	$ 0.25	$ 0.25	$ 0.25	$ 0.26	$ 0.28
Interior Construction	$ 20.08	$ 20.60	$ 20.89	$ 21.54	$ 22.02	$ 20.21	$ 21.19	$ 21.82	$ 22.47	$ 23.54
Services	$ 31.73	$ 31.72	$ 32.31	$ 32.66	$ 33.06	$ 33.95	$ 35.03	$ 36.58	$ 37.49	$ 41.12
Conveying	$ 3.49	$ 2.85	$ 2.89	$ 3.00	$ 3.10	$ 3.14	$ 3.22	$ 3.26	$ 3.40	$ 3.59
Plumbing	$ 9.51	$ 9.89	$ 10.14	$ 10.35	$ 10.24	$ 10.51	$ 11.08	$ 11.98	$ 12.11	$ 13.23
HVAC	$ 9.27	$ 9.37	$ 9.54	$ 9.38	$ 9.57	$ 9.77	$ 9.87	$ 10.11	$ 10.28	$ 11.51
Fire Protection	$ 2.18	$ 2.20	$ 2.22	$ 2.17	$ 2.20	$ 2.28	$ 2.36	$ 2.39	$ 2.59	$ 2.72
Electrical	$ 7.28	$ 7.41	$ 7.52	$ 7.76	$ 7.95	$ 8.25	$ 8.50	$ 8.84	$ 9.11	$ 10.07
Subtotal Building	$ 66.58	$ 67.86	$ 69.16	$ 70.73	$ 71.94	$ 72.49	$ 74.03	$ 76.30	$ 78.28	$ 86.30
Contractor Fees	$ 16.65	$ 16.97	$ 17.29	$ 17.68	$ 17.99	$ 18.12	$ 18.51	$ 19.08	$ 19.57	$ 21.58
Architect Fees	$ 4.99	$ 5.09	$ 5.19	$ 5.30	$ 5.40	$ 5.44	$ 5.55	$ 5.72	$ 5.87	$ 6.47
Total Construction Cost	$ 88.22	$ 89.91	$ 91.64	$ 93.72	$ 95.32	$ 96.05	$ 98.09	$ 101.10	$ 103.72	$ 114.35

Source: *Means Square Foot Costs* (Kingston, Mass.: RSMeans, 1996–2005).

Exhibit 12 Construction Cost Indexes for the 15-Story Hotel Prototype

	1996	1997	1998	1999	2000	2001	2002	2003	2004	2005
				Percentage Change from Prior Year						
Substructure		6.9%	-1.8%	4.7%	2.7%	2.6%	4.2%	2.4%	-1.6%	8.1%
Shell		5.1%	3.0%	3.5%	1.9%	9.2%	-3.3%	0.4%	2.6%	18.9%
Superstructure		6.7%	3.7%	2.3%	1.2%	11.8%	-6.1%	-0.5%	2.1%	25.6%
Exterior Closure		1.0%	1.6%	6.4%	4.1%	3.0%	4.3%	2.6%	4.0%	3.4%
Roofing		4.5%	0.0%	8.7%	0.0%	0.0%	0.0%	0.0%	4.0%	7.7%
Interior Construction		2.6%	1.4%	3.1%	2.2%	-8.2%	4.8%	3.0%	3.0%	4.8%
Services		0.0%	1.9%	1.1%	1.2%	2.7%	3.2%	4.4%	2.5%	9.7%
Conveying		-18.3%	1.4%	3.8%	3.3%	1.3%	2.5%	1.2%	4.3%	5.6%
Plumbing		4.0%	2.5%	2.1%	-1.1%	2.6%	5.4%	8.1%	1.1%	9.2%
HVAC		1.1%	1.8%	-1.7%	2.0%	2.1%	1.0%	2.4%	1.7%	12.0%
Fire Protection		0.9%	0.9%	-2.3%	1.4%	3.6%	3.5%	1.3%	8.4%	5.0%
Electrical		1.8%	1.5%	3.2%	2.4%	3.8%	3.0%	4.0%	3.1%	10.5%
Subtotal Building		1.9%	1.9%	2.3%	1.7%	0.8%	2.1%	3.1%	2.6%	10.2%
Contractor Fees		1.9%	1.9%	2.3%	1.7%	0.8%	2.1%	3.1%	2.6%	10.2%
Architect Fees		1.9%	1.9%	2.3%	1.7%	0.8%	2.1%	3.1%	2.6%	10.2%
Total Building Cost		1.9%	1.9%	2.3%	1.7%	0.8%	2.1%	3.1%	2.6%	10.2%

Source: *Means Square Foot Costs* (Kingston, Mass.: RSMeans, 1996–2005).

Exhibit 13   *ENR* Construction Index 12-Month Rolling Change

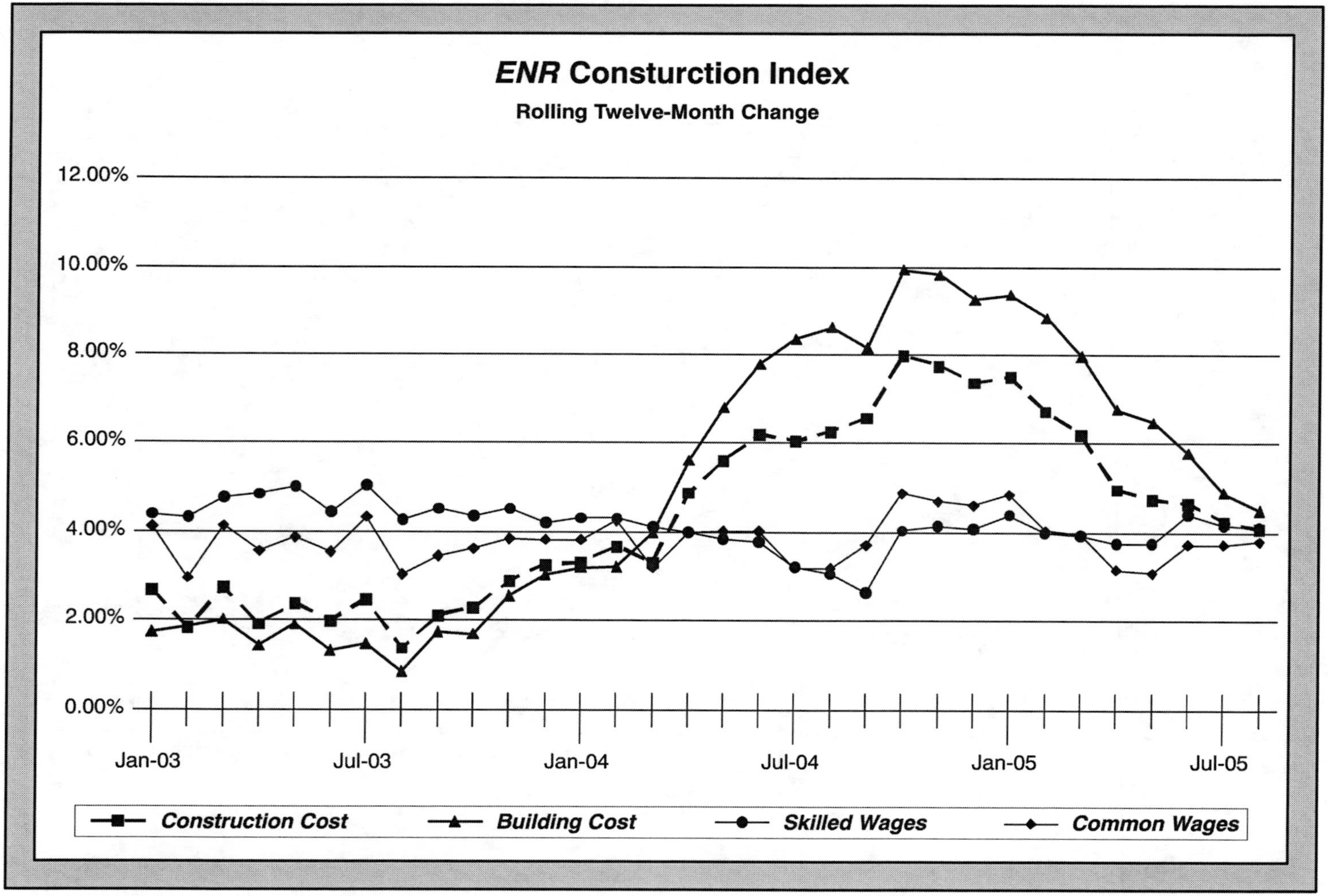

ENR Consturction Index
Rolling Twelve-Month Change

Legend: Construction Cost — Building Cost — Skilled Wages — Common Wages

Y-axis: 0.00%, 2.00%, 4.00%, 6.00%, 8.00%, 10.00%, 12.00%
X-axis: Jan-03, Jul-03, Jan-04, Jul-04, Jan-05, Jul-05

Asset Management 101:
Lessons Learned and Thoughts to Share

By *Lori E. Raleigh, ISHC*

Lori E. Raleigh is the founder of The Travers Group, a hotel investment and asset management advisory firm, and is currently serving as the Executive Director of the International Society of Hospitality Consultants (ISHC). She is frequently a guest speaker at industry conferences and events and has written numerous articles on hotel investments, asset management, and evaluating brand and franchise affiliation programs. Ms. Raleigh currently serves on the board of directors of the American Hotel & Lodging Association, the New York University Preston Robert Tisch Center for Hospitality, Tourism and Sports Management Advisory Board, Florida Gulf Coast University's Resort & Hospitality Management Advisory Board, the New England Real Estate Journal Advisory Board, Real Estate Forum's Hotel Industry Advisory Board, and National Hotel Executive's Finance Editorial Advisory Board. She is a member of IREFAC and is also a member and past president of the Hotel Asset Managers Association. Other memberships include the Urban Land Institute and the Association of Hospitality Financial Management Educators. Ms. Raleigh is a graduate of Emmanuel College and holds an MBA from Boston College. She is listed among Who's Who in American Colleges & Universities.

ASSET MANAGEMENT IN THE HOTEL INDUSTRY has changed substantially over the years. With its early roots going back to the mid-1980s, asset management first developed as a specialty area of expertise due in large part to the emergence of passive forms of ownership (i.e., limited partnerships, institutional ownership of hotels, etc.) and the extremely weak performance of hotels as an investment alternative.

From the mid-1980s to the early 1990s, hotels in general made little or no economic sense as investments. During this time, many hotels were struggling to break even, let alone generate a return on investment. In 1991, the worst performing year in the history of the hotel industry, the industry reported a record loss of $5.4 billion and many investors faced the challenge of funding significant deficits.

Asset management during this challenging time tended to focus on crisis management, restructuring hotel investments, and the polarity (as opposed to consensus/alignment) of interests of the various parties (i.e., owners, lenders, managers, and/or franchisors). While this approach served to address crisis issues and helped manage owner/investor downside risk and exposure, it was not necessarily geared to building long-term relationships with managers and franchisors or to maximizing the overall performance of a hotel investment.

Fortunately, in recent years, the focus of asset management has out of necessity changed dramatically because of the increased complexity of hotel investments, the current operating environment, and the changing needs, objectives, and expectations of investors. Today, asset management represents a highly specialized and dedicated area of expertise, requiring keen analytical and problem-solving skills, forward thinking and strategic planning expertise, strong communication skills, and the ability to work well with and motivate others to accomplish results.

Unfortunately, there are not necessarily clear-cut right or wrong solutions to many of the problems, issues, and challenges that asset managers face. Asset management is more of an ever-evolving discipline encompassing other asset managers' best practices as well as—for better or worse—learning from one's own mistakes.

The purpose of this chapter is to share thoughts about some important asset management issues. The chapter begins with an overview of the investment climate—a critical fundamental barometer for hotel investors and asset managers—and highlights some key issues to be addressed when underwriting a hotel investment. The chapter also discusses opportunities for improving hotel investment performance and important issues to keep in mind from an investment/asset management perspective going forward.

Hotel Investment Climate

During the past 20-plus years, hotels have been in and out of favor as an investment alternative. Understanding where we are in the investment cycle and how and why we got there is a critical part of managing a hotel investment. Accordingly, we begin this chapter with a brief overview of the current investment climate along with a discussion of some of the key issues affecting the availability of capital to the hospitality industry.

According to Smith Travel Research, the hotel industry is in the "sweet spot" of a rebound that began in the summer of 2004. With demand growth currently exceeding supply growth, the outlook for further revenue growth looks excellent, at least in the immediate future. Assuming no further erosion in profit margin (which has been a huge challenge since 2000), along with the benefit of positive operating leverage in a strong revenue growth environment, the industry appears poised to realize substantial improvement in bottom-line financial performance.

It is important to note, however, that there are areas of potential vulnerability and at this point in the cycle, it is important to stay focused on net operating income performance fundamentals and to monitor alternative investment performance and capital market trends.

Following is a brief overview of where we are relative to hotel industry profit, the recovery/restoration of real estate values following the events of September 11, 2001, and the capital markets.

Hotel Industry Profit

The hotel industry reported record total revenue of $113.7 billion for 2004 and an approximately $3.9 billion or 30 percent increase (from $12.8 billion to $16.7 billion) in profitability. Despite record revenue, however, bottom-line performance is nearly $6 billion or 25 percent below the $22.5 billion profit level achieved in 2000. Further improvement in industry profit is expected for 2005, but it most likely will be 2006 before the industry reaches the record profit levels achieved in 2000.

Why the Shortfall in Bottom-Line Performance? Between 2000 and 2004, total revenue increased by $1.6 billion or 1.4 percent (from $112.1 billion in 2000 to $113.7 billion in 2004). During this same timeframe, total expenses increased by 8.3 percent from $89.6 billion in 2000 to $97 billion. The industry has therefore experienced substantial margin erosion since 2000. From 2000 to 2003, the industry average profit margin decreased by 5.9 percentage points or by 14.5 percent (i.e., from 40.9 percent to 35 percent) due to the escalation of operating expenses and to increases in labor, benefit, insurance, and energy expenses in particular. Although the average industry profit margin increased by 1.6 percentage points in 2004, it is important to note that it is still nearly 4.3 percentage points or 10.5 percent below 2000 levels despite the record revenue reported in 2004.

Revenue Growth. In light of the substantial increase in operating expenses, the industry has been dependent upon revenue growth as the primary driver of improvements in bottom line performance during the 2001–2004 timeframe. The further improvement in industry profit forecast for 2005 also is expected to be attributable in large part to revenue growth.

Value Restoration

Hotel valuation is a function of many factors, including net operating income or profit levels, interest rates, investor expectations, capitalization rates, and alternative investment performance.

We are at a very interesting juncture in the hotel investment cycle. Although industry profit is still approximately 25 percent or $6 billion below the record profit level of $22.5 billion reported in 2000, hotel valuations on an industry average per-room basis are close to, and in some instances have exceeded, 2000 levels.

It is important to note that the recovery of value has been in large part attributable to the very favorable interest environment and significantly lower capitalization rates and investor return expectations—factors that essentially are beyond the direct control of the hotel industry.

What does this mean? With both capitalization and interest rates essentially at all-time lows, the industry will need to look to growth in net operating income to realize further improvement in pricing and valuation levels.

Availability of Investment Capital

There are three major factors currently affecting the availability of capital to the hotel industry: a surplus of investment capital in general, weak alternative investment performance, and the yield performance of hotels relative to alternative investments.

Surplus of Investment Capital. There currently is a huge surplus of investment capital, in large part attributable to the accumulation of both institutional pension fund and individual retirement plan assets. Total retirement assets—including defined benefit plans (i.e., traditional employer-guaranteed income retirement plans) and defined contribution plans (i.e., 401(k) or employer/employee contribution savings plans) along with individual retirement accounts—currently are valued at more than $12 trillion. Given the enormous amount of pension and retirement fund capital, even seemingly minor shifts in the investment allocation of retirement assets into and out of the hotel sector can have a significant impact on the availability of capital to the hotel industry.

Alternative Investment Performance. The availability of capital to the hotel industry is dependent upon hotel investment return performance, in particular relative to the comparative risk and return performance of alternative investments. During the past 15–20 years, the industry has been in and out of favor at various times. In 1991, the hotel industry reported negative returns at a time when an investor could earn a much higher return from a certificate of deposit with minimal or no risk. At this time, hotels understandably made little economic sense as investments.

From 1991 to 2000, the hotel industry reported successive improvements in bottom line performance and profit grew by more than $28 billion during this timeframe (from a $5.4 billion loss to a record $22.5 billion in pretax profit). During this timeframe, hotels catapulted from being undesirable to very attractive investment alternatives. Following the events of 2001, the hotel industry once again experienced a flight of investment capital due to the dramatic deterioration in operating fundamentals and return on investment.

More recently, the hotel industry has come back in favor as an investment alternative. While this is attributable first and foremost to significant improvements in bottom-line performance, it is important to keep in mind that the hotel industry also currently is the beneficiary of the weak performance of alternative investment classes.

Net operating income or yield and total return on investment performance for hotels both have declined quite dramatically from mid-1990s levels. However, returns on alternative assets have declined as well and currently real estate in general and hotels in particular are outperforming alternative investments, including equities.

Yield Performance

Pension fund investment capital increasingly is focusing on yield vs. capital appreciation performance to fund contingent liabilities (i.e., retirement pension obligations) and individual investors nearing retirement are also looking for yield investments. With an estimated 77 million baby boomers approaching retirement age over the next several years, the search for yield can be expected to continue to be a huge issue going forward.

Shrinking Yield Alternatives. Investing for yield has become very challenging. The average dividend yield in the stock market is just over 2 percent. Certificate of deposit rates, although having increased recently (now in the 3.75–4 percent range, depending upon the term), still leave a bit to be desired from an investment perspective.

The bond market is confusing at this point in time, particularly in light of the disconnect in yields versus treasury activity. The dramatic compression of the yield curve (the spread between short- and long-term interest rates), albeit following ten successive quarter-point increases during the past several months in the Fed funds rate, is confusing from an investment perspective and has been called a "conundrum" by Federal Reserve chairman Alan Greenspan.

Investing in corporate debt, traditionally viewed as a safe haven for fixed income/yield investors, has also posed challenges and resulted in substantial losses for many investors. With the write-down of over $35 billion in debt, many of WorldCom's fixed-income investors lost more than 90 percent of their principal. WorldCom went from institutional-grade debt yielding 7 percent to junk status virtually overnight. In 2004, there was substantial exposure for many investors with the downgrading of General Motors debt from institutional to high-risk or speculative status. Ginnie Mae and Fannie Mae, which traditionally have represented opportunities for investing for yield, also are under increased scrutiny.

In light of the challenge of investing for yield, real estate in general and hotels in particular have emerged as a diversification/alternative investment for yield investors.

Underwriting the Investment

It is very difficult and can take many years to recover from the poor underwriting of a hotel investment. Accordingly, performing adequate underwriting and due diligence up front is a critical part of the acquisition/purchase of a hotel.

The due diligence process should include (at a minimum) a review of the market, the underwriting of the both the asset or real estate and business or operating components in a hotel investment, and an evaluation of the management and affiliation alternatives for the hotel.

Sensitivity analysis is also a critical part of the underwriting process. It is important to understand how changes in key assumptions can affect projections for even minor changes in key variables (e.g., market share, revenue growth, or margin assumptions) and dramatically affect bottom-line performance projections/estimates.

Following are some issues to think about when underwriting a hotel's real estate component and evaluating affiliation alternatives for a hotel.

Underwriting the Asset or Real Estate Component

For many years, the hotel industry focused primarily on underwriting the competitive market and operating fundamentals of a hotel. Only in more recent years have investors and asset managers recognized the importance of also underwriting the asset or real estate component in a hotel investment.

What Types of Issues Need to Be Evaluated? Issues that need to be evaluated from a real estate perspective include value volatility, the age and condition of the property, the cost to maintain and upgrade the property, barriers to competition and other land value/alternative use considerations, existing and potential functional obsolescence issues, and insurance coverage, taxation, and regulatory issues.

Reconciling Different Approaches to Value. The value of shares of public hotel companies and publicly traded hotel real estate (real estate investment trusts) are essentially valued by the market on a regular, ongoing basis. In sharp contrast, information on private (as opposed to publicly traded) hotel values and investment performance is extremely limited and is based primarily on research and/or available transaction data. Privately held hotels are estimated to account for more than 75 percent of hotel inventory.

When we think of the "value" of a hotel, traditionally we think of its appraised or market value. It is important to keep in mind, however, that there are different approaches to determining appraisal value (i.e., the replacement cost, comparable sales, and the capitalization of income or discounted cash flow approach to value). In today's environment, these different approaches can potentially yield very different values, depending upon the particular situation and certain key assumptions.

In addition to appraised value, there are also the concepts of highest and best use value, net asset value, assessed value, investment value, and liquidation value. Depending on the situation, these may also need to be evaluated and reconciled.

Real Estate Replacement Cost Considerations. One frequently hears that a hotel is a good investment because it can be acquired at a substantial discount to replacement cost. While purchasing a property below its replacement cost can be very beneficial (particularly with regard to new supply), it does not ensure the financial success of a property. This can be an issue of concern when comparable competitive hotels have lower replacement costs.

Occasionally, the income approach to value can suggest a higher value than replacement cost. While there may be instances when paying a premium to replacement cost is justifiable (e.g., when there are strong barriers to competition or alternative use considerations), it is important to keep in mind that replacement cost generally should represent the upper limit of value.

Alternative Use Considerations. For many years, hotels represented the "highest and best use" for a property. This is not necessarily the case today. In fact, in many high-end urban markets and resort destinations, mixed use and/or condominium use have emerged as the highest and best use. This new reality can present an opportunity for some hotel investors and a challenge for others, depending upon the market dynamics and whether one is buying or selling a hotel.

Functional Obsolescence. Functional obsolescence—the need to replace or upgrade a capital item prematurely due to changing needs or the competitive environment rather than the asset's actual physical deterioration—represents a major challenge for many hotels today. From rewiring older hotels to replacing dated armoires and televisions to updating/redesigning group meeting space and/or food and beverage outlets to meet changing customer expectations, many hotels are undertaking or will need to undertake major and potentially costly alterations to resolve obsolescence issues.

It is important to identify competitive product obsolescence issues up front and include the potential cost involved in addressing them as part of the underwriting and purchase price/investment basis of a hotel. Typically, the cost of this type of work is not accounted for in either the operating or capital budget plans for the hotel when they are first developed.

Absorbing the cost of addressing unforeseen obsolescence issues that are not accounted for in the original capital budget may have a substantial negative impact on financial performance and return on investment.

Capital Asset Preservation. The hotel industry lags far behind the residential and commercial real estate community in managing and preserving the physical assets of a hotel investment. Capital asset preservation, or extending the life of capital assets via improved preventive maintenance programs, is an area with substantial potential for the hotel industry to improve investment return performance. For example, the ability to extend the life of carpet in a hotel by one or two years via appropriate product selection up front and diligent preventive maintenance can represent a 20–30 percent reduction in the amortized or capital cost to replace the carpet. Unfortunately, many hotel operators and owners tend to focus on short-term operating financial results and do not invest in preventive maintenance to preserve and extend the life of furnishings and other capital assets.

Evaluating Franchise/Affiliation Alternatives

With the cost of affiliation representing the single largest expense category after labor for many hotels, the decision to be an independent or affiliated hotel (and, if affiliated, determining which affiliation is best) is one of the most critical decisions in a hotel investment.

In the United States, it is estimated that approximately 55 percent of all hotels are branded and approximately 67 percent of hotel room inventory is affiliated. For many hotels, affiliation can represent the difference between financial viability and failure. However, it is important to keep in mind that affiliation does not ensure successful performance. In fact, some hotels, depending upon their location, market positioning, and business segmentation, actually perform better as independents.

There are three primary reasons to consider an affiliation: (1) the ability of a particular brand or affiliation to generate incremental business (business the hotel could not otherwise capture on its own); (2) the ability of a franchisor or affiliation to capture or generate higher rated business for a hotel; and (3) the potential to generate business more cost effectively than a hotel could on its own.

Evaluating the merits of a franchise or affiliation should begin with a review of the competitive market, the positioning of the hotel in the market, and an in-depth analysis of the business mix. Various market segments may require different marketing strategies and sales and promotional programs. There are many alternative potential sources of business and distribution channels for capturing and/or generating different types of business.

When evaluating the merits of affiliation, it is important to evaluate the potential of a particular brand to generate specific types of business (group, leisure, corporate, etc.) to meet the needs of a particular hotel. It also is important to assess the potential for a brand or affiliation to capture or generate incremental business.

Evaluating the Cost of Affiliation. The cost of a franchise or affiliation can vary substantially, depending upon the perceived value of the brand and the scope of services and programs provided. While the overall cost of most franchise and affiliation programs currently offered is between 7 and 9 percent of revenue, the total cost can vary substantially from less than 2 percent to 10 percent or more, depending upon the specific programs a particular affiliation or franchise company is offering or requiring.

Typically, the cost of a franchise or affiliation includes up-front, royalty, marketing, and reservation fees. Other costs that may need to be accounted for include expenses involved in implementing and maintaining the affiliation (e.g., signage, upgrading to comply with system standards, or providing amenities), promoting the affiliation (e.g., honored or frequent guest programs), and meeting technology standards. Additional program offerings and related fees might include special marketing support and promotional programs, sales representation programs, and special revenue- and yield-management programs/systems. It also is important to understand clearly any potential termination fees and/or liquidated damage expense exposure.

Challenges in Evaluating the Costs and Benefits of Affiliation. One of the primary statistics traditionally used for evaluating a franchisor's or chain's performance has been the volume of business generated by the brand's toll-free number and on-line reservation systems. However, there are shortcomings to this approach. It can be difficult to make performance comparisons between affiliation alternatives based on reservation system performance for franchisors, and chain organizations have different ways to account for reservation activity—including, for example, call volume, conversions, cancellations, gross versus net bookings, etc. Additionally, this approach does not take into account the cost of generating the business.

Determining the actual total cost of generating a booking can be difficult. Then there is the added challenge of dealing with inconsistencies in how costs are accounted for from one brand to another. For example, the total cost allocations may or may not include expenditures associated with frequent or honored guest programs, brochures, advertising, technology support, and other promotional costs involved in generating business through a central and/or Web-enabled reservations system.

It often is difficult to determine whether business generated through the franchise's or chain's reservation system truly represents incremental business rather than bookings that a hotel could generate on its own. For example, group business represents a major market segment for many hotels. Although group meeting business may have been booked directly by the on-site hotel sales staff, reservations for meeting attendees frequently are included in brand reservation-system counts, especially in situations where attendees are responsible for making their own reservations (which typically is the case for association group business).

Alternative Approaches for Evaluating the Overall Economics of Affiliation. In light of the difficulties inherent in evaluating a franchisor's or chain's reservations/booking performance, it is important to identify alternative ways of evaluating the costs and benefits of affiliation. Possible alternative approaches might include assessing the bottom-line versus the top-line impact of franchise or affiliation fees, estimating the net effective cost of business generated by a franchise or affiliation, and estimating a breakeven point that suggests the volume of business needed to support the cost of a specific franchise or affiliation.

Assessing bottom-line versus top-line impact. The cost of a franchise or affiliation traditionally has been measured in terms of its impact on the top line expressed as a percentage of revenue. While this ratio is a reasonable approach for comparing the nominal costs of one franchise or affiliation program to another, it does not take into account the fact that the profitability of different types of hotels can vary significantly. Thus, the impact of franchise or affiliation fees can vary dramatically when fees are evaluated from a bottom-line perspective.

Estimating net effective cost. Another method of evaluating the costs and benefits of a franchise or affiliation program is to determine the net effective cost of business generated by the franchise or chain organization. Net effective cost can be defined as the ratio of franchise fees to the percentage or volume of business generated though the franchise or affiliation. For example, if franchise fees are equivalent to 10 percent of total revenue, and a franchisor is generating 25 percent of the business for a hotel, the cost is $.10 \div .25$, or .40 (40 percent) for the business actually generated by and/or attributable to the franchise or affiliation.

Estimating a break-even point. Another way to evaluate the financial contribution of a franchise or affiliation program is to estimate the incremental volume of business needed to break even, or just cover the cost of a franchise or affiliation.

Evaluating Potential Conflicts of Interest. In making the decision to become a franchisee or chain-affiliated property, the investor also should take into consideration potential conflicts of interest between the franchisee and a franchisor or chain. Conflicts might arise between competing properties with the same brand and/or among properties of different brands if a system has multiple brands.

Assessing the Independent Alternative. The decision to align a property with a particular franchise or affiliation is often arrived at by evaluating the merits of one brand versus another. However, the decision-making process also should evaluate the comparative merits of operating independently.

An interesting way to think of hotel products is to place them on a continuum. At one end are hotels with little opportunity to differentiate themselves from similar types of properties. At the other end are hotels and resorts that are considered to be one-of-a-kind properties. Affiliation alternatives and the merits of affiliation differ substantially, depending on where an individual hotel lies along this continuum.

Certain limited-service and highway properties have few ways to differentiate themselves from their competitors. For these hotels, a franchise or brand affiliation often is critical to financial success. For hotels at the other end of the continuum (such as specialty properties with unique locations, high-end resorts, properties in strong urban destination markets, or four diamond/star properties), a franchise or affiliation may not be necessary. In fact, for these hotels, a franchise or brand affiliation potentially could be detrimental and undermine their ability to attract certain market segments and clientele, such as high-end social and corporate business travelers, selected types of group business, and incentive meeting business. Often, these types of guests prefer to stay at a unique property, rather than a franchise- or chain-affiliated hotel or resort.

For many years, there were few opportunities for independent hotels to tie into a global reservations system or into national or international marketing, sales, and promotional programs. Programs that were available tended to be expensive when sold on a stand-alone basis, making it more cost effective to purchase sales, marketing, and reservation support services through a franchise or chain affiliation. In recent years, however, many firms have emerged that specialize in providing services in these areas. Today, there are numerous alternatives available for purchasing reservation system support (for toll-free number and Web-enabled booking systems), direct sales and trade show representation services, advertising and public relations expertise, or Web marketing expertise.

Depending upon the specific needs of an individual hotel, the cost of purchasing such services on a stand-alone basis can be significantly less than the cost associated with a franchise or chain affiliation. Additionally, the Internet has had a dramatic impact on the marketing and promotion of hotels. Although brand Web sites offer potential advantages over individual hotel Web sites—in particular, they provide opportunities for much greater customer reach—one can also argue that the Internet has substantially leveled the playing field for independent hotels.

Pricing flexibility and integrity. It is difficult for chains to develop and implement national positioning, pricing, and promotional strategies and programs that meet the specific needs of all properties within their systems. The absence of a brand can afford an owner greater flexibility in positioning a specific hotel against its competition. As an independent hotel, the property has the opportunity to explore its strengths and points of differentiation from the competition in terms of location, size, character, ambiance, design, and/or level of service.

Independent positioning allows for greater flexibility in establishing rates and control over rate integrity. As a member of a chain, a hotel's pricing strategy must be consistent with the overall positioning and perception of the chain. It is very difficult for franchisors or chain organizations, especially those having more than one brand, to develop national pricing strategies that address the needs and objectives of all hotels within their systems. Rate integrity, inventory control, allocations to intermediaries, and opaque versus transparent pricing have emerged as major issues and challenges, particularly in light of the dramatic increase in online bookings.

Opportunities for Improving Return on Investment ————

There essentially are four ways to improve investment return performance, including increasing revenue, decreasing expenses, decreasing the investment basis of a hotel, restructuring the cost of capital, or using a combination of these.

Opportunities for Revenue Growth

Favorable demand versus supply fundamentals can be expected to provide both room night growth and pricing opportunities for the industry. There are opportunities for some hotels for further revenue growth via improved yield management. Historically, hotels have focused primarily on yield management from the top down. For many hotels, there is untapped potential to improve revenue performance by managing yield from the bottom up. It is important to keep in mind that increasing the lowest rate for a hotel by x dollars can potentially have the same impact on improving average rate as increasing the highest rate by x dollars. For many hotels, lower-rated business accounts for a larger percentage/volume of business and even modest increases in rates for lower-rated business can have a substantial impact on bottom-line performance.

There is also an opportunity for some hotels—resorts in particular—to improve revenue performance by increasing total revenue per guest and/or per occupied room. This can be accomplished both through pricing strategies and increased capture or utilization of outlets and facilities by in-house guests. For example, in resort hotels with substantial group business, there often is the potential to increase spa utilization (and total revenue/spend per guest) by customizing programs to meet the specific needs of a particular group and promoting the programs (e.g., spouse spa service programs, fitness programs, etc.) to attendees before the arrival of the group.

Managing Expenses

Labor (including benefits) represents the single largest expense for hotels. Many hotels could better manage their labor expenses by improving their forecasting and more effectively managing their fixed and variable labor expenses and their overtime expenses. Many hotels have invested substantial time and money in sophisticated labor management systems, yet lack the expertise to use them properly. Accurate forecasting—a critical component of a labor management/scheduling program—remains a huge challenge for many hotels.

Marketing and distribution expenses combined typically represent the second largest expense category after labor. Many yield management programs focus on maximizing revenue and do not take into account the cost associated with generating business or the actual profit contribution of the business. All rooms revenue dollars are not created equal because the cost of generating business can vary dramatically by source of business. For example, the incremental cost of a booking for a repeat customer may be less than 1 percent. In sharp contrast, the cost of a new customer booking generated by an advertisement in a major publication offering triple mileage points and booked through an intermediary via a toll-free number potentially can exceed 25 percent of the rooms revenue. Thus, the profit contribution (revenue less distribution expenses) of one source/type of business versus another can vary dramatically.

The Internet has brought attention to the importance of understanding all of the costs associated with business generated from a particular source. Internet business has grown dramatically and currently accounts for approximately 25 percent of the total room nights industry wide. It is important, however, for a hotel to apply this same thinking to all sources of business to identify opportunities for cost savings.

Operating Leverage

In light of the recent improvement of hotel industry fundamentals, the performance of many hotels has improved or can be expected to improve substantially due to the impact of positive operating leverage. Operating leverage (the ratio of fixed costs to variable costs) can work for or against a property. After the sharp declines in revenue in late 2001 and 2002, many hotels, in particular ones with high operating leverage (more fixed costs), experienced substantial profit margin erosion because they could not cut costs commensurate with declines in revenue. On the other hand, during periods of revenue growth (rate growth in particular), properties with high operating leverage have the potential to dramatically improve or leverage bottom-line performance once fixed costs are covered.

Capital Asset Preservation

Historically, the hotel industry has lagged far behind other industries in managing the physical assets underlying a hotel investment. For many hotels, there is substantial untapped potential to improve hotel investment performance by mitigating capital reinvestment exposure through better preventive maintenance programs and improved capital investment decision-making.

Asset Management Going Forward

As we move into the future, it will be a good idea to keep a number of points in mind.

Staying Focused on Business Fundamentals

The industry has benefited greatly from the extremely favorable low interest and cap rate environment—both factors that are not within the immediate control of the industry and that can be expected to moderate in the future. Going forward, it will be important that the industry stay focused on demand and supply along with key net operating income growth fundamentals to sustain values and realize potential further improvements in values.

Keeping an Eye on Alternative Investment Risk versus Return Performance

The risk premium (the spread between hotel returns and alternative investment returns) is narrowing. It is important for the hotel industry to continue to monitor the return on investment of hotels relative to alternative investments for signs of further narrowing and/or imbalances in the risk versus return performance levels (for hotels) versus potential alternative investments (for investors).

If the rates for CDs and other fixed income/yield investments continue to improve, risk versus return expectations can be expected to shift.

A change in investor risk versus return expectations could have a substantial impact on both real estate valuation (which in many instances currently reflects a premium for yield/income performance relative to alternative investments) and the availability of capital to the real estate industry in general (including hotels). As a practical matter, in many instances today's capitalization rates for real estate would be hard to justify if treasuries and/or CD rates break the 6 percent barrier.

Related Industry Performance: The Airline Crisis

The hotel industry is highly dependent upon what is going on in closely related industries and the challenges currently facing the airline industry can be expected to impact the hotel industry. The performance of many hotels is very dependent upon both lift capacity (or the availability of airline service) and the cost of air travel.

For many years, the airlines' Saturday night stay-over requirements had a huge impact on hotels' day-of-the-week demand patterns. After the events of September 11, 2001, many destinations saw significant reductions in lift capacity. Total U.S. lift capacity is still approximately 6 percent below pre–September 11 levels.

Labor issues, along with the recent dramatic increases in fuel costs, have presented huge challenges for the airline industry. Several major U.S. carriers are in severe financial distress and the 10 largest airlines in the United States collectively posted losses of $4.9 billion in the first half of 2005. The losses are not sustainable and ultimately we can expect fallout and further consolidation/restructuring within the airline industry.

It is important that the hotel industry closely monitor the situation because restructuring in the airline industry can be expected to affect the hotel industry significantly. For some hotels, changes in the airlines' routes, airfares, and lift capacities will represent major challenges. For others, such changes will represent opportunities.

Human Resources Challenges and Opportunities

With the growing emphasis in recent years on the transaction side of the business, many hotels have lost focus on one of the most critical components of a hotel investment—the employee.

It is important to keep in mind that the hotel business is a people business. Neither the most glamorous of hotels nor the most sophisticated or creative financial transactions can ensure success in the hotel industry. Rather, it is employees—well-trained and motivated employees—who ultimately make the difference in a hotel investment. Human resources management issues—recruiting, training, and motivating employees and managing turnover and labor costs—can be expected to continue to present challenges. However, human resources management, from both an expense and guest satisfaction perspective, also represents one of the most significant opportunities for improving investment return performance.

Mixed-Use Resorts

By *Rick S. Kirkbride, ISHC*

Rick Kirkbride, Chair of the Resort, Restaurant & Recreation Practice Group, represents real estate development companies, institutional lenders, investment banks, opportunity funds and other capital providers, owners, and operators. His practice encompasses the development, acquisition and sale, finance, leasing, operation, management, licensing, branding, repositioning, roll-up, foreclosure, workout and restructuring of hotels, condo hotels, resorts, branded condominiums, private residence clubs and timeshare projects, fractional jets, spas, restaurants, casinos, golf courses and country clubs, tennis stadiums, theme and amusement parks, yachts, fishing, shooting and vineyard-based leisure activities, and other hospitality, recreational, and real estate–based entertainment properties and businesses in North America, Latin America, the Caribbean, Europe, and Asia. He speaks on various hospitality topics at seminars and conferences throughout the world and has written articles for, and is quoted frequently in, legal and hospitality industry–related magazines and newspapers.

Mr. Kirkbride is the founder and chair of the UCLA Annual Real Estate Finance & Investment Conference and has been an instructor for UCLA Extension on Hospitality Law. He also serves as General Counsel to and a member of the Planning Committee of the American Lodging Investment Summit; is a member of ULI and is Vice President at Large of its Hotel Development Council; and is a member of the International Society of Hospitality Consultants. Rick previously served on the Planning Committee of the UCLA California Restaurant Industry Conference and the Steering Committee on China of the International Travel & Tourism Council; was Chair of the Timeshare Committee and Vice Chair of the Hospitality Committee of the American Bar Association; and was a member of the Executive Committee of the Real Property Section of the Los Angeles County Bar Association and President of its Real Estate Development Subsection.

As EVERYONE IN THE HOSPITALITY INDUSTRY today knows, during the last several years there has been a growing trend to develop new mixed-use projects that include not only a hotel component but also a fractional-interest or timeshare component, a residential component (i.e., undeveloped residential lots or whole-ownership condominiums), and/or a retail or other commercial component. The purpose of this chapter is to provide a broad overview of not only the major issues and difficulties, but also the goals and business strategies in developing a mixed-use project including the creation and launch of a new brand. For the purpose of this chapter, we will assume the new brand is to be known as "RRR." The project, in essence a launch of the greater RRR brand, presents two objectives: (1) in the short term, developing and structuring the RRR resort (the "Resort") and (2) in the long term, building an RRR brand that offers the ultimate in luxury hospitality-focused real estate at all its destinations.

The Value of a Brand ——————————————————————————

A hotel brand is the distinctive identifier of the product line it embodies. A brand is shaped both by the information that brand developers aim to convey to travelers and by the attributes that a traveler ascribes to it based both on his or her perceptions and experiences. Effective brand-building, beginning with the development of the brand and continuing with every traveler's individualized experience, is thus critical to capitalizing on any specific facet of the travel experience.

Brand-building begins with establishing uniformity of the brand operating standards among the various brand locations such that each property succeeds in consistent delivery on the brand promise—from sales and marketing to hotel personnel. To guests of a well-branded hotel, each hotel appears as if it is owned by the brand, not by disparate individual hotel owners.

Developing the RRR Brand

RRR is intended to be at once a wellness retreat with a hideaway feel and a boutique hotel with Hollywood cachet, offering one the opportunity to introduce an unprecedented luxury brand with spa services and amenities, personalized service, and first-class accommodations all set against a historic and nature-driven backdrop.

An initial sketch of the RRR brand requires careful examination of the following matters (some of which are beyond the scope of this chapter):

- How will the RRR brand distinguish itself from the competition and create for itself an identity separate and distinct (will it be through the "wellness" focus)?

- Will the RRR image dictate one destination style (spa based?) or might other destinations include golf, ski, etc. (either with or without the specialty spa)?

- How will the RRR brand convey the sense of luxury that high-income travelers demand while maintaining a focus on wellness for travelers of all ages and encapsulating the desired aesthetic?

- Will the RRR structure be uniformly horizontal (i.e., sprawling "village" style)?

- Will RRR create a management staff seeking out hotels to manage? Will it create the RRR brand for licensing?

While hotel rooms at the Resort hotel will be available to anyone who can afford to stay there, the driving mechanism in RRR's pricing model will be the exclusivity that comes with owning a residence or a fractional or membership interest in the Resort's unrivaled surroundings. The typical RRR purchaser will be affluent, most likely earning more than $1 million per year. Most potential RRR purchasers can afford to purchase a vacation home outright, but likely would not use a vacation home frequently enough to justify its purchase. Potential RRR purchasers prefer the five-star services and amenities associated with first-class hotels and are willing to pay top dollar for them, especially when such amenities are centered on an unconventional or alternative concept not commonly found at other resorts. They tend to already visit resort destinations multiple times each year and prefer the added exclusivity, luxury, conveniences, amenities, and personal service that comes with purchasing a real estate interest in, or a right to longer-term use of, such a product.

Purchaser selection is particularly important at the early stages of the Resort development, both for setting a standard with respect to Resort clientele and for greater brand-development purposes (establishing the demographic of future RRR purchasers). Targeting guests who have previously visited similar projects is among the best ways to attract celebrity attention or entice wealthy individuals seeking the celebrity lifestyle at the earliest stages of development and sales. Additionally, a focus on the Resort's spa will attract another subset of the high-end travel market.

Overview of Resort Products

In today's marketplace, it is not enough to offer well-appointed accommodations and exceptional amenities in a true hotel-resort. Today's high-wealth traveler seeks the comfort of a home away from home and the personal attention of a private club, in addition to the conveniences of a first-class hotel. Exhibit 1 presents four basic product types that are the obvious options for a resort of the size and horizontal layout of the Resort and RRR brand. The following sections discuss these options as well as one that is not included in Exhibit 1 (for reasons that will become apparent).

The Luxury Hotel Product

In the case of a true hotel imposed on a horizontal structure, the developer retains ownership of the various hotel units. Although there are many disadvantages to structuring an entire project as a short-term-stay hotel, including greater difficulty in obtaining financing and the burdensome requirement of keeping money locked up in the hotel long term, it is almost necessary to have a hotel as one part of the resort in order to have transient occupants paying to use resort amenities, eat at the restaurant, use spa services, etc. In order to ensure the developer reaps the benefits of the maximum number of income streams at the resort, the resort must have a minimum number of hotel rooms and generate revenue from hotel guests' use of amenities to help finance those amenities.

The Timeshare Product

Although the timeshare product is not among the more appropriate options available to RRR listed in Exhibit 1, it is useful to understand this product to better understand why a fractional product might be appropriate for RRR. The timeshare product provides for the exclusive use of accommodations for a particular number of days each year. It usually is sold in blocks of one or more weeks and may also be referred to as interval ownership or vacation ownership. (The term "timeshare" in fact has a negative connotation for some, stemming from abusive practices of developers in the 1960s and 1970s, mostly in connection with developments in

Exhibit 1   Resort Product Types

Product Type	Ownership Interest	Features	Pricing/ Other Revenue	Financing Issues	Possible RRR Unit Type
Hotel	Developer retains ownership	Developed and operated by developer or a management company on the developer's behalf	Room revenue, restaurant, spa, all other pay-for-use amenities	Developer may need to obtain true acquisition and development loan	One-bedroom huts, oceanfront room blocks, beach cottages
Fractional Ownership/ Club	Deeded condominium interest with a related fractional right of occupancy or Nonequity license to use without a real property interest or Equity club membership with use rights	Larger units than hotels (fully equipped kitchens, etc.) Longer fractions and lower marketing costs than timeshare	2.0 times price of a wholly owned unit divided by number of fractions Developer may run resales and be entitled to annual management fees and transfer fees when memberships are sold between members	Can be built in phases with membership agreements as collateral for financing to construct additional units	Spa cottages, condo hotel or larger hotel units
Condo Hotel	Fee ownership with limitations on use rights Viewed as a security under U.S. law	Mandatory centrally-managed rental pool Higher density of units Uniform FF&E across the units	Lower price than branded estates, but higher than average prices per square foot because of hotel amenities Developer may be entitled to HOA management fees and/or rental program management fees	Can be built in phases with purchase agreements as collateral for financing to construct additional units	Laguna or bay villas that may be subject to the project's rental program when vacant
Branded Estates	Fee ownership of the subdivided lot and owner-constructed home	Voluntary rental pool Owner may benefit from some hotel services and amenities Developer may avoid the risk of construction defect liability	Highest prices Developer may be entitled to licensing and management fees and/or a percentage of rental income	Self-financed when purchase agreement is executed by deposits made under the contract Developer need not front development and construction costs	Three-bedroom villas, oceanfront villas, bay villas

Florida.) Interval owners typically own either a fee interest in the subject property with a related right of occupancy or a license to occupy with no real property estate.

Interval buyers typically pay a purchase price based on (among other factors) the location, nature, and quality of the project; the length of the use period being purchased; and the developer's acquisition, development, and marketing costs. Subsequently, interval owners generally are required to pay assessments for maintenance fees and, if applicable, for membership and participation in exchange programs that allow interval owners to exchange their use periods at their particular resort for the use of similar projects around the world.

Every timeshare project must employ a managing agent who oversees the daily operation of the project pursuant to a written agreement. In many jurisdictions, this agreement is separate and distinct from other management agreements that may be relevant to the operation of the overall project facilities, including, for example, a rental management agreement for units owned by the developer.

Timeshare intervals may be fixed as to unit and annual occupancy period, or may float as to each. A fixed-period interval would provide the owner thereof the right to occupy a particular unit (fixed unit) or one of a category of units (floating units) during the same period of time on a recurring basis (e.g., week 51 each year in Unit 303 or week 51 each year in any three-bedroom unit). A floating-period interval would provide the owner thereof the right to occupy a fixed or floating unit at any time (based on availability) or anytime during a particular season on a recurring basis (e.g., any three-bedroom unit during the high season, with the specific unit and week to be determined by availability according to an established reservation procedure). If floating intervals are used, unused intervals may be rented by the timeshare owners association to the public, with the revenue derived from such rentals accruing to the association.

The invention of the exchange company—particularly Resort Condominiums International (RCI) and Interval International (II)—revolutionized the timeshare industry by greatly expanding the pool of potential purchasers. Before the existence of exchange companies, a timeshare owner was limited to occupying the particular timeshare property in which he or she held interest (the home resort) and had to be willing to commit to visiting the home resort on a recurring basis. By affiliating with an exchange company, however, a timeshare property can provide to its owners the right to deposit or bank their occupancy rights at their home resort with the exchange company and instead occupy another resort within the exchange company network (as a result of an owner from that resort banking his or her occupancy rights). A number of timeshare developers have created their own internal exchange programs to provide owners with a preferential and often discounted right of exchange. Note that creation of an internal exchange program can supplement or replace an affiliation with such external third-party exchange programs as RCI or II.

The purchase price of timeshare interests is typically lower than the purchase price of fractional interests (and therefore attracts a less affluent purchaser than fractional interests). As a result, the quality of the timeshare product and its amenities is usually lower than that of a fractional-interest product. Because the Resort will be developed according to first-class hospitality principles and priced much higher than the average timeshare product, timeshare ownership would not be the best product choice for the Resort and the RRR brand.

The Luxury Fractional-Interest Product

Although no fractional products are exactly alike, a fractional structure typically is characterized by relationship-based sales, a purchaser's right to 6–12 weeks in a unit, and increased costs over timeshare. The basic structure of a fractional-interest product is very similar to that of a timeshare product, but timeshare interests have fallen out of favor among high-end resort developers.

The luxury fractional-interest product is a high-growth segment of the lodging and leisure industry that typically combines the benefits of upscale luxury home ownership with the amenities and exclusivity of a first-class hotel. The product involves the creation of long-term exclusive rights to use real property for short-term recurring fixed or floating periods (which operate exactly the same as in a timeshare product). Fractional ownership can exist either as a license of specific-use rights or fractional ownership of the underlying real estate accompanied by use rights. Frequently, the luxury fractional-interest product is marketed as a private residential club (particularly when the resort offers luxury amenities) to attract those purchasers interested in "membership."

While similar to the fee-interest timeshare product described above, the upscale fractional-interest product can be distinguished from traditional timeshare properties in at least four ways. First, the amenities, services, and furnishings provided at an upscale fractional-interest resort usually far exceed those offered at a timeshare property both in scope and quality. For example, in addition to hotel-style amenities, the luxury fractional-interest product frequently will also offer concierge services, laundry services, housekeeping services, room service, and reservation services for local attractions and restaurants. Second, the living units frequently will feature custom interior designs and gourmet kitchens. Third, the marketing strategies used to attract clientele to luxury fractional-interest properties include far fewer hard-sell tactics than do the marketing strategies for timeshare properties. Fourth, the fractional-interest ownership structure generally enables the consumer to purchase a larger share of a vacation ownership unit—usually between 5 and 26 weeks—whereas the share for timeshare ownership interest usually is limited to one to two weeks.

The gross sales price charged by high-end fractional-interest developers for their products and services generally is around twice the cost of each residential unit. This premium on sales price reflects high returns to the developer as well as the relatively low (as compared to traditional timeshare product) expense of offering the luxury fractional-interest product for sale. For example, the less aggressive marketing tactics that distinguish the luxury fractional-interest product from the traditional timeshare product result in an overall marketing and sales expense that typically is only 10–25 percent of the sales price, as opposed to 35–50 percent for a typical timeshare unit.

The Club Product

Essentially, a club is similar to the fractional structure, but is set across multiple sites. A club membership can be an equity or a nonequity membership. Generally speaking, luxury residence clubs take one of three basic structures: (1) a deeded condominium interest structure, in which the club member actually acquires an ownership interest in the real property operated by the club; (2) an equity club, in which real property is owned by a nonprofit corporation and club members own shares of the corporation; or (3) a nonequity club, in which the developer retains ownership of the real property and only conveys to the club members a right to use such property. The deeded condominium interest structure has been the most commonly used structure for residence clubs. The primary reasons for choosing this structure in the U.S. have been marketability (caused by the buyers' familiarity with and greater willingness to buy this structure), sales tax exemption in many states, and the tax-deductible status of deeded condominium mortgage interest.

Note, however, that private club memberships trigger regulation by both state timeshare regulations and federal and state securities laws. When registering the private club under state timeshare laws, several states require that all of the properties in the club—not just the particular property in which the purchaser is buying an interest—register. Additionally, if private club memberships are not tied to a specific real property interest, the mortgage interest deduction may not be available to prospective U.S. purchasers. Of course, if sales are made predominantly locally or in Europe, these issues may not be relevant.

If a developer is particularly concerned with benefiting from the appreciation of a resort's real estate, it should attempt to retain ownership of as many resort components as possible, while still creating various income streams. If the developer of RRR takes this approach, it should consider creating a club structure with the following elements:

- *Trust Company.* The developer should establish a club by creating a legal trust and conveying into the trust relevant brand intellectual property and the actual property or properties. Purchasers will become members of the club and their memberships actually will be beneficial interests in the trust company. The trust company (not the development entity) should serve as the management entity for the club. The trust company, pursuant to an agreement executed with the developer, should make and carry out the day-to-day operational decisions for the club and club properties.

- *Club Memberships.* The trust company should sell club memberships in some to-be-determined fraction based on the desired number of members per club unit.

- *Trustees.* Under a typical model, a trust company should have between three and five trustees, each of whom will serve as a fiduciary to club members and will assume all operational and management responsibilities for the club and the properties. The initial trustees will be appointed by brand executives, with the election of replacements performed by the club members on an annual basis.

- *Term.* The term of the trust company and, in turn, the club, should be perpetual (or such lesser term as may be mandated by law).

- *Reservation and Use Rights.* Club membership interests should be floating as to both time and unit. Subject to availability and applicable reservation and use policies, any member may reserve any club unit at any time. Exhibit 2 lists sample availability and reservation restrictions for the RRR resort.

- *Homeowners Association.* A homeowners association (HOA) should be established for each property and each should enter into a management

Exhibit 2   Sample Availability and Reservation Restrictions for the RRR Resort

While the club is operated so as to permit the Members, to the greatest degree possible, to stay at any property at any time for as long as they want, the club documents will provide, as a technical legal matter, for restrictions such as the following:

1. No Member will have the right (but, subject to availability and possibly the payment of supplemental amounts, shall be permitted) to stay in residence at an RRR property longer than *x* weeks (the "Maximum Annual Stay").

2. No Member may reserve a Club Unit more than 12 months in advance.

3. No member may reserve more than two weeks in any particular RRR property during that RRR property's high season; provided, however, if within 30 days prior to the Member's high season reserved stay there remains availability at the property, the Member may reserve additional time in excess of the initial two weeks.

4. Without a Member in residence, only the children, grandchildren, parents, and siblings of a Member may stay in or use a Club Unit at an RRR property.

5. Members wishing to stay in an RRR property for a period in excess of the Maximum Annual Stay may do so upon payment to the Trust Company of a weekly fee.

6. Both the participation by Members in external third-party exchange programs and the rental by Members to third parties of RRR Club membership interests will be prohibited.

agreement with the trust company, which will in turn have the right to enter into a submanagement agreement with a third-party manager (unless the brand forms its own management company) to carry out the maintenance and repair of each property and the collection for and the payment of the costs thereof, including utilities, taxes, and all casualty insurance and general liability insurance in customary amounts.

- *Additional Payments by Members.* In addition to the purchase price payable to the trust company for each membership in the club over the life of the club, members also should be responsible for HOA fees, annual trustees' fees, and commencing on the fifth anniversary of the first sale of memberships in the club, a profit participation in favor of the developer equal to some percentage of the gross sales price upon the resale of a club interest by a member to be paid upon the recordation of each assignment of beneficial interest by the selling member.

- *Alterations.* The trust company alone (and no individual member) will be permitted to construct, alter, add to, renovate, and/or demolish any club unit or property structure at any time, subject to the approval of the trustees.

In addition, the following documentation should be used to effectuate the creation and govern the ongoing operations of the club:

- *Formation Documents*—Articles of incorporation and bylaws for the club association.

- *Consumer Documents*—The reservation agreement, purchase and escrow agreements, and rules and regulations governing the reservation and use privileges for each club member.

- *Management Agreement*—An agreement between the trust company and manager stipulating that the manager will operate and manage the club property.

- *Declarations and Trust Documents*—Documents outlining the rights and obligations of the trust company and the reservation and use privileges for each club member.

- *License and Use Rights Agreements*—Agreements between future developers and the trust company that allow the branded private club property to be operated and marketed as a branded club property using brand intellectual property. Under the license agreement, a licensee would have to obtain approval of its facilities and all uses of the brand to ensure that the brand's quality will be preserved.

- *Rental Agreements*—Documents that provide for club use of condo/villa units when vacant.

- *Budgets and Pro Forma*—Operating budgets for each component of the resort, including the club.

Considerations in Structuring a Club. A developer must be aware of several factors when setting out the legal structure of the club.

Approval and resale rights. The developer should consider retaining the right to approve all purchasers of club memberships, including resale purchasers. This will create a perception of exclusivity that can enhance marketability of the memberships. The governing documents should provide that the club manager can establish the resale price. The ability to set the resale price is very important in a club structure since resales are likely to start occurring before the developer has sold out all of its inventory. If club members can set their own resale prices, they may offer resales at much lower than the price charged by the developer and adversely affect the developer's ability to sell its remaining inventory.

Amount to be repaid to a selling club member. A major factor in the marketability of residence clubs is the ability of a selling club member to participate in any appreciation on the market value of his/her club membership. Clubs with deeded condominium interest structures or equity structures tend to be more marketable because their members have an opportunity to participate in any appreciation in value of the membership. That said, it is only one factor among many that influences why purchasers buy into a club structure. More often than not at this price point, purchasers are more interested in lifestyle and cachet than investment potential.

Accounting. From an accounting perspective, a deeded condominium interest or equity club structure may be preferable for the club if the developer does not want the club and the parcels on which units are constructed to remain on its books as an asset. Because the developer will convey title to the club units under a deeded condominium interest structure, the units do not depreciate on the developer's books. Depending on the developer's accounting preferences and other financial plans, this may prove quite attractive.

Condo Hotel Product

In a condominium-hotel structure (also known as a condominiumized hotel, a condo hotel, a resort hotel condominium, or a condotel), units are condominiumized and sold off individually, with a mandatory centrally-managed rental pool program imposed on owners. A typical condo hotel project, therefore, has the look and feel of a hotel, including a front desk offering rental services, bellhops, a concierge, daily housekeeping, and room service, but units are owned by individual condominium purchasers rather than the developer. The developer retains ownership of the common areas, the maintenance and repair costs for which are allocated among condominium unit owners (via their condominium assessments), based on their pro-rata shares. The condo hotel manager on behalf of the developer (or the developer in its capacity as manager) provides hotel services to the condo hotel pursuant to contractual arrangements between the developer and a condominium association, which shall be formed to represent individual condominium unit owners collectively. A management agreement may provide that:

- A portion of the revenue received from nightly sales of rental pool units (when vacant) flows through to condo owners after a management fee is assessed.

- A manager receives its management fee up front and uses its portion of the rental revenue stream to offset cleaning, maintenance, and overhead costs and contribute to profit.

- An agreement is to be executed between the condominium association and manager providing for a furniture, fixtures, and equipment (FF&E) reserve maintained by the manager.

- The FF&E packages in the rental pool condo units must conform to the manager's standards.

- A minimum 60-day notice of arrival is required to guarantee availability to owners.

- A rotational room assignment program should be used to ensure equal distribution of bookings to all units in the rental program.

- Owners are restricted to a maximum of eight weeks of personal use during the year (subject to limitations based on U.S. law described below).

- Normal wear and tear is the responsibility of the unit owner and replacements are to be made from a unit's reserve account.

In exchange for participation in the rental pool, the individual unit owner shares in the rental income. The rental agreement may either be a unit rental plan under which each unit owner shares only in the rentals on his or her particular unit or a rental pool plan under which all of the owners share in the total rentals charged for all units. In either case, condo hotel purchasers find the condo hotel

Pricing the Fractional-Interest or Club Product

A key business objective in selling a luxury fractional-interest or club product is obtaining the maximum price sustainable in the market. The ability to accomplish this objective depends on several fundamental business decisions. (Note that where the term "fractional interest" is used, the same logic also applies to club memberships.)

Size of the Fractional Interest. Initially, the size of the fractional interest to be sold must be determined. As a general matter, fractional-interest size depends on the length of the high season at the property and the number of peak-season weeks that can be made available to the purchaser. In general, luxury fractional-interest sizes range between $1/4$ and $1/12$. Size will vary by the type of resort destination involved as well—ski resorts with a high season of only a few months typically have $1/7$ ownership interests, while warm climate destinations with a much longer high season will have smaller fractional interests, generally around $1/12$. Because the success of the luxury fractional-interest product requires a feeling of exclusivity, short intervals, which make the price of the fractional interest accessible to more people, should be avoided.

Fixed vs. Floating Use. The fixed interest is a fee interest in the subject property with a related right of occupancy. The floating interest is a license or membership right of occupancy in a fractional-ownership project. Thus, with the floating interest, instead of reserving occupancy within one single unit, purchasers may reserve occupancy within any of the units within the particular class of units in which they have purchased an interest. Because floating interest tends to provide more flexibility in the reservation process, most luxury fractional-interest products are sold at least in part as floating interests. Clubs, specifically, tend to be floating.

Pricing the Fractional Interest. The price of the luxury fractional-interest product also must be determined. In general, the purchase price of a high-end fractional interest depends upon (among other factors) the location and nature of the product (i.e., urban hotel or resort), size of the fractional interest, size of the units (i.e., number of bedrooms or square footage), and the developer's acquisition, development, and marketing costs. There are two widely used methods of pricing a high-end fractional interest.

- **Average Daily Rate.** The first pricing method seeks to back into a fractional-interest price by determining what the average daily rate would be for the units in which fractional interests are being sold if those units were used for rental. After assuming a basic daily rack rate using market statistics for comparable properties and discounting that rate to account for the fact that many consumers will never pay the full rack rate, a weekly rack rate is determined. The weekly rack rate is then calibrated to represent the size of the fractional interest (i.e., for a $1/13$ ownership interest, the weekly rack rate is multiplied by 4; for a $1/4$ ownership interest, the weekly rack rate is multiplied by 13). This weekly rate is then multiplied by 10 to reflect a standard rule of thumb drawn from the timeshare industry that the fractional-interest price should be approximately ten times the weekly rack rate. (Note that this is a *description* of a common practice and not a recommended *prescription or direction* to be followed as some sort of industry standard.) As an equation:

(continued)

(continued)

Price = Assumed Daily Rack Rate × Discount Rate × 7 × Number of
Weeks in Interest × 10

- **Markup/Multiplier.** The second method of pricing fractional interests is to determine the price at which the unit in which fractional interests are being sold would be sold if it were sold as a single, wholly-owned unit. Once this figure is calculated (generally by multiplying the unit's square footage by the construction cost per square foot), a markup is added. This markup, expressed as a multiplier (commonly between 1.5 and 2.0 times the single unit price), represents the compensation to the developer for the higher marketing, sales, and administrative costs incurred, for the additional services and amenities provided, for the higher risk involved, and for the higher profit margin desired as a result of selling fractional interests in a unit, rather than selling that single unit as a whole. After adding in the compensation mark-up, dividing the total cost of the unit (with markup) by the number of fractional interests to be sold in the unit will yield the price per fractional interest. As an equation:

$$\text{Price} = \frac{\text{Square Feet in Unit} \times \text{Cost per Square Foot} \times \text{Markup}}{\text{Number of Fractional Interests to Be Sold}}$$

structure attractive because it serves as a second home with the luxury of hotel services and rental income can partially or wholly offset the owner's costs.

For the developer, a condo hotel structure provides a faster return, a possible immediate exit if the developer does not take on the role of manager, and higher sales prices per square foot by marketing the hotel amenities.

Note that if sold in the United States and marketed as an investment (by virtue of either a mandatory rental program or the pooling of rental income across multiple units), the U.S. Securities and Exchange Commission (SEC) considers interests in condo hotels to be securities. Unless there is an exemption, units must be registered as a security with the SEC and with the states in which they are offered. Under the U.S. Internal Revenue Code, the owner of an investment rental property (which usually includes condo hotels) may use the property for personal purposes for up to the greater of 14 days or 10 percent of the time that the property is rented to others. For example, if the property is rented for 200 days, the owner could use the property for personal purposes for up to 20 days. Since the property is operated as a hotel, the use dates available to an owner are flexible and may be scheduled based on the owner's desires and the demand and market for renters. This often is not the case with timeshare and fractional-interest ownership where the time period may be fixed each year. (See this chapter's appendix for a more in-depth discussion of U.S. securities laws and fractional interests.)

In sum, the condo hotel structure is advantageous in that it allows for product consistency, fewer ownership conflicts (since owners do not live in the units), and an even distribution of revenue (since units are a regular part of hotel inventory). There are, however, complex accounting and management issues (and potential U.S. securities issues) involved and the developer does not benefit from any appreciation in the value of the units because it accrues to the individual unit owners.

Branded Estates

Branded estates are becoming a standard component of the luxury resort. Branded estates are owned by individual owners but are constructed according to the developer's requirements, thus ensuring that each individual home is consistent with the overall resort setting. Most importantly, branded estates present a self-financing opportunity for the developer that allows it to earn additional income streams in the form of management and other fees.

Developers typically develop branded estates according to one of two paradigms, both of which begin with the purchase of a subdivided lot. In the first option, the purchase price includes the estate lot and a to-be-constructed home that the developer only begins to construct once a purchase agreement has been executed, so the proceeds from the sale can fund construction. In the second option, the purchase price includes only the price of the estate lot and the purchaser constructs his or her own home with a captive contractor and in accordance with the plans and specifications approved by the developer. In both options, the developer does not have to front the costs of developing the branded estates. Only in option two, however, does the developer avoid the risk of construction defect liability. Additionally, option two allows the developer to close on the land and use the proceeds of the sale to build other resort product units and/or hotel amenities. Although each individual owner, not the developer, constructs each home, the developer succeeds in establishing a uniform look and feel for the resort by requiring that owners construct their homes according to developer-approved plans and specifications that dictate the design and construction of each unit; plans and design guidelines should be attached to each lot purchase agreement. In this way, the developer can achieve architectural harmony within the resort without having to risk building the homes before they are purchased and avoiding potential construction defect liability.

Therefore, branded estates are essentially self-financed: the proceeds of the sales of the lots would be applied to construction of the units because construction would not commence until a purchase agreement is executed.

In addition, branded estates present additional opportunities for developer revenue. First, a developer can contract with the branded estates' HOA to manage the association and perform the association's obligations to the homeowners on its behalf. If a developer chooses to do so, management fees typically amount to 10 percent of the HOA budget. Second, a developer can create an optional rental program into which homeowners can enter their units when they are not in use. The developer will then obtain both a management fee for managing the rental program and 50 percent or more of the rental proceeds (calculated once the developer-manager has obtained its management fee). Note that if homeowners choose to place their units in the rental program, they also will be required to equip them with developer-approved FF&E. Otherwise, homeowners have the freedom to

Exhibit 3   Sample Branding Fee Schedule

Gross Sales Price of Residence Lot	Branding Fee
Less than or equal to 100 percent of the base sales price	1.5 percent of the gross sales price
More than 100 percent, but less than or equal to or less than 110 percent of the base sales price	1.5 percent of the gross sales price, plus 5 percent of every dollar over the base sales price
More than 110 percent, but less than or equal to 120 percent of the base sales price	1.5 percent of the gross sales price, plus 10 percent of every dollar over the base sales price
More than 120 percent of the base sales price	5 percent of the gross sales price, plus 20 percent of every dollar over the base sales price

design the interior of their units any way they desire and are subject only to uniform exterior requirements.

Third, the brand is entitled to a branding fee in connection with the sale of branded estates (payable as of the closing of the sale of each residence lot). To determine the branding fee, the parties should first determine the per-square-foot base sales price (excluding extras and change orders) of each branded estate. Subject to the brand's review and approval of a comparable resort, the base sales price for the branded estates will be the prevailing per-square-foot sales price (excluding extras and change orders) of the units in the comparable resort at the time the branded estates are offered for sale. With respect to each branded estate sold by the developer, the developer might pay the brand a branding fee (under the assumption that you would create a brand separate from the current development company) according to terms such as those set out in Exhibit 3.

Branded estates are attractive to purchasers because, depending on the ultimate layout of the resort, owners may benefit from use of hotel amenities (subject to a use agreement and the payment of use fees). Potential access to hotel amenities coupled with exclusive ownership of real estate in an unparalleled setting allows a developer to charge higher sales prices per square foot than it could for similar real estate in another location.

Mixed-Use Projects

The above-described products commonly are combined at one site to create a mixed-use project that provides the developer with a variety of income streams and, in turn, financing vehicles. A mixed-use project comprises at least one traditional hotel component and one or more other components. Resorts today are hybrids of investment properties, second-home properties, and hotels.

Because of the combination of different product types and use rights in mixed-use projects, developers should prepare an amenities use agreement to be used in conjunction with a detailed master resort declaration for the development to provide some insight into the provision of services and amenities that will be available to each of the hotel guests, club members, and owners either with or without charge. All amenities and services should be described in full in a resort declaration, including a sample listing of each, and then divided into at least three different categories of availability, each of which will be priced and charged differently to the consumer. In resort declarations we have provided for developments similar to the RRR Resort, we have divided the amenities and services into the following categories:

- *Basic Services.* Basic services would be those services that are minimally necessary for the resort to function (i.e., landscaping, utilities, security services, etc.) regardless of the brand associated with the resort. The cost of these basic services would be paid for as part of the homeowner, condominium owner, and club association assessments.

- *Upgraded Services.* Upgraded services would be those provided by the hotel owner/manager to the owners and club members specifically as negotiated by the owner/manager and the relevant association(s) and only during the period that the hotel is managed by a particular manager that provides such services. The cost of these upgraded services would also likely be part of each association's assessments.

- *À la Carte Services.* À la carte services would be those provided by the hotel owner/manager to the owners and club members specifically to the extent negotiated from time to time (e.g., spa services, grocery stocking, airport transfers). À la carte services would be completely discretionary at the election of the hotel owner and each individual owner and club member and would be paid for by that owner or club member on a per use, per diem, or other periodic basis, pursuant to separate written agreements by and between them.

One of the benefits of categorizing a resort's amenities and services in this way is to minimize the hotel owner's exposure to lawsuit in the event that it (or the hotel's manager) elects to eliminate and/or modify one or more of the amenities and services previously provided. To the extent one or more of the governing documents and the amenities use agreement can dispel any notion of an owner or club member's entitlement to certain services, it is less likely that the hotel owner will be held liable in the event that it elects to terminate the provision of one or more services. Finally, the governing documents should make clear whether the hotel owner or one (or more) of the associations will be providing amenities and services.

Proposal for the RRR Product

In light of the preceding discussion, we would recommend that the RRR Resort should be a mixed-use project consisting of four distinct components that are developed, constructed, and operated pursuant to the highest standards of quality and service: a five-star luxury hotel, a condo hotel, wholly-owned branded estates subject to an optional rental program, and a residence club. Of course, these products can be interchanged among the various unit types (after an in-depth examination of the Resort's financial projections). In fact, it might make the most sense, in order to fulfill financing needs and respond to market demand, to begin with sales of the condo hotel units on one end of the Resort and residence club product on the other and let the market dictate how much of the Resort should account for each.

Note that, in creating a club, a developer has many options. Given the finan - cial and brand-building goals for the project, RRR might want to create a club focusedaroundt heResort 'sst at e-of-t he-art spainst eadofaresidenceclub. This structure takes into account the lifestyle theme of the Resort and emphasizes a unique spa focus, rather than conventional luxury-hotel focus.

To the extent RRR can market a five-star product with unparalleled real estate and facilities, a mix of product types at various price points and targeting an inter-national as well as local clientele, and providing outstanding personal service and spa amenities in a setting unmatched by other travel destinations, it will be able to demand the highest possible market rate for its products. Determining the right combination of the various products described above depends upon project pro formas, and to what extent it will be possible to deliver the hotel services across the various components of the resort.

Appendix
U.S. Regulatory Hurdles

If an organization like RRR sells its product in the United States, it faces certain regulatory hurdles.

State Timeshare Registration

Each state, to varying degrees, requires that any sale of real property within that state (regardless of the property's location) that provides a purchaser with either a recurring use right or a fee interest in a subdivided property be registered with the state as a sale of a timeshare estate. This timeshare registration requirement is broadly written in most states and typically requires private clubs as well as interval exchange programs to register their products before bringing them to market. Because the timeshare registration requirement is so broadly written, it is extremely difficult to avoid. In California, for example, essentially any trust, stock cooperative, timeshare program, fractional-interest product, private club, or other subdivision of real property into five or more units will require registration with the California Department of Real Estate. This registration is both costly and onerous, in that each state in which a developer intends to sell its product will, to varying degrees, have approval rights over the product's structure, budget, pricing, documentation, marketing efforts, and general operation. In California, for example, the state Department of Real Estate must approve as "fair and reasonable" the proposed budget for each product registered under the state's timeshare regulations.

As a result, avoidance of the timeshare registration requirement is desirable to the extent possible. However, because the net of the registration requirement is cast so widely, avoidance is virtually impossible. The documentation and creativity required to avoid timeshare registration can result in costs and burdens equal to or greater than those incurred through compliance with timeshare registration. Moreover, if such documentation and creativity appears to be motivated by avoidance strategies, a state is all the more likely to force regulation (and perhaps penalties) on the developer.

For example, in order to avoid a California timeshare registration (which requires, essentially, that any fractional-interest product containing more than five units or memberships be registered as a timeshare), RRR would have to create multiple distinct fractional-interest products, clubs, or exchange programs, each of which would contain no more than five units. RRR could, for example, create a different product for each floor of each property, with none of such fractional-interest products (whether club, exchange program, or straight fractional-interest product) containing more than five units. The subdivision of the RRR product into multiple units, each of which offers multiple (although not more than five) units has the potential to create exorbitant legal and transactional costs. In order to maintain the appearance of multiple fractional-interest products, each of which with fewer than five units, each product would have to have separate management contracts for the operation of each RRR property, each product would have to have separate marketing and sales efforts, and each product would have to enter right-to-use agreements, not only across RRR properties, but also by and between the products being offered within each RRR property. The result of all of these efforts is likely to be the confusion and distrust of the prospective purchaser, who may be put off by apparent scheming. In the end, it is likely to be more beneficial for RRR to simply avoid such efforts by complying with state timeshare registration requirements.

Federal Securities Laws

If RRR's owners are subject to a mandatory rental program or if revenue is pooled across multiple units, it may be subject to U.S. federal securities laws.

Fractional Interest as a Security

The SEC has held that the coupling of a real property interest with an offer or agreement by a developer to perform or arrange for rental and/or other services that enhance the value of the real property interest constitutes an "investment contract" under the Securities Act of 1933, and is thus required to be registered as a security unless a statutory exemption permits otherwise. As a result, particularly when coupled with a rental pool arrangement, in which owners are led to expect a profit from the rental of the real property interest they are purchasing, the SEC will tend to require fractional-interest products to be registered as a security.

Rule 506 Exemption

The SEC exempts from its registration requirements offerings of securities that are not "public offerings." For example, under the SEC's Regulation D, Rule 506, private placements are not required to register as a security with the SEC if certain definitional parameters are met. To fall under the Rule 506 exemption for private placements, the following two criteria must be met:

- "There are no more than or the issuer reasonably believes that there are no more than 35 purchasers of securities from the issuer in any offering under this section."

- "Each purchaser who is not an accredited investor either alone or with his purchaser representative(s) has such knowledge and experience in financial and business matters that he is capable of evaluating the merits and risks of the prospective investment, or the issuer reasonably believes immediately prior to making any sale that such purchaser comes within this description."

Accredited Investor Excluded

According to Rule 501 of Regulation D, the following purchasers are excluded for the purpose of calculating the number of purchasers under Rule 506:

> (i) Any relative, spouse or relative of the spouse of a purchaser who has the same principal residence as the purchaser;

> (ii) Any trust or estate in which a purchaser and any of the persons related to him...collectively have more than 50 percent of the beneficial interest (excluding contingent interests);

(iii) Any corporation or other organization of which a purchaser and any of the persons related to him...collectively are beneficial owners of more than 50 percent of the equity securities (excluding directors' qualifying shares) or equity interests; and

(iv) Any accredited investor.

The fourth of these categories of excluded purchasers would be of particular interest to RRR. Under Rule 501, the following two types of individuals are included as accredited investors: (1) "Any natural person whose individual net worth, or joint net worth with that person's spouse, at the time of his purchase exceeds $1,000,000" and (2) "Any natural person who had an individual income in excess of $200,000 in each of the two most recent years or joint income with that person's spouse in excess of $300,000 in each of those years and has a reasonable expectation of reaching the same income level in the current year."

Because the individuals to whom RRR will be marketing its fractional-interest product almost certainly will meet one or both of these definitional criteria for an accredited investor, they will not need to be included in the determination of whether RRR will be exempted from the securities registration requirements of the SEC. As a result of such purchasers being excluded from the determination, it is more likely that RRR will be offering a private placement than a public offering, thereby making it more likely that RRR will be exempted from having to register its fractional-interest product as a security.

Additional Structuring Issues

Even if a substantial number of RRR's prospective purchasers are accredited investors, there still may be a sizeable number of prospective purchasers who are not. As a result, RRR must be careful not to exceed the limit under Rule 506, which only permits an exemption for offerings made to 35 or fewer offerees. If RRR structures its fractional-interest product across all its future properties (rather than creating fractional-interest products and offerings for each particular property), when taken together across all of its properties, the number of prospective purchasers who are not accredited investors may well exceed 35. Because it will facilitate an exemption under Rule 506 of Regulation D, it may be in RRR's strategic interest to create multiple smaller offerings of its fractional-interest product (e.g., one offering per property, one offering per unit type, etc.), rather than one large single offering of its product.

6

Impact

By *Rachel J. Roginsky, ISHC,* and *Jared H. Kelso*

Rachel J. Roginsky is a principal and co-owner of Pinnacle Advisory Group and Pinnacle Realty Investments. Pinnacle Advisory is a national hotel consulting firm, while Pinnacle Realty is a full-service transaction firm specializing in selling hotels and sourcing both debt and equity for hotel assets. Over the past 25 years, she has provided advisory services for lenders, hotel owners, management companies, and investors throughout the United States. These services include market and economic feasibility studies, operational analysis, appraisals, litigation support, and asset management for hotels and hospitality related assets. Additionally, Ms. Roginsky has four years of operational and management experience with Walt Disney World and a major restaurant chain. She is a graduate of and a regular guest lecturer at The School of Hotel Administration at Cornell University, is a board member of the Massachusetts Lodging Association and the International Society of Hospitality Consultants, has written numerous articles in business and hospitality industry periodicals, and is quoted regularly in newspapers such as the Wall Street Journal, the Boston Globe, and the NY Times. Ms. Roginsky is also certified as an arbitrator and mediator for Hospitality Alternative Dispute Resolution.

Jared H. Kelso is a consultant at Pinnacle Advisory Group, a national hospitality consulting firm. He has conducted numerous impact studies across the United States, in addition to a host of other feasibility, due-diligence, and operational consulting assignments. Prior to joining Pinnacle Advisory Group, he served as a manager at the New York Marriott Marquis. Mr. Kelso received an undergraduate degree in Hotel Administration from Cornell University.

THIS CHAPTER ON territorial encroachment, commonly known as "impact" in the hospitality industry, is an update of the chapter entitled "A Critical Analysis of Hotel Impact Issues" in the first edition of this textbook, published in 1995. The landscape of the hotel industry has changed dramatically in the ten years since the original chapter was published. A wave of purchases in the mid-1990s consolidated many brands under one parent company. Promus and Patriot American Hospitality no longer exist and Doubletree is now part of Hilton Hotels Corporation. Soon after its formation in 1991, Starwood Hotels & Resorts Worldwide, Inc., moved forward with a purchase of Westin Hotels & Resorts from the Aoki

Corporation and Sheraton Hotels from the ITT Sheraton Corporation. Marriott joined the consolidation wave with its purchase of The Ritz-Carlton Hotel Company, LLC, and The Renaissance Hotel Group in the mid-1990s. However, as hotel franchisors have sought to distinguish themselves from their competitors while simultaneously maintaining strong supply-side development, the number of brands across the United States has exploded, while the number of franchisors has actually gone down through acquisitions, mergers, and strategic partnerships.

How have these changes in the hotel landscape affected the issue of impact? First, it is important to define impact. To those who fully understand the concept and implications of current impact policies, the word represents a commitment to protecting franchisees' rights. To developers looking to expand a franchisor presence in a specific market, the word frequently can signify delays and challenges in the franchise approval process. To franchisees, the word frequently represents the erosion of their key asset—demand generated through their brand's central reservation system (CRS). But what, exactly, is impact? Most franchisees, while familiar with the term, fail to grasp the intricacies of their respective franchisors' policies and even mistake base impact for incremental impact. The following definitions of the two types of impact that can affect hotel owners are based on the 1995 text and are consistent with today's policies.

Base impact is defined as the effect of new competition on an existing property, usually resulting from the addition of hotel rooms to the competitive market. For example, the opening of a 220-unit Westin property could cause base impact on an existing 240-unit Renaissance Hotel if it is part of the same competitive market. Another example could involve the repositioning of an existing hotel. Let's assume the Gateway Hotel and the Hilton Hotel both have been open for many years. However, the Gateway Hotel is in poor condition, markets primarily to transient discount business, and has a lower rate structure than the Hilton. If the owners of the Gateway Hotel decide to undertake an extensive renovation and rebrand the property as a Marriott, the Hilton Hotel could suffer from increased competition. In this case, no new rooms will be added to the market, but *competitive* rooms will be created. Upon the rebranding, the two properties would be competing directly for the same rated business and the Hilton could be subject to base impact.

Incremental impact is defined as the effect of new competition on an existing property due to the addition of hotel rooms that operate under the same brand or franchise company or that access the same reservations system. For example, the addition of a Best Western hotel located ten miles away from an existing Best Western could cause incremental impact, depending on the demand characteristics of the area. It is critical to distinguish between the two types of impact. While any new supply may cause base impact, new supply within the same franchise or reservations network may cause base *and* incremental impact. The additional impact incurred due to the dilution of the franchise company–generated business is the incremental impact.

Hotel owners frequently fail to recognize this difference. Franchisors focus on *incremental impact only* when deciding whether to approve a franchise application. While most impact studies will include calculations of base impact, the franchise company's concern is not, nor should it be, with base impact. Let's look at this from a franchisor's standpoint. Franchise companies generate revenue from the fees that hotel owners pay to them for the benefit of associating their asset with a nationally recognized brand, an expected level of standards, and an established reservations network. Thus, more hotel rooms generate more fees. If a new Courtyard property opens just two miles from an existing Courtyard and takes business away from the existing Courtyard, the franchisor (Marriott International) still receives fees on that room night. Furthermore, any new business that the recently opened Courtyard generates that would not otherwise have stayed at a Marriott property now is generating fees. Thus, on a basic level, it is to Marriott's benefit to continue adding new supply to the market.

A Discussion of Key Issues

To give you a better idea of some issues that may arise or have arisen with regard to impact, we're going to briefly describe a number of developments and scenarios.

Consolidation in the Industry

As waves of consolidation sweep the industry, the number of franchise companies continues to shrink. A prime example is Starwood's pending purchase of the Le Meridien brand, which would bring its total number of brands to eight. The average franchise company now has more than seven brands. By way of example, the 16 brands under the Marriott umbrella include Marriott Hotels & Resorts, JW Marriott Hotels & Resorts, Renaissance Hotels & Resorts, Courtyard by Marriott, Residence Inn by Marriott, Fairfield Inn by Marriott, Marriott Conference Centers, Towne Place Suites by Marriott, SpringHill Suites by Marriott, Marriott Vacation Club International, Horizons by Marriott, The Ritz-Carlton Hotel Company, LLC, The Ritz-Carlton Club, Marriott ExecuStay, Marriott Executive Apartments, and Marriott Grand Residence Club.

Expansion of Brands by Existing Franchisors

This very same expansion of brands that drives more fees to franchisors creates a potential problem for hotel owners. New market-targeted brands enable developers to continue to add hotel rooms to a market where a franchise company already may have a strong presence. However, in some circumstances, especially in soft markets, these brands are competing with each other. Under the Hilton umbrella, Homewood and Embassy both offer a suite product; are they competing? Within the Marriott system, does a full-service Renaissance compete with a full-service Marriott? Similarly, InterContinental Hotels Group's Candlewood might compete with a Staybridge or Holiday Inn Express if the rate structures and geographic locations are similar.

Currently, several new brands are under development or recently have opened. These include the Hotel Indigo concept by InterContinental Hotels Group, Cambria Suites by Choice, and the Project XYZ concept by Starwood. Hyatt is in the process of rebranding all of its recently purchased AmeriSuites as Hyatt Place properties. All of these brand developments have played, and will continue to play, a role in impact issues.

Evolution of Central Reservation Systems and Shifting Distribution Channels

As brands and their parent companies simultaneously grow and consolidate, so do the distribution channels generating room nights for the hotels. When this chapter was first written, the Internet was just coming into its own and Choice Hotels and the Holiday Inn Company were preparing to unveil online bookings for the first time. Now JupiterResearch estimates that 20 percent of all hotel bookings will take place on-line in 2005.

As Internet bookings grow in popularity, they are replacing traditional booking channels. This is a trend that can be expected to continue as technology-comfortable generations begin to earn more and spend money on travel. According to TravelCLICK's eTrack report for 2004, brand Web sites were the source of 71.4 percent of the brands' centrally booked Internet reservations, compared to 66.5 percent in 2003. For the first time ever, Hilton reported that bookings via Hilton.com outnumbered bookings through call centers in October 2004. Hilton estimates that 15 percent of its bookings will be made on Hilton.com in 2005, versus 13 percent in 2004. According to its Uniform Franchise Offering Circular (UFOC), Marriott.com bookings also increased significantly in 2004, generating 9 percent of Marriott's overall bookings.

This growing trend of brand Web site bookings has created a new issue for analyzing impact. Since InterContinental Hotels Group first broke ranks with third-party intermediaries and established the Lowest Internet Rate Guarantee, these bookings have grown exponentially and Web site placement issues have become increasingly important. Each major company handles its bookings differently. Marriott.com will run a search by "distance to city center" and return results by distance whether they are Residence Inns, Courtyards, or SpringHill Suites. Hilton.com, however, returns results by brand under the default search. All Hilton Hotels within a 20-mile radius will be listed, then all Doubletrees, then Conrads, then Embassy Suites, and so on down to Homewood Suites. Thus, searching for all brands in New York City on the Hilton Web site will display a full-service Hilton in New Jersey before displaying the Hampton Inns within Manhattan.

As most brand Web site booking engines search by distance to city center in some way, owners increasingly are becoming concerned with where their hotel appears in the list of results. What if a developer is planning a hotel in a secondary location within a downtown area, but located three blocks closer than other properties to the city center as defined by the booking engine? A leisure traveler who is not familiar with the destination may assume that the first hotel to appear on the Web site is, in fact, the best location in town. Thus, issues could arise as other area hotels that are better located proximate to demand generators are pushed down the Web site.

Expansion of Points Programs

Another key issue that has affected impact over the past ten years has been the proliferation of points programs offered by various franchisors. The premise of points programs is that by awarding customers redeemable points every time they book a

Exhibit 1   Major Franchise Company Reward Programs

Franchise Company	Reward Program	Millions of Members	Percent of Reservations
Marriott	Marriott Rewards	21+	56%
Starwood	Preferred Guest	16+	29%
Hilton	HHonors	18+	33–50%
InterContinental Hotels Group	Priority Club	26+	30%
Choice	Choice Privileges	4+	15%
Wyndham	Wyndham ByRequest	2.3+	20%

room under a specific brand, the national franchisor is creating a brand-loyal customer who has added incentive to continue to book with it. Of course, this brand-loyal customer may result in an incremental loss of room nights for existing area owners. While many business travelers may have membership with more than one points program, they are less likely to have four or five, because the potential benefit from each lessens with additional memberships. Exhibit 1 details several major rewards programs, the number of members, and overall percent of rooms booked at that chain by points members.

New Supply in the Market

New supply in a hotel owner's competitive market is the most common reason for investigating impact. When a developer applies for a franchise license, franchisors are bound by contract to notify other area owners, with each company having its own policy regarding who must be contacted and who has the right to object. The issue seems simple on its face: new supply within any competitive set will cause a drop in occupancy or rate at the existing hotels. The impact issue here revolves around how much *incremental* impact there may be. The issue is rarely as simple as it appears. For example, assume that ABC Developer has applied for a license to build a limited-service property in Suburbia, USA and that an existing extended-stay property under the same franchise umbrella exists two towns away. The owner of that hotel may object and request an impact study. While these two hotels normally target different segments, the existing extended-stay product is not operating at an ideal mix of business because the majority of its business is transient, rather than true extended-stay. This issue holds true across a variety of brands. All-suite products and extended-stay products, while designed with a focus on different segments, often can compete directly for business. After all, both properties feature suite rooms and, in fact, may be operating at similar rate levels. In many cases, the demand in the local market—not the product itself—will dictate who competes with whom.

Another complex example of a potential impact situation involves multiple developers who apply consecutively for franchise agreements. Assume a limited-service property exists in a downtown location. Developer A has applied for a permit to develop a property under the same brand. At the same time, Developer B is planning a mixed-use project in the next town that will include a full-service property, also under that same umbrella. Developer A submits an application and the existing owner requests an impact study. In this case, let's say the findings reveal marginal impact of three points on room revenue. Two weeks later, Developer B files for an application. The owner again requests an impact study. However, in this case, the impact of *only* Hotel B upon the existing hotel is reviewed. Marginal impact of, say, 3.5 percent is determined to be accurate and supportable. Now the existing hotel is anticipating a 6.5 percent drop in rooms revenue from incremental impact of both proposed hotels, although neither separate impact study showed significant decreases to rooms revenue.

Conversion in the Market

Conversions within a market also may cause incremental impact and present a host of challenges when analyzing the market. For example, let's assume there is a potential impact situation in a major metropolitan area that is experiencing a supply shortage and, consequently, an excess of demand. An existing hotel—let's call it Hotel A—is located approximately two blocks from a less desirable asset that has undergone several brand changes over the course of the past three years. The new owners of an independent hotel—Hotel B—have filed for conversion approvals with the franchise company. The existing hotel owners in the market are notified, as per the guidelines of the franchise company's impact policy. Existing Hotel A responds promptly with a letter of objection to the franchisor regarding impact resulting from the conversion of Hotel B. However, Hotel A is operating well in excess of 85 percent occupancy. Furthermore, other products under the same flag in this major metropolitan area are operating at similar levels. As such, the level of turndown demand is significant. The owner of Hotel A contends that if he loses one room night on any given weekend, there is impact. Furthermore, Hotel B's position on the brand Web site would give it an advantage and could drive down Hotel A's rates, which consistently are higher than the rest of the market. Developer projections for the conversion hotel support this claim.

Two issues arise here. One is the timing of the existing turndown demand. Is it all generated on peak weekends and holidays and as such, truly couldn't be accommodated by the existing Hotel A, or was it spread out throughout the year? The second issue lies with determining how much of that excess demand represents actual, bookable room nights. Considering that the potential conversion asset already has a base of business, the chance of impact seems minimal on its face. However, careful analysis based on the timing of demand in the market and such issues as Web site placement could cause impact during soft seasons and weeks in the market. Thus, the issue is less clear than it may first appear.

New Product/Brand

Given the consolidation of franchise companies and the rapid expansion of the brands under their umbrellas, new brands can be a concern for existing hotel owners. Although franchisors will develop a brand to target a specific market and support its development with statistically valid data, consumers may see some brands as quite similar. While literature on SpringHill Suites and Residence Inns clearly distinguishes the brands from each other, consumers may not view these distinctions the same way. For example, both hotels offer suite products and, depending on the market, they may operate at similar rate levels. Likewise, do Comfort Inns and Quality Inns compete if they have similar locations, similar products, and similar rate structures? While the products are designed to target different markets, the owners of the actual properties have a great deal of latitude in the upkeep of their products. As a result, a new Quality Inn may in fact compete directly with a Comfort Inn. However, not all impact policies allow for impact across brands.

Brand Acquisition

Although less prevalent, hotel companies have added entire portfolios to their systems. Take Starwood's pending purchase of Le Meridien, for example. These companies both operate properties in the luxury tier. While both companies have solid bases of business and existing assets that preclude base impact, the addition of Le Meridien to the Starwood reservations network has the potential to cause impact on specific existing properties. More importantly, future W or St. Regis developments could now encounter impact with Le Meridien properties. As of the date of this writing, no brand impact policy covers this scenario.

The Impact Policy

While all the major brands have implemented and updated their impact policies, impact issues require constant reevaluation. The majority of brands have dedicated significant resources and staff to addressing the concerns of franchisees. These typically are vice presidents of fair franchising or franchise services departments. They are responsible for administering the impact policy and maintaining relationships with existing franchisees. The impact policy can be broken down into four key parts: notification/timing, the objection process, evaluation, and decision.

Notification/Timing

The key issue with notification and timing involves determining who is to be notified of a pending application to develop a new hotel or convert an existing one. Do all hotels within a 20-mile radius receive notification? Is a Comfort Inn owner notified if a developer has submitted an application for a Clarion? What if the existing property is a Comfort Inn and Suites rather than a standard Comfort Inn? In other words, is impact limited to same-brand competition, or is it considered for all brands under the same franchisor? Who decides whom to notify? Is it the corporate franchise relations department, or is it regional franchise representatives? Does everyone who is notified have the right to object? The answers vary from hotel company to hotel company. Some notify all their brands within a certain radius. Other impact policies state explicitly which brands compete, while others notify only the three closest hotels to the applicant property. Another method allows only franchisees in good standing to object.

Once a franchisor has clearly established who is notified of a pending license application, a decision must be made regarding how they are notified. Are all involved parties sent a letter? Do all owners receive a phone call? There certainly have been cases in which existing owners have claimed not to have received a letter, so what exactly is the franchisors' legal responsibility? The notification process should be spelled out clearly in the franchise document and understood by every franchisee.

The Objection Process

Once notification letters are sent or phone calls are made, notified owners typically have a specific number of days to respond. However, not all parties necessarily have objection rights. Several franchisors notify all brands in the market as a courtesy, but allow only certain properties to object. Typically, those who are allowed to object have 10–20 calendar days to do so in writing. Frequently, they must establish why impact could occur and formally request an impact study. Most franchise companies have forms to facilitate this process. This critical issue should be defined clearly in the impact policy.

Evaluation

Once the objection process is complete, the franchise company must move forward with the evaluation of impact. Each hotel company has a different methodology for this process. Several major firms have elected to do internal studies, typically conducted by their feasibility departments. Others have an approved list of outside consultants who (ideally) are well qualified to perform the study. Formal arbitration is a third possibility, though it is not used as frequently as in the past, since impact policies have evolved to define incremental impact more clearly.

When outside consultants are used, the question of cost arises. Who should pay for the study? In many cases, the franchise company will pay all fees and expenses for all studies. However, this policy can lead to frivolous studies in situations where the lack of impact is clear, but an owner has nothing to lose by objecting. One of the more effective policies requires the objecting owner to deposit money to cover the cost of the impact study. If the study reveals significant incremental impact, the franchise company will reimburse the owner. This method encourages owners to seriously consider the market and their competitive position within it before objecting and requesting that a study be undertaken. A clear methodology regarding who performs the study, who selects that party, and who has input in the study also should be defined in the impact policy.

Decision

Several key questions affect the final outcome of an impact study. One of these questions is who makes the final decision. Is it a single person within the franchise company or the local franchise representative? Does a panel of participants review the study and decide? Do owners have any recourse if a decision is not in their favor? In the interest of impartiality, we recommend a panel of executives, including a feasibility or development analyst, the fair franchising or franchising relations department head, an operations vice president, and at least one other senior-level person within the organization, review all impact cases.

The next issue is determining the incremental impact threshold at which an application will be denied. Is this threshold based on occupancy alone or does it include rooms revenue? Is it based on total net revenue impact, which could include impact on other operating departments within a hotel? Is this threshold fixed at a certain point—say, 5 percent of rooms revenue—or is it flexible based on the situation?

Another key factor that involves the threshold point is whether incremental impact is a deal-breaker. In other words, does a conclusion of four points of incremental impact require the franchisee to terminate the deal, or is there room to negotiate fees? If negotiation is possible, who is responsible for this process?

Impact policies should be analyzed closely by potential brand owners, and the franchisor's commitment to protecting its owners' rights should be discussed at the onset of an engagement. While ultimately the policy, and therefore the power, lies with the franchise company to decide on its growth practices, a clear understanding of these issues will lead to a healthier franchisor/franchisee relationship.

The Impact Study

Although companies have different policies regarding who has the right to object and who will undertake the impact study, the basis by which to evaluate and quantify impact remains similar. While, ideally, an impact study should serve to maintain a positive relationship between franchisor and franchisee, often relations can be strained in a "go/no-go" situation and the value of a fair franchising representative becomes clear. The critical steps in conducting an impact study include:

- Evaluating the existing property.

- Analyzing the competition and competitive market.

- Profiling the applicant property.

- Profiling the franchise company and relevant brands.

- Projecting occupancy and average daily rates for the existing hotel.

- Determining the impact.

Evaluating the Existing Property

The first step in determining incremental impact upon an existing hotel is to evaluate the existing property. Several factors should be taken into consideration, including:

- Location, access, visibility, proximity to demand generators, condition, pricing, amenities.

- Market mix at subject property.

- Demand generated through the CRS.

- Demand generated through global sales force.

- Percent of demand that is local accounts versus national accounts.

- Percent of guests that are reward program members.

- Repeat accounts.

Location, access, visibility, condition, amenities, and pricing generally are the first issues that an impact consultant will review, as they usually are made clear by a visual inspection of the property. The impact consultant should create a direct comparison to the applicant property. If the property is a highway hotel, which has better access to the highway? Which is more visible? Does one hotel have a pool, while the other does not?

The second issue to analyze is the existing property's market mix. What percentage of its demand is generated from corporate, group, and leisure segments? Will the applicant hotel operate with a similar market mix? If one property will operate primarily within the leisure segment and the other sits in an office park and does 80 percent corporate transient business, impact will be mitigated.

CRSs, national corporate accounts, and points programs all potentially relate to incremental impact. Demand generated through a CRS can be, to some extent, linked directly to the strength of the brand and essentially is why owners pay franchise fees. If an existing hotel generates only 10 percent of its demand through the CRS and the majority of business is transient, incremental impact may be mitigated. However, CRS contribution for the major hotel chains ranges from 20 to 60 percent, with an average of approximately 45 percent contribution. Typically, room nights generated by the CRS command slightly higher rates as well.

Major franchise chains also generate group sales leads through their national sales force. For example, many of the largest companies in the United States have corporate accounts with brands and their employees are required to stay at that brand's properties. This business is generated at a national level and can be highly susceptible to impact. For example, assume ABC Corporation has its headquarters in Portland, Maine. ABC Corporation employees are required to stay at Starwood properties per a national corporate account agreement. However, there is no Starwood hotel in downtown Portland, so they must travel to South Portland to stay at the Sheraton. Assume now that Starwood-branded Four Points Sheraton opens downtown. Although the product clearly is different, the convenience of having a hotel in downtown Portland outweighs the benefits associated with a full-service hotel. As such, all their employees book rooms at the Four Points. This creates incremental impact for the Sheraton South Portland because of the national sales agreement with ABC Corporation, even though the properties might not have competed otherwise.

Another factor to review for hotels with a strong focus on corporate transient guests is the percent of local versus national corporate account business. Local accounts may tend to be more loyal to specific properties, rather than brands. For example, a consultant who visits Parsippany, New Jersey, frequently may choose to continue to stay at a hotel with a familiar staff, rather than relocate to a newly opened hotel that is closer to his or her office.

Finally, a key issue that must be addressed is the percentage of rewards members that stay in any one hotel, which can indicate brand-loyal guests who are particularly vulnerable to incremental impact.

Analyzing the Competition and Competitive Market

The second step an impact consultant would take revolves around understanding the competitive market, including hotel supply and demand in the area. The following items should be analyzed:

- Brand profiles
- Competition and management company profiles
- Occupancy and rate data
- New supply
- Demand trends/market mix
- New demand generators
- General economic health of area

Clearly understanding the competitive supply in the market and its historical performance is critical. Without this base of historical performance, the consultant has no basis for projecting future market trends. However, other factors also should be analyzed, including future development plans and future renovation plans for the market. Conversations with as many market participants as possible should be undertaken, including competitive management, local economic development officials, and local planners who issue building permits and approvals. These discussions will allow the consultant to paint an informed picture of the market for the next few years.

Profiling the Applicant Property

A thorough understanding of the applicant-developer's development plans is required. An interview with the applicant-developer should include:

- Location.
- Complete facility plans including total number of units, amount of meeting space, food and beverage facilities, amenities, room mix, and brand.
- Timing of development.
- Developer's projections.
- Developer's marketing plan.

The applicant profile will allow the consultant to compare the applicant directly to the existing hotel and analyze base and incremental impact.

Profiling the Franchise Company and Relevant Brands

The impact analyst must have a thorough understanding of the strength of the franchise company. The following information should be requested of the parent company and reviewed:

- Data from earnings claims (found in the UFOC)

- Average occupancy and rate for brand

- Average CRS contribution on system-wide basis

- Average CRS contribution for brand

- Average CRS contribution for local branded hotels in relation to objecting property

- Turndown demand for local branded hotels

- Reservations booked *by distribution channel* for local area branded hotels, with specific emphasis placed on brand Web site bookings

- How the franchise company decides placement of hotels on its Web site

Several caveats should be noted when analyzing this data. The national average occupancy and rate data should be viewed as supplementary information. It is interesting to compare it to the local market. Does the franchise company send more business to the local market than the national averages? Is the CRS contribution at the objecting property in line with national averages? If it is, national averages may present the best parameter to project the CRS contribution to the applicant hotel. With that piece of information, a consultant can begin to build a penetration of the local franchise-generated business based on additional supply.

Another issue of relevance is the presence of turndown demand in the area. Turndown demand is recorded through the CRS and generally is overstated. For example, a consumer checking to see if rooms are available will generate a turndown for each hotel he or she checks when, in reality, this only represents one booking. Also, turndown demand isn't sorted by day of the year, so when evaluating this in relation to impact, the analyst must make assumptions as to the timing of this demand. This requires the analyst to adjust turndown reports downward to get a clearer picture of surplus demand generated by the CRS in the market. The greater the surplus, the less incremental impact to the existing hotel, as it is clear that the franchise company is generating room nights that the current supply in the market cannot accommodate.

The last issue—one of brand Web site placement—is a concern that did not exist ten years ago. An understanding of how specific hotels are ordered on the franchise company's online booking channels often can prove useful. For example, assume that two existing assets with the same brand affiliation are located on the outlying beltway of a major metropolitan area. The two hotels are located in markets that are distinctly different from a conversion applicant. While all three hotels are located on or near the same beltway, the applicant property is located closer to the center of the metropolitan area than the existing two. As such, leisure guests searching the brand's Web site for hotels in this city would be led to believe that the applicant hotel is located closer to the city (and thus is more desirable) than the existing hotels. Since this is a significant portion of business for the existing hotels, an incremental impact situation could be created that would not exist on other distribution channels that don't display hotel properties side-by-side.

Projecting Occupancy and Average Daily Rates for the Existing Hotel

Once the relevant information is gathered and analyzed, a projection of occupancy and room rates should be prepared. Projections should be done under three scenarios:

- "As-is"—Assumes the applicant does not exist

- Base Impact—Assumes the new rooms (or newly competitive rooms) will not be affiliated with any objecting property's brand/franchise company

- Incremental Impact—Assumes the applicant's hotel rooms will be under the same brand or franchise company

A report detailing the above points and providing a clear methodology for the impact determination should be prepared. Depending on the company, these reports may be confidential or are shared with the objecting hotels before a decision is reached.

Determining the Impact

The final step in the impact process involves quantifying the amount of base impact and the amount of incremental impact. After analyzing the existing hotel and surrounding competitive market, the consultant should have an accurate idea of what this is. However, one issue that frequently arises with the final determination of impact is the timing of such impact. Will the applicant property impact the existing asset in only one year? Will impact decrease over time? Should the impact be considered throughout the projection period? These questions should be answered on a case-by-case basis. One market may be improving steadily and have a bright economic outlook that will mitigate the effects of impact, but another may be in decline with no promising economic development options on the horizon, so the applicant and objecting hotel will continue to compete for a shrinking base of business. Ideally, the analyst will have considered several methods of determining incremental impact that will form a supported position regarding the actual amount to be expected.

Issues with Impact Studies

Differing Methods of Analysis. While this chapter details the overall steps for analyzing and determining impact, there is no uniformly accepted model that returns an "answer" for a given set of inputs. Rather, impact analysts develop their own sets of tools that they feel are useful under different circumstances. Indeed, we apply several different types of analysis depending on the property type and market situation.

In an effort to streamline and standardize the way impact is viewed, Best Western has developed a financial model that includes clear inputs and quantifies impact based on comparative rankings between the two properties under consideration. This method has some advantages—specifically, it provides a clear, straight-line method for analyzing impact. However, this model may not take into account the vast complexities of specific markets, demand flow patterns, future supply issues, and shifting distribution channels. More importantly, the input is only as good as the research conducted by the analyst and the interpretation of such research can be subjective.

Another method to analyze impact is the percent vulnerable method. This methodology analyzes demand by business segment (for example, local transient, rack, local negotiated corporate, corporate group, association, national corporate, and third-party intermediary). The consultant then determines what percent of that business is vulnerable to impact, or what percent the applicant property could actively target. Then the consultant determines what percent is likely to be booked by the applicant hotel. This method is particularly suited to hotels with a diverse base of business. This method also allows the applicant hotel to affect segments in different ways. For example, assume the applicant hotel will have larger, newer meeting space than the objecting property, but will be located further from the major demand generators than the existing property. This method would allow for the penetration of group business, while acknowledging that local corporate business is less likely to relocate. Corporate business can even be broken down to the company level. Mapping out the locations of the top ten or twenty demand generators can also be helpful because it allows the analyst to clearly understand the relevance of location and project with much greater accuracy the potential loss of room nights to a new competitor. A national corporate account located closer to the applicant hotel may be more likely to relocate than a local corporate account located closer to the existing asset. Thus, an accurate breakdown of potentially lost demand can be made with this analysis.

Another impact analysis method involves a breakdown of all CRS business generated in the target market for the past several years. Detailed CRS data can be provided by the franchise company and used to paint a clear picture of how each hotel performs relative to the reservation system. Do all hotels receive 100 percent penetration of the demand being generated through the CRS? Where does the subject stand? If the room count of same-brand hotels increases, but the net rooms generated remains the same, what is the impact in terms of room nights to each of the existing assets in the market?

The impact analyst should use several methods for analyzing and projecting impact. The final estimate of impact should be supported in as many ways as possible.

Lack of Available Research. While an impact analyst can expect to receive a well-prepared information packet from a hotel in a major metropolitan area, specific statistics often are unavailable from less sophisticated owners or from small, more rural hotels. Hotel owners in budget, rooms-only hotels often are unable to provide the impact analyst with such specific data as top ten accounts for the past five years, or a specific profile of walk-in business. Referral chains such as Best Western do not track the occupancy levels and room rates of their associated hotels. While analysts can hope for sophisticated tracking software to be in place at the objecting asset, often they must do without and make projections based on in-depth knowledge of the market and experience.

Subjectivity. Despite the various methods of determining impact available to the analyst, the practice is inherently subjective. As such, owners, franchisors, managers, and impact analysts often can disagree on the interpretation of the same facts. However, through diligent market research and thoughtful analysis, a well-supported projection can be made. This inherent subjectivity is the reason that qualified, independent consultants should be utilized, rather than parties with an interest in the proposed project.

E-Commerce

By *John D. Burns, CHA, ISHC*

John D. Burns, *identified by* Lodging Magazine *as one of the experts changing the travel industry, founded Hospitality Technology Consulting in 1992. As HTC's president, he heads this international consulting service specializing in assisting hotel chains and independent hotels in optimizing central reservations and electronic distribution programs. Born and educated in Canada, he has worked for firms such as Hyatt International, Ramada Inc., and THISCO (later Pegasus Solutions). Mr. Burns is active in organizations including ISHC, HFTP, and HSMAI, is a past Board Member of the Hotel Electronic Distribution Network Association, and received that organization's Outstanding Contributor Award in 2002 for support of the association's activities. He has authored numerous articles and speaks frequently to a variety of industry audiences.*

THIS CHAPTER WILL PROVIDE an overview of e-commerce for the hotel investor and covers the definition of e-commerce; the evolution of e-commerce, including the development of Internet commerce and its embrace by the hotel industry; the importance of e-commerce to the hotel industry; the key elements of a successful e-commerce program, including striking a balance with traditional channels and selecting and optimizing e-commerce opportunities; and future trends in electronic distribution.

What Is E-Commerce?

A common definition of e-commerce (short for electronic commerce) is simply any business conducted over the Internet. In the hotel industry, e-commerce extends beyond the Internet to include other forms of electronic distribution as well—principally the global distribution systems (GDSs), including Sabre, Galileo, Worldspan, and Amadeus. For some e-marketers, GDSs have become a secondary issue in e-commerce, but they delivered approximately $13 billion in hotel revenue in 2004 and about $66 billion since 1998, according to TravelCLICK.

Whatever its definition, e-commerce is certainly having an impact on the economy in general and the travel sector in particular. According to University of Texas Internet Economy Indicators, global e-commerce revenue has reached more than $550 billion since 1998 and is growing at a rate of more than $1 million every minute. There can be no doubt that this new sales opportunity is one in which the hotel industry must compete—like it or not—and to which it must assign already scarce resources.

As a new marketplace for the presentation and sale of accommodations, the Internet has caused major changes in the hotel industry's standard business practices. For example, e-commerce has produced a marketplace with nearly complete rate transparency. By visiting individual sites or by using travel metasearch sites, prospective guests can (and do) compare rates. E-commerce is also simultaneously transforming the traditional market segments with which hotel marketers had grown comfortable. The fences that once defined those segments have crumbled. Potential guests in each segment know—and want—everyone else's rates, so demand segmentation and forecasting has become much more difficult. A hotel's competitors can and do use Internet-based rate search tools to determine what rates are being offered, compare them with their own, and make adjustments with the hope of gaining a competitive edge.

Anyone selling in the e-commerce marketplace is already aware that the Internet is also an entirely new person-to-person communication environment. It has fostered instant feedback and has become a medium where rumors, opinions, and ideas about value and customer service can be compared and explored. The Web changed the speed with which everyone expects an answer. "Instant" is now the expectation, whether it is an immediate purchase, a confirmation of a reservation, or the quick resolution of a problem.

But e-commerce is certainly not only about challenges. Although challenges abound, they are more than balanced by tremendous opportunities. The Internet has substantially redefined the marketplace by delivering worldwide marketing exposure, allowing independents to compete effectively with the largest brands, and enabling a new level of client/vendor relationships. Still, the e-commerce environment is a typical marketplace—obscure, biased, unfair, powerful, promising, and fast-changing.

A book—indeed, a shelf of books—could be written about e-commerce. The reality is that they would be out-of-date before they were published. We cannot attempt to examine every facet of e-commerce and its many implications for the lodging industry. Instead, we will identify and discuss some of the major issues that e-commerce raises for hoteliers. Our hope is that a better understanding of the environment will lead to better decisions about options, vendors, and activities.

We must also limit our discussion to focus on the outward/external impact of e-commerce on the hotel industry and its efforts to sell accommodation. Issues related to internal impacts—the relationship between a brand and a property, for example—will not be addressed except where they substantially affect external distribution.

How Has E-Commerce Evolved?

The early days of the Internet have sometimes been likened to a "gold rush" where everyone grabbed their picks and shovels and headed off on their own to make their fortune. The current situation is probably better compared to attempting to scale Mt. Everest—a detailed plan, base and advance camps, and skilled guides are required and real dangers lurk. What's more, the evolution from gold rush to complex expedition has occurred (and continues) at "Internet speed," making it a challenge for hoteliers to keep up.

In less colorful language, the early Internet was in many ways a do-it-yourself environment. Perhaps someone from the information technology department or a front desk clerk who was good with computers developed a basic Web site with text drawn from sales collateral, existing photography shot for print collateral, and maybe even an e-mail reservation request form. The site was submitted to the few Internet search engines that existed and everyone sat back to wait for the arrival of the first reservation.

The current environment requires a far more sophisticated approach, including a substantially larger investment in both time and money. An e-commerce plan has become a key corporate strategy to ensure profitability. Cadres of talent, including Web site designers, search engine optimizers, photographers, writers, and e-commerce marketers, are pulled into the process and corporate coffers are opened. Consultants by the score offer their services as guides to specialized niches as well as for general marketing services.

How did we get from do-it-yourself to an all-encompassing e-distribution/e-commerce corporate marketing strategy? It has been a steadily developing process built on a foundation of technology development that started in the 1960s.

The First Steps

Holiday Inn, under the leadership of Kemmons Wilson, is generally credited as the organization that revolutionized hotel reservation processing. In a program designed to both boost the value of owning a Holiday Inn franchise and to provide improved guest service, Holiday Inn opened a central reservation office and installed toll-free reservation phone numbers. This introduced a new level of centralization and structure to the previously property-centered reservation process. For the first time, availability and rate information for all of the brand's hotels was easily accessed at a central location. Other chains soon followed Holiday Inn's lead. In the ensuing years, hotel companies and reservation service bureaus developed the first generation of computerized central reservation systems (CRSs) with which to facilitate management of the growing volumes of availability, rate, and descriptive information.

The next important step was the addition of hotel booking capability to airline reservation systems. Originally developed for use by airline staff, access terminals for those systems were soon installed by the airlines on the desks of their travel agent partners. These reservation systems evolved into what are now the GDSs. Between the time when hotel reservations processing became available to travel agents through the GDSs in the early 1980s and the present, the GDSs have worked with the hotel industry—particularly with the Hotel Electronic Distribution Network Association (HEDNA)—to expand their content and ease of use and to improve the GDSs as hotel booking channels. According to HEDNA, almost 50 million hotel reservations were being booked annually in the GDSs by the year 2000.

The GDSs' ability to instantly confirm hotel reservations resulted from increasingly sophisticated communication links between hotel company CRSs and the GDSs. The links were initially constructed directly between a hotel company's

CRS computer and the GDSs with considerable difficulty and expense. They were later accomplished through the use of an intermediary service called a switch.

The development of these communication links and fully automated reservation processing in the GDSs (through their links with hotel companies' CRSs) provided the crucial technology and operational processes that enabled the next major development in electronic distribution of hotel rooms—sale through the Internet.

A New Marketing Environment

While the Internet had been available as a communication vehicle for military and educational research since the early 1970s, the introduction of the World Wide Web in 1990 ushered the Internet into widespread general consumer use. What we have come to know as the Internet, with its graphics and easy user navigation, resulted from work done by Tim Berners-Lee—a scientist working at the CERN research center in Switzerland. Although his Internet browser was designed to assist his fellow scientists in locating and exploring the wealth of information available on the Internet, it permitted anyone with access to a computer and a modem to easily navigate that information.

Equally important, while the original Internet was a text-dominated information system, Berners-Lee's work brought a new level of ease of use and graphical richness, allowing vendors to appealingly present their products on the Internet.

The Hotel Industry Embraces the Web

The hotel industry was an early adopter of this new sales opportunity. In the mid-1990s, hoteliers began to display basic information on the Internet. The embrace of this new technology was somewhat out of character for an industry that has not always welcomed technology advances. Whatever the stimulus for this early acceptance, it sparked rapid growth in the number of hotels offering information (although not necessarily reservation processing) on the Internet. Hoteliers quickly saw that, at a minimum, the Internet could constructively supplement their printed collateral and their person-to-person sales efforts.

Over the next ten years, hotel Web sites rapidly evolved from minimal displays to our current information-rich, sophisticated e-distribution presentation and booking centers. This progression could be likened to moving information from a black and white newspaper classified ad to a sophisticated television commercial in prime time. These changes have moved Web sites through several stages:

- Stage 1—Basic presence on the Web with very limited descriptive information, often listing a toll-free telephone number for reservations.

- Stage 2—Expanded information including an e-mail reservation request form and more photographs.

- Stage 3—Online reservation processing displaying accurate availability and rates with immediate confirmation numbers (accomplished through room allocations or automated links to the CRS).

- Stage 4—Upgraded content presenting all facets of the hotel, including expanded and improved facility descriptions and graphics, use of video tours and 360° photos, search capabilities, maps, local attraction information, and Webcams.

- Stage 5—Sites building and maintaining relationships through frequent guest recognition program information available on the site and the use of cookies to identify returning visitors. Users can create profiles containing information on their preferences and retrieve information on their current reservations. The appearance of the site evolves, now actively merchandising the property by portraying the hotel as a key contributor to a rich, positive guest experience.

- Stage 6—Some sites add limited packaging capability that may include air and car reservation options and begin to offer advance reservation of golf tee times, spa appointments, restaurant reservations, and other services. The Web site becomes a fully functional alternative to calling a hotel, CRS, or travel agent for information and reservations.

New Merchants Arrive on the Scene

In the mid-1990s, hotel companies and operators of independent properties were not the only ones who saw the potential power of e-commerce for the hospitality industry. Commission-based online travel agencies such as Expedia and Travelocity came to market.

Travel agents, wholesalers (who received substantial discounts in return for their promotional and sales efforts), and niche "distressed inventory" merchants were longstanding participants in the hotel industry's distribution scene well before the age of the Internet. The Internet and its emerging travel marketplace prompted some of these established organizations to adapt their business models to this emerging hospitality sales arena. The new market also caught the attention of nontravel suppliers and entrepreneurs alike, encouraging them to target the travel distribution marketplace.

The commission-based retail approach used by traditional travel agents was the initial business model adopted by megavendors such as Travelocity and Expedia as well as numerous lesser known (and in many cases now long-forgotten) companies.

Among the best known e-versions of the traditional wholesaler-style model is 1-800-HOTELS (which later became Hotels.com). This wholesale arrangement, eventually labeled the "merchant model," consisted of contracts between the wholesaler and individual hotels. In these agreements, the hotel agreed to provide a generally small block of rooms on most dates at a substantially discounted rate. The original merchant-model vendors pitched their services to hoteliers as help with last-minute sales of accommodations to highly price-sensitive leisure travelers, offering an opportunity to sell rooms that would likely otherwise go unsold to a small and hard to reach niche market.

The economic slowdown that occurred in 2000 coupled with the dramatic impact of the September 11, 2001, attacks on the travel industry propelled two significant developments: much greater participation in merchant model programs by hotels and implementation or substantial expansion of merchant-model programs by retail distributors. Many in the hotel community attribute the mounting success of Hotels.com as the primary indicator to others of the impressive size and profitability of this market segment and identify their growth as inspiration for this merchant model program development.

Other Distribution Models Evolve

As the e-equivalents of conventional retail and wholesale distributors matured, other e-styles were also evolving. The first—now widely known as the "opaque" model—was something of a grab bag in which travelers committed to buying a product after specifying general parameters of property or rate acceptability. This model was first launched by priceline.com and later offered by Hotwire in a slightly different version. The opaque model offered hoteliers an additional e-commerce option in which the room price was initially masked, protecting the brand from value perception erosion.

Not surprisingly, sales techniques that were successful in others areas of e-commerce (or, for that matter, in the traditional marketplace) were also applied to hospitality sales on the Web. These included development of auction and last-minute travel sites.

In recent years we have also seen the development of Web sites operated by supplier alliances. Among the best known examples is the group of six hotel companies who developed Travelweb (now owned by priceline.com). Such sites gave participating hotel companies the opportunity to offer specially priced accommodations directly on an aggregated site with multiple brands and wider selection without incurring the rate discount costs inherent in the merchant model.

What Is the Importance of E-Commerce for the Hotel Industry?

The evolution of a variety of e-commerce distribution channels has provided hotels with a range of opportunities to choose among in hopes of tapping the Web's potential. Hoteliers can apply modest resources to simply maintain their sales or pursue more extensive and astute e-commerce practices that can result in substantially increased sales.

The barrage of statistics encountered in the trade press documents the importance of e-commerce sales to the hotel industry. In early 2005, for example, Travel-CLICK reported that room night reservations booked through the Internet and the GDSs combined grew at a rate of 7 percent in 2004 and that the average daily rate for those bookings also rose almost 7 percent. It also reported that Internet reservations received via hotel companies' CRSs grew by 22.8 percent in 2004 with hotel brand Web sites accounting for almost 72 percent of reservations processed through the CRS. Note that these figures do not reflect direct-to-property Internet bookings.

While many factors (including a more robust economy and proliferation of computer use) have led to growing e-commerce sales, the evolution of hotel Web sites from simple supplements to static printed sales collateral into sophisticated sales tools has been an instrumental factor as well. The ability of hoteliers to readily adjust their rates and to add such new sales vehicles as dynamic packaging is also facilitating this growth.

Now a major factor in selling individual traveler reservations, e-commerce has also begun to revolutionize the corporate booking process. Businesses are migrating to easy-to-use desktop self-booking systems that allow the business traveler to make instant travel reservations (including lodging bookings) without the participation of a travel agent. Likewise, corporate meeting planners and convention organizers have joined in embracing the e-commerce option. Hoteliers have responded with meeting planner request-for-proposal functions, online catering and audiovisual equipment requests, rooming list submission capabilities, and more.

Steadily evolving Internet technology has also fostered lower cost, more extensive communication between corporate offices and properties. This increased communication flow takes the form not only of e-mail, but also user screens that enable property staff to easily maintain their own rates and availability data in CRSs, Internet-based PMS/CRS interfaces, and easy online recruiting and hotel supply purchasing services.

Distribution Costs

The e-commerce evolution has had a profound impact on the hotel industry's distribution costs. Historically, hotels often viewed distribution costs as a secondary issue in the costs of doing business. The Internet, in a tantalizing dichotomy, expanded the opportunity to sell directly to the traveler (theoretically lowering the cost of distribution) while simultaneously ushering in an era of such deep-discount (or high overhead) options as the merchant model.

Hoteliers traditionally have chosen to offer their lodging through the widest possible array of sales channels, and each channel offers its own sales opportunity and cost of sale. These sales opportunities and associated costs should be central considerations in determining channel participation, rate setting, and inventory allocation. Exhibit 1 illustrates how distribution costs vary from channel to channel. It also demonstrates how hurdles (such as full prepayment requirements) have been incorporated into discount rates in order to protect higher yielding rates.

What Are the Key Elements in this E-Commerce Opportunity?

The new distribution and sales opportunities offered to hoteliers by the e-commerce environment are numerous and constantly evolving. These opportunities challenge hoteliers to evaluate their potential and then use the best of them in a deliberate and productive balance with traditional sales and marketing opportunities.

Hoteliers, like many others, were intrigued with the Internet as it began to take shape as a consumer shopping environment. They asked, "Might this be the ideal low-cost (or no-cost) hotel sales marketplace? Might it quickly and decisively

Exhibit 1 Distribution Costs by Channel

Channel	Business Model	Charge to Guests	Gross Revenue to Hotel	Distribution Costs to Hotel	Net Revenue to Hotel	Comments/ Restrictions
Voice—Central Reservation Center	Retail	$100	$100	CRS fee ($12)	$88	No prepayment requirement or cancellation penalty
GDS	Retail	$100	$100	Travel agent commission (10%=$10) + CRS fee ($12)	$78	No prepayment requirement or cancellation penalty
Web— Brand/Rep. Co. Direct	Retail	$95	$95	CRS fee ($12)	$83	No prepayment requirement or cancellation penalty
Web—Hotel direct	Retail	$95	$95	PMS IBE* fee ($2)	$93	No prepayment requirement or cancellation penalty
Web—Third-Party	Retail	$95	$95	Commission (10%=$9.50)	$85.50	No prepayment requirement or cancellation penalty
Web— Brand/Rep. Co. Direct	Restrictions Apply	$90	$90	Reduced CRS fee ($5)	$85	Prepayment required; no refunds
Web—Hotel Direct	Restrictions Apply	$90	$90	PMS IBE* fee ($2)	$88	Prepayment required; no refunds
Web—Third-Party Merchant Model	Restrictions Apply	$90	$67.50	-	$67.50	Prepayment required; no refunds
Web—Third-Party	Opaque	$65	$45	-	$45	Prepayment required; no refunds

* PMS IBE—Internet Booking Engine provided by PMS vendor and linked directly to Property Management System.

replace the traditional sales channels to allow hotels to sell directly to travelers, eliminating costly intermediaries? Might it even allow hotels to terminate their brand affiliations and compete at little cost in a global, bias-free, merit-based marketplace?"

The last several years have demonstrated that the Internet is not a sales utopia. E-commerce and electronic distribution are complex and rarely inexpensive. Breaking through the information clutter to deliver a sales message to a potential guest is difficult, and costs for intermediaries, designers, technicians, and advisors abound. Nonetheless, as we have seen, use of the Internet for travel research and booking is increasing steadily. Internet bookings are already a significant proportion of every hotel company's business mix.

Striking the Traditional Channel vs. E-Commerce Balance

The addition of the Internet to the lodging sales environment was a new and significant disruption to what had become a reasonably predictable, if not altogether static, sales process. In the end, however, this increased difficulty does not matter. The rules have changed somewhat, but the objective remains the same—to fill rooms while achieving the optimum occupancy-to-rate ratio.

Hoteliers have always strived to maximize room rate and occupancy. To do so, they increasingly are applying the analytical methods of the emerging revenue management discipline as they examine market segments—corporate, leisure, government/military, SMERF (social, military, educational, religious, and fraternal) groups, meetings and conventions, tour and travel, crew, and so on—to estimate each segment's volume potential and the rate tolerance for each individual property. Once this potential is calculated, rates are set and inventory is allocated to achieve the desired occupancy rate/goal.

Internet-enabled rate and information transparency has disrupted the conventional marketplace. It has made the tasks of defining and estimating segment-by-segment potential and administering segment-by-segment sales immeasurably more difficult for hoteliers. Members of every one of the longstanding market segments now want to reserve their accommodations (and sometimes related facilities—a golf tee time or conference room, for example) online. Moreover, segment members increasingly have access to rates, special offers, and extensive competitive information for their segment and (more disruptively) for other segments.

In the new e-commerce–inclusive sales environment, the first challenge is to estimate the proportion of bookers in each market segment that will prefer to research electronically. The next is to estimate the proportion of each segment that will prefer to book electronically. With these estimates in hand, achieving the balance in resource assignment and inventory allocation between the traditional and e-commerce sales channels can be accomplished.

Having estimated the electronic research and booking demand, the next step is to focus on e-commerce sales optimization. The objectives are to identify the available sales practices, options, and opportunities; to select from them appropriately; and to then use them with maximum productivity. In an ideal world, a hotelier could participate in every e-channel or Web site that potentially would be able to produce revenue for the property. In the real world, a successful e-commerce strategy must identify a manageable mix of channels and Web sites that will meet sales goals.

A Successful Web Site

In moving to identification and discussion of a hotelier's e-commerce options, the hotel or brand Web site is the logical point to begin. Branded hotels generally must participate in the chain's Web site. Independent properties use their representation company's Web site as well as, in many cases, their individual property's Web site.

Hotels and hotel companies are eager to attract visitors to their Web sites and to have those visitors reserve their lodging online. Generally speaking, these sites represent the booking channel with the lowest overhead cost, since they rarely involve third-party commissions or processing fees. In many (although not all) cases, the net revenue remaining after payment of such site operation expenses as design fees and booking engine costs is higher for Web site–direct reservations than for bookings from other channels.

A successful Web site that is persuasive and productive is neither easily developed nor permanent. It requires a commitment of time and money to update the site on a recurring basis as the technology available to support the site, the functions that it can offer, and the style of presentation evolve. Competitive pressures make these changes unavoidable.

The characterization of a successful Web site as persuasive acknowledges the influence that Web sites have on travel buying decisions. The substantial proportion of travelers who use the Internet for prebooking research purposes (even though they may ultimately choose to book their reservations nonelectronically) compels hotel Web site developers to provide extensive descriptive content. That information should describe the property in detail—its rooms, public spaces, food and beverage facilities, recreational opportunities, retail outlets, etc. A well-managed site anticipates as many travelers' questions as possible and provides answers on the site. The restaurant descriptions, for example, should be complete and compelling so that guests will want to dine there rather than outside the hotel. If the corporate market is being targeted, businesses in the area should be listed along with their distance and directions from the hotel. Information on business amenities should be described in complete detail.

Of equal importance to the presence of that information is that the information presented is phrased in a sales-oriented manner. Travelers seek reassurance that their basic needs will be met and confirmation that the facility will provide the comfortable, productive, stimulating, or relaxing environment they seek. They also look for confirmation that their needs will be satisfied in a manner that confirms the price/value relationship. The property must be attractively and compellingly presented so that potential guests do not make the decision to look elsewhere.

A review of a variety of hotel Web sites—both for independent and branded properties—still reveals too many instances in which the traveler must select the hotel in spite of the Web presentation. The facility is presented in such lackluster and unappealing fashion that the selection (in cases where it is in favor of the property) is driven by such other factors as location and price.

As mentioned earlier, successful Web sites must not only be persuasive but also productive. Productivity is measured as bookings completed. The core determinant in enhancing productivity is the quality of the booking function, often referred to as the booking engine or Internet booking engine (IBE).

It is essential that the booking engine be easy for the site visitor to locate. Hotel Web site designers now realize that there need not be only a single path to frequently sought important information. This is absolutely true of the booking function. Most hotel Web sites have evolved from offering a single "reserve now" option on a "reservations" page of the site to offering one or more "book now" opportunities on every page.

Once the booking function has been selected by the site visitor, a clear, short path through the booking process is essential. The obviousness of the booking pathway is essential whether the reservation sequence is presented via a series of screens (progressing through room types, rates, selection, addition of personal booking details, etc.) or via a group of panels on a single booking page. Described by such terms as "ease of navigation" and "intuitiveness of design," the goal is to minimize the steps the booker must take to complete the reservation process.

The booking engine is also enhanced by the presence of the opportunity to read room descriptions (without the need to leave the IBE to check information), review package options, and reserve specialized features—a nonsmoking room, feather pillows, or a king bed—during the booking process itself. The user should not be required to send a post-transaction e-mail to communicate a special request or live with the uncertainty of a requested but unconfirmed feature or service.

Increasingly, Web sites and booking engines are being enhanced further to support reservation processing beyond those for accommodation. Where facilities for capturing nonroom revenue exist at a property, descriptions of these opportunities are being presented and reservation opportunities provided. This is occurring following the completion of a lodging reservation, during the reservation process itself, or independent of the room reservation function.

In the supplementary revenue opportunity spectrum that spans preordered room service deliveries and dining reservations, golf tee times, spa treatment reservations, and so on, the leading Web sites offer limited to extensive booking opportunities. Often, sales facilities for logo wear, branded toiletries, and even such soft goods as bedding are presented on the Web site as well.

While the global reach and opportunities of e-commerce have long been espoused, recognition of the multilingual character of the world and the interest of travelers in reading about hotels and completing their reservations in a language other than English has been slower to take root. This situation is now changing as parallel versions of Web sites in a variety of languages are developed and launched by hotel companies and, in some cases, by individual independent hotels.

The complexities associated with multilingual operation are numerous. They certainly include translation of Web site contents and booking engine functions (including even error messages) into a number of languages. They also include maintenance of currency conversion tables, response to e-mail inquiries in the guests' selected language, and dealing with the guests' expectations of availability of multilingual staff during their visit to the property. In addition, not all hotel companies fully understand the cultural differences that may influence potential guests who visit their sites. A bikini-clad woman may entice some but may well offend others.

Every successful e-commerce strategy begins with the definition of the goals to be met. While the e-commerce strategy may well be drafted at the senior levels of corporate or hotel management, meeting the goals of the strategy is left to the sales staff, the revenue manager, and the reservations management and staff. The e-commerce strategy may well run aground in the day-to-day (or sometimes hour-to-hour) implementation of sales and revenue management techniques if specific responsibilities for coordination and cooperation are not mandated.

Successful Web sites are not completed once and then left to function unattended thereafter. Each of the six phases of Web site evolution required some redesign and redevelopment. In each case, successively greater levels of design expertise, copywriting talent, and technical acumen were required. This pattern of periodic need for site redevelopment and increasingly more specialized expertise to support it should and must be expected and budgeted for.

Beyond a Well-Developed Web Site

A hotel's (or hotel company's) e-commerce program now extends far beyond the operation of its own Web site. The variety of third-party Web sites in which they can participate includes retail (such as that of a local convention and visitors bureau), merchant-model (such as Expedia.com or Hotels.com), opaque (such as priceline.com or Hotwire.com), auction or last-minute (such as luxurylink.com and lastminute.com), and package sites (such as site59.com). These opportunities are categorized by their business models. In parallel, there are scores of special interest Web sites offering one or more of these business models in their booking functions.

Within most third-party sites, there are multiple levels of participation and expense. The task for hoteliers—and it is a recurring one as the options evolve, with old ones disappearing and new ones emerging—is to evaluate the likely return on investment of different site types and degrees of participation. Hotels use various criteria in considering prospective sites. For example, do the hotel's style and the interests of its potential guests match the demographics of the site under consideration? An illustration might be a deep-discount style site catering to low-budget travelers that would be inappropriate for a four- or five-star hotel company. Other factors often considered are the third-party Web site's reputation, customer service standards, and booking engine sophistication, as well as terms of payment for accommodations reserved and reservation fees for those bookings.

The number of sites in which a hotel can effectively participate varies. The key issue in determining the number of sites in which to participate is the property's ability to effectively present the hotel. That is to say, where can the availability and rates be maintained in a timely manner and kept fully synchronized with the PMS? Effective presentation is also indicated by the comprehensiveness and timely maintenance of descriptive information.

Sites that draw inventory from PMSs, CRSs, or GDSs, deliver confirmed reservations to the destination hotel through those systems, and require little additional maintenance generally are included with little further thought. Sites that require management of availability or rates through an extranet (generally an Internet site that is accessed by the reservations or revenue management staff) or deliver reservations via fax or e-mail involve a greater level of participation by the staff of the property. Forrester Research reports that hotels attempt to participate in an average of seven sites, while HTC Research reports that some reservation managers believe that the maximum number of these sites that can effectively be administered is five.

With the array of other duties imposed by e-commerce participation, it is easy for hoteliers to overlook the information that is presented about their property on third-party Web sites. The information on those sites may have been collected when the hotel was first listed and not subsequently refreshed with more up-to-date details or a more appealing presentation. Hotels should actively monitor third-party sites and request revision of their information, particularly if it no longer supports the property's e-commerce strategy. Third-party sites should be willing to promptly make such changes. Additionally, problems arising from inaccurate or misleading information or booking problems on third-party sites should be tracked by the front desk, sales, or reservations staff, and their immediate correction should be demanded of the site operator.

In an April 7, 2005, article on www.ehotelier.com, Yahoo! Travel general manager Yen Lee said that customers want unbiased information. Because many individuals believe that pictures don't lie, graphic data is going to be (for some companies) the single make-or-break difference between e-commerce success and failure. Many hoteliers continue the practice of emphasizing their signage and lobby area when potential guests want to see what their rooms (and not just the suites) really look like.

As hoteliers strive to portray their properties more appealingly and successfully, a word of caution is warranted. Today's travelers are becoming more sophisticated in their use of the Web. In searching for accommodations, they increasingly are on the watch for any sleight of hand, retouched photography, or exaggerated descriptions. A misleading rate or exaggerated facility presentation has the potential, like biased rate displays on third-party sites, to create skepticism and ultimately antipathy to a property or brand.

Potential guests sometimes browse through user feedback sites like www.tripadvisor.com to check reviews of a property to ensure that it matches the glowing words and photographs on the property Web site or elsewhere. We recently heard about a hotel that rushed to open three weeks early because there was the potential of adding $50,000–$60,000 in revenue. Unfortunately, things did not go well with the rushed opening. It resulted in a substantial number of postings to the TripAdvisor Web site. The hotel took months to recover from the negative reviews.

Hotels face the challenge of determining how to enhance the information on their Web sites, of assessing whether their Web presence already meets its users' needs. One effective approach is to review the Web sites of competing hotels looking for innovative ideas. Another is to view "best of breed" sites to identify what features could be added to a Web site. Finally, visit user feedback sites to identify areas for improvement.

Effective Presentation of Rates

Consumers are perennially interested in getting the best rate or best value. For many hotel companies, the answer to this challenge has been to develop Web guarantee offers that assure potential guests that the rate displayed on their own Internet site will be the lowest available. Such an approach can be very successful. Keep in mind, however, a recent KPMG report described in the May 16, 2005, issue of *Business Travel News* indicated that among the hotels surveyed, only 27 percent with such a "best rate" guarantee actually offered the lowest rate on their Web site. One factor in this situation may be that the updating of inventory and rates on the Web does not consistently reflect the policy set by senior staff. When the junior reservations staff who often are responsible for day-to-day maintenance of availability and rates in e-commerce channels are not trained and kept fully updated on those policies, discrepancies can occur.

Potential customers are also increasingly using third-party travel metasearch companies like SideStep, Kayak.com, or Mobissimo. These companies' sites present lists of available rates in a side-by-side comparison in an attempt to aid travelers in their search for the best rate for their travel choices. The complexity of hotel rates, involving as they do eligibility qualifications (such as AAA rates or AARP rates) and stay restrictions (such as a three-night minimum stay), sometimes corrupts the rate research and comparison process. These metasearch site results sometimes can present questionable rate comparisons that confuse potential guests. This confusion can also result from displays of rates that appear lower since they do not include reservation fees or have prepayment requirements or other limitations. Periodic monitoring of travel metasearch sites by hoteliers can help determine where and when rate comparisons are being correctly or incorrectly made.

Hotels face similar challenges as they themselves use competitive rate search tools in an attempt to determine their competitors' rates and to possibly better understand their competitors' sales philosophies. Use of competitive rate search tools (such as AnyRate, Electrobug, RateTiger, RateGain, and TravelCLICK's RateVIEW) using apples-to-apples comparisons can be an effective technique to ensure that the most attractive rates are being displayed in comparison with competitor rates, although the data must be validated to ensure its accuracy.

Limited and Dynamic Packaging

Recent research by PhoCusWright Inc. indicates that when it comes to purchasing packaged travel, most travelers prefer to assemble their vacation components themselves. Dynamic packaging technology has emerged to assist consumers in assembling their own vacation packages. Traditionally, tour companies assembled package components and sold static packages at a preset price. With the dynamic packaging approach, consumers pick the individual package components (a flight on Airline A, a car from Car Rental Company B, three nights in a suite at Hotel C, and four nights in a deluxe room at Hotel D, for example). A price for the package is then determined. In many instances, buyers can pick from a menu of additional options for sightseeing, theme park and museum admissions, theater tickets, and so on. While the travel agency megasites were the first to institute such self-packaging offerings for their clientele, hotel companies have followed with implementation of limited and sometimes full dynamic packaging functions.

Even without implementation of dynamic packaging software or use of third-party linked sites, hotels can offer limited packaging through their Web sites that will satisfy the desires of many of today's travelers to reserve hotel services into a customized vacation experience. Web site functionality can be enhanced to include the option for guests to add such hotel-supplied components as meals, spa treatments, or sporting activities to their reservations. Hotels can also contract with outside organizations to provide services that are not available on site and offer these products as part of limited packaging opportunities on the hotel's Web site. The goal is to fulfill the potential guest's desire for an experience as well as to enhance the revenue generated to the hotel during each guest stay.

Using Outside Expertise

As the depth and complexity of e-commerce marketing has increased, scores of companies have stepped forward with a range of services that can help hoteliers deal with what can be a complicated undertaking. Internet marketing organizations typically offer a range of services, often including Web design and Web site hosting, site optimization, search engine optimization (SEO), development and placement of pay-per-click (PPC) advertising or placement campaigns, Web site traffic analysis, and consulting services related to distribution site selection, presentation, and participation strategies.

Most hoteliers already have been approached by companies seeking to provide Internet marketing services. In some cases, hoteliers have been reluctant to use these services partly because they may be unsure of what can be accomplished by such work and because of the potential need for continued use of these services.

No matter how informative and persuasive a hotel or hotel company's Web site, there is no guarantee anyone will visit it. First it must be found. While brand awareness drives some visitors, the majority (about 70 percent according to Forrester Research) of Web users preface a review of a hotel Web site with use of a search engine. Research results indicate not only that search engines are major factors in traffic to hotel Web sites, but that most search queries entered into these engines by their users include neither a hotel name nor a brand name.

One service that has become increasingly more sophisticated is SEO, a process that attempts to increase the likelihood that a search engine will find a Web site and that it will rank highly on that search engine's results display. A thorough SEO program analyzes site content in light of the mechanics of search engines and reengineers the site (including the wording of site content) so that its search engine display is enhanced. Sometimes the process is as simple as changing page titles, metatags, and keywords. With search engine technology varying and constantly changing, however, SEO generally involves an ongoing effort to keep a site at its highest possible level in search engine results.

One technique within search engine optimization is PPC advertising. PPC advertising involves paying a site for a preferred spot (sometimes a preferred ranking in a search results listing, sometimes in a separate listing where advertisers are identified as such, or sometimes as separate button or block ads on the results page) on that Web site. The purchaser of PPC advertising pays only when a site visitor clicks on the listing. The advertiser potentially gains new viewers of its own Web site without a substantial outlay of upfront advertising costs. Similar approaches are paid placement (which involves purchasing a spot at the top of the search results) and purchase of keywords (which involves buying the rights to display a hotel's site at the top of search results when the hotel's purchased keyword is entered). Both involve potentially more expense than PPC advertising because of the limited number of these opportunities and the stiff competition for them.

Internet marketing organizations will argue that once a site has been optimized for search engines and visitors are linking to the site from PPC advertising, their work is still not complete. They will suggest that site visits should also be tracked and analyzed to determine whether the site is accomplishing its sales goals and where potential problems for visitors are occurring. In addition, some firms offer data bank services where information on site visitors can be stored and used for future marketing decisions.

In some cases, Internet marketing organizations also own and offer or promote third-party vendors' products or services for such functions as channel management, competitive rate searching, revenue management, guest relationship management, and other services.

The variety of services, depth of each offering, and expertise in delivery varies from vendor to vendor. Two points are important to consider when evaluating Internet marketing service vendors. The first is that the distribution environment is evolving quickly—some aspects of it change every day—as new vendors emerge, new programs are announced, or new alliances are formed. The repeatedly demonstrated commitment of the vendor to maintain awareness and respond where appropriate to these sometimes peripheral, sometimes mainstream developments is a central determinant of their long-term value to their hotel industry clients.

The second point is that some configuration of these services and some level of competence are offered by most hotel brands and representation companies. What is more, these services are often fully funded (or, at least, partially subsidized) by other fees already paid by the hotel. Where these services are not offered directly, preferred vendor relationships resulting in fee discounts may be in place. Before finalizing a service agreement with a third party, hoteliers would be well advised to review and evaluate available brand and representation company service options.

Guest Relationships

Internet technology enables direct communication between a supplier (such as a hotelier) and a customer (a guest). With this ability comes a host of privacy, response time, and expectation management concerns. A pre-arrival dialogue can be created, but it must be modulated so as to provide timely information while avoiding excessive and potentially overbearing contact. Provided the guest has agreed, that dialogue—taking the form of a generic or customized news update and offers—can continue in anticipation of repeat visits, referrals, or both.

Cutting-edge Web sites offer ever-expanding opportunities to create preference profiles and store personal information, eliminating the need for reentry of this data for every new reservation. Automated communication of pre-arrival welcome messages and reminders about on-property or nearby facilities (sometimes complete with special offers) are becoming more common. Also more commonly seen are post-visit e-mail contacts thanking the guest, making special offers to encourage a return visit, and, in some cases, seeking an evaluation of the guest's recent stay.

While the temptation to use the Internet for this style of direct promotion is strong, it has become entirely a permission-based opportunity. Strict controls already exist on the use of information obtained from customers in the European Union. In the United States, the Controlling the Assault of Non-Solicited Pornography and Marketing (CAN-SPAM) Act of 2003, which went into effect in January 2004, requires the sender of "any e-mail whose primary purpose is commercial" to have the prior permission of the recipient of such a message.

What Is the Future Direction of E-Commerce?

The e-commerce marketplace is obscure, biased, unfair, powerful, promising, and fast-changing. Predicting future directions in such an environment is difficult. However, the following developments appear highly likely.

The percentage contribution of e-commerce to overall reservations will continue to grow. Hotel companies will see a lower percentage of overall reservations arriving through their call centers and hotel-direct contact. Rather than disappear, those central reservation offices will evolve into multi-faceted customer service centers assisting with Internet and voice reservations, particularly as their complexity increases with the addition of packaging components.

This new marketplace threatens such long-established travel vendors as traditional travel agencies. Expedia is now the third largest travel agency in the United States after American Express and Carlson Wagonlit, a ranking attributed primarily to leisure travel bookings. In the coming months and years, such third-party megasites as Expedia and Travelocity will play a steadily larger role in corporate travel reservations as well as in the meeting and conventions market. Corporate self-booking tools (many of which are provided by Expedia, Orbitz, and Travelocity) will be widely adopted in companies both large and small. This changing relationship of third-party travel sites with corporate meeting and convention planners will encourage hoteliers to provide more extensive services on their own sites. Starwood Hotels and Resorts, for example, recently instituted an online program that allows small meeting planners to not only book their rooms online, but also to order food and beverage services and audiovisual equipment.

Travel agencies are not going away. The more aware and adept organizations are changing their business practices to emulate and challenge their emerging e-based competitors.

The travel research process will be further disrupted and permanently changed by the travel metasearch sites. While many of today's travelers are attempting to find lodging by going to a search engine (such as Yahoo!), entering a phrase such as "hotel in Cleveland" (remember that about 70 percent of all hotel searches begin this way), then searching through the thousands of entries to find the best accommodations for their particular price point, future lodging seekers will change the pattern. The metasearch sites will gain popularity as more travelers become familiar with their ease of use, including the need to only enter a city name, add such selective criteria as distance from the airport, and then wait for a comparative listing of available hotels and their prices. Over time, these metasearch sites will emulate other third-party sites with the increased use of paid placement as well as on-screen advertising that pushes individual listings from the top of these side-by-side comparisons if they do not participate in these paid promotions. It is probably a safe prediction that others will adopt the metasearch site model as Google and AOL move to offer travel search and booking services.

Hoteliers will continue their attempts to disintermediate the intermediaries. In the early days of the Internet, many travel sites offered themselves up as "disintermediaries" that facilitated direct commerce between a purchaser and supplier. For example, a traveler could disintermediate a travel agent (and a GDS and a switch) by purchasing travel directly from the Web. Those sites eventually evolved into the Expedia and Travelocity of today and themselves became another type of intermediary for hotel suppliers. Hoteliers will continue their efforts to remove third parties from the travel booking process (i.e., disintermediating them) by attracting bookers directly to their brand Web sites in an effort to reduce their cost of sales. Statistics published in the *International Herald Tribune* on May 31, 2005, suggest that hotel owners and managers will have increasing success in this endeavor, with third-party site bookings growing at a rate of 18 percent in the first quarter of this year, while supplier site bookings are growing faster at 22 percent.

Some hotel companies will develop comparison shopping capabilities on their own brand sites to assist potential guests in determining alternative rates and demonstrate that their rates represent a better value, particularly when compared to rates offered elsewhere that require prepayment and/or impose a cancellation penalty.

Hoteliers will reinforce relationships with frequent guests by providing them not only with a best available rate guarantee but also with points incentives for booking on the brand or hotel Web site and making rewards unavailable for bookings made on third-party sites.

When demand cycles lower, the travel agency megasites will resume a major distribution role as the industry seeks to sell available inventory. When this situation occurs, those megasites will have changed to compete in a greater number of market sectors.

Travelers' research and buying pathways will continue to evolve with the use of an increasing number of Internet devices that are not computers (telephones, personal digital assistants, televisions, etc.). Hotel companies will be challenged to provide the information, the speed, and the necessary e-commerce sales approaches that will fit everyone, everywhere.

The increasing availability of computer access around the world will not only expand the opportunity to reach a larger audience through e-commerce marketing, but also challenge and reshape conventional marketing, sales, and interaction methods. To date, most hotels' Internet sites offer text in a limited number of languages and do so in a Euro-American style. Hotel companies must address this deficiency in order to become successful with e-commerce worldwide.

E-commerce will almost certainly face stricter regulation to protect against abuse from fraud and misrepresentation, expanding on current EU and U.S. privacy and spam restrictions.

Application of revenue management principles and techniques will continue to grow. This trend will be facilitated by adoption of application service provider models by revenue management service vendors providing new levels of affordability. The roles of the reservation manager, revenue manager, and director of sales will continue to evolve. Sales work and business relationships will be restructured in a bottom-line focused, revenue managed environment. Rooms revenue management will evolve into "total-spend revenue management." Hoteliers will continue to attempt to apply revenue management processes through the electronic channels.

Lodging companies will be repeatedly called on to demonstrate the value of their brands as some hotel owners contemplate the merits—although not always the risks—of independent operation coupled with use of the Internet as their primary distribution mechanism.

SEO will decrease somewhat in importance for many hoteliers, particularly those in large metropolitan areas. As more and more Web sites use these tools, the likelihood that they will be effective for any one particular Web site will decrease because of the finite number of places in the top group of search engine listings.

Hoteliers and their online marketing gurus will search for new ways to promote traffic to Web sites to supplement search engines, including more sophisticated use of links to nontravel, nonhospitality Web sites, creative use of PPC ads on nontravel, nonhospitality Web sites, and increased promotion of Web site content through other media.

Conclusions

Without a doubt, e-commerce is a fundamental component of a hotel's marketing program. It is a component that can significantly enhance a hotel's profitability if successful managed. For the foreseeable future, the role and significance of e-commerce for the hotel industry can only increase. However, e-commerce is also a complex undertaking that requires a sophisticated understanding of its opportunities and challenges. Earlier in this chapter, e-commerce was compared with an expedition to climb Mt. Everest. A growing number of hoteliers are likely to agree with this assessment. The challenge for each hotelier is to balance this rich opportunity with the risks involved, which can be substantial. The resources available must be wisely assigned to a Web presence as well as to the professional advice, technical support, and staff training required to meet the challenging goals of any e-commerce marketing plan.

8

Labor Productivity Management

By *David W. Heath, ISHC*

David Heath is Senior Principal and Chief Operating Officer of Heath & Company Hospitality Advisors, LLP, a professional services firm providing operational and development consulting services for the hospitality industry. He has an extensive hospitality management background and his consulting experience includes operational consulting as well as market and financial analysis for hotels, resorts, restaurants, and private clubs. His areas of specialization include analysis of operational effectiveness with a view toward improving the overall profitability of hotels, resorts and private clubs through innovative marketing and enhanced internal controls; design, development, and implementation of state-of-the-art automated labor productivity management systems for hotels and resorts, strategic planning, market repositioning, and workouts for distressed hotels, resorts, and clubs; and development planning, market evaluation, and financial analysis for hotel, resort, restaurant, and planned community developments.

At the outset of his career, Mr. Heath worked for more than ten years in various management capacities in hotel and restaurant operations with, among other companies, Hyatt Hotels and the Ritz-Carlton Hotel Company. Before establishing his own firm, he managed the Florida hospitality consulting practice of Arthur Andersen LLP and directed numerous consulting engagements in Florida and the Caribbean. Mr. Heath earned a B.S. in Hotel Administration at the University of Massachusetts at Amherst and an M.B.A. at Northeastern University in Boston. Mr. Heath has conducted continuing education seminars on Internal Controls for Hotels and Restaurants for the American Institute of Certified Public Accountants.

LABOR IS THE LARGEST and most controllable cost hotels incur. Labor costs (including benefits and payroll taxes) in some full-service luxury hotels can amount to more than sixty percent of total revenue. Variable cost items like food, beverage, energy, repairs and maintenance, and amenities can and should be controlled, but it is often difficult to generate major savings in these line items without negatively affecting the customer experience. Reducing marketing and promotional expenditures can increase profit in the short term, but also can reduce total revenue in the long run. Expenses like insurance, property taxes, and interest are fixed and often can't be reduced at all, at least in the short- and medium-term.

Managing labor costs often is the single most effective way to increase profit. Unlike many other businesses, hotels traditionally have used a variable labor force to accommodate the ebbs and flows of customer demand. Hotel workers traditionally have been accustomed to working a full work week (and occasionally overtime) when their hotel is busy and working less than a full week during slower demand periods. Labor costs can be controlled effectively by scheduling the appropriate number of employees in each department to provide desired levels of customer service. The optimal number of employees is influenced by several factors, including seasonality of demand, local labor market conditions, state and local laws, and union work rules, where applicable.

Monthly labor planning receives considerable emphasis in many hotels. Monthly revenue and expense forecasts are reported to corporate offices, owners, and financial markets. Labor is, of course, a key component. Weekly work schedules, however, are the critical decision-making point in terms of labor cost control. Payroll dollars are spent, in effect, when the weekly schedule is made.

This chapter focuses on labor management in the hospitality industry and addresses the following topics:

- The labor management process
- Forecasting
- Labor standards
- Scheduling
- Time and attendance
- Labor management reporting
- Paying competitive wages
- Improving productivity

The Labor Management Process

Because of the critical nature of weekly labor planning, we will focus on this aspect of the labor management process. We break the labor management process into five elements, as follows:

- *Forecasting.* Understanding how much business to anticipate is the critical first step in labor management. Managers can't effectively plan their labor requirements without first knowing how much customer activity to anticipate, whether in arrivals, departures, rooms occupied, or restaurant or banquet covers. Forecasting is the critical first step in the labor management process.

- *Labor Standards.* Labor standards are rules or guidelines for staffing the hotel at varying levels of volume. Every hotel has some form of labor standard. Sometimes these staffing guides or standards are as simple as a roster or list of fixed positions, others take the form of informal rules of thumb, and still others take the form of detailed labor standards specifying precisely how many employees to schedule at each level of customer activity.

- *Scheduling.* The effectiveness with which labor standards are used in conjunction with accurate weekly forecasts often will determine the overall profitability of an entire hotel. The weekly work schedule is the linchpin.

Exhibit 1   Key Volume Indicators for Hotels

Indicator	Affected Departments
Rooms occupied	Housekeeping
Arrivals and departures	Bell, door, front desk
Hotel guests	PBX, concierge, food and beverage
Banquet covers	Banquets, door, food and beverage
Outlet covers	Food and beverage, room service
Beverage outlet sales	Beverage outlets
Drinks served	Beverage outlets
Laundry pounds	Laundry
Spa treatments	Spa
Salon treatments	Salon
Golf rounds	Golf

- *Time and Attendance.* The accurate tracking of employee time and attendance is an important management responsibility and central to the labor management process. Ensuring that employees punch in as scheduled, take breaks in accordance with hotel policies (and state and local law), and depart at the appointed hour is essential to labor cost control.

- *Labor Reporting.* Letting managers know how well they have controlled costs is essential to achieving profitability. Managers need timely and accurate feedback in terms of labor cost performance in order to achieve financial objectives and improve efficiency and profits.

Forecasting

Knowing how many customers to anticipate is the critical first step in the labor management process. Without a fairly sound idea of how much volume to anticipate, managers can't plan their labor requirements effectively. The result often is overstaffing and lower profit levels or understaffing and poor service. It is important to forecast weekly business volume for all key volume indicators listed in Exhibit 1. Most hotels do an adequate job forecasting arrivals, departures, and rooms occupied. Existing reservations and historical trend data made available from the hotel's central reservations and property management systems enable the revenue manager to estimate upcoming rooms activity with a reasonable level of accuracy.

Forecasting banquet volume most often is similarly straightforward, at least in the short term. Weekly catering forecasts, while often subject to last minute "pop-up" events or last-minute cancellations, report business already on the books and generally can be relied upon for accuracy.

Forecasting Restaurant and Ancillary Volume

Developing forecasts for restaurants, spas, and golf operations can be more complex. A popular hotel restaurant may attract customers from the local community as well as from guests staying within the hotel. These pools of customers from inside the hotel and from the local community have few demand characteristics in common other than the desire to eat in the same restaurant. Hotel occupancy will have little influence on the behavior of local patrons and vice versa.

To develop an accurate restaurant forecast, most often it is advisable to differentiate and forecast local demand separately from hotel guest demand whenever outside customers make up a significant component of total demand for the restaurant. The best predictor of outside patronage will likely be recent history of outside patronage. If, for example, a hotel restaurant has had 80 outside guests the past six Saturday nights, it may be prudent to assume (all other things being equal) that 80 is a reasonable forecast of outside guests for the next Saturday night.

Banquets and Restaurant Volume

Banquet activity also will affect the forecast for a hotel restaurant. Consider two similar Saturday evenings in a particular hotel. On each evening, the hotel is full with approximately 500 guests. On the first Saturday evening, there are no banquet functions so all 500 hotel guests will be seeking a place to dine, either within the hotel or at another local establishment. A percentage of these guests will likely eat in the hotel's restaurant. This percentage is called the *capture ratio*. If 100 of these guests dined in the hotel's restaurant, the capture ratio for this particular Saturday night was 20 percent. If we measure and study this statistic over time, we may find that the average capture ratio often is a valid predictor of hotel guest demand for a restaurant.

On the second Saturday evening, the hotel also has 500 guests, but 300 of them are attending a banquet in the hotel's ballroom. It doesn't make sense to apply the capture ratio of 20 percent to the total guest population if 300 guests are unavailable because they are attending the banquet. To forecast the number of guests likely to eat in a hotel restaurant, the number of *available* guests must first be calculated. The number of available guests is equal to total hotel guests less guests that are unavailable because they are attending a banquet or other event.

The following formula accounts for outside guests and banquet activity when forecasting restaurant volume:

$$\text{Forecasted Guests} = (\text{Total Hotel Guests} - \text{Banquet Guests}) \times \text{Capture Ratio} + \text{Outside Patrons}$$

Applying this formula to the two examples above yields the following:

	First Saturday	Second Saturday
Hotel guests	500	500
Less: Hotel guests attending a banquet	0	300
Available guests	500	200
Capture ratio	20%	20%
Anticipated hotel patrons	100	40
Anticipated outside patrons	80	80
Total forecasted covers	180	120

The principles presented here for a restaurant also can be applied to a hotel's golf or spa operation. The key is to track and separately forecast local volume and hotel guest activity.

Beverage Outlet Forecasting

When forecasting for a beverage outlet, generally it is most useful to forecast revenue. Tracking sales revenue from outside guests in a beverage outlet can be a little more complicated than in a restaurant. A simple way to differentiate hotel guest volume from local patronage in a beverage outlet is to assume that room charges (sales charged to guestrooms) are from hotel guests and that credit card and cash transactions are from local patrons. While this approach is not always 100 percent accurate, studies have found it to be generally reliable.

Sales per available guest often is used instead of a capture ratio to predict hotel guest patronage in a beverage outlet. For example, if in a particular beverage outlet, average daily hotel guest sales (calculated from room charges) is $4,000 and the average number of hotel guests over the same time period is 500, the average sales or spend per guest is $8. This statistic can be used as a predictor of future volume in much the same way the capture ratio is used in a restaurant. Operations should monitor this statistic closely over time to identify trends by meal period (lunch, dinner, or late night) and by day of the week. Outside guest sales can be tracked in much the same way as they are for restaurants. If, for example, a beverage operation has averaged $2,000 in sales to local patrons over the past several Saturdays (calculated from cash settlements and credit card charges), then $2,000 may be a reasonable estimate of local customer sales for the next Saturday evening (all other things being equal). The beverage outlet's forecast might look like the following:

	Saturday Forecast
Hotel guests	500
Less: Hotel guests attending a banquet	300
Available hotel guests	200
Sales per hotel guest	$ 8
Anticipated hotel beverage sales	$1,600
Anticipated sales to local patrons	$2,000
Total forecasted sales	$3,600

Applying Human Judgment

Forecasting is as much art as a science. Most often, raw forecasts like those presented above will need to be adjusted based on the experience and judgment of the manager preparing the forecast. The manager may want to make adjustments based on what he or she knows about the particular group staying in the hotel, outside and local events, or even the weather forecast.

Tracking Forecast Accuracy

An important final component of the weekly forecasting process is tracking and analyzing forecast accuracy. It is advisable to formally review the accuracy of business volume forecasts for rooms, banquets, restaurants, and ancillary departments. In the absence of feedback, forecast accuracy is unlikely to improve. Understanding the various factors that may have affected customer volume is the single best way to improve accuracy going forward.

Asset Managers and Forecasting

A hotel asset manager may want to ask the on-site hotel management team the following questions about forecasting:

- Is a weekly forecast prepared for all hotel activity areas including rooms, catering/banquets, and food and beverage?

- How does the food and beverage forecasting methodology take local patronage into consideration? The effects of banquets on outlet demand?

- Are capture factors or ratios used? How? How often are they are updated?

- How often is forecast accuracy formally reviewed?

Labor Standards

Labor standards are formal or informal rules or guidelines for staffing the hotel at varying levels of volume. They are used to ensure that quality standards are maintained while profit goals are achieved. Labor standards can take the form of detailed staffing guides specifying the number of hours to be consumed in relation to one or more volume indicators. Examples of common indicators of customer volume in hotels include arrivals, departures, rooms occupied, guests, restaurant and banquet covers, beverage or bar sales, and laundry pounds.

Developing Labor Standards

To be effective, labor standards must be based on work-to-time relationships. Examples of work-to-time relationships include rooms per labor hour, covers per labor hour, or laundry pounds per labor hour. There are a number of ways labor standards are developed. The most common approach is the experiential approach. Based on the hotel or hotel brand's experience, a standard has become the norm within a particular company. For example, the standard for room attendants within a particular brand has evolved over time to be 16 guestrooms per eight-hour shift. There may not be much science behind it, but the standard remains because it seems to have worked well in the past.

The market approach is another commonly used method for developing labor standards. In this approach, managers will evaluate local labor market conditions and set their labor standards accordingly. While this may sound like a lazy approach, it may make sense in a number of instances. If a new hotel is opening in a market where labor unions are active or where other competitive hotels are already organized by labor unions, management may want to set labor standards, work rules, and benefits to approximate those of local union properties to reduce the likelihood of union organization at the new hotel.

A more scientific method of establishing labor standards involves time and motion studies. In a time and motion study, the actual work employees perform is measured in terms of quantity, frequency, and reasonable time expectancy. In the simple example of a room attendant, a time and motion study may reveal the following:

Position:	Room attendant
Assignment:	Guestroom cleaning
Volume:	One guestroom
Frequency:	Once daily
Reasonable time expectancy:	30 minutes

The reasonable time expectancy can be determined by actually timing employees performing tasks at different hours of the day and different days of the week to estimate a reasonable amount of time for the task to be completed. It is beneficial to record many observations in order to be confident of a reasonable time expectancy. For example, assume that in an eight-hour shift, one room attendant should be able to clean 16 rooms. However, all work-related tasks need to be incorporated into the labor standard. Our room attendant may have other noncleaning tasks to perform that also need to be taken into consideration. Room attendants may be required to attend a morning meeting or stock their supply carts and may be entitled to one or more paid or unpaid breaks during their shift. The time required for these other activities might be summarized as follows:

Breaks:	60 minutes (30 minutes unpaid)
Morning meeting:	10 minutes
Cart loading:	10 minutes
Travel time to and from floors:	10 minutes

In an eight-and-a-half hour shift (eight hours paid), a room attendant may have only seven hours available to clean rooms. In this case, the standard may be set at 14 rooms per shift.

A time and motion study at the front desk may reveal that it takes approximately three minutes to check a guest in and two minutes to check a guest out. Again, other factors need to be considered before deciding on an appropriate labor standard for front desk agents. Meal breaks will need to be considered. Also, an increasing number of guests bypass the front desk when departing the hotel by using television check-out in their guestroom, so the labor standard for front desk agents will need to consider only the percentage of guests actually checking out at the desk. To make matters even more complicated, weekend leisure guests may be less likely to use the television check-out option than the typical weekday business traveler. It may be necessary to create different standards for weekdays and weekends or to base the standard for front desk agents at least in part on the number of leisure guests scheduled to depart the hotel.

If all this sounds complicated, that's because it can be. There are a number of software vendors that incorporate labor standards as part of their electronic time and attendance systems. These systems generally work well. Additionally, there are several reputable industrial engineering and consulting firms that specialize in the implementation of labor management systems and the development of labor standards for the hospitality industry. The American Hotel & Lodging Association and the International Society of Hospitality Consultants are excellent sources for identifying reputable firms.

A sample staffing guide for a front office department appears as Exhibit 2. The guide includes both fixed and variable components. Labor hours are added with increases in business volume, including arrivals, departures, rooms occupied, and total guests. These guidelines can be used by a department manager on a weekly basis to ensure that service levels are maintained while profitability goals are reached.

Unions and Labor Standards

Labor standards are sometimes dictated by union contracts. In many urban hotels, collective bargaining agreements with local labor unions will indicate the units of output an employee is expected to produce. For example, a union contract may specify that room attendants will be required to clean no more than 16 rooms per eight-hour shift or that banquet servers will be required to serve no more than 30 guests during a buffet luncheon. Labor standards in union hotels may not always be specifically detailed within the union contract, but the hotel's past practices often are as binding as if the standards were written directly into the labor agreement. It can be difficult, though not impossible, to change labor standards in a union hotel. Productivity improvements can be negotiated with the union and most often are achieved successfully when the affected employees share the financial benefits derived from the desired increase in productivity.

Asset Managers and Labor Standards

A hotel asset manager may want to ask the on-site management team the following questions about labor standards:

- Does the hotel use documented labor standards to manage labor costs?
- How were they developed?
- Are the labor standards in daily use by department managers?
- Do standard labor hours vary in step with changes in business volume?
- How and how often is actual performance measured against the standard?

Scheduling

Preparing the weekly employee work schedule is one of the most important managerial tasks performed in a hotel department. The weekly schedule is the critical decision-making point where labor hours need to match anticipated volume. If too few employees are scheduled, customer service suffers; if too many are scheduled, potential profit is lost. All too often, insufficient attention is paid to the scheduling process. Scheduling sometimes is delegated to an employee without the proper training to adequately match scheduled hours to forecasted volume.

Exhibit 2 Sample Front Office Staffing Guide

Title	Front Office Manager		Assistant Front Office Managers		Front Desk Agents		Bellmen	
Job Code	0011-21		0011-91		0011-25		0011-26	
	Fixed Positions		Fixed Positions		Fixed Positions		Fixed Positions	
	Fixed Empl's	Hours	Fixed Empl's	Hours	Fixed Empl's	Hours	Fixed Empl's	Hours
Fixed	1	5.71	2	11.43	1	8.00	2	16.00

	Arrivals			Arrivals			Arrivals			Arrivals		
	Volume	Empl's	Hours	Volume	Empl's	Hours	Volume	Empl's	Hours	Volume	Empl's	Hours
							1	1	8.00	100	1	4.00
							35	2	12.00	125	2	9.00
							70	2	16.00	175	3	17.00
							105	3	20.00	9999	3	17.00
							141	3	24.00			
							176	4	28.00			
							225	4	32.00			
							9999	4	32.00			

	Departures			Departures			Departures			Departures		
	Volume	Empl's	Hours	Volume	Empl's	Hours	Volume	Empl's	Hours	Volume	Empl's	Hours
							1	1	8.00	100	1	4.00
							35	2	12.00	125	2	9.00
							70	2	16.00	175	3	17.00
							105	3	20.00	9999	3	17.00
							141	3	24.00			
							176	4	28.00			
							225	4	32.00			
							9999	4	32.00			

The scheduling process is greatly enhanced when the hotel's labor management system includes an accurate weekly forecast and clearly defined labor standards. To prepare the schedule, the manager need only apply the labor standards to the upcoming week's business volume forecast to determine the required hours and prepare the schedule accordingly. In an increasing number of hotels, senior managers take the time to review weekly schedules to ensure that quality and profitability targets will be achieved.

Evaluating the Weekly Work Schedule

Comparing scheduled hours to standard is an important control for ensuring that payroll dollars are being spent effectively. A scheduled vs. forecast report compares scheduled hours to the number of hours that *should* have been scheduled given the upcoming week's business volume forecast and the labor standards for the particular department. This critical step enables management to ensure quality customer service while controlling payroll dollars before they are spent.

Automated Scheduling

Several reputable software vendors have developed automated systems for preparing weekly work schedules. When the automated scheduler is integrated into or interfaced with the hotel's time and attendance (time clock) system, employees can be restricted from punching in early or when not scheduled. This additional control can typically save up to one half of one percent of hourly payroll.

Artificial Intelligence Scheduling

In recent years, several vendors have begun marketing artificial intelligence (AI) schedulers to hospitality clients. These systems use mathematical algorithms to match qualified employees to forecasted business volume to produce an *optimal* work schedule. Producing an optimal schedule requires three elements: (1) a weekly volume forecast, (2) clearly defined labor standards, and (3) employee profiles that include skill sets and availability. Currently, reviews of AI scheduling systems are mixed. Maintaining employee profiles with skill sets and availability often is found to be more cumbersome than producing a traditional work schedule that meets labor standard targets. Additionally, the draft work schedules produced by AI schedulers often require significant manual adjustment.

Asset Managers and Scheduling

A hotel asset manager may want to discuss the following questions about employee scheduling with the on-site management team:

- What mechanisms are in place to ensure that weekly work schedules will achieve quality and profitability goals?

- Do senior-level managers review employee work schedules before they are posted?

- Does the hotel employ a scheduled vs. forecast report to evaluate scheduled hours based on labor standards and anticipated business volume?

- Are employee work schedules loaded into the time clocks to prevent employees from punching in early and when not scheduled?

Time and Attendance

Hotels increasingly are relying on automated time and attendance systems to track and record employee hours. Until recently, only full-service hotels could afford the luxury of an automated system. However, today's Web-based applications require only minimal hardware, so even small limited-service hotels with just a few employees can take full advantage of an automated system. Electronic time clocks can be connected to the hotel's property management system and to the Internet to make use of time and attendance software applications that are physically located thousands of miles away at corporate headquarters. The advantages of automated time and attendance systems over manual time clocks and sign-in sheets include fewer errors and improved efficiency because on-site management spends less time processing payroll.

When selecting a time and attendance system, it is worthwhile to evaluate the following labor management features offered by various vendors:

- Business volume forecasting

- Incorporation of labor standards

- Automated scheduling

- Labor management reporting, including forecast accuracy tracking, labor hours forecasting, scheduled vs. forecast reporting, and actual vs. standard hours reporting

Employee Meal Breaks

In many hotels, employees receive an unpaid meal break at some point during their shift. Employees often are required to punch out for their break. In a surprising number of cases, employees forget to punch out and can be overpaid (sometimes at overtime rates). Missed meal breaks at some hotels have amounted to hundreds of thousands of dollars in excess payroll on an annual basis. While more sophisticated time and attendance systems have features to track missed meal breaks, every hotel should have controls to ensure meal break compliance.

Asset Managers and Time and Attendance

A hotel asset manager may want to discuss the following questions about the hotel's time and attendance system with the on-site management team:

- What labor management features does the hotel's time and attendance system offer?

- What mechanisms are in place to prevent employees from punching in early and when not scheduled?

- What controls are in place to ensure that employees remember to punch out for their unpaid breaks?

Labor Management Reporting

Performance often declines in the absence of feedback. This is especially true when it comes to labor management. Department managers need timely and accurate feedback to assess how effectively they are managing labor. Some hotels compare actual labor hours to budgeted hours or to the monthly forecast. This works reasonably well, as long as actual business volume is approximately equal to budget or forecast. Significant variances between actual business volume and budget or forecast make comparisons of actual labor use to budget and forecast less meaningful.

For example, if a hotel's occupancy exceeds budget by ten percent, should labor hours and labor costs stay the same as budgeted costs or should they increase? By how much? In most cases, labor costs have both fixed and variable components. In other words, some labor costs remain unchanged regardless of volume (e.g., one general manager), while other positions are variable and need to be increased in step with business volume (e.g., room attendants need to be increased in proportion to rooms occupied). So the answer is that when volume increases by ten percent, labor hours should increase by somewhere between zero and ten percent.

Productivity and Labor Utilization Ratios

Some hotels and hotel companies rely on productivity or labor utilization ratios to evaluate labor cost performance. Productivity ratios are calculated using the following formula:

$$\text{Productivity} = \frac{\text{Units of Output}}{\text{Labor Hours}}$$

Examples of productivity ratios are rooms per labor hour, covers per labor hour, and pounds of laundry per labor hour.

Labor utilization ratios are the inverse or reciprocal of productivity ratios. Examples of labor utilization ratios commonly used in hotels are hours per occupied room and hours per cover. Labor utilization ratios are calculated using the following formula:

$$\text{Labor Utilization} = \frac{\text{Labor Hours}}{\text{Units of Output}}$$

If occupancy exceeds budget by ten percent, should our productivity ratio stay the same or should we expect some productivity improvement as the result of increased economies of scale? If so, how much increased productivity should we expect? Productivity and labor utilization ratios alone will not tell us. A more precise answer requires a more precise approach.

Standard Costing

Hotels can develop a reasonably precise estimate of what labor utilization should be by applying the same labor standards used for scheduling to evaluate our actual labor utilization. By applying labor standards to actual business volume, hotels can calculate standard labor costs (i.e., the number of hours that *should* have been used given actual business volume and our labor standards). If actual labor hours are approximately equal to standard hours, hotel managers can be comfortable knowing that they have delivered desired levels of service at or near an optimal cost.

Essential Labor Management Reports

The following labor reports are especially important parts of an effective labor management system:

- *Forecast Accuracy Report.* Tracking forecast accuracy is a critical step in developing better forecasts. After all, if we never look back and evaluate our performance, how can we improve? Understanding how and why actual business volume differed from forecast enables managers to become better forecasters. A sample forecast accuracy report is shown in Exhibit 3.

- *Weekly Labor Forecast.* The weekly labor forecast applies the hotel's labor standards to the upcoming week's business volume forecast, providing a target number of hours for each position each day. Developing a weekly labor plan based on anticipated volume and the hotel's labor standards is an effective means of ensuring that quality standards are maintained while profitability targets are achieved. A sample weekly labor forecast is shown in Exhibit 4.

- *Scheduled vs. Forecast Report.* Once work schedules have been prepared (preferably using an automated scheduler), the scheduled vs. forecast report compares hours scheduled to the number of hours that should have been scheduled based on the upcoming week's forecast and the hotel's labor standards. Reviewing the scheduled vs. forecast report on a weekly basis is an important step in proactive labor cost control. A sample scheduled vs. forecast report appears as Exhibit 5.

- *Actual vs. Standard Hours Report.* Perhaps the most critical labor management report is the actual vs. standard hours report. This report answers the question of how many hours a hotel used compared to how many it should have used given its actual business volume and the hotel's labor standards. A sample actual vs. standard hours report appears as Exhibit 6.

Asset Managers and Labor Management Reporting

A hotel asset manager may want to discuss the following questions about the hotel's labor management reporting process with the on-site management team:

- What reports are produced to help managers control labor costs before the fact?

- What information do department managers receive to let them know whether they are doing a good job controlling labor costs?

- Do current labor reports compare actual hours to standard hours?

Exhibit 3   Sample Forecast Accuracy Report

Forecast Accuracy Report
For the week ending:
December 13, 2002

		Saturday 12/07/02	Sunday 12/08/02	Monday 12/09/02	Tuesday 12/10/02	Wednesday 12/11/02	Thursday 12/12/02	Friday 12/13/02	Weekly Accuracy Score
Rooms Statistics									
Arrivals	Forecast	247	91	52	86	86	77	78	
	Actual	272	94	68	100	97	134	89	
	Variance %	10%	3%	31%	16%	47%	74%	14%	72%
Departures	Forecast	227	215	49	44	257	46	85	
	Actual	236	225	65	60	269	66	121	
	Variance %	4%	5%	33%	36%	5%	43%	42%	76%
Rooms Occupied	Forecast	444	320	323	365	174	205	198	
	Actual	430	307	314	342	184	218	190	
	Variance %	3%	4%	3%	6%	6%	6%	4%	95%
Guests	Forecast	888	480	485	548	261	308	396	
	Actual	727	519	511	536	249	325	329	
	Variance %	18%	8%	5%	2%	5%	6%	17%	91%
Conference / Banquet Group									
Breakfast Covers	Forecast	0	0	200	200	200	0	0	
	Actual	0	0	225	225	225	0	0	
	Variance %	0%	0%	13%	13%	13%	0%	0%	95%
Lunch Covers	Forecast	0	0	200	200	55	55	120	
	Actual	0	0	225	225	55	55	125	
	Variance %	0%	0%	13%	13%	0%	0%	4%	96%
Dinner Covers	Forecast	0	0	385	45	0	125	0	
	Actual	0	0	435	43	0	127	0	
	Variance %	0%	0%	13%	4%	0%	2%	0%	97%
Coffee Breaks	Forecast	76	0	915	800	350	165	120	
	Actual	76	0	990	805	390	250	330	
	Variance %	0%	0%	8%	1%	11%	52%	175%	65%
Reception Covers	Forecast	0	0	350	45	0	125	12	
	Actual	0	0	385	43	0	127	12	
	Variance %	0%	0%	10%	4%	0%	2%	0%	98%
Food Sales	Forecast	$840	$0	$45,940	$18,040	$8,215	$12,820	$3,894	
	Actual	$854	$0	$40,211	$21,310	$10,232	$14,394	$7,805	

Exhibit 4   Sample Weekly Labor Forecast

Weekly Labor Forecast

DEPARTMENT	Job Code	Saturday 02/26/05	Sunday 02/27/05	Monday 02/28/05	Tuesday 03/01/05	Wednesday 03/02/05	Thursday 03/03/05	Friday 03/04/05	Total
ROOMS									
FRONT OFFICE									
Front Desk Associates	0011-21	48.00	68.00	32.00	32.00	68.00	56.00	56.00	360.00
Front Office Supervisor	0011-91	28.57	28.57	28.57	28.57	28.57	28.57	28.57	200.00
Expeditor	0011-23	8.00	0.00	0.00	0.00	0.00	8.00	8.00	24.00
Limo Drivers	0011-25	16.00	16.00	16.00	16.00	16.00	16.00	16.00	112.00
Bell Staff	0011-26	32.00	50.00	16.00	16.00	50.00	41.00	42.00	247.00
FRONT OFFICE TOTAL		132.57	162.57	92.57	92.57	162.57	149.57	150.57	943.00
HOUSEKEEPING									
Housekeeper	0012-03	256.00	296.00	224.00	224.00	224.00	168.00	256.00	1,648.00
Housekeepman	0012-04	32.00	32.00	32.00	32.00	32.00	32.00	32.00	224.00
Public Area Attendants	0012-06	60.50	60.50	60.50	60.50	60.50	60.50	60.50	423.50
HOUSEKEEPING TOTAL		348.50	388.50	316.50	316.50	316.50	260.50	348.50	2,295.50
RESERVATIONS									
Group Res. Coordinator	0120-70	28.57	28.57	28.57	28.57	28.57	28.57	28.57	200.00
RESERVATIONS TOTAL		28.57	28.57	28.57	28.57	28.57	28.57	28.57	200.00
TOTAL ROOMS		509.64	579.64	437.64	437.64	507.64	438.64	527.64	3,438.50
F&B									
F&B GENERAL									
F&B Admin	0190-01	2.86	2.86	2.86	2.86	2.86	2.86	2.86	20.00
F&B Purchasing Clerk	0190-02	17.14	17.14	17.14	17.14	17.14	17.14	17.14	120.00
F&B GENERAL TOTAL		20.00	20.00	20.00	20.00	20.00	20.00	20.00	140.00
MAIN KITCHEN									
Baker	0190-05	92.19	66.19	69.69	89.69	49.69	45.19	106.69	519.30
Cook	0190-07	133.17	98.67	92.67	110.67	67.17	56.33	136.33	695.00
Station Attendant	0190-08	108.73	85.90	94.57	104.57	76.23	69.23	122.58	661.82
Supervisor	0190-91	60.00	60.00	60.00	60.00	60.00	60.00	60.00	420.00
MAIN KITCHEN TOTAL		394.09	310.75	316.92	364.92	253.09	230.75	425.60	2,296.12
STEWARDING									
Utility	0190-09	112.00	102.00	112.00	112.00	92.00	86.00	112.00	728.00
STEWARDING TOTAL		112.00	102.00	112.00	112.00	92.00	86.00	112.00	728.00
PABLO'S									
Pablo's Night Cleaners	0211-09	11.43	11.43	11.43	11.43	11.43	11.43	11.43	80.00

Exhibit 5   Sample Scheduled vs. Forecast Report

Schedule vs. Forecast Detail

For the week ending Friday, April 15, 2005

DEPARTMENT	CODE	SCHEDULED HOURS	FORECAST HOURS	VARIANCE TO FORECAST	PERFORMANCE TO FORECAST
FRONT OFFICE					
Front Desk Associates	0011-21	372.00	392.00	20.00	94.9%
Front Office Supervisor	0011-91	192.00	200.00	8.00	96.0%
Expeditor	0011-23	32.00	32.00	-	100.0%
Limo Drivers	0011-25	108.00	112.00	4.00	96.4%
Bell Staff	0011-26	240.00	252.00	12.00	95.2%
FRONT OFFICE TOTAL		944.00	988.00	44.00	95.5%
HOUSEKEEPING					
Housekeeper	0012-03	1,656.90	1,640.00	(16.90)	101.0%
Housekeeping Aide	0012-04	216.00	224.00	8.00	96.4%
Public Area Attendants	0012-06	408.00	423.50	15.50	96.3%
HOUSEKEEPING TOTAL		2,280.90	2,287.50	6.60	99.7%
RESERVATIONS					
Group Res. Coordinator	0120-70	199.10	200.00	0.90	99.6%
RESERVATIONS TOTAL		199.10	200.00	0.90	99.6%
TOTAL ROOMS		3,424.00	3,475.50	51.50	98.5%
F&B GENERAL					
F&B Admin	0190-01	40.00	20.00	(20.00)	200.0%
F&B Purchasing Clerk	0190-02	121.70	120.00	(1.70)	101.4%
F&B GENERAL TOTAL		161.70	140.00	(21.70)	115.5%
MAIN KITCHEN					
Baker	0190-05	247.40	427.30	179.90	57.9%
Cook	0190-07	810.45	644.67	(165.78)	125.7%
Station Attendant	0190-08	453.30	563.90	110.60	80.4%
Supervisor	0190-91	413.70	420.00	6.30	98.5%
MAIN KITCHEN TOTAL		1,924.85	2,055.87	131.02	93.6%
STEWARDING					
Utility	0190-09	612.10	638.00	25.90	95.9%
STEWARDING TOTAL		612.10	638.00	25.90	95.9%
PABLO'S					
Pablo's Night Cleaners	0211-09	80.00	80.00	-	100.0%

Exhibit 6   Sample Actual vs. Standard Hours Report

Weekly Labor Detail

For the week ending Friday, April 15, 2005

DEPARTMENT	CODE	ACTUAL HOURS	STANDARD HOURS	FORECAST HOURS	VARIANCE TO STANDARD	VARIANCE TO FORECAST	PERFORMANCE TO STANDARD	PERFORMANCE TO FORECAST
FRONT OFFICE								
Front Desk Associates	0011-21	408.00	432.00	392.00	24.00	(16.00)	94.4%	104.1%
Front Office Supervisor	0011-91	184.00	200.00	200.00	16.00	16.00	92.0%	92.0%
Limo Drivers	0011-25	159.70	112.00	112.00	(47.70)	(47.70)	142.6%	142.6%
Bell Staff	0011-26	170.80	302.00	252.00	131.20	81.20	56.6%	67.8%
FRONT OFFICE TOTAL		922.50	1,078.00	988.00	155.50	65.50	85.6%	93.4%
HOUSEKEEPING								
Housekeeper	0012-03	1,656.90	1,680.00	1,640.00	23.10	(16.90)	98.6%	101.0%
Housekeeping Aide	0012-04	285.30	224.00	224.00	(61.30)	(61.30)	127.4%	127.4%
Public Area Attendants	0012-06	374.60	423.50	423.50	48.90	48.90	88.5%	88.5%
HOUSEKEEPING TOTAL		2,316.80	2,327.50	2,287.50	10.70	(29.30)	99.5%	101.3%
RESERVATIONS								
Group Res. Coordinator	0120-70	199.10	200.00	200.00	0.90	0.90	99.6%	99.6%
RESERVATIONS TOTAL		199.10	200.00	200.00	0.90	0.90	99.6%	99.6%
TOTAL ROOMS		3,438.40	3,605.50	3,475.50	167.10	37.10	95.4%	98.9%
F&B GENERAL								
F&B Admin	0190-01	40.00	20.00	20.00	(20.00)	(20.00)	200.0%	200.0%
F&B Purchasing Clerk	0190-02	121.70	120.00	120.00	(1.70)	(1.70)	101.4%	101.4%
F&B GENERAL TOTAL		161.70	140.00	140.00	(21.70)	(21.70)	115.5%	115.5%
MAIN KITCHEN								
Baker	0190-05	475.00	474.30	427.30	(0.70)	(47.70)	100.1%	111.2%
Cook	0190-07	722.00	744.00	644.67	22.00	(77.33)	97.0%	112.0%
Station Attendant	0190-08	596.00	608.43	563.90	12.43	(32.10)	98.0%	105.7%
Supervisor	0190-91	413.70	420.00	420.00	6.30	6.30	98.5%	98.5%
MAIN KITCHEN TOTAL		2,206.70	2,246.73	2,055.87	40.03	(150.83)	98.2%	107.3%
STEWARDING								
Utility	0190-09	612.10	688.00	638.00	75.90	25.90	89.0%	95.9%
STEWARDING TOTAL		612.10	688.00	638.00	75.90	25.90	89.0%	95.9%
PABLO'S								
Pablo's Night Cleaners	0211-09	64.00	80.00	80.00	16.00	16.00	80.0%	80.0%
Pablo's Lead Hostess	0211-10	41.20	40.00	40.00	(1.20)	(1.20)	103.0%	103.0%
Pablo's Hostess/Host	0211-12	66.60	80.00	80.00	13.40	13.40	83.3%	83.3%

Paying Competitive Wages

Paying competitive wages without overpaying has always been a challenge for many hotels. In union hotels, wages are dictated by the union contract. In non-union hotels, it is important to pay competitive wages compared to other hotels in the local market. It traditionally has been the responsibility of the human resources department to contact neighboring hotels to compare hourly wages and salaries for various positions. For many brands, this was a yearly duty, often conducted at annual budget time. Today, services like WageWatch, Inc. (www.wagewatch.com) offer wage and benefits comparisons for local markets around the United States at a nominal cost.

Asset Managers and Wages

A hotel asset manager may want to discuss the following questions about the hotel's wage scale with the on-site management team:

- How do salaries and wages at our hotel compare with those of other hotels in the competitive market?

- Does the wage strategy at our hotel position salaries and hourly wages above, below, or at the median of other hotels in the local market?

Improving Productivity

Given that labor is the single greatest cost incurred in any hotel, hoteliers are always seeking new ways to improve efficiency. The balance of this chapter looks at several of the best practices we have seen to increase productivity. Not all of the following methods will work in every situation, especially in hotels with labor unions, but they all deserve consideration.

Front Office Performance Cross-Training and Cross-Utilization

An excellent way to improve productivity in the front office is to train employees to perform multiple functions. When employees are cross-trained in front desk, private branch exchange, reservations, concierge, club floor lounge, and even bell and door attendant procedures, an operation will be less likely to run overtime, will operate more smoothly, and provide better service. In addition, employees will benefit from learning more skill sets and by being able to work in a variety of jobs, rather than in just a single position.

Room Attendant Empowerment

Until a few years ago, in most hotels, housekeeping supervisors were assigned to go behind and check virtually every room after it was cleaned by a room attendant. In the early 1990s, a number of brands began to experiment with self-inspection (i.e., empowering qualified room attendants to inspect their own work). Considered radical at the time, self-inspection has become the norm in many full-service hotels. When inspections of every room are replaced by random, documented inspections, quality most often improves and productivity increases as fewer supervisors are needed.

Room Attendant Incentive Programs

Probably the hardest job in any hotel is cleaning guestrooms. Room attendants often clean anywhere from 14 to 18 or more rooms in an eight-hour shift. Some more innovative operators have begun to offer incentives to reward room attendants for increased productivity. Some of the more innovative programs include:

- *Pay-Per-Room.* In the pay-per-room program, employees receive a fixed dollar amount (often equal to one half hour's pay) for each room they clean. A minimum quota is set, but most program participants clean far more than the minimum and are rewarded financially for the extra work. The hotel can operate with fewer full-time employees, saving expensive benefit costs. Participants are required to maintain acceptable quality scores as a condition for continued participation in the program.

- *Eight and Skate.* Under an "eight and skate" program, employees are permitted to leave work once they have completed their work for the day (typically one additional room over the standard quota). The hotel benefits through the increased productivity associated with one additional room cleaned and because program participants complete and turn their rooms over to the front desk for occupancy more quickly, thus reducing lines at check-in. Room attendants are free to leave work early—an important benefit for working parents. One hotel became the preferred employer in its local market after implementing an eight and skate program, ending a longstanding problem of recruiting and retaining room attendants.

Requirements for the successful implementation of incentive programs are: (1) a consistent quality-control program to ensure that cleaning standards are met and (2) voluntary participation so employees do not feel coerced.

Hotel Laundry Incentive Programs

One innovative general manager was concerned that his hotel's laundry crew did not seem to be meeting its production potential. He challenged the laundry crew to increase productivity from 80 pounds per hour to 90. The hotel estimates laundry poundage at 17 pounds per occupied guestroom and one pound per cover. Each morning, productivity for the previous day was posted outside the laundry manager's office on a big calendar. After one month, laundry productivity jumped to 95 pounds per labor hour. The general manager rewarded each laundry employee by personally handing him or her a new fifty-dollar bill. By the second month, productivity exceeded 100 pounds per labor hour and has remained at that level ever since.

Telephone Call Centers

It's surprising how many employees are stationed throughout a full-service hotel waiting by the telephone for a guest to call. Many full-service and luxury hotels have room service order takers, housekeeping office coordinators, bell dispatchers, reservations agents, engineering dispatchers, private branch exchange operators, and even restaurant reservations agents. A number of brands have begun combining these positions to form a centralized call center. While these super service agents require a higher level of training, the benefits in terms of improved service and increased productivity most often are well worth the effort.

Restaurant Position Consolidation

Hoteliers can take a lesson from many freestanding restaurateurs. Many restaurants reduce overtime, increase scheduling flexibility, and improve productivity by combining the traditional positions of food server, busperson, and food runner into a single job. These employees are all paid server wages and take turns filling each of the roles and sharing in pooled gratuities.

Staggered Start Times for Restaurant Crews

It's become increasingly common for hotel restaurants and other departments to have preshift meetings (sometimes called line-ups) to convey information about daily specials and other topics at the start of a shift. Managers often will bring in the entire restaurant crew up to two or more hours before opening to set the room, schedule meal breaks, and have a preshift meeting. In this way, the entire restaurant and its crew can be ready when the doors open. The problem is that in most cases, restaurant volume often starts out slowly and peaks at some later point in the shift. In many cases it makes more sense to stagger employee start times to match customer arrival patterns and find a more efficient way to convey preshift information. One hotel restaurant was able to reduce total hours by the equivalent of two full-time employees just by adjusting the starting times of the dining room crew.

Creative Recruiting

Being short-staffed can be a major drain on quality, productivity, and profitability. Being short-staffed often increases overtime. When there is no one to work, quality can suffer and customers may decide to take their business elsewhere. Savvy hoteliers know that the ideal employee probably already has a job and is unlikely to walk through the door to drop off an application. Innovative managers increasingly are using proactive and creative recruiting techniques, including the following:

- One general manager had special recruiting cards printed and distributed to department managers. As the managers dined and shopped in the local community, they were encouraged to hand out the recruiting cards and an invitation to stop by the hotel and apply for a job whenever they encountered a superior service person.

- At another hotel, the human resources manager contacted clergy members in neighborhoods where current staff members lived to let them know that the hotel had openings for stewards and room attendants. The response provided an ample supply of suitable candidates.

- The front office manager at another property went on "shopping trips" to a nearby mall to chat with personable department store sales clerks. The manager would explain the advantages of working in the hospitality industry and invite worthy candidates to stop by the hotel and fill out an application.

Security Officer Quality Inspections

At many full-service hotels, security officers make rounds of the building throughout the day and night. Having security officers complete detailed quality inspection checklists of guest floors, storage closets, lobby, public areas, restrooms, and back-of-the-house areas is an excellent way to take maximum advantage of the security team's mobility. These inspection checklists are especially effective when crafted in a way that provides a performance score. Completed inspections can be routed to the appropriate department and scores tallied and tracked over time. The program works best when recognition programs and contests are incorporated to reward superior performance and high scores.

Preventive Maintenance to Boost Engineering Productivity

The old saying "a stitch in time saves nine" is especially true when it comes to maintaining a hotel. The hotel's engineering department should have documented and ongoing programs for maintaining guestrooms and equipment. Hotels that fall behind in preventive maintenance require increasingly more (and more expensive) emergency repairs. It often is valuable to review and analyze guest calls and emergency repairs. Such a review often will reveal recurring systemic problems that can be incorporated into the hotel's preventive maintenance program. At one hotel, the chief engineer was able to reduce emergency calls by ten percent by replacing smoke detector and television remote control batteries as an ongoing part of the hotel's guestroom preventive maintenance program.

New Food and Beverage Paradigms for Hotels

By *Bob Puccini* and *Rick Swig, ISHC*

Bob Puccini *is Chairman and CEO of The Puccini Gr oup, a leading restaurant design and development firm specializing in full-service concept development, construction management, operations management, and interior design. With more than 30 years of experience in all aspects of restaurant development, he has become the industry leader in the conception, design, and development of destination restaurants within boutique and luxury hotels. Bob's specialization in creating personality restaurants has evolved as a result of his development career beginning with the Que Pasa group of family restaurants for the San Diego–based El Torito Company in the 1970s. He later led the U.S. national expansion of the wildly successful Acapulco restaurants. In 1989, Bob joined the Kimpton Hotel and Restaurant Group as Senior Vice President of Restaurants. In a partnership with Bill Kimpton, Bob gr ew the restaurant division from four restaurants to eighteen restaurants and over 100 million dollars in revenue during his tenure. In 1996, Mr. Puccini left Kimpton to start his own restaurant design, operations, and consulting firm, The Puccini Group. In 2005, he was inducted into the World Travel and Tourism Council and is a member of Foodservice Consultants Society International and the International Society of Hospitality Consultants. He holds a BA in Political Science and Economics from San Diego State University and spent 1969 in Brazil with the Peace Corps.*

Rick Swig operates RSBA & Associates, which was founded in 1986. Since that time, he has provided advisory services to both major hotel operating companies and owners of individual hotels and portfolios. Along with his asset management and consultancy work, he has been an investor in hotels since 1989. His background also includes a career with Fairmont Hotels.

RSBA & Associates is a consultancy firm for the hospitality industry. Primary activities include hotel operations reviews, asset strategy development, general operational troubleshooting, and asset management. Clients include individual and institutional asset owners, as well as hotel operating and management companies. Engagements have included work on hotels with both urban and resort locations with business and/or leisure services.

FOOD AND BEVERAGE IS an integral part of hotel operations. The products and services go beyond providing the fundamental perfunctory three-meal, banquet, and room service to guests. Hotels may choose to operate their food and beverage facilities on their own, engage a third party through a lease, franchise/license agreement, or management contract, or use a hybrid of these options to separate the retail restaurant operation from banquet or room-service functions. Regardless of the business structure, a well-implemented program will maximize benefits that extend beyond profitability to the general market positioning and merchandising of the hotel.

Historical Background

Food and beverage service in hotels has a great history of importance within the commercial realm of hospitality. It can be argued whether commercial overnight accommodations came as a result of the world's oldest profession (ancient languages often used the same words for inns and brothels) or as an outcropping of services provided by roadside taverns, but in any case, lodging and the provision of food and beverage have long been integrated components. The code of Hammurabi, written around 1700 B.C., includes references to lodging and taverns. Hospitality has evolved over centuries, but a core value always included the delivery of food and beverage to patrons seeking shelter during their travels.

In more contemporary times, at least in Europe and the United States, there is a significant history of hotels serving as the social center of urban society by providing fine food and beverage services in restaurants and in grand ballrooms. Luxury hotels were the traditional outlet for the merger of society, culture, and hospitality. It is estimated that by 1883, hotels in the United States were serving more than 200,000 corporate travelers.

Such U.S. hotels as The Waldorf=Astoria and the Plaza in New York, the Palmer House in Chicago, the Biltmore in Los Angeles, or the Palace Hotel and the Fairmont in San Francisco offered more than simply a good night's sleep. They became the centers for social, business, and cultural affairs with theaters, nightclubs, hairdressers, and haberdashers operating along with the finest restaurants and ballrooms in their respective cities. Dining in those fine hotel dining rooms became something to which many social climbers aspired. This fashion peaked in the late 1950s and early 1960s as suburban living, along with retail food and beverage development, began to grow.

Cultural Changes in America Since 1950

During the 1950s, American culture was one of harmony, sameness, mass-produced items, and very little desire or ability to create niche products. There were three dominant automakers, and each manufacturer had just a handful of models. The same was true for home appliances and furniture. The few great hotels that existed in many cities generally were bastions of design and uniqueness, within a conservative context for the community. Restaurants generally were considered for special-occasion dining-out experiences and had menus that were largely traditional in content.

American culture started to change, however, in the 1960s when the suburbs were developed with the help of emerging regional shopping centers. The new inner city was clean, modern, and safe, and the baby boomers started to grow up. As that great bulge in the population started to emerge from its teens, the desire for more personal satisfaction began to develop. "Personal" and "unique" were in.

The 1970s saw maturing baby boomers going into business and bringing their desire for style and differentiation into those businesses. Manufacturing less homogeneous products became easier with the advent of primitive computers. As the 1970s moved to the 1980s, there was a convergence between technology, higher incomes, two-income families, smaller families, and the desire to have things "my way." Federal Express started its first flights in 1973. Pottery Barn emerged when it was purchased by a major retailer in 1986 and stylish designer home furnishings took off. Since that time, instant gratification and style have become reality, not just expectations. Demand for unique and creative design is escalating, aesthetics are not a luxury, and instant availability is the norm.

As suburban growth fueled shopping centers, it also fueled growth in popular restaurants as adjunct tenants in the shopping centers. At the same time, hotels based on pure functionality were added and their focus on food and beverage dissipated. The result was that hotels catered more to the needs of business travelers and less to the emotional needs of the social diner. Therefore, three-meal hotel restaurants looked and acted like breakfast rooms. Meanwhile, the suburban freestanding restaurant market continued to grow as a result of dual-income households, more commuting time, and smaller families. Time became more precious, money a little more plentiful, and eating out more justifiable.

Theme restaurants evolved quickly with millions of dollars being spent on décor, training, uniforms, and real estate to position dining out as a home meal replacement. This really started in the late 1960s with regional chains and then grew dramatically in the 1970s. Such large conglomerates as W.R. Grace & Co. brought character and décor into chain restaurants. This was often missing in hotel restaurants.

As the 1980s emerged, many managers and chefs who were trained so well by chain management learned that they could make a good living with their own restaurant. This resulted in a new type of restaurant that again focused on unique style and local flavor. These entrepreneurs in the 1980s and 1990s yielded a professional group of independent restaurants that reached into virtually every conceivable food, style, and décor niche imaginable. Like the automobile, housewares, apparel, and home furnishings industries, the restaurant business became a product of its culture.

Hotels, on the other hand, remained stuck in the old paradigm of providing food and beverage to the public because they were required to do so. Full-service hotels in fact struggled not to become commodities themselves as low-cost hotels for business travelers in suburban markets became popular with the larger chains.

There was also the issue of profit. During the early 1990s when there was too much hotel supply and not enough demand, hotel operators focused on reducing expenses by cutting services in retail food and beverage departments. The quality and competitive distinctiveness of individual hotel restaurants diminished along with expense and service. If freestanding commercial restaurants did not already dominate individual marketplaces, hotel operators basically let them win. Large full-service brands reduced the number of outlets from several to one (possibly with a lobby bar), while Marriott and Hilton introduced their Courtyard and Garden Inn brands with limited food and beverage options. According to Smith Travel

Research, dining-out spending has grown from $42.8 billion in sales in 1970 to a projected $475.8 billion in 2005, while the lodging industry's portion of this has grown from an estimated $887 million in 1970 to an estimated $20.3 billion in 2004.

The overall effect of this growth in the freestanding restaurant market, whether it was in quick-service, casual-dining, or white-tablecloth restaurants, was a dramatic increase in the public's standards and expectations. Unfortunately, typical hotel restaurants failed to keep up with minimum criteria, as independent and branded freestanding restaurants increased their standards.

Cultural Evolution and Expectations

Culture and lifestyle changes are driven by variables related to a variety of influences, including economic trends, technology, personal style, and family size, among others. When any of these variables change, the marketplace adjusts to reflect new consumer needs and wants.

Social and economic factors account for the increase in dining-out spending. Dual-income families have emerged as a norm, particularly in the United States. This is as a result of more women in the workforce. Women—particularly those with families—in the workplace have led to distinct changes in the fabric of the dining-out public.

The most obvious result of an additional family income is the increase in the average household income. Adjusted for inflation, the median U.S. household income more than doubled between 1960 and 2000. There was also real growth in the economy. Additionally, the average family size has become smaller, which is a result of the declining American birth rate.

These two factors have created a third phenomenon—the time drought. In many cases, the lack of time has prohibited the previous norm of the traditional home-cooked family meal. Dining out and convenience meals have become in many ways less expensive than eating at home due to the opportunity cost of time used in preparation and clean up. This fundamental shift in the behavior of the American family has made an evening meal at a local restaurant or burger stand a regular occurrence, rather than a special event.

The psychological impact of the breakup of the family meal period in the home will probably be analyzed for decades to come by sociologists and anthropologists. The immediate effect is a boom for restaurateurs that does not, in most cases, include hotel operations.

The growth of suburban markets and the media's continual broadcast of image messages have created cultural influences on style. Members of the general public now have a general sense that real life can and should reflect the lives of their "peers," who are portrayed in various media campaigns. This peer group aspiration coupled with the aforementioned economic drivers and the proliferation of stand-alone dining establishments, whether fast food or fine dining, has turned a social trend into a new dining reality.

This style and design phenomenon is not limited to the United States. It has become a worldwide movement during the last 20 years. For example, at least five new home and lifestyle magazines have started publication in Australia since 2000 to join an existing 15 lifestyle magazines. On a worldwide basis, more than 40 design magazines have begun publishing since 1995. In Japan, where design schools did not exist in 1970, there are no less than nine of those schools. South Korea, likewise, had no design schools in 1970, while today there are ten. Italy's first design school opened in 1983 and today there are nearly 25 schools.

The focus on unique and creative design has escalated enormously in the last 30 years. Design aesthetics are no longer a luxury, but a universal human desire. Demand for design aesthetics is now reflected not only in fancy boutiques and along trendy retail streets, but in shopping malls, theme parks, airports, movies, television, and restaurants. This reinforces the conversion from trend to lifestyle norm being forced upon restaurant operators in virtually every corner of the globe. This includes locations on rural islands that host spectacular resort dining experiences to cities that house myriad unique and stylish dining establishments. Hotel operators have been followers in matching the food and beverage style trends and aesthetics of their freestanding restaurant competitors.

Unfortunately, as restaurant diners were seeking better aesthetics and dining experiences, hotel restaurants were evolving mostly as symbols of obligatory and mediocre food and beverage services. This created a cycle in which both overnight-stay and local customers sought their food and beverage services outside of a hotel environment. This created a downward revenue spiral for hotel restaurants and they no longer could achieve profitability.

Hotel restaurants have been forced to shift their operational focuses in the last decade to include an emphasis on freestanding restaurant concepts. In many cases, they have evolved from individual boutique or destination restaurants into nationally branded fine dining chains.

With the general exception of such luxury hotel brands as Four Seasons and Ritz-Carlton, most higher-end properties have been faced with shedding their generic reputations for providing stale, uninspiring retail food and beverage products and services. Hotel operators have been forced to seek methods of keeping their overnight-stay guests on property for three meal periods, while attracting a solid customer base from the local community as well. There has been a shift of focus from providing a "typical" hotel restaurant experience to creating a defining food, beverage, and entertainment experience to complement the lifestyle expectations of all constituencies.

This evolution required a change in the vision for the execution of a successful food and beverage program. This included a shift from the idea that food and beverage was a requisite supplementary and money-losing hotel amenity to the concept that a retail food and beverage department within a hotel could be profitable as a freestanding commercial revenue center with its own distinctive positioning. Additionally, there was a regeneration of the idea that a restaurant provides an additional selling and positioning point for a hotel operation. As a result, there now exists an independent approach to restaurants within hotels, which includes both the development of distinctive concepts and the inclusion of management and chefs with independent backgrounds and thinking to create an entrepreneurial spirit.

Upscale hotel operators recognize that they must expand their food and beverage concepts beyond their own ideas and the traditional operating parameters or pigeon holes of their hotels to embrace an independent restaurant concept. This is also necessary to leverage the development of a restaurant and expand the hotel's market visibility and positioning.

Hoteliers cannot and will not attract local customers or their own overnight guests without paying keen attention to lifestyle trends, style, and product quality in the form of attractive restaurant environments and menu products. Additionally, if the operators of the restaurant—whether hotel employees or outside practitioners—are not held accountable for competing directly for market share against unaffiliated freestanding restaurants, an independent operating culture will not develop.

There are historical precedents for third-party or independent restaurants within hotels. The first outsourcing or co-branding occurred in the late 1940s between Western International Hotels and Trader Vic's. Even then, there was opportunity for both the hotel operator and the restaurant company to link two strong brand names to enhance the profile and quality of each.

Contemporary Trends

Clearly, then, hotel operators have not, for the most part, developed strong reputations for their food and beverage operations in recent years. Hotel management is justifiably more focused on selling rooms at a 75 percent departmental profit than food and beverage at a 25 percent or less departmental profit. While hotels send their marketing messages mostly outside of their immediate local marketplaces, restaurant operators send their solicitations primarily to local customers with point-of-sale promotions and merchandising. While hoteliers have in many cases considered food and beverage as an ancillary function, restaurant operators have no choice but to make their facilities their one and only focus.

Hotel operators have struggled for years with unprofitable and sometimes unmanageable food and beverage operations. Although struggling to improve matters, hotel operators often accepted the status quo and undesirable circumstances. The impact of the early 1990s recession led to the emergence of limited-service and moderate-service hotels. These hotels operated without full-service food and beverage facilities and forced full-service hotels to more carefully scrutinize their situations. This scrutiny resulted in the following activities: downsizing or eliminating food and beverage operations, developing proprietary concepts, leasing out space to local restaurateurs, franchisees, and restaurant companies, and directly buying the rights to franchise a nationally recognized brand.

Tension has emerged during the evolution of food and beverage service within hotels between the need to support the hotel's brand image and the customer's overall hotel experience with the intention to generate profit from the food and beverage department. Herein lies the fundamental difference between hoteliers and restaurateurs.

Within the hotel paradigm, the rooms department rules and drives home the notion that the revenue from rooms is the dominant source of sales and profit. If 75 percent of every room's gross revenue dollar goes to profit, how can the 15 to 25 percent profit earned by restaurants be important? Hotel operations require a housekeeper for every 14 to 16 rooms and someone to check guests in and out, while restaurants require servers for every five tables plus buspersons, cooks, chefs, bartenders, and hosts, making it far more labor intensive to earn a profit.

Another traditional hotel paradigm is many operators' belief that food and beverage is a commodity like bath towels or televisions—a staple amenity for a hotel operation. Conversely, restaurateurs view their restaurant as an emotional experience that can affect both the body and soul of their guests.

In spite of much of this recent history of food and beverage in hotels, hoteliers are starting to realize that a strong restaurant image can enhance the value of their hotel rooms as well as generate profits. One of the leaders of the new hotel restaurant movement was Bill Kimpton, with his concept for a well-balanced upscale boutique hotel that includes both fine guestroom accommodations and a distinctive food and beverage operation. Kimpton was not trained in either the hotel or restaurant business and his lack of preconceived notions presented the perfect opportunity to become an innovator.

Kimpton saw an opportunity to break from the traditional formula of rooms and food and beverage and as a result, he restructured the paradigm. Kimpton's intention was to create street entrances for the hotel's restaurants. He recognized that restaurants inside of hotels would further perpetuate the hotel restaurant stigma, as customers presumed that hotel-operated restaurants were not as good as restaurateur-operated outlets.

This hotel vision, which was based on Kimpton's years of travel as a mortgage banker, included the creation of a warm, comfortable place to "sell sleep." Each sleep environment was to be developed in conjunction with an associated restaurant, designed for popularity in the local community, and attractive to the room guests.

This vision, now a tradition, still continues through the Kimpton development culture after 20 years and requires the marketing design and focus of their hotel's restaurants to correspond with local consumption. Restaurants appear as separate from the hotels. This separate nature extends to the hotel's and restaurant's operation as separate business entities, including separate profit/loss sheets and separate management and operating cultures to offer an additional form of theater to the overall hospitality presentation.

Kimpton restaurants have often become more successful in their own right than the hotels in which they are placed. This has been due to the combination of creative chefs, stimulating ambiance, strong service, and the goal of operating competitively. This has generally translated into financial success, a unique selling point, and marketing visibility for the hotel.

In upscale hotel operations, restaurants are now expected to reflect guest expectations for both a hotel and a distinctive freestanding restaurant. The restaurant is the opportunity to merge the high brand standards for both entities.

There are major challenges with the integration of an "independent" restaurant concept into a hotel format. While the restaurant may offer a unique and definitive product orientation, hotel guests may still require staple products and services. The major challenges are breakfast, banquets, and room service. These three areas may present conflicts between hotel operators and their potential outsourcing partners. Hoteliers look at the service benefits of room service, breakfast, and banqueting, while restaurant operators may not have the same alignment of goals. There is the ongoing perception and reality that, while breakfast potentially can be profitable, room service is just an around-the-clock liability. Additionally, there are stereotypes—whether accurate or not—that either restaurateurs do not understand hotel culture or that hoteliers are too set in their ways, inflexible, and complacent to understand an entrepreneurial restaurant operation.

Some hotels have sidestepped these challenges by providing separate accommodations for these three elements, while others have accepted the challenge to extend the restaurant's theme into these departmental extensions. Obviously, the size and scale of the individual hotel operations define strategic and tactical implementations for supplementary services.

Food and Beverage Operating Arrangements

Hotel operators are now benefiting from the success of breaking traditional molds and seeking alternative methods of delivering retail food and beverage products. There are several emerging models, including self-operation, leasing to a third party, and forming a joint venture with a restaurant's brand manager to operate the primary hotel restaurant under a nationally recognized name or identity. As a result, a hotel guest, either local or overnight, may have the option of eating at a Shula's Steak House in a Sheraton, Daily Grill in a Westin, Ruth's Chris Steakhouse in a Hilton, Bice in a Four Seasons, or other nationally recognized restaurant brand within the confines of a nationally recognized hotel brand product. Alternatively, celebrity chefs are the focal point of many "independent" restaurant operations in branded or independent hotels throughout the country. This has created both mutual brand enhancement and customer demand for the cooperative entities.

Whether driven by customer convenience and need for staple services or by demand for a distinctive environment for effective positioning and marketing, hotel operators have realigned their thinking on their approach to food and beverage services within a hotel. A variety of ways to redefine food service have evolved. These arrangements can be classified as one of five types.

Self-Operation

The most common type of hotel food and beverage operation is self-operated. Such outlets are characterized by the following traits.

Legal Organization. Self-operated outlets are run by either the hotel's owner or its management company. All food and beverage is integrated into the entity that owns and operates the whole facility. This could include the separate operation of a restaurant franchise within the hotel.

Profit and Loss Responsibility. Profit and loss (P&L) responsibility lies with the hotel department that accounts for revenue and expenses. These expenses may not include many such shared expenses as utilities, marketing, maintenance, and general and administrative overhead. In this case, profitability is not "real profit," but rather a departmental line item that might or might not contribute to the overall welfare of the hotel.

Operational Responsibility. Operational responsibility traditionally is assumed by a food and beverage manager. In larger hotels, this person frequently is an administrator with equal or even more focus on the high-volume catering and banqueting functions that contribute the most sales and profit to the hotel. Dining room functions traditionally are directed by outlet managers, who are responsible for the staffing and general operation of the dining room rather than the full combination of product, service, and ambiance. The executive chef, along with the food and beverage director, is most often responsible for menus and plate presentation. Dining room managers generally are not required to be seasoned restaurant operators.

Concept Direction. Food and beverage operations in larger self-operated organizations have focused mostly on banquet operations because meeting, catering, and banqueting demand provides the greatest portion of food and beverage revenue. The restaurant outlet's revenue potential often is viewed as too insignificant in the context of overall food and beverage performance. As a result, the principal functions of the dining outlet are to serve breakfast and provide a convenience for guests who choose to have lunch or dinner in the hotel. Hotel room service revenue for dinner often is as great as the dining room revenue.

Advantages/Disadvantages. The benefit to self operation is control. Within a hotel with a high volume of meeting space or within a resort with multiple food and beverage outlets, self operation provides flexibility to accommodate demand peaks from group or seasonal travelers. Smaller hotels, likewise, benefit from the ability to respond to the frequently fluctuating demands of their guests. The disadvantage of the traditional self-operated hotel restaurant, in which demand ebbs and flows with occupancy, is the potential lack of entrepreneurial behavior to adapt to these changes and attract business from the local community.

An Example of Failure in Self-Operation. A large international chain of hotels saw its dining room outlets as a means to serve breakfast and as a convenience for lunch and dinner. Paramount in its mind was the need to satisfy guests with its accommodations and first-class locations. Its food and beverage program was geared to mass feeding due to a high volume of guests from meeting and convention facilities, while outlet operations were minimal to reduce the strain on management. The food and beverage outlet thus became an afterthought, which stimulated customer migration out of the hotel and held little potential for attracting local community demand.

Sales in the restaurant were approximately \$2.3 million per year and the departmental gross operating profit (GOP) was around 18 percent. The bulk of the positive GOP was derived from \$6 million in catering revenue. The net result in a profit and loss statement that included all of the actual costs to the restaurant—not just departmental costs—was an actual cash loss to the food and beverage department.

Example of Success in Self-Operation. An international chain operator focused on the development of a cool boutique hotel environment. Emphasis was placed on the hotel bar as the focal point of the operation during nonbreakfast periods. This created the platform for positioning the hotel to the local community and out-of-town guests. The restaurant and in-room dining were more focused on the hotel guest.

The low cost of a bar is ideal for economical operations. By creating a high-revenue bar with simpler operations, the hotel took advantage of markets where there were an abundance of younger, more price-sensitive travelers and where the restaurant was positioned to support the overall concept of the hotel. Because the cost of the beverage product and labor in a bar operation are relatively low, revenue and profit are greater. The labor cost for providing a drink, whether alcoholic or not, generally is the labor expense for a bartender and a cocktail server, which can be less than $18 per hour. Food service requires a chef, several cooks, a dishwasher, a busperson, and a server and generates labor expenses of up to $90 per hour. (This does not include preparation, dishwashing, or the capital expense of cooking.)

Lease

A leased operation is characterized by the following traits.

Legal Organization. Leased food and beverage operations may be either single-restaurant-outlet leases or total-facility leases. In larger hotels, management may lease out more than one restaurant space (as long as there are separate kitchens), while continuing to maintain control over the "base" hotel food and beverage operations of room service, catering, and/or breakfast. In smaller hotels with leased food and beverage facilities, the tenant/operator generally is responsible for all food and beverage operations in the hotel.

Leases generally specify a fixed minimum rent plus a percentage rent, which is contingent on the contribution of the hotel owner/operator to the initial restaurant improvements. It is not unusual for the tenant/operator to pay one rent level for the restaurant, another for the catering operation, and another for the bar or lounge.

Profit and Loss Responsibility. The P&L responsibility is in the hands of the tenant/operator. His or her responsibility is to pay rent, common area maintenance expenses, and operating expenses, which typically would include the operation's direct utility expenses, sales taxes, and a pro rata share of property taxes and/or insurance.

Operational Responsibility. Direct day-to-day responsibility for operations is in the hands of the tenant/operator. In smaller hotels, however, there is a keen interaction between the hotel operator and restaurant operator when there are shared food and beverage activities that relate directly to hotel guests and their experience in the hotel. Depending on the terms of the lease, the hotel operator may or may not have control over the way hotel-related food and beverage operations are conducted. Criteria dictated to the tenant/operator generally are more qualitative and less quantitative, so the food and beverage operation will not have to compromise profitability as a result of standard hotel demands.

Concept Direction. The concept direction in a leasing scenario generally is driven by the tenant/operator, but initially is approved by the hotel. Quite often, any substantial deviation from an initially defined concept may be considered a breach of the lease, so the tenant/operator should carefully determine a concept that can be durable in light of the demand fluxes of a particular location, occupancy changes, banquet demands, room service, and local community sales opportunities. It is also important to determine the level of skill in the employee market because a lack of properly skilled applicants has the potential to limit a concept.

Advantages/Disadvantages. The biggest advantage to a leased operation is that it brings income to the hotel without hotel management having to assume the difficult task of operating a food and beverage program. This reduces hotel management, general and administrative, utility, marketing, maintenance, and other expenses. Another benefit is in the improved reputation and positioning that the right operator can create through fine food products and services. These may even positively overshadow the hotel at the local community level and can become a public relations bonanza. The greatest liability associated with leasing out a hotel's food and beverage program is the potential inability of the tenant/operator to perform to the expected level of operation. Generally, this accompanies a financial breach, which results in the deterioration of the operation and the hotel operating the outlet until a permanent replacement is found. Alternatively, failure may not be accompanied by a financial breach, which is equally problematic because the tenant/operator continues paying rent. It then becomes difficult to replace the tenant/operator and the food and beverage operation may continue to damage the hotel's reputation. Regardless of the failure, a poor restaurant operator can hurt a hotel's reputation.

Example of Failure in Leasing. The owner of a small urban hotel leased the hotel's food and beverage operation. The tenant/operator was subsequently heavily fined for a human resource infraction and then filed for bankruptcy. During the course of the bankruptcy proceedings, the food and beverage facility deteriorated both physically and operationally, so the hotel and its reputation suffered.

This restaurant generated $3.1 million per year in sales and $20,000 per month in rent. The pressure from the fine caused a severe cash flow problem, which required the tenant/operator to file for protection under Chapter 11 bankruptcy laws. The court ordered the rent to be reduced until the lessee could emerge from Chapter 11. The rent was then reduced to $8,000 per month for a two-year period. Additionally, the restaurant's repair and maintenance program was limited to bare essentials so the facility's maintenance and cleanliness were severely diminished with a direct impact on hotel guests.

Example of Success in Leasing. A 100-room urban hotel leased its operationally plagued food and beverage operation to a local restaurant operator with multiple outlets in the same city. The new lessee rescued the food and beverage operation, which had lost money previously, and leveraged the reputation of its other restaurants to create demand for its new affiliate. The decision to lease removed the operational headaches, provided substantial rent, and enhanced the image of the hotel.

The hotel owners benefited from the installation of a high-profile restaurant to enhance the three-star status of the hotel and serve the needs of the local community and hotel guests. The tenant/operator leased the space for the higher of a triple net flat rent of $9,000 per month or 5 percent of its gross revenue. The restaurant stabilized at $5 million gross revenue per year and exceeded all expectations.

Management Contracts

A hotel restaurant operating under a separate management contract is characterized by the following traits.

Legal Organization. Management contracts for food and beverage operators are similar to hotel management or operating agreements in that they outline very distinct operating parameters for long periods of time. These parameters may apply only to the restaurant outlet or may cover the entire food and beverage operation. Each detail must be carefully considered. One of the keys to a management agreement is outlining responsibility for the expense of building and improving the facility. Generally, the hotel owner provides all or most of the improvement funds for the restaurant and catering spaces. These facilities, however, generally are built to the specifications of the contracted operator (or the franchisor), so there is little concept and design flexibility.

Profit and Loss Responsibility. The outside operator/contractor has P&L responsibility for the specific food and beverage operation. The hotel owner or operator ultimately is accountable for satisfactory accomplishment of revenue and profit goals of the food and beverage program as a whole. The budget may be departmentally driven or a full stand-alone P&L, in which all expenses for the restaurant operation are either allocated or expensed directly to the restaurant/food and beverage program. If an outside operator/contractor is responsible for performance, there may be a means to remove the operator when budget is not achieved, but the propriety of the restaurant, ownership of the name, and community standing may make a change in operator more difficult than a contract would lead one to believe.

Operational Responsibility. The day-to-day operational responsibility is with the outside operator/contractor, but operation is always in conjunction with the hotel operator/owner. This relationship requires the utmost in cooperation and understanding of common goals. These goals generally are articulated in the annual budget or business plan, which takes into account the operating needs of the hotel and the sales and profit consequences of those demands for the operator/contractor. The business plan, for example, may take into account the need for the hotel to serve breakfast very early in the morning to accommodate the occasional guest's early departure. It also may take room service into consideration, including the cost of room service attendants for breakfast, lunch, dinner, or even 24-hour service.

Concept Direction. The concept direction is first considered by hotel owners/operators when they select a management company. Selection may be based on style of operation and quality of restaurant concepts or experience with hotel food and beverage operations. For whatever reason it is chosen, the selected operator/contractor generally is responsible for the concept and the restaurant generally is built to the operator's specifications, within budget requirements or contract specifications.

Advantages/Disadvantages. The benefit of having a management contract is that the hotel operator can focus on room sales, occupancy, and guest service. Another advantage of selecting an outside operator/contractor is the delivery of a turnkey product, including product standards and guidelines, design and concept plans, recipes and menus, operating service manuals, and collateral designs, without need of further refinement. The right operator/contractor may bring a style and quality to the restaurant that the hotel could not have developed on its own. The hotel may also benefit from the operator/contractor's marketing, reputation, and existing local community goodwill. Because management contracts frequently provide for compensation as a percentage of sales, the operator/contractor is highly motivated to increase sales. If there is additional compensation for bottom line profit, the operator/contractor also receives a bonus for creating profit for the hotel.

In the best case, the hotel gains a restaurant of high local repute without the distraction of operating a food and beverage program, while it also benefits from above-average sales and profit from the operator/contractor. The downside of this arrangement parallels the downside of a lease agreement. The restaurant operator/contractor, no matter how experienced, may fail to provide the right program for the operation of the hotel. As with a leased operation, the removal of the operator/contractor and termination of the contract can become difficult. The hotel owner and outside operator/contractor must consider failure as a contractual component that is measurable on multiple levels, including financially. The parties also should not enter into a financial structure that is destined for failure due to unrealistic or lofty financial goals.

Example of Failure with Management Contracts. The owner of an upscale suburban hotel with 100 rooms hired a management company and invested in a restaurant with regional name recognition and distinction. The 124-seat restaurant and bar achieved extraordinarily high sales, but failed to achieve profit because of unusually high shared expenses with the hotel. The owner canceled the contract with the food and beverage management company and took over running the operation with reduced expenses and quality standards, resulting in lost sales and profit.

Taking advantage of a well-known restaurant concept is wise as it generally garners more immediate business from the community. When the management company is burdened with exceedingly high fixed overhead from the owner, the operation can be set up to fail. This regional group accepted a fixed overhead that exceeded $50,000 per month and, even though this relatively small restaurant achieved sales of nearly $3.6 million per year, it could not yield a net operating profit. The management company compromised the operation in such a manner that sales were affected and revenue decreased to little more than $2.4 million two years after opening.

Example of Success with Management Contracts. The owner of a 200-room urban hotel with a mediocre reputation for food and beverage engaged a separate management company with a strong local reputation to manage the hotel's restaurant and banquet function. The restaurant became a success and the quality of operation caused customers to book rooms at the hotel so they could get reservations at the restaurant.

This hotel decided that it wanted to create a destination restaurant. The restaurant was a positioning statement for the four-star hotel's success. An exclusive designer and high-profile chef created a restaurant that was truly unique. After spending $2.5 million on a restaurant, which was built to the designer's and operator/contractor's specifications, revenue eclipsed $12.0 million and restaurant clientele had to book rooms in the hotel to get much sought after reservations in the restaurant.

Joint Ventures

A hotel restaurant operating as a joint venture is characterized by the following traits.

Legal Organization. A joint venture is a hybrid of a lease and management contract with the restaurant operator contributing cash or cash equivalent to the development of the hotel's restaurant and food and beverage operations. Both the hotel owner and restaurant operator then share in the potential success or failure of the food and beverage operation. The restaurant operator may be removed for poor performance, but there are financial consequences to the hotel owner for doing so. Joint ventures typically are products of smaller hotels or smaller markets where sharing the cost of developing a restaurant is advantageous to both the restaurateur and the hotelier.

Profit and Loss Responsibility. The direct P&L responsibility for the food and beverage program rests in the hands of the restaurant operator, but as in the case of the management contract, there is a shared responsibility in that the hotel guides the criteria for success based on its needs and these needs are reflected in the annual budget and business plan. These plans account for the hotel's needs that affect the restaurant's sales and profits (free breakfast, for example) and compensate the operator of the food and beverage program accordingly. Restaurant operators generally have a higher profit potential under this arrangement, as their risk is higher based on their initial capital contribution.

Operational Responsibility. Although the specific operational responsibility rests with the restaurant operator, it is shared with the hotel manager to a greater extent than it is in the context of a pure management contract. The hotel owner/operator has more input into the operations based on the hotel's needs.

Concept Direction. Generally the restaurant operator has the sole responsibility for creating the concept and operational direction of the restaurant. Insofar as restaurant operators have contributed capital to the project, their vision of the restaurant generally is overriding.

Advantages/Disadvantages. The greatest advantage to a joint venture is that the restaurant operator has capital at risk and therefore is highly motivated to protect that investment with care for the quality of operations and bottom line profitability. The disadvantage is seen when the hotel's location or product is substandard to the restaurant operation, which results in limited potential for sales and profit.

Example of Failure with Joint Ventures. A 100-room hotel in an urban market traditionally had operated its own food and beverage outlet. It was approached by a celebrity chef with funds from local investors to create a joint venture, in which the chef would operate the hotel's food and beverage outlet with the hotel. The restaurant was a failure and the celebrity chef soon departed, leaving his investors behind and the hotel operating a concept that it did not understand and could not maintain.

Financial participation is no guarantee that either partner can or will sustain the relationship when times are tough. In this case, the chef lost his enthusiasm for the project when he could not pay himself and faced criticism from his partners. The result was his withdrawal and the hotel was forced to re-conceptualize the operation and review its operational procedures at considerable cost. The hotel was unprepared to assume the operation and its vision. A $100,000 annual triple net lease turned into a $200,000 annual loss and an operational nightmare for the hotel.

Example of Success with Joint Ventures. A small 40-room motel in a suburban community wanted to upgrade its profile by providing a full-service restaurant for its guests and the community. The hotel had not previously provided full food and beverage service. By introducing a full-service restaurant, the motel increased its average daily rate by 30 percent with no negative impact on occupancy. Catering, which had heretofore been outsourced, and the restaurant managed to both pay a 5 percent rent and provide a profit to the hotel owner and the joint venture operator.

Franchises

A hotel restaurant operating as a franchised operation is characterized by the following traits.

Legal Organization. A franchised operation can be hotel-operated, leased, or operated under a management contract. The franchise agreement is very restrictive as to how the restaurant looks and operates, how much money is spent annually on marketing, and how that marketing is done. Guidelines for operation frequently do not include breakfast and do not provide for banquet and catering capabilities.

Profit and Loss Responsibility. This depends on the type of arrangement with the franchisor. The designated operator has responsibility for the P&L. Operating costs are maintained through the supplier pipeline, regimented recipes, and designated operating requirements. More often than not, franchised restaurant concepts are not able to provide full room service and catering capability.

Operational Responsibility. Franchisors typically train franchisee management and provide regional supervision to maintain their brand standards. Day-to-day responsibility rests with the local management team and ultimately with that management or ownership structure. In the case of failure, the franchisee is responsible unless there is some reason to believe that the franchisor has failed in its efforts to market and maintain a high standard that was expected by the franchisee.

Concept Direction. This is directed entirely by the franchisor according to distinct brand standards.

Advantages/Disadvantages. The chief benefit of a franchise is certainty of product, track record, and operating procedures, which presumably would indicate a high likelihood of success. The operator has the added advantage of the brand's reputation, customer base, and national marketing efforts. The risk relates to a weak franchisor that is not prepared to support the efforts of a franchisee adequately or the possibility of a brand weakening due to forces outside of the franchisee's control.

Example of Failure in Franchising. A hotel operator entered into a franchise relationship with a nationally known brand and made significant financial investments in improvements to the existing restaurant for conversion to the brand's standard. During the subsequent course of operating the nationally recognized franchise, the operator adopted a philosophy of cheating on certain franchise standards in an effort to economize. The restaurant, as a result, did not maintain the expected product and service standard, and loyal brand customers abandoned the restaurant and the hotel.

In this case, be careful of the strength of the franchisee. A brand name may ensure initial business, but loyal brand customers are also likely to be highly indignant when the brand does not produce at the level of their expectation. In this case, the franchisee cut back on specified quality levels and hastened his fall by disappointing his guests. The result was a high opening trail and loyal customer base for the first year and a subsequent reduction in sales and profit once the brand standards were compromised.

Example of Success in Franchising. A hotel achieved approximately $400,000 of annual revenue through its self-conceived and operated restaurant, which was open for lunch and dinner. The hotel entered into a franchise/license agreement with a national restaurant chain and invested $850,000 in capital improvements to comply with the franchise's design requirements. The franchise fee and related expenses amounted to a license fee of 10 percent of gross revenue per year. In the first three years of operation, revenue grew as follows: $2.8 million in year one, $3.7 million in year two, and $4.6 million in year three.

Outsourcing Options and Considerations

Hoteliers have had to adjust their traditional inclination not to give up control of important food and beverage outlets. This becomes especially tension filled when a hotel has already ventured a unique model and customers have failed to overcome their discriminatory attitudes toward hotel restaurants. Although outsourcing food and beverage operations presents many positives related to brand extension, marketing, and profitability, many hoteliers still feel that the loss of operating control and their inability to provide input is extremely unattractive.

Hoteliers are faced with either giving up control or losing the opportunity to stimulate traffic and reputation through an outside venture.

The easiest means of giving up control is to find a nationally successful brand to operate restaurant activity, which generally includes the lunch and dinner meal periods and leaves breakfast, catering, and room service for the hotel to operate. When the restaurant is leased or franchised, a separate room frequently is required for breakfast service because the lessee does not want to contaminate its concept with nonbrand meal periods or offerings. The hotel operator, except in smaller hotels, may rely on its restaurant lessee's menu for room service and catering. As the boutique hotel concept came of age, this uniqueness became part of the signature and charm of this segment of hotels. In smaller hotels with fewer than 250 rooms, reliance on the restaurant operator is acceptable, but in larger hotels, there are guest service issues or the need to provide distinctive catering or breakfast options that may present a conflict with the signature restaurant's style.

Las Vegas has become a center for restaurant outsourcing, as hotels understand that they can keep their guests within their casinos, while attracting customers from the community and other hotels with their destination restaurant appeal. The Las Vegas hotels have used outsourcing to underscore their positions as destinations within a great destination, which also creates incremental revenue opportunities through the food and beverage operations or their gaming options.

Similarly, traditional hotels in less distinctive destinations have recognized that by franchising, leasing, or other forms of restaurant management they have sustained the attention and incremental spending of their overnight-stay guests, who have most recently found more attractive alternatives outside of the hotel, and local customers, who become regular diners as well as referrals for overnight stay customers. Every market has a popular restaurant that sets the standard for a quality experience in the community. Price threshold or product positioning is not limited, as a community's most popular restaurant may be a TGI Friday's or a Chili's, as opposed to an upscale brand, such as a Morton's, a Ruth's Chris Steakhouse, or a prestigious regional operator.

While well-known chefs or consultants may draw more elite "foodie" crowds, there is a feeling from some hotel operators that more generic brand recognition is the way to solve their food and beverage challenges. Regardless of philosophy, the end game is the same. Hotel food and beverage still must be geared to outside and nonhotel customers. If the outside customer cannot get interested, how can a hotel operator expect an in-house guest to opt to stay inside the hotel instead of seeking a more notable experience outside the hotel?

Business structures for leases, management contracts, or other consultative formats may be geared to the performance and success of the restaurant. These can range from a celebrity chef/consultant/operator receiving a fixed fee with a percentage of revenue or net income to a leased operation paying a fixed fee or a percentage of overall revenue. The value-added proposition for these formats is the less easily measurable impact of incremental hotel room sales and general positioning impact for the hotel. The real value of these arrangements is that they create a pay-for-performance relationship between the hotel and the operator. It is important to recognize that personality and ego are both essential to a successful restaurant operation but potentially can contribute to its downfall if misdirected. It is critical that the hotel's and operator's goals be aligned and that a shared financial arrangement helps to govern that relationship and understanding. It is important to ensure that the operator is focused on sales and profits, while not compromising quality and service. Balance between the two forces is critical to a successful relationship. The wrong relationship is exemplified by a high-quality restaurant that loses money for the sake of chefs' or operators' ego standards.

Hotels are now outsourcing a variety of support departments from laundry to security to maintenance. The major challenges with outsourcing the food and beverage department are the risk of tarnishing brand image and service standards and the integration of nonhotel employees or alternative standards into the standard practices of the hotel.

Preparing for a Good Relationship

The fundamental steps toward establishing the best mesh between an outsourced food and beverage outlet and a hotel seem to be as follows:

- Develop a financial risk analysis and a needs analysis in consideration of the strengths and weakness of the current operation and its direct competition.

  - What are hotel customers' needs and expectations?

  - What food and beverage concept aligns with the hotel's positioning?

  - Would conversion of the hotel's restaurant improve profitability?

  - Would conversion of the hotel's restaurant improve competitive edge?

- Develop an implementation strategy or vision that considers structural changes for the organization, timeline for conversion, teambuilding, marketing, and financial controls.

- Identify known or available restaurant/food and beverage service operators with common service standards and target markets plus local experience or the ability to support a site-specific infrastructure.

- Institute a defined selection process with criteria including important contract negotiating points, anticipated budget for tenant improvements or start-up costs, and contract outline for use in the distribution of a request for proposal (RFP).

- Determine a strategic path for RFP distribution; the interview and selection of a franchisee, manager, or vendor; and conversion of food and beverage program.

- Establish accountability and control standards to measure the productivity and success of two merging cultures.

Deal Structure

The two major issues in deal structuring may be slightly contradictory. A hotel owner should focus on maximizing rent while also working to support the lessee's financial health and welfare to prevent a downturn in restaurant operations, lessee turnover, and business interruption, which would deteriorate the overall quality of the hotel operation. Consider the following issues when preparing a lease agreement:

- Create financial structures that will help the operator sustain the health of the business (i.e., low base rent plus a moderate percentage rent or shared profit risk).

- Increase base rent based on a percentage of total rent paid during a previous annual period.

- Consider the deferral of rent obligations in lieu of providing cash for initial tenant improvements.

- Set a restaurant opening date with defined penalties for not meeting the commencement period.

- Consider staged increases in percentage rent for initial annual periods to ensure the tenant's financial health through business stabilization.

- Require an escrowed fund for renovation and replacement.

- Require the tenant to pay its fair share of real estate taxes and building insurance.

- Clarify rights to building improvements upon breach of lease or completion of term.

- Create a series of short-term lease periods with an option to continue based on prescribed performance attributes that would consider both product and financial issues.

Miscellaneous Contract Issues

The miscellaneous issues in developing a restaurant's lease structure are as important as the financial issues. The relationship between the hotel operator and the restaurant operator must be seamless for the benefit of all parties. The concept of "us versus them" must be eradicated through a detailed lease agreement. The same holds true for third-party management and franchise agreements. The following items should be considered in any lease agreement between a hotel owner and a restaurant operator:

- Select an operator with a solid track record of operation in the local market or with leased hotel restaurant operations.

- Verify the ability of the restaurant operator to financially sustain the operation during any stabilization period.

- Ensure that the restaurant operator has a defined product, format, and strategy.

- Ensure that the restaurant operation will complement the level of product quality, service, and market positioning of the hotel operation.

- Establish defined hours of operation to meet hotel guest needs, with specific determination of meal periods, operating hours, or potential holiday and special event conflicts.

- Confirm the restaurant's responsibilities with regard to conference services and catering services with clear definition of selling, pricing, servicing, and collection responsibilities between hotel sales staff and restaurant operators.

- Define room-service meal period coverage, hours of operation, menu selection parameters, pricing, extent of services, and collection and control of room service equipment (room service tray pick-up, for example).

- Predetermine pricing policies and allowances for vouchers and coupons for tour group operations, special packages, and complimentary food or beverage programs.

- Identify storage space for perishable food and beverage items or operating equipment, including restaurant and catering elements.

- Specify financial responsibility for maintenance and replacement of non-restaurant equipment (banquet chairs, tables, and props, for example).

- Ascertain the location for restaurant-related refuse with clear rules regarding compacting, processing, and removal.

- Specify and identify mutual use of hotel and restaurant identity (name, logo, etc.) in advertising, collateral, and public relations.

- Specify the use of the hotel's name in the address of the restaurant.

- Create an approval process for all mutual marketing and public relations collateral.

- Identify technology issues with regard to the restaurant's integration into the hotel's telephone and possibly property management systems.

- Ensure that hotel guests will have the ability to bill charges to their guest-rooms, while prescribing a method by which the restaurant can determine the creditworthiness of any guest.

- Define the process for the restaurant's collection of hotel guest charges with consideration of a withholding for credit-card processing and other collection-related fees.

- Establish that the restaurant operation will have separate utility meters. If separate metering is not available in every physical area the restaurant operation uses, then a formula for allocation must be defined.

- If the restaurant requires use of hotel parking facilities, clarify policies and processes for validations, predetermined availability of dedicated parking spaces, and expense for valets or other staff for restaurant-related demand.

- If restaurant requires use of hotel laundry facilities, clarify the process for related charges and inventory controls.

- Determine minimum communication standards between restaurant and hotel management regarding occupancy forecasting, special events, special needs, service coordination, and cooperative marketing programs.

Conclusion

The hotel business has evolved significantly since 1700 B.C. and the time of Hammurabi. Moving along the chronological timeline, hotel restaurants have changed and actually moved "back to the future," as consumers have changed their thoughts, lifestyles, and habits regarding retail food and beverage consumption.

Operators have rediscovered the validity of the 1950s philosophy that positions a hotel's restaurant and other food and beverage attributes as a centerpiece of a local market's food and beverage scene, as opposed to a commodity for the simple purpose of feeding overnight hotel guests. This local focus creates financial benefit for the hotel due to additional food and beverage demand and more effectively positions the hotel for overnight travelers and local customers.

The reconnection with this philosophy requires that hotel operators stay abreast of the ever-changing market and embrace continuing changes in market tastes, rather than getting stuck in a rigid way of thinking about product or service. This view represents a general paradigm shift in thinking about hotel food and beverage solutions and formats.

Along with the shift in thinking about product, service, and décor, there are changes in the way hotels manage their food and beverage operations. Outsourcing is now an accepted option, whether in the form of a lease or a third-party management contract. Alternatively, hotels with the wish to operate their own retail food and beverage outlets, but without the concept development prowess to do so successfully, have turned to franchising or licensing from respected operators of familiar national brands. With proper planning and care, these third-party structures are able to operate seamlessly and profitably within other traditional hotel formats, which would include not only retail food and beverage but room service and banqueting as well.

Hotel restaurants with mundane food and beverage, service delivery, or décor are unnecessary and unacceptable, as they bring down both the competitive and brand value (independent or nationally recognized) of the operations they serve. Recent trends indicate hotel operators' acceptance of a high-profile, well-designed destination restaurant within their hotels that can create a draw to the hotel, enhance the hotel's image, and maintain a competitive position within their marketplaces.

10

Technology Trends and Issues

By *Jon Inge, ISHC*

Jon Inge is an independent consultant in hotel technology. He has over 25 years experience with hotel systems, gained through working with both vendor and hotel companies and, for the last nine years, through his own consulting practice. Based in Seattle, Mr. Inge works with clients from eight-room hotels to international chains on all aspects of selecting and using property systems. He compiles a bi-weekly e-newsletter on hospitality technology, and his articles appear frequently in the trade press. He is a regular speaker at industry conferences, has been a member of the AH&LA Technology Committee for the last five years, is a founding member of the HTNG initiative, and is a member of the International Society of Hospitality Consultants.

WHAT DO HOSPITALITY INVESTORS WANT from their technology systems? Typically, the answer would include accurate and comprehensive data that tells them how well the property is performing, enough functionality, flexibility, and power to help management keep producing those great results, and reasonable (i.e., low) costs of installation and support.

The challenges of providing this are many. The more complex operations and marketing become, the more data is needed in both depth and breadth from more systems, each specializing in a different area. Consolidating this data, either through interfaces or by manual reentry, is often difficult, error-prone, and open to changes in meaning from one system to another. Further, the many different systems required at a property often each need their own server hardware and communications networks, making for complex, expensive implementation and support scenarios.

Fortunately, recent trends in technology show that it's possible to reverse this pattern. This chapter discusses current advances that are producing more powerful and flexible systems, better data links between them, improved analysis tools, less costly implementation, and more affordable, effective support.

Hospitality investment and management show no signs of becoming simpler. Resorts continue to add such new facets as condominium units, membership clubs, fractional ownership, spas, golf, tennis, and all kinds of other activities. Business-oriented properties need ever more comprehensive information about their individual and corporate group customers. Guests are encouraged to expect more personally tailored service, and distribution channel management has become impossibly complex as marketing efforts target increasingly more specialized segments. Despite the current optimism in the hospitality market, competition is still fierce, and continued close attention to cost management and operating efficiency is required for investors to see an acceptable return on their funds.

To manage all of these influences, hotel systems have continued to grow in power and flexibility. The number of different systems required, however, has itself become a major problem. The demand for data consolidation and analysis has skyrocketed as managers and owners need a more comprehensive and detailed view of their guests and operations. Each individual system has a different and incomplete view of the guest or operation, but pulling data together into a complete view is tedious and error-prone, and there simply are too many systems for most hotels to manage or support cost-effectively.

Fortunately, a turning point toward more effective systems that are simpler to manage and less expensive to implement has arrived with the convergence of several trends, including:

- More comprehensive systems functionality, often overlapping and blurring traditional distinctions between roles so fewer systems are needed.

- New interface technologies, providing more powerful and flexible ways for systems to work together.

- Greater cooperation between vendors to take advantage of this.

- More reliance on centralized systems that allow simpler on-site requirements and more cost-effective support.

- More accurate and complete databases of operational and guest profile information, with better analysis tools to provide real-time business intelligence (BI).

- Increased use of unified cable and wireless networks, allowing for a simpler, less expensive, and more effective property infrastructure.

- The still-growing impact of the Internet in simplifying communications, making more information available more easily to travelers, and in raising guests' expectations about hotel service, data availability, and the standard of technical services available to them during their stay.

- Significant upgrades in guestroom technology.

Systems Trends

Comprehensive systems are not so much a trend as a fact of life. As long as managers and marketers keep coming up with new ways to attract guests and new services to offer them, vendors will enhance their systems to cope and improve on the concepts. Before we discuss specific system trends, note that two underlying trends are supporting a very welcome growth in systems integration and effectiveness: more powerful and flexible interface technology and a greater willingness on the part of vendors to work together to take advantage of it.

With most vendors moving to Internet Protocol (IP) communications and such Web services as EML-based messaging, interfacing is changing radically for the better. Instead of each vendor writing a very specifically formatted string of data elements to send to each version of each system with which it needs to exchange data, a single self-describing and more complete description of a guest-driven event can be published for use as required by any other system that needs to know about the event. For example, when a guest checks in, the property management system (PMS) can publish a message listing the guest's name, room number, number of nights, room rate, package plan, and preferences. Any other system affected by a check-in can then extract from that message just the data elements it needs to use. The longer-term potential for this technology is that systems eventually will be able to identify themselves when they connect to a network and exchange enough standard information to communicate without human intervention.

It's most encouraging to see how much vendor cooperation has grown over the last year or so. Often prompted by strong-minded hoteliers, several ad hoc partnerships have sprung up between vendors with complementary products working together to offer more complete and better-supported combinations of systems.

More formal initiatives have promoted this trend by providing neutral territory where competing vendors can meet to work on common problems. The Open Travel Alliance (OTA) has linked hotels, airlines, and car rental companies to resolve data-exchange issues for the whole travel industry. The Hotel Technology Next Generation (HTNG) initiative has taken a more pragmatic approach, with hoteliers working directly with vendors in sponsored workgroups to identify practical, real-world sets of systems and interfaces that they will buy and implement. The initial focus was on more comprehensive PMS/sales and catering (S&C)/private branch exchange (PBX)/pay-per-view (PPV) links. The next three workgroups are focused on guestroom technology, PMS/revenue management system (RMS)/central reservations system (CRS) distribution management, and the use of Web services for property systems communications. Other groups include the Accepted Practices Exchange, which is working on meetings technology, and the Open Building Information Exchange, for such building infrastructure systems as climate control, access security, and utilities.

Property Management Systems

PMSs are still the core of on-property guest data management and continue to expand to include more depth in guest information and preference tracking, group block bookings, charge routing flexibility, housekeeping schedule flexibility, and myriad other, smaller improvements.

In addition to the expected growth in detailed functionality, many PMSs now include whole modules that were long the preserve of specialized systems. What used to be a very rooms-oriented system will now quite often also include point-of-sale (POS) functionality and S&C, spa management, condominium owner accounting, and club membership management modules. As PMSs grow to cover these other operational areas, hoteliers need fewer systems to provide the same breadth of guest data and the data is more accurate because it hasn't needed to be translated from one system to another.

However, no system currently provides everything a hotelier needs, and indeed it may not be appropriate or desirable to replace an existing well-performing system with an equivalent module from a more comprehensive system. Interfaces, therefore, are and will remain a fact of life for every property.

Reflecting the marketing trend toward dynamic packaging, vendors now provide much more flexibility in the packaging capabilities of their systems. This manifests in both external and internal choices. The ability to build packages on the fly offers guests more choices in building their own combinations of such services as spa appointments, golf, tennis, horseback riding, dining reservations, room upgrades, and so on, while previous practice usually restricted sales to preconfigured combinations. This has come about both through the increased scope of PMSs (since many of these package components are now an integral part of the system's database) and through better PMS interfaces with the specialized activities management systems.

External to the hotel's operations, dynamic packaging offers travelers a way to book nonhotel components of their trip (airfare, rental cars, golf, cruises, etc.) directly from the hotel's Web site. In contrast to the internal package flexibility, which usually is provided by direct linking between the systems, these external links usually require a third-party specialist system to gather the information from each source and aggregate it for the user. This will become simpler as more systems adopt OTA specifications for guest profile definitions and data transfer across all air, car, and hotel providers, but that will take several years. For now, the process usually takes place behind the scenes so that the user isn't aware of the challenges.

CRS/PMS Roles

A fundamental shift has occurred in the relative roles of the two main hospitality systems—CRSs and PMSs. The latter have long been considered the core of hotel automation, since they are the on-property hubs that capture all information about a guest's stay, including reservations, room selection, check-in, all activities and charges posted to the folio, check-out, and accounts receivable. CRSs used to be seen mostly as limited-function tools to help call center agents forward a guest's booking to a property.

However, there has been a major shift in focus to concentrate on central customer relationship management (CRM) databases of guest profile and history information, both for a more complete view of guest activities and preferences and database-driven targeted marketing. Coupled with this is the more fragmented distribution world where traditional global distribution systems have been supplemented with myriad Internet-based booking sites requiring a detailed knowledge of how different guest market segments book through different channels. As a result, the CRS/CRM combination has become the main focus of most hotels' marketing and booking efforts.

The PMS is still vital in its role of managing every aspect of a guest's increasingly complex stay at a property, especially in the resort world, but it is now seen as the system that tracks and compiles guest data while the guest happens to be on site. After check-out, all relevant data is forwarded to central databases for consolidation and whatever further action might be required.

With this growing awareness of the value of complete, consolidated information, and the desire to increase accuracy and efficiency by reducing the number of times data is transferred between systems, it's inevitable that vendors will blur the lines between CRSs and PMSs by combining the two, along with whatever other modules each considers most relevant. MICROS Systems, Inc.'s OPERA Enterprise Solution, for example, includes CRS, PMS, S&C, and CRM modules within the same application and database. Long-established PMS vendor Hotel Information Systems has developed a modern, Web services–based CRS/CRM system and is converting its PMS to the same platform for more complete integration between the two. The trend toward centralized systems hosted at one site away from the properties and accessed over dedicated networks strongly encourages a more global view of these systems and how they ought to be integrated for maximum effectiveness.

Rate Search and Channel Management Tools

With the trend toward personalization of travel showing no signs of slowing down, the number of specialized travel Web sites has grown exponentially. These range from the very specific (e.g., hiking treks in the Himalayas) to the very general (e.g., cruises) and from hotel chains' brand sites (e.g., www.marriott.com) to all-purpose travel search engines (e.g., www.expedia.com). It's no surprise, therefore, that as the number of different target market segments has increased, distribution channel management has become one of most complex and difficult tasks hotel management faces.

An abundance of rate-search services has become available to hoteliers to fulfill their need for accurate, up-to-the-minute information about how their hotels compare to other hotels in their peer group. These services typically report posted information for various dates and market segments and feed this information directly into an RMS to provide on-screen assistance. However, being sure that an accurate apples-to-apples rate comparison is being completed remains an issue, as does making sure that the most important distribution channels for the hotel are all being tracked, since they may be different for different hotels. In addition, most of these tools initially have focused only on the one-way process of gathering information.

To help revenue managers supply the right mix of rooms and rate availability on the right distribution channel sites at the right time for the right customers, automated revenue management tools have become increasingly sophisticated. However, actually posting the recommended rates and room availability to the individual sites still remains largely a manual process.

Electronic interfaces between the PMS or CRS and the various sites have been slow to develop, and hotels often must use a separate extranet for each channel that needs updating. The progress that has occurred has been led by IAC Travel via its Newtrade Technologies division, which is developing direct interfaces from its two main sites (www.expedia.com and www.hotels.com) to major chains' CRSs and to the main PMSs. Several other vendors have developed channel management tools that allow a revenue manager to distribute rate and room availability updates to multiple Web sites chosen by the hotel from a single screen. High-profile programs currently include EZ Yield, Hotel Booking Solutions's hobooBox, and TravelCLICK's Channel Manager.

Not surprisingly, channel management tools and rate search tools are being merged into a single service more and more often. In addition, distribution channel management functionality increasingly is being built into CRSs and PMSs with their growing capabilities and integration with RMSs.

While these tools are useful, permitting distribution through a larger number of sites and relieving reservation staff of some data maintenance duties, they are not yet perfect. They may use unauthorized links to the channel sites through terminal emulation and they sometimes do not link to all of the sites with which a hotel or chain would like to work.

Revenue Management

Automated revenue management is still primarily a property-level application, though it is being more and more widely accepted as a legitimate tool for less than four and five star properties and properties under less-than-high-occupancy conditions. Both traditional and new vendors now offer it in remotely hosted format, which has made it considerably more cost effective.

Given the increased awareness of the importance of considering all aspects of a guest's or company's business with the hotel, revenue management now extends past consideration of the free independent traveler (FIT) market segment to also include evaluation of and recommendations about group activity. There's also a strong interest in managing a city-group of hotels as a single unit, varying revenue management factors to steer business to the hotel where it will do the most good for the group as a whole.

Since RMSs are still the domain of specialized statistical programming vendors due to the uniquely complex mathematical demands, their vendors are forming tighter links with other vendors in semiformal working partnerships. Although much work still remains to be done, RMSs are becoming more closely integrated with other systems (PMSs, CRSs, S&C systems, and eventually spa, golf, and other activity management systems) and outside data sources (competitive rate search engines, Smith Travel Research, TravelCLICK, etc.), which will result in more accurate and better focused recommendations.

However, with increased integration comes the need to not micromanage the hotel's operations on an automated basis and to maintain a real-world perspective. If all hotels in a peer group track each other's rates and have integrated their systems to automatically post updates to remain competitive in response to changes, setting the response brackets too fine could result in the systems chasing each other's tails and achieving no result beyond overloading the computer systems.

One issue of some concern is that the role of reservation manager is morphing into that of revenue manager, too frequently with little training and follow-up support. While all reservation managers practice revenue management to some extent, the complexity of the current environment mandates specialized training and a full awareness of the impact integrated systems have on each other.

Web Sites

In the never-ending battle to capture travelers' attention, hotel, chain, and third-party Web sites are becoming more elaborate in functionality and (fortunately) better designed. Improved descriptions are now accompanied by steadily better photography, including 360-degree panoramic tours, often sourced from a central image library maintained by the hotel chain. This library, which typically also includes general descriptive information about a hotel and its function space, is also often interfaced to automated request for proposal–response systems to allow a faster turnaround of inquiries for contract bids.

Online booking engines are also becoming more streamlined and user-friendly, more often allowing travelers to retrieve and modify their bookings directly. Many also provide the ability for frequent-guest program members to access their accounts and update their profiles online. The latest innovation is the addition of packaging capabilities that extend from the opportunity to reserve additional on-property services (spa, golf, dining, etc.) to fully dynamic packaging capability in adding air transportation and/or car rental to the core lodging booking.

Internet Marketing

While the proportion of reservations made on brand Web sites is increasing, many travelers still check several other options before making the actual booking, continuing to increase the already strong influence of search engines. If the guest can't find a hotel's site, he or she can't book from it.

As a result, search engine optimization (SEO) services have grown quickly in number. Initial results can be very rewarding, but steady maintenance is also required as travelers' search phrases change over time and different search engines enhance their ranking techniques.

Many hotels supplement the relatively passive SEO approach with use of search engines' pay-for-position advertising capabilities to improve their positioning on search lists and add advertisements to search engine result displays. These capabilities are becoming more sophisticated as vendors add rules-based functionality. In the past, it was common to display an ad whenever a search phrase mentioned a specific city or location. Travel dates can now be considered so a hotel's ad appears only on its low-occupancy dates.

Self-Service Kiosks

Self-service check-in kiosks are finally becoming mainstream. After a series of minor trials over the last 20 years, their recent widespread acceptance at airline counters has encouraged many hotel chains to commit to them on a widespread basis. Most current designs are deliberately limited to retrieving reservations, checking in the guest, producing a guestroom key, and handling check-out and folio printing.

However, the opportunity and technology exist to add several more options to these functions, including:

- A hotel room layout plan to help guests select a room with specific attributes or location.

- Group delegate check-in messages and printable agendas.

- Upselling the guest to a higher rate room or package.

- Printing airline boarding passes at check-out.

However, care needs to be taken not to overly complicate the user interface and delay both the guest using the kiosk and those in the queue forming behind him or her.

Similarly, it's tempting to provide full Internet access so that guests can research local restaurants and attractions, printing out directions and maps as needed. Again, there's the risk of such usage blocking guests wanting to check in or out using the device, and these concierge-like activities are best handled on a dedicated kiosk further removed from the front desk.

Kiosks are never going to be the answer for every guest, and they probably won't save any staffing costs since hotels still need to keep front desk staff available to answer queries. However, they have a very definite place in the lobby of extended-stay and limited-service properties where the front desk may be unattended at night, and there's a good-sized segment of guests who will be very happy to use them in most other types of operations.

Audiovisual Meeting Technologies

With a general move from annual larger, national presentation-style meetings to more frequent smaller, regional collaborative-style meetings, there's been a corresponding trend toward maximizing their effectiveness through technology. They're not being replaced by video conferencing, as was feared a few years ago; instead, video conferencing and other advanced hotel-based systems are used to get the maximum value out of the on-site meeting. Examples include:

- Simulations that lead multiple small workgroups through a series of experiences to enhance their decision-making skills in competition with each other. Their decisions and results are compiled and later analyzed centrally for everyone's benefit. An example would be a group of motorcycle dealers separated into teams with each going through a simulation of operating a dealership for five years. A moderator would introduce such challenges as parts shortages, an economic downturn, or a labor strike.

- Video teleconferencing that provides two-way audio and video, mostly for groups of 12 or fewer.

- Webcasting that uses the hotel's high-speed Internet access to broadcast events on the Internet, either in real time or later, so remote participants can browse into the event and watch and hear the presenter and presentation materials.

- Webconferencing that allows participants to interact with the presented materials (document sharing) and, if necessary, the application itself (application sharing). The most popular of these service providers are WebEx and Microsoft's Live Meeting (formerly Placeware).

- Digital events that include any or all of the above, plus audio and video conferencing, Web newsletter input from listserv distributors, and feeds from weblogs and news sites. Digital audiovisual input/output is fast becoming an essential and integral part of business life. Providing a flexible, powerful infrastructure to meet clients' needs is the way to attract their business.

Technologically, the move from analog to digital audiovisual equipment has only become stronger as prices for the latter have fallen. Digital signal processing greatly simplifies systems through combining the functions of several previously separate components into one unit, provides far more flexibility and control over the signal processing, requires less rack space and air-conditioning, and takes less labor to install. The systems themselves are becoming more intelligent and communicative with each other, providing for more interconnectivity and integration with telecommunications services, including the Internet.

However, in contrast to hotel management systems, this has led to increased competition among manufacturers who were once collaborators and a counterintuitive trend away from standards-based communications protocols. While the industry has reluctantly accepted standards for communications, manufacturers are competing to maximize the performance of their equipment at the cost of standards compatibility. This can cause problems if audiovisual equipment is hooked up to the same network as other hotel systems and can make it very difficult to make substitutions of equipment on the fly.

Challenges also occur in the specifying and contracting world where each party has its own "right" way of designing the systems. Installation and support will be easier if a complete system is acquired from a single vendor, but this usually restricts the ability of the hotel to make any changes or enhancements without going back to the vendor.

Electronic signage is fast expanding in the hospitality arena as well. Visual information systems or electronic reader boards located in public assembly areas perform several functions. They are used primarily to provide information on the location and times of the meetings and activities and for the hotel to promote such amenities as golf, spas, gift shops, and food and beverage outlets.

Public area displays are typically flat panels, often with door-side alphanumeric or LCD displays adjacent to each meeting room entry. These messaging systems can also be integrated with PMSs and S&C systems to distribute meeting information to the appropriate guestrooms.

As for the infrastructure in the meeting rooms—power, telecommunication and Internet services, cabling, and connectivity—standard practice is to install multiple bundles of Category 5e cabling tie lines to all function spaces with fiber to the larger rooms. All lines are brought back to patch panels in the audiovisual equipment room so any connector can be assigned any service in any room at any time.

It is also important to provide wired high-speed Internet services in addition to the ubiquitous Wireless Fidelity (WiFi). All presentation or meeting functions that are Internet-based must be wired; wireless usually will *not* be sufficient for security concerns, and many corporate clients and government agencies do not permit it in their meetings.

This cabling infrastructure must be able to provide telephone services as well. Corporate local area networks (LANs) can be securely accessed via dial-up switched services. The current best practice for video teleconferences is still via such switched services as integrated services digital network (ISDN) and T1 lines. This will be the case for at least the next few years.

It's also critical to start with the right foundation of good architecture, interior design, and infrastructure. Even the best technology can't fix a bad (e.g., noisy, dim, or poorly designed) meeting space. For all the possibilities for digital audiovisual systems, quality meetings start with a high-quality sound system (for voice) based on an array of ceiling speakers. All meetings need voice reinforcement, and there is no better way to provide high intelligibility in the typical flexible function space than this approach.

VoIP Telephone Systems

Voice over Internet Protocol (VoIP) telephone systems transmit voice communications over Internet-based data networks and have received a great deal of publicity. They do have several significant advantages under certain circumstances. Since they're just another form of computer, albeit one that happens to look like and behave like a telephone, they can be run on a shared data network like any other system and can be integrated with other systems in increasingly sophisticated ways.

The advantages are that they're cheaper to install and maintain (since the work can be done by a standard PC/network technician instead of a telephone specialist), phone calls can be administered quickly, flexibly, and remotely, and they can be integrated very effectively with other systems. Since the PBX operator doesn't have to be on property, it's quite feasible for one call center to handle all calls, voice mail messages, and call accounting functions for several properties from one central site. Phone extensions can also be linked to the PMS so, for example, a guest can have the names of other members of her group displayed on her guestroom phone for one-touch dialing to their rooms, can access her group meeting agenda on the phone, and much, much more.

Another common VoIP advantage often mentioned is that it's very simple to move a telephone instrument or extension—just plug the phone into a network point anywhere else, sign in to the PBX, and it's recognized with the same extension, speed-dial numbers, and ring tones as it had before. While valuable in a commercial office environment, this feature has far less application in the hospitality world, because while administrative phones may need to be moved from time to time, guestroom phones won't.

The major drawback so far is cost. While the systems themselves are competitively priced, the guestroom phones are significantly more expensive than traditional units ($200–$300 each at present, compared to $70–$120), since they must contain basic computing and display capability. This differential will undoubtedly fall over the next few years, and the flexibility and data integration of these systems will become even more attractive. For now, though, they make much more sense for new installations than as retrofits in existing properties.

Two other issues to be addressed are call pricing and security. In contrast to the historic approach of pricing calls by time and distance, future pricing for IP-based telephony is likely to be based on the bandwidth used. Many details remain to be worked, though, such as taxes and surcharges. For example, VoIP is currently classified as an information service and is free of those charges, but this will almost certainly change.

Security also requires careful planning and management. The risks of telephone fraud are high enough already, but are limited mostly to excessive charges from unauthorized use. Once the phone system is part of the main data network, and especially as it becomes increasingly integrated with the data systems, all access points and levels of authorized usage must be far more tightly controlled and secured.

Overall, VoIP telephone systems will continue to experience slow acceptance in the lodging arena because there's still a huge working inventory of analog and digital systems that will be around for many years to come. The first area in which VoIP will benefit lodging will be the call center because it provides individual flexibility and control, which translates directly into agent responsiveness to customers. Even if it's still early in its development and the lodging industry will in general lag behind the business world in adopting it, VoIP is definitely here to stay.

Centralized Systems

Despite improvements in the breadth of systems functionality and system interaction, more systems with more functionality are required to handle more mixes of operating environments with higher demands for data accuracy, analysis, and uptime. Few properties are able to afford the resources to support this complex mix cost-effectively on their own and the complexity of operating and supporting the current mix of on-site systems is reaching breaking point. As a result, centralized systems in which users access a computer system situated somewhere other than in the workplace are once again receiving significant attention.

Advantages

A centralized approach allows resources to be concentrated for maximum effectiveness, providing a more supportable and reliable environment with better data and operational standardization. The many advantages include greater reliability and availability, more consistent performance, better vendor support, better security, the avoidance of capital exchange battles, ease of new application introduction, and—for multi-property operations—huge improvements in data consolidation and reporting, simpler interfaces, easier integration of new properties into the system.

Greater Reliability and Availability. Very few individual properties can afford to run their critical applications in the kind of access-secured, fully protected environment available from professional hosting companies, with the software running on duplicated, redundant servers with duplicated power supplies, back-ups, 24-hour monitoring, and full protection against viruses and spam, all designed to keep the systems available and performing efficiently all the time. Sharing the costs of such an environment between many hotels or even hotel chains makes it affordable and practical for each.

A frequent concern expressed over centralized systems is their vulnerability if the communications link goes down. However, the experience of many companies already using them is that link reliability is the least of their problems, especially compared with the challenges of keeping site-based hardware and software running. In the United States, communications link reliability often approaches 99.998 percent, a highly acceptable figure. Many software applications are often down for longer periods than that just to load enhancements.

More Consistent Performance. Hosted environments also enhance performance stability. Since the hosting companies have more powerful servers than individual properties, they also will have more reserves of power and will be better able to smooth out peaks in demand since the hotels won't all require peak performance at the same time. There will be some common high-demand periods during the night audit and end-of-day processing, but the lack of concurrency in the peak demands of check-in and check-out provides a performance cushion for everyone.

Better Vendor Support. Technical support is more available and of higher quality at a central site since it's more feasible to spread the costs of 24-hour skilled technicians across multiple properties. Upgrades and patches are installed consistently by the vendor technicians at their own location, not by multiple IT coordinators at the properties when they have time and maybe not in complete accordance with the instructions. If there are problems with a new release, a central system can be rolled back quickly to the previous release without complications.

The vendor also has more incentive to perform high-quality testing before implementing any patch or upgrade, since any such change will immediately affect many properties. Smaller properties should see a higher level of support responsiveness because any problem they experience will likely also affect the biggest multi-property users, who will exert considerably more influence on the speed of identifying and resolving the issue.

Better Security. Firewalls, anti-virus and anti-spam software, user authentication, and remote access management for sales managers are all better managed on a skilled, professional level rather than left to overworked management and staff.

Avoidance of Capital Expenditure Battles. If a hotel is paying for its systems with a monthly or transaction-based fee, the annual competition with other departments for capital funds simply goes away. The hosting fee should include regular updates to the servers to keep them current, and while the hotel will still need to budget for regular workstation upgrades or replacement, this can be covered in a lease program. Since centralized systems require only a browser or thin-client application instead of a full PC software suite, workstations can be simpler and less expensive. In many cases a simple thin-client appliance can be used instead of a PC, reducing both purchase and support costs.

Ease of New Application Introduction. A prime benefit for many hotel chains is the ability to introduce a new system to the organization quickly, a huge benefit when a property is reflagged and needs to be brought into the chain as quickly as possible. As long as the hotel already has a standard PC/browser environment, just typing the new system's address into the browser establishes a connection. Of course, there is still much operational work to be done in training the staff in the new system and in the standard data parameters used by the new management company, but the technical issues become almost insignificant.

Benefits for Multi-Property Operations

Data Consolidation and Reporting. All of the above benefits accrue to a single hotel just as much as to a multi-property organization, but the latter also enjoy other advantages, whether they decide to host a system for their properties themselves or rely on the vendor. Key among these are the twin benefits of having standardized data across all properties for consistency and accuracy, and far simpler consolidation of that data allowing for accurate, timely comparative reporting, data analysis, and guest profile consolidation. Sharing operational data so all hotels in a group can see which are performing well and which are underperforming in certain areas also brings in peer pressure as a powerful driver of improved efficiencies and profitability.

Simpler Interfaces. A multi-property chain using a centralized PMS can implement single interfaces to its CRS, to a centralized RMS or S&C system, to the Internet for Web bookings, and possibly even to a centralized VoIP telephone and call accounting system, instead of having to implement and manage one of each at every property. Some interface links still need to remain on site to non-centralized implementations of POS, PBX, PPV movies, and so on, but the improvements in reliability and supportability by concentrating as many as possible centrally are obvious and enticing.

Easier Integration of New Properties. When a new property joins a group with an already-defined standard system configuration, it is significantly more efficient and faster to produce a copy and customize it for local variations than to build a new one from scratch. Since it's hosted, it's already installed on the servers, leaving one less major task to perform.

Feasible for Smaller Properties. Centralization can make it feasible to implement systems in smaller properties where they were previously cost-prohibitive. A classic example of this is PPV movies. Few vendors have ever been keen to install their revenue-sharing systems in properties of less than 150 rooms because they seldom generate enough revenue to justify putting the central equipment on site. If the service is delivered over a network from a remote central site, the only cost is that of servicing the additional rooms and it is purely incremental. Other examples of potentially significant cost savings are VoIP telephone systems and the centralization of call accounting and voice messaging.

Service Level Agreements

Service level agreements (SLAs) are essential to ensuring the effective delivery of services, but they need to be approached with a sense of reality from both sides. Vendors need to understand how critical their service is to the hoteliers and the true impact of downtime. Hoteliers also need to understand that achieving those last few percentage points toward 100 percent uptime can get very expensive. An uptime of 99.5 percent might sound good, but it means that service is likely to be unavailable for 0.5 percent of a year, which is nearly two days. Fortunately it's relatively affordable to get to 99.95 percent uptime and most services offer this, though perhaps not in all parts of the globe. Each hotelier has to strike a balance between cost and the impact of occasional interruptions.

Clearly there must be financial penalties if the vendor fails to meet the guaranteed uptime, but these too must be kept in proportion. They have to be significant enough to get the vendor's attention, but a hotel can't impose consequential damages on the vendor even if downtime causes it to lose a major piece of business.

Vendor-Hosting vs. Self-Hosting

If hoteliers decide that the centralized system concept makes sense for them, there's still the decision of whether to contract for their own hosting services or contract with the software vendor to use theirs. It's basically a trade-off based on their degree of comfort with the vendor's ability to provide the service reliably and the degree of control they want to have over the whole process.

Self-hosting lets hoteliers keep their data stored on their own servers and allows them to test every new software release independently of the vendor before loading it. However, the trade-off is that they must then manage three separate support agreements and SLAs: one each with the software vendor, the hosting company, and the communications provider.

The alternative is to contract directly with the vendor to take full responsibility for all three aspects of providing the service to the properties—software, hosting, and communications. With only one SLA to deal with, it is then the vendor's responsibility to fix problems within tightly defined time limits, wherever they lie.

Some might suggest that if they can't rely on their vendor to deliver bug-free releases, they don't trust them to host the whole delivery process. Keep in mind that vendors will be using outside hosting and communications vendors and facilities just as a hotel would. The more hotels hosted on their servers, the more incentive they have to improve the quality of their releases, since more clients will be immediately affected by any problems. They'll also be quicker to roll back to an earlier release if a bug surfaces.

Support should also see significant improvement since hosting multiple clients gives the vendor more direct feedback from more properties using the software under a variety of circumstances and they'll be able to track what's happening directly on their servers without having to interpret third-party reports of circumstances from the users. Smaller hotels especially ought to see an improvement in support since they'll be sharing the software with larger groups that put more pressure on the system in daily use and more pressure on the vendor to fix problems.

It's not a simple choice. If a hotel hosts its own servers, the vendor can still have remote access to them to monitor unusual events and track down problems, though without the direct feedback from other hoteliers' usage. If the vendor hosts them, hotels can still access their test servers to verify the quality of new software releases before authorizing their introduction. Some hotel chains centralize many systems but still install PMS servers at the properties, often in secure rooms and monitored remotely by central support technicians. This complicates both support and the roll-out of software updates, but it does remove concerns about data inaccessibility at the properties in case of communications failure. It all has to do with a hotel's comfort level and individual circumstances.

Communications—Internet vs. Dedicated Lines

With the rapid expansion of broadband coverage, encryption, and the adoption of virtual private networks, many centralized hotel systems work very well over the Internet. Once a property has a reliable broadband connection from a trusted Internet service provider, the connection can be used for access to many remote applications as well as for general Internet usage by guests and staff. A back-up link (dial-up or ISDN) with automatic failover is always a good idea.

For PMSs and POS systems where response time and dependability are critical, the Internet is really viable only for smaller properties. While it's remarkably resilient and designed from the start to automatically reroute around broken links, its performance can vary with general traffic demands. Going with a dedicated communications network for these systems pays dividends in predictability and reliable performance for most properties, and such networks have become surprisingly affordable as their usage has spread.

Web-Native vs. Web-Enabled

The vendors are likely to describe their centralized systems as either Web-native or Web-enabled. Web-enabled systems usually are more established and provide remote access over the Internet or other IP-based network by using Citrix or Microsoft's Terminal Services on the workstations. These off-load the actual software application processing work from the workstation to the central server and use the workstation as a display device to show the changed screens, but they don't change the way the underlying application works.

In contrast, Web-native systems are usually newer, have been written using more modern languages and approaches, and are inherently designed for use by browser-equipped PCs via any IP-based network. The browser is used to reach the central site, but the application then usually loads a small client application on the workstation to handle screen displays and whatever minor local processing might be required.

Since they tend to be more recently developed, Web-native systems don't always have the rich functionality or established reliability of the Web-enabled ones. However, they're likely to be better positioned for future development, especially for integrating with other systems. Either approach means that simpler and less powerful "thin-client" workstations can be used at the property level than are required for traditional client-server software architecture, a major advantage for the centralized approach.

Commitment

One objection raised to the concept of buying software as a service is that the payments never end—hotels sign up for a minimum commitment (usually three years) but continue to pay as long as they use the software. With the more traditional practice of buying and installing a system, of course, payments stop eventually—but only for the most visible costs. The hidden operational costs of running on older, under-supported, poorly-integrated systems on hardware that's not kept up-to-date and running efficiently will keep increasing whether accounted for or not. Paying a monthly fee for reliable, well-managed, perpetually up-to-date systems allows hoteliers to concentrate on using those tools to run the operation more effectively and imaginatively. The payback in terms of time and focus is well worth the investment.

Business Intelligence

The demand for accurate, comprehensive operational data and intelligent analysis tools has never been stronger. Revenue may be on an upswing, but profits have not grown at the same rate and the intelligent management of expenses and costs is as critical as making the right operational and marketing decisions. Given this, the need for the central consolidation and analysis of operational and guest profile data—in other words for performance management and BI tools—continues to grow.

What makes this more challenging is the increased complexity of the business (mixed-use buildings add many more property owners into the mix, for example), the pressure on margins from rising customer-service expectations, and the unpredictability of travel volumes due to wars, government actions, and terrorist threats and actions. Owners, investors, and operators all need real-time access to the critical measures driving the business to provide timely, useful information to decision makers, identify problems while they are still small, and assess trends as quickly as possible as they develop.

The two biggest trends recently have been time compression and reporting flexibility. We've moved from monthly Smith Travel Reports that arrived three or four weeks after the close of the month to weekly reports and, most recently, to daily data reporting. Many multi-property data consolidation tasks now include Web-based data entry and reporting, with preliminary data distributed early in the morning and audited data available before the end of the day.

At the same time, with the multi-owner complexity of many (if not most) properties, the number of people needing their own sub-set of the data continues to expand. A multi-hotel operation typically will need to provide reporting and analysis tools for management staff at property, regional, headquarters, and brand management levels, as well as for functional area management on site, development, owners, asset managers, investor relations, and so on. Modern systems can provide all these clients with data in their own formats quickly and at secure Web sites so they can access their reports and drill down to the underlying detail, wherever they happen to be.

The better BI systems now have more data-collection options, are able to attach to any open data sources (PeopleSoft, Oracle, DB2, Microsoft Access, Smith Travel Research databases, etc.), have flexible, straightforward drag-and-drop ad hoc query builders, and allow companies to preconfigure their own online analytical processing (OLAP) cubes to give line managers access to fast, flexible analysis with full drill-down. Dashboard views are easily constructed to give near-real-time indicators of key performance measures and can guide users through the entire budgeting/forecasting process by property, region, or other breakdown.

The data collection challenge has grown both in scope and complexity as more and different systems are used to collect and track data about more aspects of hotel operations and guest activities, both inside and outside the property. Relevant information sources typically include the PMS, POS systems, S&C systems, spa/golf/other activities management systems, CRM software, accounting, payroll, comment cards, Smith Travel Reports, TravelCLICK, PKF Consulting's Hospitality Research Group, financial indices, currency exchange rates, and so on.

The extraction of data from all these disparate sources and its normalization and consolidation must all be resolved before BI tools can help provide intelligent decision guidance. Most hotel systems now have at least rudimentary (and often quite sophisticated) data extraction and export tools, but there's also been strong growth in the number of systems that have their own built-in BI analysis tools or optional third-party modules providing similar functions. Most PMSs now have at least a custom report generator, plus data export facilities for more detailed analysis. The more comprehensive CRSs, PMSs, and S&C systems have their own data warehouses, often with predefined OLAP cubes.

However, despite the growth of more comprehensive systems that reduce the need for data translation between different vendors' products and the significant benefits of cross-industry data definition standards established by such groups as OTA and HTNG, the operational challenges of collecting clean and complete data at the point of entry show no signs of diminishing and will always remain the primary obstacle to accurate data analysis. This drive for data consistency is obviously the key reason so many hotel chains require their properties to use standard systems for all critical areas of operations and is also a strong incentive for them to consider using centrally hosted systems for all properties to access instead of each having their own.

Network Infrastructure

Two related trends are combining to make hotel network infrastructure simpler, cheaper to install, more powerful, and more flexible. Network technology itself continues to provide more capability, both wired and wireless, and intervendor cooperation is allowing more systems to run over fewer links, reducing the number of separate networks required and lowering implementation costs.

The combination provides significant advantages. The most common cabling standard now in use calls for Category 6 (Cat 6) network wiring to each guestroom and to the various administration points, with a fiber optic backbone back to the central servers. This higher-performance cable can accommodate more traffic than the earlier Cat 5 standard and allows more systems to share a single line to the guestrooms, an approach called a unified network. At the same time, the various guestroom technology vendors either have moved or are moving from a mix of Ethernet and coaxial cable types to IP communications, and many are cooperating with the HTNG workgroup to define how their various products should interact.

A typical unified network would run a single Cat 6 cable to each guestroom to carry the signals required for the telephones, the guest's high-speed Internet access (whether direct to the guest's laptop or through the television), free-to-guest television and audio programming, mini-bars, electronic door locks, thermostats, and so on. Clearly this requires the full use of appropriate digital systems and would be an expensive retrofit, but for new build properties it provides significant savings in implementation and equally significant flexibility in the systems that can be transmitted over it.

The main exceptions at this time are the providers of PPV movies. Concern over possible piracy of their copyrighted programming currently requires separate coaxial cabling to each room, despite the technological feasibility of distributing video content over Cat 6 cable. This is expected to change as copyright management software becomes more widespread and practical and eliminates the need for coaxial cable to be installed at all.

Outside the guestrooms, the use of the LAN for the property's closed circuit television monitoring and security system can also provide enhanced functionality and flexibility. With camera input viewable via the network, a monitoring station can be established at any PC, not only at the guards' desk. This allows flexibility in the night shift monitoring positions and provides multiple viewing options for management, from providing support for housekeeping or front desk staff to automatic alarming for night personnel based on motion detection at any camera.

High-speed wireless networks—the ubiquitous WiFi—are also becoming more powerful and practical. Each new iteration provides greater range, more bandwidth, and better security. The growing public demand for wireless Internet access shows absolutely no signs of slackening. It's now almost an imperative for every hotel to offer wireless access in at least its public areas, if not also the guestrooms. From a practical viewpoint, it's also a cost-effective way to extend administrative network coverage to hard-to-reach areas of the property, where cabling costs would be prohibitive.

The security of wireless networks has also improved to the point where it's much more practical to share a single network between guest Internet access and several administrative and operations programs. The latter can include restaurant POS, housekeeping, engineering, and management systems. In all of these applications, the use of wireless handheld personal digital assistant devices can put essential information in the hands of key staff without impeding their mobility. Few hotels exploit this opportunity at present, possibly due to the costs of ensuring wireless coverage throughout the property, but using the same network as the guests' wireless high-speed Internet access makes it much more cost-effective.

New cell phone antenna repeater systems and Nextel repeater systems are also becoming more common to enhance guest and employee communications systems, including the implementation of Blackberry and other wireless e-mail communication devices for staff communications and trouble ticket records. This can eliminate the need for separate radio communications for staff.

One emerging trend with great potential to change the landscape is WiMAX, a new wireless networking protocol that promises to provide both greater speed and a range of up to 30 miles compared to the current WiFi limits of a few hundred feet. If all travelers will eventually be able use WiMAX to connect to the Internet on a mobile, city-wide basis, the need for hotels to provide their own access points will diminish considerably. At this stage, though, it's not clear how effectively WiMAX will penetrate building structures, and some kind of bridge device may be necessary to link an exterior WiMAX signal to an internal WiFi network for guest use.

The trend toward hotels using more digital systems on common IP networks and having permanent high-speed connections to the Internet makes it feasible to offer such systems remotely, instead of requiring them to be installed at the hotel property itself. Hotel networks and PC workstations can—and, in cost-effective operations, really should—be monitored remotely by outside maintenance and support companies. With the trend toward VoIP telephone systems and digital video programming, for example, it becomes very cost-effective to provide these systems from one central location, sharing the server and support infrastructure between all properties served.

Guestroom Technology

Certainly one of the most visible trends in hospitality technology has been in upgraded guestroom technology, both in terms of the guest experience and in the impact on investment needs to meet them. Recently, high-speed Internet access has become a mainstream requirement and now flat-panel television displays and the ability to play back programming from the guests' own portable devices are leading the way.

The old paradigm in which hotel guestrooms offered a technology environment superior to that found in most guests' homes (mostly in having larger-screen televisions and a selection of first-run PPV movies) has been totally eclipsed in the last few years. More travelers are familiar with the size and clarity of large-screen flat-panel displays (either in their own homes or in general business and commercial use), are used to being able to select from a very wide range of movies with full pause/rewind control over play, and increasingly carry their own wide selection of music and even video programs with them on portable devices.

Movie/Television Standards

PPV movies moved to digital technology relatively recently, storing the programs on computer disks instead of in racks of videotape players, thus providing much more flexibility and control. Guests can now select from the full range of movies in the system instead of just those not currently being watched by others and have full pause/rewind control from the guestroom set. Digital storage allows other programming to be added relatively easily, and premium television series episodes, instructional videos (golf, yoga, etc.), and music CDs are usually available. However, the advent of flat-screen displays has made possible a quantum leap in providing far higher quality viewing of movies, even if regular television programming is often rendered at lower quality than with a conventional set.

This last point is important, but transitional. The change from standard to high-definition (HD) transmission formats will take a while to work through. Until then, the display of analog programming often will suffer as receivers and displays are optimized more to the demands of higher-definition digital formats. One issue is the difference in screen aspect ratios, from traditional 4:3 to 16:9 for HD. All HD format televisions can stretch the image to fill the wider screen, but they distort it in the process.

We are in a transition period where both analog and digital broadcasts of HD programming coexist on off-air, cable, and satellite systems. HD transmissions have been in a chicken-and-egg situation for several years, with broadcasters reluctant to invest in higher-cost HD programming until a sufficient base of installed HD receivers can display it, but sales of the latter being slow because of the lack of suitable programming.

The Federal Communications Commission has set July 1, 2007, as the end of this transition period. At that point, any programming available in both analog HD format and digital HD format must drop the analog version. Hotels with traditional coaxial cable infrastructure will be required to install converters on their head-end equipment to switch the digital signals to analog for distribution, just as domestic consumers will have to do for their home sets.

Hotels that have IP-based infrastructure to distribute video content over the digital data network will already be able to distribute this higher-quality digital signal. It's impossible to tell how long it will be before digital HD transmissions become the norm, but the unprecedented rise in sales of large-format flat-panel displays for home use is definitely encouraging; people are clearly willing to pay for quality.

Flat Panels and Alarm Clocks

The early plasma-screen displays were seized on by several chains as a way of distinguishing themselves, but were very expensive. Despite having dazzlingly sharp, vibrant displays, they had drawbacks regarding weight, heat, noise, images burning on the screen, and a relatively short life, with color and contrast both fading after a few years. However, they were visually striking, both in themselves as well as in terms of their image quality.

Just as importantly, they've allowed a rethinking of guestroom design toward a sleeker, more open modern style, since expensive, custom-made armoires are no longer required to conceal their main structure. That factor combined with falling unit prices and much improved reliability (both plasma and LCD) has made them the standard for new construction or complete refurbishing projects. Justifying them for retrofits is more challenging, of course, especially if the guestroom television sets are relatively new.

One way to increase their appeal is to let them be used for other purposes than just television/movie display. One obvious use might be as a display for a guest's laptop computer. While this is technically simple, there are social and operational drawbacks. Most computer users are comfortable with having the screen at a conventional distance from their eyes, and many older users have reading glasses prescribed for that distance. Transferring one's focus to a more distant screen, even if significantly larger, can be more strain than it's worth. Many guests also like to have the TV on for occasional glances at the news or sports events while they're working on their computers and obviously can't do that if the screen is in use for their laptop. One of the design advantages of flat screen displays is that they are mounted flat on a wall, visually and physically out of the way, but very difficult to see from the conventional location of a guestroom work desk. Guestroom configurations will need to be rethought to accommodate these uses.

More promising is the ability of these displays to accept connections from guests' portable video devices, such as DVD players, game players, and personal video players/recorders. Similarly, many guests carry portable music players and are used to a far higher quality of music reproduction and greater choice of material than is provided by the typical hotel room alarm clock/radio, which has become legendary for both its poor quality and awkward and cryptic controls. Adding a CD player to the clock allows guests to play their own selection (or those borrowed from the hotel), but far more useful nowadays is the ability for guests to plug in their personal music players (iPods and other MP3 players) and play them back over the guestroom equipment while recharging the units.

This is likely to drive a demand for higher-quality audio speakers, too. This might be resolved by allowing the radio unit to play back through the speakers often built in to flat-panel displays, and indeed some luxury hotels do provide full 5.1 theater surround-sound to enhance the viewing and listening experiences. Care in speaker placement and in providing audio insulation between rooms is essential to minimize audio intrusion into adjacent guestrooms.

This guest-device connectivity is expected to become a standard quite quickly. Current examples include Hilton's introduction of its own design of clock/radio to all guestrooms, which features music player plug-in connections as well as (praise be!) simplified clock and alarm controls, and Marriott's decision to install over 50,000 flat-panel displays in its guestrooms, with connectivity for guests' laptops, game players, and portable video players.

Device Integration

High-speed Internet access has quickly become a key factor in guests' decisions on where to stay and, as a result, virtually every hotel brand has made it a mandatory amenity. For many hotels, the cost of providing wired access to all guestrooms has been significant (unless spare conductors of high enough quality have been available in the existing wiring), but the flexibility and lower cost of wireless connectivity would have made it a popular alternative even without the strong guest preference for its freedom and cableless simplicity. Wired connections are still faster and more secure, but for most guests wireless is fast enough and much more convenient. Internet access through the television is becoming more practical with the higher resolution flat-screen displays—it's very rudimentary with conventional television sets—but it's more flexible to provide a separate high-speed Internet access link as well. This way one guest watching a movie need not be interrupted while another checks the Internet for local restaurants.

One emerging trend that could still manifest in different ways is the integration of the various pieces of guestroom technology with each other and with the hotel management systems. A familiar example is the provision of video check-out, with the guest's folio being displayed on the television and check-out processing in the PMS being initiated from that screen. More advanced integrations involve using the television to play wake-up calls and voice mail messages, display guest messages and faxes, and provide details of a conference attendee's meeting and function room agenda. Integration with VoIP phone instruments allows the names of other members of a guest's group to be displayed on the phone after he or she has checked in for simple one-touch dialing to their rooms, arranging ad hoc conference calls, or sending voice messages to all or some of them.

This type of integration can only grow—what's still unclear is what combination of devices will prevail for the guest to use. VoIP telephone set vendors are providing larger and clearer displays on their phones and can offer Internet access, but clearly work with fairly tight space restrictions. Other vendors offer separate "concierge" workstations, either as small wired workstations or as battery-powered tablet-style PC units, for guests to use both for Internet access and hotel services. Clearly, however, there's a limit to how many technology devices are desirable in a guestroom and some shake-out and consolidation of functions is inevitable.

On a less visible level, door locks, occupancy sensors, thermostats, and mini-bars have either shared cabling or have used infrared links to link their sensors for some years. This increases operations efficiency through setting thermostats back when a room is unoccupied, reducing network costs, and advising the mini-bar restocking staff as to what items need to be replenished in which rooms.

One of the most significant developments in this area promises to be the work being carried out by the HTNG workgroup on integrating all the different systems that appear in the guestroom. Several vendors have made a good start, both as noted above and in relation to sharing a single, common network cable among all systems, but the workgroup has brought together hoteliers and vendors representing all of the above systems and more to agree on the most practical and useful sets of functions to be standardized.

The Future

After complicating our lives with ever-increasing levels of narrowly focused functionality, technology seems to have crossed an integration threshold. This promises to lead to even more effective systems that, for once, are easier to manage and less costly to implement. It's a hopeful prospect.

Appendix 1: Other Sources of Hotel Technology Information

Further information can be gathered from a variety of resources. Some trade magazines focus exclusively on technology, such as *Hospitality Upgrade* and *Hospitality Technology*. The more general publications such as *Hotel & Motel Management*, *Hotels, Lodging,* and *Lodging Hospitality* all have sections that cover technology developments and issues, and a number of electronic newsletters provide valuable regular updates, including Hotel Online, Hospitality Net, Hotel Interactive, and others. The American Hotel & Lodging Association's Technology Committee publishes a series of Primers as introductory guidelines on hotel technology, which give a good grounding in the fundamentals.

One of the most comprehensive and useful annual trade shows is the Hospitality Industry Technology Exposition and Conference, sponsored each June by Hospitality Financial & Technology Professionals and focused exclusively on all aspects of hospitality technology. The International Food Service Technology Exposition (FS/TEC), sponsored each October by *Nation's Restaurant News* and Accuvia, covers systems used in the food service industry. The International Hotel/Motel & Restaurant Show, held each November in New York City, also incorporates a significant technology section within its equipment, services, and supplies coverage.

Consultants can also provide valuable, independent advice and help in technology selection and implementation. If you decide to use their services, be sure to select carefully, checking references and distinguishing between generalists and regular specialists to ensure the most appropriate match of approach and experience for your needs.

Appendix 2: Acronyms

BI—business intelligence, the collection of consolidated data and its flexible analysis for decision support

CRM—customer relationship management

CRS—central reservations system

HD—high-definition

HTNG—Hotel Technology Next Generation, a hotel-sponsored initiative to encourage vendors to develop integrated sets of systems for purchase by hotels

IP—Internet Protocol, the general term for the technology used for Internet communications

LAN—local area network

ISDN—integrated services digital network

OLAP—online analytical processing

OTA—Open Travel Alliance, a travel industry group defining standard guest/traveler profiles and data exchange messages between the airline, car rental, and hotel industries

PBX—private branch exchange, a property-based telephone system

PMS—property management system

POS—point of sale, for food and beverage and retail outlets

PPV—pay-per-view (movies)

RMS—revenue management system

S&C—sales and catering

SEO—search engine optimization

SLA—service level agreement

VoIP—Voice over Internet Protocol, the transmission of voice communications over Internet-based data networks

WiFi—Wireless Fidelity

XML—eXtended Markup Language

11

Condo Hotels

By *David M. Neff, ISHC, and Adam T. Berkoff*

David M. Neff is the Co-Chair of the Lodging and Timeshare Practice Group at the 2,700 lawyer firm of DLA Piper Rudnick Gray Cary, which has more than 50 offices throughout the world, of which 20 are in the United States. Based in the firm's Chicago office, he has practiced law for almost 20 years and is widely recognized as one of the leading hotel lawyers in the country. He represents hotel owners, lenders, management companies, and franchise companies in a wide variety of issues including acquisitions and dispositions, franchise disputes, management contract negotiations, condo hotel structuring, general litigation, workouts, and bankruptcies.

Mr. Neff has spoken frequently at industry conferences such as the NYU Hotel Investment Conference, Americas Lodging Investment Summit, the Atlanta Hotel Investment Conference, the Lodging Conference, and the Asian American Hotel Owners Annual Convention and for leading hotel organizations such as the International Society of Hospitality Consultants and the Hospitality Asset Managers Association. He has published many articles in such industry publications as Hotel & Motel Management, Hotel Journal, Lodging Hospitality, Hotels' Investment Outlook, Hotels, AAHOA Lodging Business and AAHOA Hospitality. He currently is the President of the International Society of Hospitality Consultants.

Adam T. Berkoff is a partner in DLA Piper Rudnick Gray Cary's Real Estate group and the head of the firm's Condominium and Complex Mixed-Use Development Practice Group. He concentrates his practice in the areas of real estate development, condominium development and conversion, mixed-use high rise development, acquisition and disposition of real estate, commercial financing (both lender and borrower representation), and office park/retail center development. Mr. Berkoff has vast experience in representing developers of residential condominiums, commercial condominiums, and hotel condominiums. He is an adjunct professor in the DePaul University Real Estate Center. He received his law degree at Marquette University in 1994 where he served as Executive Editor of the Marquette Law Review. He received his Bachelor of Arts degree with Honors and Distinction from the University of Wisconsin-Madison in 1991.

ONE OF THE HOTTEST RECENT TRENDS in the hotel industry has been transforming traditional hotels into condominium hotels (condo hotels). This chapter explores many facets of condo hotels in a question-and-answer format. Keep in mind, however, that the following is not meant to consist of legal advice in connection with any specific matter. Readers are advised to consult with legal counsel in connection with all condo hotel issues.

Question   What are condo hotels?

Answer   Condo hotels are hotels that operate just like any other hotel property, except that ownership of the hotel is held by various owners instead of just one company. Basically, you have a condominium ownership structure layered over a typical hotel.

Question   How do they differ from timeshares?

Answer   Timeshare is taking someone's ownership of a unit or a piece of property and selling off increments of time in that interest. For instance, if I owned a condominium unit and I were to timeshare it, I could sell off a quarter of a year, a week, or a day, such that someone could occupy my unit for that period of time. Condominium ownership is actual fee-simple ownership of a unit in a condominium. So in the condo hotel construct, you have a hotel building in which you have any number of guestrooms and the condo hotel purchaser owns one of those guestrooms. As in any other condominium, the unit owner does not actually own the walls, but does own the wallpaper; the unit owner does not own the floors, but does own the carpeting; and the unit owner owns everything in between—all the air rights. If it were a timeshare, the unit owner would not own any of that. The unit owner merely would have a right to occupy that space for a given period of time.

Question   What are the benefits of a condo hotel from a developer's perspective?

Answer   The biggest benefit is financeability. In a traditional hotel arrangement, a borrower or developer essentially is asking the lender to lend it money based on what the lender thinks the hotel is capable of generating in terms of cash flow. When you are approaching a lender about financing a condo hotel, the lender can look at it very differently and consider it to be more analogous to a residential condo loan in which the lender is not basing its underwriting on the hotel owner's ability to rent rooms, but instead on its ability to sell units. If the owner can generate a number of presales, the lender may be willing to make the loan on that basis because it usually will be taken out after the owner has completed a certain number of initial sales. Lending for a traditional hotel product is going to be on a much longer loan term. A second advantage for a developer, depending upon how the condo hotel is structured, is sharing in the ongoing revenue from the units, in addition to being paid the purchase price of the units. In addition, the developer typically passes on some—or in some cases all—of the operating expenses of the hotel to the unit purchasers. Another advantage for a developer is that it probably will make more money by selling off individual units than selling the entire building as a hotel.

Question   What are the benefits of a condo hotel to unit owners?

Answer   Securities law issues aside, one of the benefits of a condo hotel is the potential income to be derived from the unit when the owner is not occupying it. Not only do owners get to stay in the place they want to stay, but they can rent the room to third parties when they are not there. Units are maintained by the hotel operator or management company at levels the unit owners expect, and the unit owners will get—depending upon how the program is structured—either some or all of the revenue from rental of their units. At the same time, depending on how the project is structured, there may be a sharing of the expense burden by the developer.

Question   Are there any tax benefits to the condo hotel unit owner?

Answer   There are certain income tax benefits that can be achieved by owning a condo hotel unit. They relate to the unit owner's ability to deduct mortgage interest, real estate taxes, and depreciation on the unit. It depends upon how many nights he or she stays there, which is why many condo hotel rental programs offer packages allowing unit owners to occupy their units for a certain number of nights to take advantage of the tax laws.

Question   Can a condo hotel also be used as a 1031 exchange property?

Answer   Yes, as long as the exchange property is of a "like kind" to the other property, which typically should be the case. As a result, someone who is trying to defer taxes on a gain from the sale of a like-kind investment property can use a condo hotel property as a replacement property.

Question   Where in the United States have we typically been seeing condo hotels?

Answer   Condo hotels primarily have been developed in resort areas such as Florida and Hawaii. They are now becoming popular in such major metropolitan areasasNew York and Chicago.

Question   What kinds of properties are we seeing go condo hotel?

Answer   We are seeing condo hotels being considered all across the board. However, most of the development continues to be of resort properties and first-class hotels in major markets. The concept has gained publicity with the Trump condo hotel projects inNew York and Chicago, both of which are very high quality condo hotel projects. Many of the top hotel chains in the country also are very interested in this concept.

Question   What kind of laws do developers of condo hotels need to consider?

Answer   They always need to be thinking about securities law concerns, which will exist any time you have a condo hotel offering. Although the U.S. Securities and Exchange Commission (SEC) doesn't consider the sale of a parcel of real estate for personal residence as the sale of a security, it takes a closer look as to whether the offering should be registered as a security when the real estate looks more like an investment. There are many SEC letter rulings stating that if you take certain precautions and sell your condo hotel product in a certain way, you can get into an SEC safe harbor where the sale of units does not qualify as the sale of a security.

Question   So what does a developer need to do to comply with the securities laws?

Answer   One of the requirements to get safe-harbor treatment for securities purposes in a condo hotel is that the salespeople cannot bring up the fact that there is a rental management program unless it is in response to a buyer's inquiry. In other words, if the buyer comes into the sales center and says, "Do you offer some program to rent my unit when I am not in town?" the salespeople can then discuss the program.

The developer also cannot emphasize the economic benefits from rental of the units or from third-party management efforts. This means the developer cannot provide projections of how it expects the hotel to do or how much money it expects the unit owner to make if he or she rents out the room. However, if asked about the rental program, the developer can provide historical operating results of the hotel and its competitors.

The developer cannot make representations regarding the tax benefits of ownership, advertise rental services, limit the unit owner's ability to occupy the unit, designate an exclusive rental agent, or pool income or expenses.

Question   Can a developer choose to comply with the securities laws and register its condo hotel as a security?

Answer   Yes, but few developers of condo hotels choose to do that because it is very expensive and requires that the units be sold only by registered securities brokers. Instead, most choose not to register, but try to comply with the law so that their sales are not considered an offering of a security.

Question   Does this mean that the salespeople must be very well trained?

Answer   Absolutely. It is vital that the salespeople understand what they can and cannot say and when they can say it.

Question   What other laws apply to condo hotels?

Answer   In addition to securities law considerations, a condo hotel developer must comply with any local condominium laws, state condominium laws, and municipal condominium disclosure requirements. For instance, there may be subdivision code requirements. In certain jurisdictions,includingNew York and California, there are a whole host of land sale registration requirements. Also, if the developer has more than 100 units of new construction or if there is significant rehabilitation of the units, it may be subject to Interstate Land Sales Full Disclosure Act requirements.

Question Do these laws vary throughout the country?

Answer The Interstate Land Sales Act and the SEC's securities laws apply uniformly because they are federal laws. State and local condominium laws and subdivision requirements and any other local condominium requirements (such as the limitations recently passed in some cities) vary from jurisdiction to jurisdiction.

Question What is the typical condo hotel structure?

Answer The typical model, which is popular in Florida, has the individual unit owners owning their rooms and the developer owning such common space as the hallways, the lobby, the front desk, and the back-of-the-house space. The developer holds that ownership either in a separate condominium unit or in a separate carved-out parcel accomplished by a vertical subdivision, which is a much more complicated endeavor than just making it a separate condominium unit. The purpose of this structure is for the developer to have control over that common space and how and when it is maintained and refurbished. Otherwise, such decisions would be in the condo association's control.

Question What kind of rental programs typically are offered to buyers?

Answer In the typical structure, the developer wants to motivate unit owners to place their units in the rental management program. Consequently, in exchange for a unit owner's participation in the rental management program, the developer often will agree to pay a certain amount of the ongoing maintenance expenses associated with that unit. Of course, the developer also takes a share of the revenue that is derived from the rental of the unit. For example, unit owners may elect a package at the beginning of the year to stay in their units zero nights a year, 14 nights a year, or 35 nights a year. If they stay in their unit zero nights a year, they get perhaps 50 percent of the net revenue any time someone stays in their unit. If they stay in their unit 14 nights a year, they may get 42 percent of the net revenue from someone staying in their unit. If they stay in their unit 35 nights a year, they may get around 30 percent of the net revenue. After deducting all of the expenses, the developer is getting anywhere from 50 to 70 percent of the net revenue from rental of the unit.

Question What legal documents does a developer need to establish a condo hotel and be able to sell units?

Answer The developer needs whatever local compliance documents are required. For instance, in Chicago that would be a City of Chicago Condominium Property Report, a condominium declaration, a pricing schedule, floor plans for the units, a condominium budget, and a host of other ancillary documents. The developer also would need to develop a rental management agreement to govern the rental program. The developer is going to need to document the relationship between the developer and the hotel management company in a management agreement. The developer also will need to develop a form of purchaser contract. The list of required documents can expand from that depending upon how the project is set up. Finally, if compliance with the Interstate Land Sales Full Disclosure Act is required, the developer also will need either to qualify for an exemption to the Act or file a Statement of Record with U.S. Department of Housing and Urban Development (HUD) that must be accepted before unit sales commence.

Question   Does any governmental agency have to approve the documents?

Answer   In some jurisdictions—such as Florida—that is the case. No approval is required in Chicago, although the documents must be filed with the city. Again, if a filing is required under the Interstate Land Sales Full Disclosure Act, HUD must accept the filing before units can be sold.

Question   What are the developer's goals in setting up a condo hotel structure?

Answer   It all depends on the developer's exit strategy. The typical example is the model prevalent in Florida, in which the developer tries to obtain the proceeds from the sale of the individual units and obtain a share of the revenues from the hotel on a going forward basis. If the developer views the condo hotel arena much like a residential condominium project, it may reject the model prevalent in Florida and instead create a condo hotel much like a residential condo. Thus, the developer may not hold the common space in a separate developer unit. Instead, common areas may be owned by the unit owners as tenants in common just like in any other condominium project. This makes sense if the exit strategy is to sell off the units and not share in the ongoing revenues. In that structure, the developer can pass through 100 percent of the expenses to the unit owners, who also will get 100 percent of the revenue.

Question   How do developers maintain control over the common areas of the hotel?

Answer   The condo hotel documents can grant a perpetual easement right to all of the unit owners to use the common space. Some developers will get more aggressive than that and, for instance, provide in their documents that if they are terminated as manager, the unit owners cannot use the lobby and/or the front desk because they belong to the developer as a separate unit. That may create some legal problems depending upon the local laws that apply to the condo hotel project.

Question   Does a typical condo hotel have a homeowners association?

Answer   Yes, there is going to be a homeowners association or a condominium association in any condominium project. The open issue is how much the developer can marginalize that condominium association. In a typical Florida condo hotel project, the developer tries to make the homeowners association very marginal by removing many of the common elements. The developer does so by putting much of the common space in the developer-controlled unit so the condo association is left in charge of only such responsibilities as insurance for the shell of the building and maintenance of a few of the building elements, like its foundation, core, and structure. The day-to-day maintenance of the lobby, hallways, and elevators and refurbishment of that space are removed from the common elements and basically taken out of the association's control.

Question   Is that going to be acceptable in all locations?

Answer   It depends on the condominium statute in the given jurisdiction. Most condominium statutes are not very sophisticated in the sense that they are decades old and were enacted at a time when legislators only contemplated residential condominiums. That does not mean the statutes are bad; it just means that they usually are silent as to some of the more complicated issues raised by condo hotels. It remains to be seen how these existing laws will be applied to the condo hotel structure.

Question   When is the homeowners association typically formed and when do the unit owners take over control of the association?

Answer   The developer typically forms the homeowners association before it closes on its first unit sale. The association needs to be in place by then to do such things as bill for assessments and maintain the insurance. The point at which the homeowners association is turned over to the unit owners depends on the jurisdiction. For instance, turnover in Illinois occurs either three years after the condo declaration is recorded or when 75 percent of the units have been sold—whichever comes first. Upon such turnover, the unit owners will elect their own board, which ends up controlling the association.

Question   Are there any limits as to how revenue or expenses are shared between the developer and the unit owners?

Answer   The developer has total flexibility on how to structure the sharing of revenue and expenses, but it cannot pool revenue or expenses without violating securities laws.

Question   How does the developer ensure that necessary capital expenditure reserves are maintained?

Answer   There are several types of reserves the developer must be concerned about. First, the developer must provide for the maintenance of condo reserves. In some jurisdictions, the homeowners association is required to maintain reasonable reserves. Of course, these reserves may not be particularly high if the association has little control over the common areas. The developer also must provide for capital expenditure reserves for the hotel. A hotel is a very expensive operation, with much wear and tear on linens, furniture, and carpeting. Many capital items are going to need replacement over time and capital expenditures may be required by the franchisor if the hotel is branded. Reserves become critical to the operations of the hotel. There are a number of ways that the developer will set up reserves. The developer typically will have unit owners pay into the reserves at the time they close on their unit purchase. In addition, a share of the nightly revenue will be set aside for these reserves.

Question   Who decides what capital expenditures are going to get done?

Answer   The decision typically is left to the developer and the hotel management company as opposed to the homeowners association because the association may not be interested in spending the money that a hotel management company might be interested in spending in order to maintain or improve the hotel. That is one of the major reasons why the developer typically tries to marginalize the association's control over capital expenditures and give itself or the hotel management company as much power as possible to control the expenditures.

Question   Are there capital expenditure budgets that are prepared?

Answer   It all depends on the jurisdiction where the condo hotel is located. In some jurisdictions, the developer is required to prepare a budget for the condominium expenses and disclose that to its buyers, but there usually is no requirement to disclose a budget for capital expenditures for the hotel. However, it is prudent for the developer to provide buyers with estimates of expected hotel expenses so buyers will have a tougher time complaining later that they were not aware of these expenses.

Question   What do developers do if the capital expenditure reserve amounts are not sufficient to do the capital improvements that are needed?

Answer   Developers should provide for a right to make special assessments for unforeseen or additional hotel capital expenditures in their condominium documents. Of course, the goal is to fund the capital reserves sufficiently to pay for all of those expenses so the developer will not have to levy a special assessment.

Question   How do developers try to maximize the number of unit owners participating in the rental program?

Answer   This is always a goal of developers. The last thing they want is to set up a condo hotel and have few of their unit owners elect to participate in the rental program. The problem is that if a developer mandates a unit owner's participation in the rental program, federal securities laws will treat the unit as a security. Some developers create a negative impact for unit owners who don't participate, which itself can become a problem with respect to securities law compliance. Other developers may instead provide for a series of enticements for unit owners to participate in the rental management program. For instance, the developer might agree to pay part of the operating expenses for the property if the unit owner participates in the rental management program. Some incentives that can get a little bit closer to raising securities issues include offering free entry into the rental program at the beginning, but charging for later entry.

Question   Can the developer require all unit owners to buy its furniture, fixtures, and equipment (FF&E) package?

Answer   Yes. There is no reason why the developer cannot obligate a unit owner to purchase the FF&E. It is purely a contractual item. Indeed, it would be difficult to sell hotel rooms—and impossible under existing brand standards—if each unit owner could furnish the unit any way he or she chose.

Question   Are unit owners always guaranteed the availability of their unit for their own use?

Answer   The ability of unit owners to use their specific units will depend upon the provisions of the developer's rental program. Most rental arrangements provide that if unit owners give the developer (or the hotel management company) sufficient notice—which may be six months or longer—they are guaranteed that their rooms will be available for their use. However, there may be blackout dates at certain times of the year and other exceptions to allow for booking of large groups. If that happens, the developer typically will provide that the unit owner will be allowed to stay in a comparable unit.

Question   Do unit owners have to pay when they stay in their own unit?

Answer   That again varies from project to project, but the answer usually is yes to some extent. The real question becomes how much. In most projects, the unit owner pays a nightly fee equal to the base operating cost for that night's stay, which obviously is significantly less than the rate that would be charged to a transient guest. Of course, if the unit owners pay the standard guest charge for their own rental, they essentially are paying themselves for any net income for that night. However, in that instance, the unit owners must pay higher occupancy taxes.

Question   How do unit owners know their units will be rented fairly?

Answer   To give unit owners some comfort in knowing that their units will be rented on a fair basis in comparison to other units in the hotel, there are software programs that attempt to allocate units so that the unit that has been most vacant becomes available most quickly for the next transient guest.

Question   For how long a period can you bind the unit owner to make a unit part of the rental program?

Answer   There is not a bright-line standard. Agreements typically last one year. Although developers would prefer much longer agreements, federal securities laws require that participation in the rental management program be totally voluntary. As a result, agreements that last for many years should allow the unit owner to get out of the agreement with sufficient advance notice if he or she chooses to do so.

Question   What happens if the unit owner fails to pay an assessment or participate in a rental program as agreed?

Answer   The unit owner can face several different consequences. The condo association may have the right to lien the owner's unit as it relates to the condominium assessments that are due. Some state laws provide that if the unit owner does not pay his or her assessment and the unit is liened, the homeowners association can go to court and obtain a forcible entry and detainer and basically evict the owner from the unit and take fee ownership. The result likely would be different if the unit owner failed to pay hotel expenses because most condominium statutes do not contemplate a structure different from a typical residential condominium. Consequently, the developer should provide for a similar lien power in the condominium documents that can be exercised against a unit owner who fails to pay his or her share of the hotel operating expenses. This is strictly a contractual lien right, not a statutory lien right. The unit owner is taking ownership subject to the condominium declaration that establishes this lien right, but there is no independent statutory authority for this lien right. Thus, it is questionable whether a unit owner could be evicted from a unit as could happen with a statutory lien right.

Question   What if the hotel has operating shortfalls?

Answer   The result depends on who ultimately is obligated to pay the operating expenses. If the operating expenses are shared by the unit owners and the developer, they all will be obligated to pay the shortfall. If all of the expenses and all of the revenues are passed through to the unit owners, then the unit owners must pay the operating shortfalls. In either model, the hotel could find itself in serious financial distress if the shortfalls are not covered. That is why the operating documents need to provide a mechanism to collect such shortfall from the unit owners.

Question   Are there any special concerns for management companies that manage condo hotels?

Answer   Yes. They need to be concerned about indemnification for any securities law violations. They also need to obtain a guaranteed minimum fee as not all unit owners may participate in the rental program, meaning there will be less income on which the management company can earn a percentage fee. In that regard, any termination rights based on income or sales must take into account that not all unit owners may participate in the rental program. There also are many issues surrounding the management company's relationship with the unit owners that must be addressed.

Question   Are there special concerns for franchise companies?

Answer   Like management companies, franchise companies will be concerned about being seen as a deep pocket for any securities law violations. They also will be very concerned—especially in conversions of existing branded hotels to condo hotels—about losing rooms to owners who don't want to participate in the rental program. They also will want to ensure that unit owners are locked into participating in the program enough in advance to accommodate large bookings that are made a year or more in advance.

Question   Do management companies or franchise companies share in any of the upside of condo hotel development?

Answer   They often get some percentage of each unit sold, especially if the unit buyer is one of their referrals.

Timeshare and Vacation Ownership—An Industry Reaching Maturity

By *Gregory T. Bohan, ISHC*

Gregory T. Bohan is a principal with Pinnacle Advisory Group and heads the firm's South Florida practice office. He actively consults with clients of all types in the lodging industry and specializes in feasibility analysis, market research, and appraisals of resorts and conference centers. Before opening the Florida office for Pinnacle, Mr. Bohan was affiliated with the Boston office of the firm from 1991 to 2003. Concurrently, he developed, owned, and operated The Inn at HighView, a full-service luxury country inn located on a mountaintop in central Vermont ski country. His consulting experience goes back to 1976 when he joined Laventhol & Horwath immediately after graduating with distinction from the School of Hotel Administration at Cornell University. Leaving L&H to join the New York office of PKF in 1980, he rose to the rank of principal and co-directed PKF's New York consulting practice until leaving the firm in 1991 to join Pinnacle and begin his Vermont adventure.

INCREDIBLE THOUGH IT MAY SEEM to those who have witnessed the process, almost 30 years have passed since the concept of timeshare or vacation ownership entered the mainstream of the lodging and resort industries in the United States. What a remarkable and tumultuous life the industry has had from infancy, through childhood and adolescence, to young adulthood, and finally, now, to maturity.

The timeshare concept—the ability for a consumer to purchase a condominium for a defined period of time—is widely recognized to have begun in Europe in the late 1960s and early 1970s. There was limited recognition and acceptance in the United States until the late 1970s, when the element of exchange—the ability for the owner to trade a timeshare unit (typically a week) for a different week of the year at the home location, for the same week at a different location, or even for a different week at a different location—began to provide widespread consumer appeal.

The timeshare industry began to expand rapidly in the United States in the early 1980s with units being developed primarily in traditional resort areas, most often via conversion of existing underperforming hotels, motels, and second-home condominium complexes. With no government regulation yet in place and the potential for rapid and substantial profit, the industry all too frequently became attractive to unscrupulous developers who saw the opportunity to make a quick

213

buck. While the majority of timeshare developers were completely honest and ethical, many developments suffered due to the use of questionable marketing techniques, lack of ongoing professional management, and lack of ongoing capital reinvestment.

By the close of the 1980s, the timeshare industry had evolved from being something reminiscent of the Wild West to being one of the most heavily regulated industries in the country. During that decade, virtually every state enacted stringent laws regarding the conduct of business in the timeshare industry, almost all of them designed to protect "typical" consumers who, because of their demographic profile (moderate income and education level), were viewed as being in need of strong protection.

The 1990s witnessed the timeshare industry's transition from adolescence to adulthood. The entrance of major well-respected lodging brands such as Marriott, Hilton, Starwood, Hyatt, and Radisson brought the playing field to an entirely new and much more professional level, helped to bring respect and stability to the industry, and fueled an expansion that was unprecedented to that time. The founding of the American Resort Development Association (ARDA), which morphed at this time from the American Land Development Association (founded in 1969), brought yet another level of respectability to the industry by promulgating industry standards and ethics. Timeshare became the fastest growing segment of the lodging industry—one that was now recognized and understood by the majority of American travelers.

In true American fashion, the timeshare industry is judged—at least in part—by its attractiveness to the investment community. By the close of the 1990s, successful public offerings by independent timeshare companies, among them Sunterra, Trendwest Resorts, and Vistana, brought the Main Street timeshare industry face to face with Wall Street and gave proof that the marriage could work.

If there were any remaining doubts that the timeshare industry had matured and was now an economic force deserving of respect, those doubts virtually disappeared in the months following the horrific terrorist attacks on the United States on September 11, 2001. Tourism and vacation travel ground to almost a standstill in the months following the attacks. Hotel occupancy in many resort areas fell to unprecedented depths and a round of rate cutting in an attempt to spur business did little to cushion the impact on the lodging industry and resort area economies. In areas dependent on tourism and the economic impact created by it, there was little reason to be upbeat—with one somewhat unexpected exception.

After the attacks, unlike the guests who had reserved at traditional lodging facilities who canceled their reservations in droves, timeshare owners stayed the course. With a mindset reflective of general thinking as follows, "I paid my maintenance; I've booked my tickets; I *own* this unit; *no one* is going to cheat me out of *my* vacation," timeshare owners, in large measure, did not alter their plans. In some resort areas where post–September 11, 2001, hotel occupancy was 40 to 50 points below what would have been the seasonal norm, timeshare occupancy was far less affected. In many cases, it was only 10 to 20 points below what would have been expected had there been no attacks. Resort areas with heavy concentrations of timeshares saw far less in the way of reduced economic activity than did those where timeshares were scarce.

Now that the timeshare industry has been witnessed as a team player that can carry its own weight and even help shoulder the burden of tough times, it has truly reached a new level of maturity. New rounds of government regulation combined with a red-hot real estate market are creating a difficult environment for continued expansion. With its newfound maturity, however, it appears that the timeshare industry has become a force to be reckoned with and is almost without doubt here for the long haul.

A study conducted by American Economics Group, Inc. on behalf of ARDA provides a snapshot of just how vital the vacation ownership industry is at present. According to the results of the research, as of January 1, 2005:

- 1,668 vacation ownership resorts were operating in the United States, an increase of approximately 5 percent from the previous tally in 2003.

- 3.87 million people owned timeshare units, an increase of 13.8 percent since 2003.

- The total number of timeshare units in the United States was 157,518, with more than 70 percent of them being two-bedroom units.

- 18,561 new units are expected to be completed during 2005.

- The top ten timeshare resort states accounted for 65 percent of resorts, with Florida being in the top position with 378 resorts (almost one-quarter of the total supply).

- The average price of a timeshare unit increased to $15,789, up approximately 5 percent from the year prior.

- The most popular type of resort location continued to be a seaside/beach location (24.7 percent), followed by golf (14.4 percent).

- Occupancy rates at the nation's timeshares in 2004 averaged 84.6 percent, far higher than the average occupancy rate of the nation's traditional hotels.

Evolution of Target Markets/Emerging Markets Today

Common sense would dictate that the target markets for timeshare development would be very similar in character to those sought by conventional hotel developers. In that sense, the critical issues typically are as follows:

- At what location that has convenient air or auto transportation would the likely guest (buyer) want or need to spend time?

- What location has an inventory of affordable land and, at the same time, features development or conversion costs such that the development will be economically feasible given the likely revenue stream or sales price?

In the timeshare industry, however, there is a very critical third consideration that rises to the very top in terms of importance:

Exhibit 1   Timeshare Industry Rescission Rates

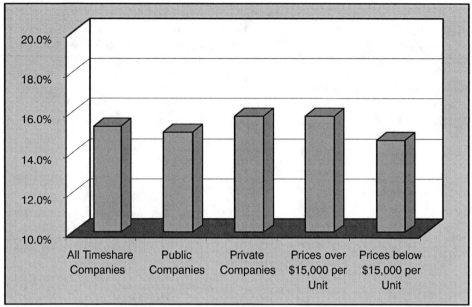

Source: "Financial Performance of the US Timeshare Industry," prepared by PricewaterhouseCoopers for the American Resort Development Association, 2004.

- What location will provide the developer of the timeshare with sufficient exposure and accessibility to create sufficient visitation traffic to generate unit sales?

The economics of the timeshare industry make it virtually mandatory for each development to be a complete sellout. Most timeshare developers typically leave one week per calendar year unsold in order to allow for regular maintenance of the units. Therefore, this implies that 51 weeks must be sold for each unit in the development. By way of example, for a 200-unit development, this translates into the need to sell 10,200 (200 × 51) unit-weeks.

Taking this a step further, it is typical in the timeshare industry for only one out of every ten potential purchasers who physically tour the resort or inspect the product at an off-site sales location to actually purchase a unit. Therefore, in order to sell 10,200 unit-weeks, more than 100,000 potential purchasers must visit the development (or its off-site sales center) to provide the necessary number of buyers who will actually produce a closed sale. In actuality, this number increases even more and approaches 120,000 since approximately 15 percent of all sales are rescinded by the buyers within the escape period on the sales contract. Rescission rates as a percentage of gross sales are fairly consistent in the industry, as shown in Exhibit 1.

Timeshare developers go to enormous effort and expense in the process of bringing sufficient traffic to the sales location. It is not uncommon for sales and marketing costs to approximate 50 percent of total sales revenues. From a strictly locational standpoint, developing a successful timeshare product is greatly facilitated by a location in an established resort or urban location that already has high levels of transient visitation. When such is not the case, marketing the timeshare product becomes a factor of marketing not only the product itself, but of marketing the *destination* as well. Costs are greatly elevated since potential sales prospects must be brought to the location or to an off-site sales location in order to entice them to purchase.

Reflecting these realities, early timeshare developments took place almost exclusively in established resort locations with good transportation infrastructure and longstanding histories of heavy visitation. During this time, Florida was a hotbed of timeshare activity. It wasn't long, however, before timeshares were being developed in the Rocky Mountain West, Las Vegas, Hawaii, Mexico (primarily Cancun), and a host of other areas.

Development of urban timeshares began in earnest in the late 1980s. Primarily taking the form of adaptive reuse of residential apartments and/or hotel conversions, the majority of this activity took place in large gateway cities such as New York, London, and San Francisco. After an initial spate of activity, development of urban timeshares began to slow, primarily as a result of rapidly escalating development and land or conversion asset purchase costs in the markets that were most attractive. The latest round of real estate price escalation, which continues as of this writing, combined with a rapid escalation of construction costs and material shortages has brought a virtual halt to these developments. In many markets, timeshare developers simply cannot compete with developers of whole-ownership condominiums or condominium hotels for scarce land, materials, and development opportunities. Rare exceptions currently exist in some widely scattered markets where prices for fractional ownership are high enough to make such projects feasible.

At present, new development is, as it has been during most of the history of the timeshare industry, primarily focused on resort locations However, there is a new twist: timeshare development is occurring, in some cases, at locations without the typically requisite high density of existing visitation and, in many cases, outside of the mainland United States. These locations include the following:

- *Caribbean Islands.* Development is escalating in traditional resort areas such as Aruba and is getting a foothold in areas that were not timeshare destinations in the past, including St. John, St. Kitts, Nevis, and St. Lucia. As in the past, airlift to Caribbean destinations is a major issue, with most flights to Caribbean destinations using Miami International Airport as the United States hub. According to developers active in the Caribbean market, congestion and a lack of low-cost carriers has resulted in Miami International being thought of as somewhat difficult and less competitive in recent years. A major expansion at Miami International Airport is expected to be completed within the year to ease congestion at that airport. While service by low-fare carriers has not increased dramatically in recent years at MIA, connections with such carriers are available through Fort Lauderdale–Hollywood International Airport, located only 25 miles to the north.

It is important to point out that one of the most attractive aspects of the Caribbean to U.S. visitors has historically been the fact that a U.S. passport was not required to travel to and from many of the island resort destinations. As of this writing, a bill has been introduced to require the use of passports for all Caribbean destinations (except, of course, Puerto Rico). Timeshare marketers rely heavily on the use of mini-vacations (mini-vacs) to bring the large volume of prospective purchasers to timeshare destinations in the Caribbean. Passage of this bill could make the Caribbean generally less attractive as a destination, especially for the sometimes spontaneous mini-vacs used in marketing.

- *Mexico.* In addition to continued development in the resort areas surrounding Cancun, timeshare development is occurring in a major fashion in Cabo San Lucas, Mazatlan, and Puerto Penasco (a newly emerging drive-in destination that is approximately a five-hour drive from Phoenix).

- *South America.* Timeshare development was well established in both Argentina and Venezuela by the 1990s, but at present development has slowed to a trickle due to problems associated with the economy and the difficulty of attracting foreign investment with such an economic climate.

- *Central America.* The resorts of Belize and Costa Rica are witnessing rapid development brought about in large measure by improved airlift from major U.S. cities. Central America is thought to be an area that offers tremendous potential in terms of attracting U.S. markets in the future.

- *China and Southeast Asia.* With its emerging middle class, China is viewed as an area where timeshare development will blossom quickly in the years to come. Unlike in Central America, the market for timeshares in China and Southeast Asia is not expected to consist of Americans. Instead, it will be dominated by Chinese nationals enjoying the fruits of a newfound wealth.

At present, large infrastructure improvements are being made in preparation for the 2008 Summer Olympics in Beijing and the 2010 World's Fair in Shanghai. Timeshare and other vacation ownership developments are following major hotel developments in places like Macao (which is home to large casino hotels including Harrah's and Mirage) and other locations on the Pearl River Delta, which is located on the Chinese mainland proximate to Hong Kong. Other areas of Southeast Asia, including Vietnam, are experiencing significant resort development with timeshare being the dominant component in many cases.

As target markets for timeshare development have been evolving, so too have the methods and means used to market timeshares.

Sales and Marketing—Facing New Challenges

More than any other aspect of timeshare or vacation ownership development, the sales and marketing of the units form the basis of success. It is not unusual for a developer to spend half of the sales proceeds on sales and marketing of the units. The effort behind generating prospective buyers is by necessity enormous because

Exhibit 2   Sales Contacts Required for Sellout of a 500-Unit Development

Number of units	500
Number of weeks[1]	51
Number of unit-weeks to be sold	25,500
Number of sales prospects necessary to generate that many sales[2]	255,000
Number of sales contacts necessary to generate that many sales prospects[3]	25,500,000

Notes:

1. Assumes one week unsold annually for maintenance.
2. Industry average is approximately one closed sale for ten prospective buyers.
3. Industry average is approximately one interested prospect per 100 sales contacts (mailing, call, etc.).

of the sheer number of prospects that must be identified. Exhibit 2 illustrates the geometric progression that arrives at the number of sales contacts that would be necessary to sell out a timeshare with 500 units—not an unusual size for the newer generation of developments. As the exhibit shows, in order to sell out a 500-unit development, more than 25 million sales contacts (direct mail, telemarketing, Internet marketing, etc.) must be made. The example above does not reflect the industry reality that approximately 10 to 20 percent of those prospective buyers who purchase a unit cancel or rescind their contract within the allowable timeframe, which means that even the effort illustrated in the table is not likely to result in a total sellout of all units. The sheer number of prospects that must be brought through the sales process is one of the primary reasons that many timeshare developments are built in phases.

While the sales and marketing process in the timeshare industry has evolved over the years, many of the original methods are still in use. In most cases, the traditional methods are being augmented with newer methods. The principal methods in use today are explored below.

Incentive Gift or Premium Offers Via Direct Mail

Early in the history of the timeshare industry, this was the most common method of generating leads. Direct mail pieces would be sent out offering gifts such as toaster ovens and blenders in exchange for attending and listening to a sales presentation. The effectiveness of this method varied widely, based in part on the quality of the mailing list and the attractiveness of the gift or premium. Very early on, direct mail sweepstakes offerings were made. If a person attended the sales presentation, he or she had a chance at winning a much more expensive premium. Early in the 1980s, sweepstakes were outlawed in Florida because each respondent's chance of winning the expensive item was slim, contrary to the impression provided by the promotion.

Off-Premises Contacts

One of the most effective techniques used by timeshare marketers has been off-premises contacts (OPCs). This method features a "people catcher" (PC) who either trolls a busy area near the resort (such as a beach or shopping district) or sets up a booth at such a busy area. The PC attempts to make contact with as many pedestrians, shoppers, or beachgoers as possible in order to offer a gift or incentive to visit the resort for a sales presentation.

Frequently, restaurants and attractions in the surrounding area provide discounted meals and entrance fees to the timeshare marketer, which are in turn provided as incentives to the sales candidates, because this promotes their business and serves as an enticement for the sales presentation. Over the years, in response primarily to complaints from consumers, activities related to OPCs have been restricted in many areas. However, the effectiveness of the technique should not be understated. Most timeshare owners of record today were recruited via either direct mail or OPC activity.

Mini-Vacs

A mini-vac is the most well-known method of sales and marketing in the timeshare industry. Potential buyers are given a short vacation—either no cost or very little cost to them—at the resort where units are being sold. In this way, they are able to feel and experience the timeshare lifestyle firsthand. The potential buyer is able to use all the facilities, enjoy the amenities, and meet individuals who already own and enjoy their units at the resort. This has historically been an extremely effective way of converting a prospect to a purchaser.

Historically, prospective buyers who took advantage of a mini-vac were required to attend what in many cases were long and arduous sales presentations during their mini-vac stay. In many cases, such presentations are now being offered as optional to the prospective buyers as timeshare marketers have discovered that this low-key approach often is just as effective as a higher-pressure sales technique. In order to use mini-vacs as an effective sales technique, the subject resort (in this case, the home resort where the buyer would be purchasing) must have sufficient vacant inventory to house the prospective buyers when they visit. As sales close, this can become a challenge. Resorts where traditional hotel rooms and timeshare are blended are at an advantage in this regard since they have their supply of traditional hotel rooms to house prospective timeshare buyers when necessary, even when the available inventory of timeshare units is slim.

Telemarketing

A spate of federal regulation, most notably the federal "do not call" list, has greatly limited the ability to use what was once a very effective sales tool. Cold calling has been virtually eliminated as a means of selling timeshares, replaced in large measure by Internet sales and marketing techniques.

Internet Marketing

In just a few short years, the Internet has become the medium of choice for consumers in choosing a very wide variety of discretionary items, including vacation experiences. It offers seemingly limitless options for browsing and searching for any consumable item and is especially effective when the impact of the visual presentation is most important, as in the case of choosing vacation options. However, while timeshares have taken a mainstream place in the minds of the vacationing public, one truth remains unchanged since the early days of the industry. As stated by one industry executive, "People don't wake up in the morning and say to themselves 'I think I'll buy a timeshare today.'"

Timeshares are not a sought-after commodity, shopped for on-line in the same fashion as books or music downloads. For this reason, it is critical for Web sites that promote sales of timeshares to be carefully designed with tags that will give them prominence when an Internet surfer searches for vacation options. For example, when a consumer performs a search using the key words "Fort Lauderdale hotel," a well-designed homepage for a timeshare development in Fort Lauderdale should bring that development's homepage to a prominent place in the listing of Web sites that appear after the search. While many search engines have gone to the pay-per-click method (i.e., charging the home page for each hit that it receives from that engine), such exposure is no longer optional in terms of successful advertising—it is essential.

Computer and Media Marketing

One of the most underused but effective methods of marketing involves a combination of old and new technology. A direct mail piece that includes a well-designed CD-ROM can provide the consumer with, for all intents and purposes, a virtual tour of a development and its surroundings. Until recently, it was critical that the mailing list be carefully compiled to include potential consumers who were likely to have home computers that could support the CD-ROM platform. In recent years, however, the sophistication of home computers has increased dramatically concurrent with a steep decline in prices. It is now likely safe to say that if a mailing list is targeted to those with home computers, then those computers will allow the potential consumer to use the CD-ROM. The sophistication of home computers may very well lead to less use of this means of marketing as increasingly complex Web sites offering often spectacular visual and interactive facets are becoming more accessible to home computer owners on a more frequent basis.

Brand-Name Marketing

In the early 1980s, Marriott was the first large hotel brand to enter the timeshare industry. Since then, virtually all of the major hospitality players have entered the field. Affiliation with a well-known and well-respected hotel brand brings instant credibility to a timeshare development. Consumers are likely to transfer the feelings they have about the hotel company—many of which were generated by advertising and/or direct experience with that brand—to the timeshare development. In many cases, timeshare developments will be located proximate to or even integrated directly into an existing resort. This provides an excellent opportunity to cross-market to guests of the hotel via the presence of a promotional desk in the hotel lobby, in-house television channel promotions, and so on. In most cases, such promotion is kept discreet and unobtrusive so as not to be viewed as an intrusion by the guests.

Strategic Alliances

Strategic alliances or affinity marketing comes into play when a timeshare operation is aligned with another company in a different industry and is able to make use of this alliance to promote the timeshare product. This has typically played out in the arena of brand-name timeshare developments, but other examples abound. For example, several years ago, Vistana, Inc., in an effort to woo the golfer market, established a relationship with the Professional Golfers Association and then developed resorts adjacent or proximate to golf courses. Such an alliance can add substantial marketing power in that the timeshare developer can make use of customer lists to reach out to potential buyers.

Referrals

For an established timeshare operation, one of the most cost-effective means of marketing and sales is to make use of the existing owner base to refer friends and relatives. In most instances, some type of gift or other consideration is provided to the owner who refers a new prospective buyer if the transaction takes place.

Off-Site Sales

Selling vacation ownership units onsite at the development location is typically the preferred option. Prospective buyers can be brought to the development site in order to experience firsthand the recreational facilities and other amenities, as well as to evaluate the quality and style of the resort. Equally important, prospective owners can see and even meet existing owners who enjoy the resort and have a sense of whether and how they would fit in.

In recent years, however, increasing reliance has been placed on off-site sales. An off-site sales center is most typically developed at a high-traffic location such as a shopping mall in a geographic location that promises to be a good source of qualified buyers. For example, an off-site sales location for a development in Florida might be built in suburban New York—a proven deep well of Florida timeshare buyers. Some off-site sales centers feature timeshare unit mock-ups for the prospective buyer to evaluate. However, even in this case, the prospective buyer cannot see or experience the actual resort. Heavy reliance, therefore, is placed on video and other media technology to create a virtual experience. Typically, off-site sales efforts will also focus strongly on the value of the exchange program to the buyer and somewhat deemphasize the sale of the home resort, while not downplaying it altogether.

Ownership Structures and Development Types ————————

Not all timeshare or vacation ownership developments feature the same type of ownership structure. As the industry has matured, the percentage of units owned in the undivided interest or fee simple structure has decreased as other ownership structures have evolved. In addition, timeshare development has evolved from the original "fixed week, fixed location" scenario to include many other development types.

Fee Simple Ownership

From a legal ownership standpoint, the most common ownership structure in the timeshare industry has historically been fee simple ownership. Once the unit has been purchased, the owner has a warrantee deed for a fixed week in a specific unit at one specific home resort. Legally, the owner of such a unit has all the same rights and privileges regarding disposition that he or she would have with any other type of real estate, including right to sell or leave the unit to an heir as part of an estate. Options with respect to the use of the unit itself, including options to rent it for use by others, are typically controlled tightly by ownership agreements.

Right to Use

In the right-to-use scenario, the timeshare unit purchaser does not actually hold the title to the unit. Rather, the developer or owner retains title and the buyer purchases the right to use the property for a certain period of time, usually up to 50 years. At the end of the right-to-use period, the "purchaser" loses all rights and privileges regarding use associated with the unit and such rights revert to the owner or developer. This type of arrangement has proved useful in offshore developments where government regulations make it difficult for nonresidents to own real estate. Nevertheless, the popularity of right to use as a vehicle for "owning" timeshare units has decreased in recent years.

In addition to the different types of ownership structures, a large variety of use arrangements that dictate how and when buyers can use the units they have purchased have evolved in the industry. These structures can be either fee simple or right to use.

One-Week Intervals

This type of use includes the most commonly understood timeshare interval—the fixed week—in which the owner has the right to use a fixed week at a fixed resort every year. Of course, many owners exchange their fixed weeks through internal exchange plans or via exchange companies such as Resort Condominiums International (RCI) and Interval International.

Because of the demands expressed by owners, an increasing number timeshare developments allow the use of one-week intervals to be split into two segments. An owner may, for example, use the first portion (Saturday and Sunday night, for example) at one time and then use the remaining portion (Monday through Friday nights) at another time. Timeshare developments are careful to make sure that such split usage does not interfere with the patterns of demand from other owners who want to use their one-week intervals in a contiguous fashion.

Some timeshare developments have even allowed owners to use one day of their one-week interval at a time. Such use has been more common in urban timeshares. The administrative burdens associated with overseeing booking patterns for such small partial-fraction uses makes them unpopular with timeshare developers.

Biennial Intervals

Developers of timeshare resorts realized many years ago that a larger potential pool of purchasers can be identified if a structure in which the purchaser is buying the timeshare unit for use every other year rather than every year is provided as an option. Such a structure can have the impact of making the purchase more affordable and, therefore, attractive to a larger number of potential buyers. For example, if potential buyers are somewhat put off by a purchase price of $25,000 for a unit that would be theirs to use every year, they may be enticed to purchase if the same unit were offered for sale with a price of $15,000 with the right to use it every other year. In particular, the popularity of this option has burgeoned in areas where travel expenses related to the vacation are likely to be high (for a unit in Hawaii if purchased by someone living in New York, for example).

For the developer, the costs associated with selling a biennial unit, particularly the marketing costs that constitute the single largest portion of selling costs, are not significantly reduced from the more standard annual unit sale. Since the sales price is, however, reduced significantly, the profit associated with this type of sale is often greatly reduced, making it far less attractive from the developer's perspective. For this reason, alternative programs, such as floating time and point systems, are more often being utilized.

Floating Time Intervals

Like biennials, floating time intervals gained popularity in response to potential purchasers' demands for additional flexibility. In the traditional arrangement, a buyer purchases, owns, and is expected to use a fixed week in a fixed unit at the home resort. A floating interval arrangement allows the buyer more flexibility regarding when, over the course of the calendar year, he or she makes use of the unit. Often, some restrictions apply regarding the available float times. Since buyers often pay different amounts to purchase a unit depending on the season, floating arrangements often limit the owner's options to other weeks within that same season (particularly in low seasons). Many resorts may also offer floating units, meaning that the buyer can make use of other units in the resort during the time he or she uses his or her unit. Having both floating weeks and floating units gives a resort additional flexibility.

Exchanging Intervals

There is virtual consensus in the timeshare industry that without the element of exchange, the timeshare industry would never have achieved the success it has to date. Since a large majority of vacationers do not chose to spend their vacation at the same location year after year, the ability to exchange units for use at other resort locations is critical in the decision to buy a timeshare. Owners may exchange for another unit or different time at the home resort—typically called an internal exchange—or they may exchange for the same time slot or a different timeslot at a different location. The exchange process is facilitated by exchange companies, such as RCI and Interval International, with whom the home resort must have an affiliation and to whom the owner of the unit must pay a membership fee.

Because unit-weeks have varying values based on the time of the year that they occur as well as the location and quality of the home resort, exchange companies serve as clearinghouses so that units of similar value are traded or exchanged and no owners feel as if they are not getting adequate trade value.

A somewhat unheralded benefit of the exchange process and a credit to the exchange companies is that the consistency of quality in the timeshare industry has improved as the frequency of exchange has increased. In order to take part in the exchange programs offered by the large exchange companies, a resort must maintain a satisfactory level of service and physical-plant quality. To be denied access to the major exchange players detracts significantly from the value of a unit.

Point-Based Ownership and Vacation Clubs

At present, the point system of ownership offers the maximum amount of flexibility to the timeshare owner. Rather than purchase fixed weeks, floating weeks, or any other rigidly defined segments, in this case the buyer purchases points that can be redeemed for time at the home resort, time at other affiliated resorts, and in many cases (with large companies like Marriott, for example), for other travel services and benefits. In this fashion, the point system is like the many frequent stay and frequent traveler programs that abound in the travel industry today.

Vacation clubs typically are structured to offer a system of related resorts in distinct destinations with diverse appeal to the buyer. Most vacation club operations rely on a point system in which an owner may use points at a number of affiliated locations within the club system. As an added layer, vacation club points are typically exchangeable through the traditional exchange process, giving the owner yet another level of flexibility.

Vacation clubs and the point systems they typically employ are greatly attractive to the consumer. From the timeshare developer and operator's standpoint, however, they are far more complex to manage and administer than the more traditional models. Recent advances in computer technology have helped to deal with this problem to a great extent. This has helped resorts that are part of these systems to maximize occupancy as well as member/guest satisfaction.

Fractional Ownership

Fractional ownership describes an ownership structure in which the buyer purchases a unit for a period of time greatly in excess of the traditional timeshare week. Many fractional programs provide the ability to purchase quarters (i.e., one quarter of the year). In the words of a prominent industry executive, "Timeshare provides a prepaid alternative to a hotel stay, while fractional ownership provides a prepaid alternative to a full-time vacation home."

In essence, most buyers of fractional shares view their purchase as one that will provide them with a vacation home at a reduced cost and with added benefits. Fractional programs, which are in some cases being marketed as "private residence clubs," typically provide all the amenities of a second home as well as full hotel services. Added benefits accrue to owners in that they may store personal items such as pictures and clothing on site when they are not using the unit. A typical ownership arrival experience might include being picked up upon arrival at the airport and arriving at the unit to find personal items displayed, the refrigerator and cupboards stocked with food and drink of one's choice, beds and bathrooms made up with linens and towels of one's choosing, and a sense that all is as it should be.

At the same time, ownership of a fractional unit relieves the owner of the maintenance concerns and headaches that ownership of a freestanding individual vacation home would entail. Such concerns can be magnified in the case where a second home in a resort area is unused for a substantial portion of the year and, therefore, no one is physically present to attend to problems such as broken water pipes, missing roof shingles, and the like.

It goes without saying that fractional ownership, with its wonderful benefits and lack of hassle, is relatively expensive to purchase.

Feasibility Analysis—Moving Outside the Box

An attempt has been made to define and to differentiate the timeshare industry from its sister lodging and resort industries. While many aspects of the feasibility analysis for a timeshare development are reminiscent of those for a more traditional lodging development, understanding the nuances of timeshare development necessitates understanding that there are subtle and not-so-subtle differences in the way in which a timeshare development moves from conceptual thought to reality when compared with a classical resort hotel development. The key sub-agendas of the typical feasibility analysis process are described briefly below and explored with regard to how they must be tailored in analyzing a timeshare development.

Site Analysis

As with any hotel or resort development, the old axiom "location, location, location" applies to the timeshare industry with respect to a development's potential for success. In general, selection criteria for a timeshare development site can be summarized as follows:

1. The geographic area of the development must, in general, be one that is attractive to large numbers of people in terms of being a location of choice for vacationing and spending extended amounts of time. For this reason, resort areas with a long history of successful visitation levels are typically targeted for timeshare development. It is more difficult to ensure timeshare success in untested, newly evolving resort areas since, in addition to marketing the timeshare development itself, the developer must market the location to increase

awareness of it. Even more importantly, one of the critical aspects of timeshare success is high volume of traffic near a location where a sales center can be located (preferably on site). For this reason, an evolving resort location without significant existing visitation creates a difficult environment for timeshare development success.

2. The site chosen for the timeshare development must be physically suitable for it. Most timeshare resorts have extensive pools and other water features in addition to recreational amenities. The site must be physically capable of providing these along with an attractive environment in order to be successful.

3. All of the necessary utilities and services must be available at the site. While this would seem like common sense, there have been timeshare developments that have run into difficulty because of lack of basic utilities. Development in the Canary Islands in the early 1980s proceeded only as fast as provision for water on many of the islands could be made—something that was foreign to the mainland developers before beginning development in the islands.

4. The site must be accessible, both at the local level (the road system) and in terms of air access from more distant locations. Many successful timeshare developments have catered to markets that are primarily drive-in markets, particularly in areas such as central Florida. However, the general rule is that adequate airlift must be in place to provide a constant flow of visitors. Particularly with respect to bringing in potential purchasers on mini-vacs, excellent airlift is critical. Not only must there be airlift in place, but it must provide convenient service to major distribution hubs without requiring a variety of unpopular connecting flights.

5. One of the most valuable site criteria that any timeshare development can have is a location proximate to an existing major hotel or resort. While timeshare developments can succeed without this, having such proximity is very helpful to achieving success. Each guest at the traditional resort becomes a potential purchaser of a timeshare unit. As noted earlier, in order to sell out a typical timeshare development, literally thousands of prospective purchasers must be identified and an existing established resort can provide many of these prospects. Large hotel and resort companies have achieved great success with developing timeshare components as an integral part of existing traditional resorts in their portfolios.

Area Review and Economic Considerations

Unlike the development scenario for transient hotels and similar to the traditional resort industry, local economic conditions in the area where a timeshare resort is developed have only an indirect impact on its probable viability. However, employment, income levels, and the general level of prosperity in the area surrounding the development can affect the ease with which a development is marketed, especially if the economic conditions result in the surrounding environment appearing unappealing or dangerous in any way.

With respect to offshore timeshare developments, including those in South America and China for example, the stability of the local economy does come into play. Since timeshares must attract investment from a large number of purchasers, a perception that the local economy in any given location is unstable and could possibly jeopardize the ability to recoup or enjoy the investment may place a negative pall over the ability to generate timeshare sales.

Supply and Demand Issues

One area where feasibility analysis differs substantially for timeshares when compared with traditional hotel developments has to do with supply and demand dynamics. In a classical hotel development analysis, the feasibility analyst performs several fundamental steps in order to project the level of performance (occupancy) for the project being analyzed. These are, in very simplified fashion:

1. Identification of the defined competitive set for the new project being contemplated. What hotels, with how many rooms, and in what areas cater to demand that is similar in nature or that could accrue directly to the proposed project? This defined competitive set could, in the case of a resort, consist of hotels in distant resort locations that are competitive with the resort area where the analysis is taking place. Alternatively, the competitive set could consist only of hotels in a neatly defined target area.

2. Gathering of data regarding the performance of the defined competitive set as a whole. On the macro level, the analyst may make use of special industry reports, such as those compiled by Smith Travel Research, for the defined set. These reports will provide occupancy and average rate data for a requested historical period. In some markets, such macro reports are also available containing information regarding the market segmentation (the percent of business coming from various market segments).

3. Gathering of detailed data regarding the performance (primarily occupancy, rate and market mix) of individual hotels and resorts within the defined competitive set. This entails site inspections and interviews with management at the hotels in the defined set, supplemented in many cases with interviews at the corporate or chain level.

4. Analysis of the data gathered in order to assess each of the competitors' strengths and weaknesses by market segment weighed against their penetration (percent of fair share) in each of the market segments.

5. Projection of penetration by segment, resulting in a projection of occupancy for the proposed hotel being analyzed. This serves as a basis for the balance of the feasibility analysis, including projection of average rate and full financial forecasts.

In the case of a timeshare analysis, the feasibility analyst is typically tasked not with projecting occupancy for the resort from transient users, but with projecting how quickly the timeshare units will sell and at what price point. For this reason, the classical supply and demand analysis format is of little use to the analyst. A key

Exhibit 3 Sample Historical Absorption Levels

	Resort at Example A Beach			Example B Beach Resort	
Year	Interval Units Sold	Percent of Total Units Sold	Year	Interval Units Sold	Percent of Total Units Sold
1998	446	7%	1990	157	5%
1999	1077	17%	1991	570	17%
2000	1472	23%	1992	1123	34%
2001	1201	19%	1993	815	25%
2002	546	9%	1994	238	7%
Total sold	4742		1995	99	3%
Left to sell	1582		1996	68	2%
			1997	40	1%
			1998	45	1%
			1999	40	1%
			2000	36	1%
			2001	21	1%
			2002	12	0%
			Total sold	3264	
			Left to sell	0	

industry executive aptly sums it up: "Timeshare is not a sought-after commodity. You can't go out and penetrate an existing pool of demand, you need to go out and *create* demand for your project."

Projection of Unit Sellout and Pricing

Because there is no pool of demand to penetrate, in order to project sellout pace, the feasibility analyst is faced with identifying comparable timeshare developments that can be used as models for the proposed development. In the case of well-established resorts with multiple timeshare developments, this can be a relatively straightforward process. In Exhibit 3, data is gathered for two existing weekly timeshare resorts that are deemed to be good models for the one being studied.

In this case, the analyst has a clear indication that the majority of unit sales occur in the first five years after the development begins the sales process, with (as shown with Example B Beach Resort) the number of units sold annually trailing off rather dramatically after that. Because of the protracted sales pace, most timeshare resorts open in phases and begin development of a second or third phase when sales of the first are well underway.

One major issue that presents a challenge to timeshare developers in terms of the sellout phase is the fact that existing owners may begin to resell their units within a relatively short timeframe, sometimes at lower prices than those being asked by the developer. Since units may be comparable to those being sold by the developer, this can have an impact on both timing of sellout and pricing.

The process of projecting pricing per week or other interval unit is similar to the process of projecting sellout timing. Comparable resorts are examined and their pricing is analyzed on a per-square-foot basis for comparably sized and located units. Seasonality and other factors are taken into account in order to project weighted average unit sales prices.

Financial Projections

Again departing from the traditional hospitality model, financial projections for the timeshare or interval developer focus not on the timeshare as an operating entity, but on the timeshare during the sellout period. During this period, the inflow and outflow of funds is unlike anything in the traditional hospitality arena. In the financing arena, the needs of the lender are also different and this is reflected in the way that financial projections are produced.

While on the surface it would appear that a timeshare is nothing more than a condominium cut into smaller, more digestible pieces, there are key aspects of the development that make it much more difficult for a lender to comprehend and synthesize. For that reason, much more scrutiny is placed upon the financial projections prepared. The following items should be considered when preparing the projections:

- Month-by-month cash flow projections are critical to show the ebbs and flows of available cash. The typical annual statement is of little use since the lender must know where the lean months will occur. Much of the revenue stream is not from the traditional source (the sale of units), so this month-by-month projection can be quite complex.

- It is not unusual for about half of the revenue derived from timeshare unit sales to be spent in marketing the project. This varies substantially from any traditional hospitality model and is an area where it takes a traditional lender some time to gain comfort.

- Should a traditional hotel or residential project get into financial difficulties, a lender may be faced with taking the project back and finding competent management to market and operate the project. In the arena of timeshare sales and marketing, it may be very difficult for the lender to find an organization that will simply step in and take over the marketing and operation of the development.

- Unlike in a traditional hospitality development, the income stream (and the place where profits for the developer can be found) for timeshare developments consists of (1) profits from the sale of the units themselves, (2) interest arbitrage on providing financing the buyers of the units, and (3) ongoing fees associated with the homeowners association.

    The portion of the income stream related to interest arbitrage is typically more substantial than the other two combined. Traditional timeshare projects have a significant number of buyers who take developer-offered financing. Developers typically finance from 40 to 90 percent of the consumers who purchase units. Exhibit 4 illustrates the percentage of total sales value that was

Exhibit 4   Percent of Total Sales Financed By Developers

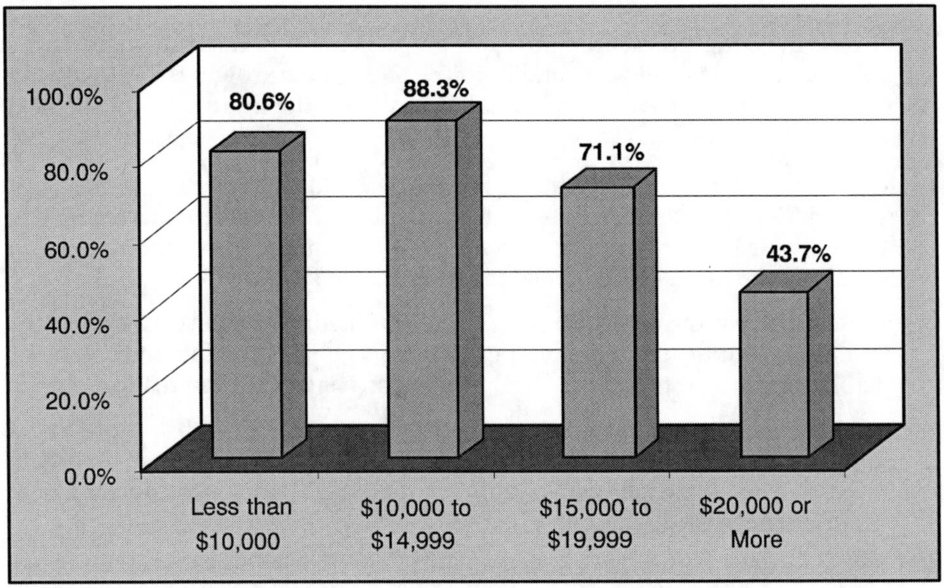

Source: "Financial Performance of the US Timeshare Industry," prepared by PricewaterhouseCoopers for the American Resort Development Association, 2004.

financed at various price points during 2003 (the most recent data available). The profit on this can be so substantial that some developers rely entirely on this as their profit and expect no profit from the sale of the units themselves. In part, profit in this area is driven by the interest rates that are charged to the consumer for the loans provided. The general rule of thumb, however, is that developers target a 20 percent profit on unit sales (remembering that approximately 50 percent of the sales price goes for marketing/administration and that the product itself costs from 20 to 35 percent of the sales price to produce). This lopsided profit potential in which the developer is likely to make more money from lending than from developing and selling presents a very difficult-to-understand financing scenario, necessitating creative and detailed financial projections during the feasibility analysis process. (Interestingly, because the demographic for fractional-ownership units is so completely different than for traditional timeshare units, there typically is little or no profit made by the developer from the process of providing loans to buyers. Lenders, therefore, tend to be less ill at ease with projections for this type of projects.)

In summary, because of the complexity of the timeshare development process and the unique way in which the developer makes profit, feasibility studies for timeshare projects share few similarities with those prepared for more traditional hospitality developments and are the subject of intense scrutiny on the part of lenders and investors.

Challenges and Opportunities for the Future ⎯⎯⎯⎯⎯⎯

By all measures, the timeshare and vacation ownership industry has grown by leaps and bounds in recent years and is poised to continue growing. The following clouds on the horizon have the potential to challenge the industry over the next several years:

- Consumer privacy laws, including the national "do not call" list, are making it more difficult to market to potential timeshare purchasers. This has resulted in timeshare marketers coming up with cross-branding and other strategies in order to keep up the pace of new prospect contacts.

- Offsetting the positive impact that Internet marketing has had on the industry, cumbersome interstate regulations continue to hinder the sale of timeshares across state lines into states where registrations have not been made.

- Rapidly escalating land and construction costs, along with a more rapid appreciation in prices of full-time residential condominiums than in timeshare prices, are making it increasingly difficult for timeshare to be the development candidate with the highest and best use.

- Resale values continue to be substantially lower than values of new units, even when product quality is comparable. As the industry matures, resales will become even more of a phenomenon, creating downward pressure on new development prices at the same time that development costs are rising.

At the same time, the following trends point toward an optimistic outlook:

- Timeshare and vacation ownership buyers are increasingly sophisticated—many industry executives consider them the leaders in the hospitality industry in terms of their product awareness and demand for increasing quality.

- Well-capitalized brand-name lodging companies and well-capitalized developers continue to work hand-in-hand to bring forth new development.

- Capital sources for timeshare and other hospitality developments are plentiful (at least at the time of this writing).

- Consumers' demand for flexibility has resulted in a new wave of product segmentation similar to what occurred in the hotel industry during the 1980s, making the complexion of the industry more interesting.

- ARDA, now a mature and well-focused trade association, has helped the industry reach a new level of self-awareness, which has produced self-policing with respect to maintaining quality and integrity.

And so, the timeshare and vacation ownership industry (the demise of which has been predicted at least several times over the course of the last 30 years) continues to grow into the new millennium. It suffers an occasional chest cold but, for the most part, it has become a healthy adult that continues to raise the spirits of its more seasoned and mature (dare we say elderly?) hospitality brethren, if for no other reason than the fact that optimism is contagious.

****

The author gratefully acknowledges the following individuals for generously sharing their time and insight to assist in the preparation of this chapter:

- Howard Nusbaum, President, American Resort Development Association
- Lani Kane-Hanan, Marriott Vacation Club International
- John Burlingame, Hyatt Vacation Ownership, Inc.
- David Gilbert, Interval International
- Michael Schiff, Resort Condominiums International
- Kathleen Conroy, HVS International

13

Sales and Revenue Management

By *Lalia Rach, Ed.D.,* and *Robert A. Gilbert, CHME, CHA*

Lalia Rach, founder of Rach Enterprises, is a trusted consultant, popular moderator, and internationally recognized speaker and is widely regarded as knowledgeable, practical, and humorous, with a genuine passion for excellence. She serves as an adviser to senior level executives at many of America's leading companies, with a focus on future trends, branding, and marketing strategies. Her clients include corporate, association, and government leaders in the hospitality, tourism, sales and marketing, entertainment, and sports industries. She has developed numerous presentations on topics as diverse as dynamic leadership strategies; socioeconomic trends; perspectives on economic development; changes in affluent markets; cultural heritage programs; organizational management; generational marketing; team building; customer service; and perspectives on urban tourism development. She also writes exten- sively on technology, management, and service, regularly contributes articles to the HSMAI Marketing Review *and other publications, and is regularly interviewed by the national news media as an expert on hospitality, tourism, and service issues. Dr. Rach is Associate Dean and HVS International Chair at the Tisch Center for Hospitality, Tourism, and Sports Management at New York University in New York City. She holds a B.S. and M.B.A. from the University of Wisconsin and an Ed.D. from The George Washington University in Washington, D.C.*

Robert A. Gilbert is President and Chief Executive Officer of the Hospitality Sales & Marketing Association International, the definitive hospitality and travel marketing association in the world. Before joining HSMAI in 1995, Gilbert was the vice president of marketing for Richfield Hospitality Services, Inc., at that time the largest hotel management company in the world, where he oversaw the corporate marketing support for all Richfield hotels, which included 170 hotels representing every price tier and product type in the industry. Gilbert holds a Bachelor of Science degree from the School of Hotel Administration at Cornell University in Ithaca, NY, and has been a member of HSMAI since joining the student chapter at Cornell. He is a frequent guest lecturer at Cornell. Gilbert serves on the Board of Directors of the American Hotel & Lodging Association (AH&LA) and the Convention Industry Council (CIC), and is also on the Board of Trustees for the World Tourism Foundation as well as the Travel and Tourism Coalition of the Travel Industry Association of America.

As THE NEW CENTURY UNFOLDS, the U.S. hotel industry has weathered the aftermath of the September 11, 2001, terrorist attacks. The attacks ended a period of unprecedented rate and revenue per available room (RevPAR) growth for the industry. Diminishing occupancy, rate, and RevPAR throughout the industry resulted in large-scale employee layoffs, mothballing of facilities and equipment, and retrenchment in all areas of spending. Less than five years after the event, hotel fundamentals in many destinations have returned to record growth of profit, facilities, and demand.

The foundation of the hotel industry traditionally has been service and hospitality. The overriding job elements for managers and employees were the quality of the welcome and the level of attention provided to every guest. Certainly the hotel was a business, but the expectation of the industry and society was that professionals and hourly employees learned on the job. As the business progressed, management ranks expanded to include sales and marketing professionals whose responsibility was to ensure a steady stream of business. The emphasis was not on the quality of the business. Value was determined instead by the constancy of rooms utilized over a day, a month, or a year. The statistic of greatest importance was occupancy—a measure in daily flux—so the focus for sales personnel was to acquire and maintain a steady flow of business through the door. A simple equation was followed throughout the industry: when demand was low, rates were lowered and when demand was strong, rates increased.

The overriding mantra for more than a century was "location, location, location," denoting that the physical location of the hotel dominated all business considerations. Whether a hotel was close to transportation (train stations, highways), in the center of a business district, at a halfway point in a journey, or at a particular destination was central to the decision process for the traveling public. It was location that brought guests, who in turn brought revenue and profitability. This concept was so firmly rooted in the hotel mindset that it was considered by many to be the only necessary "business" decision. This is not to suggest that innovation and promotion did not occur, but such change was not the norm as the industry was slow to adopt the business practices of the times.

In the mid-1990s, the *hospitality business*, defined traditionally by service, independent ownership, European management, and the "all business is good business" school of thought, evolved into the *business of hospitality*, characterized by public ownership of multi-branded companies, short-term profit orientation, the rise of revenue management, and the exploitation of the Internet as a powerful distribution channel. The U.S. hotel industry began formalizing the process by which revenue was managed and evaluated when the process of yield management, which was developed in the airline industry a decade earlier, was adapted and refined for use in hotels. As a result, the knowledge base for general managers and directors of sales is expected to include financial management, e-commerce, database marketing, and consumer behavior.

The sales component is now inexorably linked to managing profitability, valuing revenue, and qualifying customer worth. It no longer is enough to book business. Sales directors now must be able to demonstrate the long-term worth of a client. By building a dynamic relationship profile, we can analyze what may appear to be a marginal piece of business in the near term to determine its long-term significance. Among the factors to be analyzed are the extent of customer service demands, level of discount expectations, timing of the business, and the overall potential for growth. It may be that profitability is diminished greatly by a combination of increased labor costs and loss of rate during a time when demand far outstrips supply. Statistical analysis may also show that what at first glance appeared to be a coup really would be a drain on profitability.

The business of hospitality is fully engaged in the practice of revenue and cost management, which should not be viewed as ancillary to the sales process, but as the rightful evolution of the sales component. The director of sales must, as a matter of course, now have a comprehensive understanding of the distribution channels, mix of reservation channels, and selling strategies that will meet the revenue expectations of the organization. The most fundamental skill is the ability to measure a booking in terms of the business value proposition. Not all business is equally valuable, so the sales team effort must be focused on securing revenue that fits within the goals of the business, adds value on a short- and long-term basis, and does not diminish the strategic positioning of the business. All sales personnel must have a clear understanding of return on investment, mix, and performance expectations in order to make qualified decisions. Forecasting and planning, creating a selling strategy, and analyzing and understanding trends now must be embraced as principal sales management skills. In light of increased competition, social and economic realities, and consumer trends, the director of sales must be able to manage the quantity, quality, and mix of business in the pipeline and ultimately grow the business with an appropriate price-value-profit proposition.

Tradition has held that personality, the ability to network, and a killer instinct are crucial traits of a first-class salesperson. While those aspects are necessary, they no longer are the essential elements of a world-class salesperson. Successful sales professionals now must possess an intellectual capacity and flexibility that allows them to change tactics on an immediate and strategic basis.

Consider the extent of the change in the process for establishing room rates. Setting room rates during the second half of the twentieth century was a relatively one-dimensional procedure. Sales personnel checked the rates of individual competitors and used the information to create a comparison chart of rates by market type (group, corporate, rack, home-based). The chart was used by the general manager and the director of sales to determine room rates for the next three-, six-, or twelve-month period. Once the rates were set, sales personnel were sent out to find business. The key was to book any business so that occupancy would increase rather than decrease. It was a low-tech and unsophisticated but universally acceptable pricing method that reinforced a passive approach to managing and growing revenue.

The passive approach to managing the business also dominated the sales process, as the most common sales technique was the cold call. Sales personnel were expected to conduct a set number of cold calls per week. Their effectiveness and efficiency as salespeople was determined based on the number of calls without appointments made to potential sources of business. This quota focused on calls made, not business booked. Sales personnel were encouraged to book business during traditionally slow times. For non-resort properties, this would include the week between Christmas and New Year's Eve. The key was to book any business so that occupancy would trend upward rather than down. There was little regard for rate as occupancy was the key measure of success. It was a rote, narrow, uncoordinated approach that did not establish a point of differentiation and resulted in loss of revenue.

Perhaps the greatest conceptual change for managers was the idea that not all revenue is equal. There is a cost to accepting one reservation over another. Managers must consider variables and understand the nature of demand in a macro and micro sense to determine the quality of the revenue. This required a shift in thinking and positioned information as a key variable in the drive to increase profitability. Base business models were revised to manage information in a timely manner. Today a formal method for managing revenue and profitability is utilized throughout the industry to determine the most appropriate pricing and sales approach for a given demand/supply situation. Hotels, car rental agencies, restaurants, amusement parks, and golf courses now employ sophisticated technology first developed in the airline industry to monitor, analyze, and refine the pricing and sales processes.

Revenue Management Definition and Philosophies

Whether the goal is to gain market share or manage volume, revenue and yield management systems have greatly helped all types of hotels to generate additional profit regardless of the economic cycle. Any hotel without a revenue management system is losing profit, as rates are not being systematically established or adjusted. Revenue management applies to every revenue-generating department in a hotel, but this chapter will focus mostly on room revenue management.

The basic objective of revenue management is to maximize a hotel's average daily rate (ADR) when demand is high and maximize occupancy when demand is low. This can generate significant incremental profits for the hotel regardless of the market conditions. The formal application of mathematical principles embedded in a software application manipulated by knowledgeable professionals can allow an individual property, its owners, and its management company to develop a real-time forecasting and pricing strategy. Regardless of the technology, the core components of a solid revenue-management philosophy include:

- Reservation sales.
- Forecasting.
- Pricing.
- Strategy.
- Distribution.
- Measurement.

Reservation Sales

While online reservation channels have rapidly gained acceptance, phone reservations continue to be a source of bookings, so it is important to train phone reservationists at call centers or on-property to be salespeople capable of converting every inquiry into a confirmed reservation. Consumers everywhere are price-conscious and have learned not to accept the first rate quote but to counter with a request for a special rate. To complete the transaction successfully at a positive rate, reservationists must be far more than order takers. They must be capable of "selling" rate to price-savvy consumers. To accomplish this, hotels should develop professional reservation selling standards in four areas:

- Line criteria or telephone service standards
- Research and selling
- Courtesy impression
- Booking and revenue protection

To develop or improve selling standards, hotels should engage a research company at the property level to measure phone sales performance. There are many research companies that can help develop standards for individual hotels and conduct test calls to determine how well the reservations staff is doing.

Forecasting

To ensure that ADR is being maximized when demand is high and that occupancy is being maximized when demand is low, it is vital to have a forecasting process in place that identifies daily occupancy patterns in a timely, organized, and useful manner so that management can address the situation. The key components of forecasting include knowledge about the following:

- Historic demand
- Current demand trends
- Room nights lost or denials
- Reservation lead time
- Transient pick-up
- Group block commitments and status

A calendar with rooms available, rooms sold to date, and rooms forecasted to be sold should incorporate assumptions based on the key components. The calendar is used as a strategic tool by the reservations and sales departments to determine pricing strategies and allows changes that will significantly affect revenue far in advance of the actual forecast date. It will result in the exclusion of low or discounted rates during high-demand times and the offering of discount categories and lower group rates in low-demand times.

The calendar enforces a disciplined decision-making process by creating a structure and logic for pricing. To accomplish this, the calendar should use demand tags—set terminology that defines a high, medium, or low demand period or date. A demand tag is simply a label given to any particular day to signify the anticipated volume of business for that particular day. The calendar should reflect a forecasted occupancy by day at least one year in advance.

Pricing

Yield-based pricing philosophies should be designed in transient and group rate strategy schedules. Transient rates should encompass all individual rates that need to be available to service the existing and desired customer segments for the hotel. The demand tags from the forecast calendar should trigger the opening and closing of predetermined rate categories.

Group rate benchmarks should be tied to the demand tags as well. The benchmarks function as guidelines for the sales team as they negotiate group business and indicate the rate range available based upon the demand anticipated for the requested dates. Group salespeople should be given incentives to sell the highest possible rate in the lowest possible demand period. To accomplish this efficiently, they must be given the authority to negotiate without going through numerous approval channels. The forecast calendar should be that predetermined approval.

Strategy

Key hotel executives should conduct yield strategy meetings at least once a week. The objectives of these meetings are to review the forecast calendar, discuss new information (demand and competitive influences, highlights of booking and reservation activity since last meeting, etc.), and confirm or reset the demand tags. The revised forecast calendar with demand tags should be distributed to all reservations, sales, and marketing personnel.

Distribution

Distribution of hotel inventory, rates, and information is more complicated today than it ever has been. The information about an individual hotel must be managed in the chain or franchise reservation system, the global distribution systems (GDSs), Internet distribution systems (IDSs), and any other third-party systems (e.g., representation firms). In each of the systems, property inventory, rates, and information screens must be current, useful, and error-free.

The use of electronic channels to source and book hotel rooms is no longer the sole concern of travel agents. The channels now are available directly to corporations, wholesalers, and consumers. Electronic channels provide instant reservations from consumers located anywhere in the world, so the proper management of the channels is vitally important to every hotel's revenue stream. Systems vary from those that do not list a hotel on dates when no rooms are available to those that show only hotels that are indexed to the requested key feature.

The details of every system are far too extensive to review here. Consider establishing a sales position or area (depending on the size of the property) solely dedicated to the online channels with the expectation that it will monitor reservation production, develop virtual selling strategies, and manage revenue opportunities. The online channels increasingly are dominating traditional sales efforts and ultimately influence revenue growth and stability. Hotels should recognize the change and add resources to manage the input and output. All franchise reservations systems, GDSs, and Web-site systems have a variety of electronic marketing and messaging opportunities that could be used to extend the reach of managed on-line distribution efforts.

Measurement

In addition to activity and productivity reports, there are a number of measurement tools that can be used to monitor the business performance of a hotel. The areas of performance that should be monitored include the revenue activity throughout the hotel, the franchise system's and GDSs' productivity, and the competitive market set.

The revenue activity reports measure such key sales and marketing indicators as the growth in RevPAR and reservation conversion percentages per property, including reservation denials, useable denials, and regrets.

To determine the GDSs' and franchise systems' productivity, a series of reports covering net room night contribution, toll-free system statistics, and the reservation delivery per GDS, and other areas should be reviewed on a timely and constant basis. These reports vary considerably by brand, GDS, and reservation service and require an extensive orientation to understand the breadth of analysis available for review.

The performance of the hotel relative to the competitive market set is by far the most accurate measure of the success of the sales and marketing effort. Performance indicators including penetration, rate, and yield indices and the percent change of these indicators are vital comparisons to gauge the impact of decisions on the hotel's bottom line. Regardless of market occupancy, the indices reflect performance relative to the market. The indices are an objective way to measure hotel market share performance and are applicable for any type of hotel, in any price tier, chain or independent, in any market or location.

In North America and portions of the Caribbean, the source for competitive set performance and benchmark statistics is the STAR report (Smith Travel Accommodations Report) by Smith Travel Research. A typical monthly STAR report will include pages of key performance data about an individual hotel and a competitive market set with monthly and year-to-date actual data, a trend report, and a competitive set response report. The monthly and year-to-date reports include occupancy and rate information for the individual hotel, the market, the market by price tier, the market tract, market tract by price tier, the market tract by chain segment, and the hotel's competitive set. The 12-month rolling trend report includes index trend information comparing the individual hotel to the competitive set. The competitive set response report verifies which hotels in the competitive set have contributed performance data to each month's statistics. The competitive set comparison data is perhaps the most important data for ownership and management to review. The most significant feature of this data is that the management of the individual hotel defines which hotels make up the competitive set. The set can include as few as three competing hotels and the individual hotel. The sampling percentage for all hotel markets participating in the STR sampling is significant, so the competitive set data is a true measure of how the competitive set is performing in almost all cases.

Within the report, the trend of a hotel's yield index is by far the most comprehensive measurement of its sales and marketing department and revenue management initiatives. Yield index is the RevPAR of a hotel divided by the RevPAR of the aggregate competitive set. Since RevPAR is a combined measure of occupancy and ADR, the index indicates whether the hotel is achieving its fair share of revenue on a per-available-room basis. A yield greater than 100 percent indicates the hotel is achieving more than its fair share, while a yield less than 100 percent means the hotel is getting less than its fair share.

It is the combination of occupancy and ADR, or RevPAR, that represents total room revenue. Regardless of budgeting assumptions for occupancy and ADR, RevPAR relative to market conditions is the ultimate indicator of the successful delivery of room revenue. Three examples provide a comparison of the various situations that exist between the RevPAR of a hotel and its competitors.

Example 1. The hotel's RevPAR for the month of January is $84.00 and the RevPAR of the competitive set during the same month is $80.00. In January of the previous year, RevPAR was $78.00 for the hotel and $76.00 for the competitive set.

$$\text{Current year:} \quad \frac{\$84.00}{\$80.00} \ = \ 1.05 \text{ or } 105\%$$

$$\text{Previous year:} \quad \frac{\$78.00}{\$76.00} \ = \ 1.03 \text{ or } 103\%$$

This demonstrates that the hotel is getting more than its fair share of revenue and continues to improve its premium performance in the market.

Example 2. The hotel's RevPAR for the month of January is $88.00 and the RevPAR of the competitive set during the same month is $90.00. In January of the previous year, RevPAR was $80.00 for the hotel and $85.00 for the competitive set.

$$\text{Current year:} \quad \frac{\$88.00}{\$90.00} \ = \ 0.98 \text{ or } 98\%$$

$$\text{Previous year:} \quad \frac{\$80.00}{\$85.00} \ = \ 0.94 \text{ or } 94\%$$

This example shows the hotel is getting less than its fair share of revenue, but its yield management strategies have improved its position relative to the market. The hotel is growing its revenue capture at a rate faster than competitors.

Example 3. The hotel's RevPAR for the month of January is $84.00 and the RevPAR of the competitive set during the same month is $75.00. In January of the previous year, RevPAR was $78.00 for the hotel and $68.00 for the competitive set.

$$\text{Current year:} \quad \frac{\$84.00}{\$75.00} \ = \ 1.12 \text{ or } 112\%$$

$$\text{Previous year:} \quad \frac{\$78.00}{\$68.00} \ = \ 1.15 \text{ or } 115\%$$

This indicates the hotel is getting more than its fair share of revenue but the decline in the yield index indicates that competitors are growing RevPAR at a faster rate. This is *not* positive and the declining trend in yield index should not be allowed to continue. It is an indication that the hotel team may not be aggressive enough in growing either rate or occupancy.

Sales and Marketing in an Internet World

Internet marketing and electronic distribution are vitally important to the success of a hotel, a brand, and a management company. The simple financial reality that distribution costs can be as much as 30 percent of room revenue should compel owners and managers to consistently review their hotels' approach to distribution. In addition to the financial implications, distribution affects the marketing function in two crucial ways. First, distribution affects all decisions in the marketing mix (pricing, promotion, sales, and packaging) through its impact on marketing costs and relationships. Second, distribution creates a mutually dependent commitment between participants (hotels, intermediaries, brands) through an on- and off-line infrastructure that is not easily changed and very expensive to recreate.

The online channel has become part of the service delivery structure that customers are accustomed to and comfortable using for information gathering and booking. The ease of use, the transparency of price, and the capacity to compare properties are elements that empower consumers and reinforce their desire to be equal partners in, if not in charge of, the transaction.

With the advent of the Internet, the ability to market and sell hotel rooms no longer is a function of the size of the hotel or the wealth of its owners. An independent hotel can create a Web site that markets and sells rooms to anyone, which, to some degree, allows them to compete with larger branded companies. But to compete successfully and grow revenue, a hotel (independent or brand, large or small, management company or chain) must develop an integrated multi-channel approach to building and managing an electronic marketing and distribution strategy. Among the multi-channel components are:

- Central reservations systems.
- GDSs.
- IDSs.
- Hotel Web sites.
- Brand Web sites (if applicable).
- Travel metasearch sites (e.g., Yahoo! FareChase, Kayak.com, Mobissimo, Cheapflights).
- Automated and online requests for proposals.
- Group and meeting reservations Web sites.
- Sales and catering systems.
- Property management systems.

- Revenue management systems.

- Research and monitoring systems.

- Business intelligence systems (including customer relationship management).

These components are detailed in a special 2004 report published by the Hospitality Sales and Marketing Association International entitled "Demystifying Distribution."

The selection of the multi-channel components most likely will be determined by the resources (human and financial) available for use in building the hotel's electronic marketing and distribution strategy. It is far better to develop an incremental strategy that consistently incorporates additional components than to attempt an all-or-nothing approach.

Looking Forward

The impact of technology on the hotel industry stretches into every aspect of the business. The Internet has redefined distribution to the leisure and business travel segment and, in doing so, has changed the manner in which industry interacts with and values guests and visitors. The key to a successful strategy may be the level of trust the traveler has with the distribution channel as technology has allowed consumers to become more informed negotiators and decision-makers.

The primary goal for the hotel industry is profitability. This requires a comprehensive knowledge of financial and budgetary information including demand analysis, marketing programs' return on investment, cost analysis, and modeling. Advancing technology will enable any hotel to accurately and thoroughly track and forecast the lifetime value of a customer and use the information to produce rate and amenity offerings. At the foundation of the change within the industry is the fact that all actions and individuals now are measured on overall return on investment. As a result, the marketing and sales aspects of every organization are being transformed in an ever-expanding and particular fashion.

While strategy and analysis continue to expand in sophistication and availability, sales and revenue managers must stay connected to the customer. A solid relationship with customers supported by ever-increasing levels of service is equally critical to achieving revenue goals on the short- and long-term basis. The focused blending of high-tech and high-touch is crucial to meet consumer demands that product, service, and experience be compelling and consistent.

While increasingly demanding greater price transparency, consumer segments have become increasingly opaque. The lines of demarcation, more easily defined before the 1990s, have blurred as travelers blend the purpose of their trips, leaving the hotel industry to struggle with static definitions. This makes revenue analysis all the more difficult as the traditional definitions do not adequately represent the demand and make it far more challenging to provide sophisticated profiles of the guest.

Advancing technology will enable hotels to accurately and thoroughly forecast and track the lifetime value of a customer and use the information to produce desired profitability levels. As the concept of value continues to evolve, the financial analysis knowledge and skills of hotel sales and marketing professionals must strengthen.

Internet Resources

Hotel Electronic Distribution Network Association
www.hedna.org

Hospitality Sales and Marketing Association International
www.hsmai.org

HSMAI Electronic Resources
www.hsmaieconnect.org

HSMAI Revenue Management
www.revmanagement.org

HSMAI Hotel Internet Marketing
www.hotelinternetmarketing.org

New York University Master of Science in Hospitality Studies
www.scps.nyu.edu/departments/degree.jsp?degId=30

14

Alternative Dispute Resolution in the Hospitality Industry

By *Maurice Robinson, ISHC, Roger Cline, ISHC, Dana Dunwoody, ISHC, and David M. Neff, ISHC*

Maurice Robinson, CRE, ASA, is President of Maurice Robinson & Associates, LLC, of El Segundo, California, a boutique consulting firm providing advisory services to owners, operators, investors, lenders, public agencies, and developers in the hospitality and real estate industries. He has been providing dispute resolution services, hotel development consulting, market feasibility services, and appraisals for hotels and other hospitality-related real estate for over 25 years, including twelve years with KPMG and five years with PKF Consulting. His dispute resolution expertise includes training, certification, and experience as an arbitrator, mediator, and Issue Review Board chairman. He also provides expert witness testimony, development planning, and financial deal structuring for hotel real estate development and investment.

Roger Cline is Chairman and CEO of Roundhill Hospitality, a professional services firm dedicated to providing advisory and support services in the hospitality and leisure industries. He is a certified arbitrator and mediator and has extensive litigation support experience in the hospitality industry. He is an Associate Member of the American Bar Association and has extensive experience in the hospitality and leisure sectors in marketing, operations, finance, and development. Educated at London's Westminster Hotel School and Columbia University's Graduate Business School in New York, his early training commenced at the Ritz Hotel in Paris and The Waldorf=Astoria Hotel in New York. His consulting career began at Pannell Kerr Forster where he became a partner and the firm's National Director of Management Advisory Services. His experience included  *market and economic feasibility studies, strategic planning, merger and acquisition consulting, and market planning in the international hotel industry. Mr. Cline was subsequently appointed as Senior Vice President, Development at Omni Hotels and led the growth of the company from a small regional group into a large international hotel chain. Following this, Mr. Cline joined Andersen as its Worldwide Director of Hospitality Consulting Services. He is founder and Co-Chair of the New York Hospitality Council and a member of the Executive Committee of the Advisory Board of New York University's Center for Hospitality, Travel and Tourism.*

Dana Dunwoody *co-founded the law firm of Mazzarella & Dunwoody in 1991. He has also practiced with the San Diego office of Allen, Matkins, Leck, Gamble & Mallory, San Diego's Luce, Forward, Hamilton & Scripps, and Los Angeles' Cox, Castle & Nicholson. His practice focuses on trials, arbitration, and litigation of disputes concerning hotel management agreements and franchise agreements, real property, partnership, contracts, employment, and intellectual property. From 1998 to 1999, he was Chair of the Executive Committee of the then 11,000-member Litigation Section of the California State Bar, and continues to serve as an Advisor to the Section. From 1990 to 1994, he served as the Editor-in-Chief of* California Litigation News, *the Litigation Section's newsletter. He also served three years on the Board of Directors of the Association of Business Trial Lawyers of San Diego (ABTL), and is a Trial Master of the Welsh Inn of Court. He is a frequent lecturer and panelist on trial and litigation for the National Institute of Trial Advocacy (NITA), ABTL, California Continuing Education of the Bar (CEB), and other organizations. He has served as a consulting editor to the Matthew Bender text on the two-volume Contract Litigation published in June of 2005, a consulting editor for CEB's "Action Guide" series, an editor of CEB's text on alternative dispute resolution, and an editor of CEB's "The Negotiation Process." He received his J.D. in 1985 from Boalt Hall School of Law at the University of California, Berkeley, where he served as an associate editor for the* Industrial Relations Law Journal. *Mr. Dunwoody received his B.A. in Economics from the University of California at San Diego.*

David M. Neff *is the Co-Chair of the Lodging and Timeshare Practice Group at the 2,700-lawyer firm of DLA Piper Rudnick Gray Cary, which has more than 50 offices throughout the world, of which 20 areintheUnited States. Based in the firm's Chicago office, he has practiced law for almost 20 years and is widely recognized as one of the leading hotel lawyers in the country. He represents hotel owners, lenders, management companies, and franchise companies in a wide variety of issues, including acquisitions and dispositions, franchise disputes, management contract negotiations, condo hotel structuring, general litigation, workouts, and bankruptcies. He has spoken frequently at industry conferences such as the NYU Hotel Investment Conference, Americas Lodging Investment Summit, Atlanta Hotel Investment Conference, Lodging Conference, and Asian American Hotel*  *Owners Annual Convention, and for leading hotel organizations such as the International Society of Hospitality Consultants and the Hospitality Asset Managers Association. He has published many articles in such industry publications as* Hotel & Motel Management, Hotel Journal, Lodging Hospitality, Hotels' Investment Outlook, Hotels, AAHOA Lodging Business *and* AAHOA Hospitality. *He currently is the President of the International Society of Hospitality Consultants.*

BECAUSE OF THE SIGNIFICANT and rising costs involved in civil litigation, many business organizations increasingly are turning to alternative dispute resolution (ADR) as the preferred way to settle conflicts that arise either from contractual agreements or in operations. ADR has become popular because of its focus on fair and reasonable outcomes that are arrived at expeditiously, at less cost than through litigation, and in a more cordial, less confrontational atmosphere. And while hospitality may have been slower to embrace the concept than other industries, it is now becoming time to bring this important process to bear on the growing burden of litigation on the industry.

Effective risk management calls for the resolution of issues before they become full-fledged disputes. The authors encourage organizations with stakes in the hospitality sector to use ADR. An ADR plan that provides for issue review, mediation, and arbitration brings not only financial and economic benefits, but also intangible ones, including the preservation and improvement of important business relationships. Best-practice legal departments in well-managed business organizations understand the economic and non-economic benefits of effective conflict management through ADR.

In order to benefit from an ADR plan, organizations need to agree upon the forum, the procedures to be used, and the providers who will administer the process before entering into contracts. Even if such a plan is not formalized in a contract, this should not prevent parties in a relationship from agreeing to a defined ADR process to resolve a dispute.

Approaches to ADR may be viewed from the perspective of increasing of time and commitment to the outcome, from preemptive Issue Review Boards® (IRB®), to facilitated mediation, and on to final and binding arbitration.[1] There are thus three principal approaches to ADR:

- *IRB*—an informal forum that recommends nonbinding solutions to issues before they become disputes

- *Mediation*—a facilitative or evaluative process to resolve disputes with agreement reached by the parties and enforceable through arbitration or litigation

- *Arbitration*—the final, binding, and enforceable resolution of disputes (although occasionally arbitration may be defined as nonbinding with the prior agreement of the parties)

The Value of Industry Experts in Hospitality ADR

With the increasing popularity of ADR in all areas of business, it was inevitable that the hospitality industry would take note of its advantages. With the escalating costs associated with litigation, organizations involved in the hospitality sector increasingly are recognizing that disputes that arise between parties may be reasonably, fairly, and economically resolved through ADR. Hotel management and franchise agreements, for example, frequently have included arbitration and mediation provisions, but they generally have referred to standard rules and used third-party providers with little background in the industry.

Arbitrators and mediators have thus been brought into hospitality dispute resolution with little understanding of the history and dynamics of the sector. And while neutrality generally has been assured, there has been frustration associated with the frequent lack of understanding of the issues involved on the part of the arbitrators and mediators.

Recognizing this reality, the International Society of Hospitality Consultants (ISHC) has responded to serve this important need by facilitating customized dispute resolution training programs for industry experts. This effort has produced a panel of highly experienced and qualified arbitrators and mediators with extensive experience in dealing with hospitality industry issues—the best of both worlds.

Thus, the industry now has a supply of experts—the vast majority of them being current or former ISHC members with 10 to 40 years of industry experience—who have been trained and certified as commercial arbitrators, mediators, and IRB members and who are ready to support the resolution of disputes—from the simplest to the most complex.

A wide variety of complex business and real estate disputes in the hospitality industry are now arbitrated, ranging from parties' respective rights and obligations under management contracts and franchise agreements to disputes concerning capital improvements, annual budgets, the calculation of incentive and other fees, the allocation of chain-wide costs, and even the composition of competitive sets.

ADR Providers

A provider organization usually is needed to administer the dispute resolution process, such as a hearing. There are numerous providers of these services, including such organizations as the American Arbitration Association (AAA), JAMS, the International Chamber of Commerce (ICC), and the Institute of Conflict Management (ICM), which has provided the training and certification of ISHC panel members to date. While ICM is currently ISHC's preferred vendor for the provision of support services in ADR, all panel members are prepared to serve with any provider in the ADR field where the circumstances dictate or are appropriate. Some existing contractual agreements within the hospitality industry, for example, provide for the application of AAA or JAMS rules, under which all panel members would serve. It is important to note, however, that the parties involved can agree to use any provider organization to resolve a dispute, even if it is not named in the original contract.

Neutrality and Experience

Regardless of the provider, it is critical to the resolution of the disputes that the "neutrals"—those individuals empowered to resolve the disputes—possess both impartiality and industry experience. The advantages for using members of ISHC's ADR panel are not only to bring neutrality and independence to the process, but to ensure that industry experience and understanding is applied when reviewing facts, analysis, and testimony and in arriving at findings, conclusions, solutions, and awards. ISHC members are professionals who abide by strict professional standards of independence that have been well established and recognized by the hospitality industry for many years. Their independence, industry knowledge, and professional expertise make an ISHC solution to ADR desirable.

One of the primary advantages of ISHC is that its members bring vast experience covering all areas of the hospitality sector, ranging from the technical (architecture, engineering, construction, appraisal, and real estate development) to marketing, operational, financial, and economic areas to the strategic, organizational, people, process, technology, capital, and real estate property markets. ISHC is the single most comprehensive organization in which to find experts to resolve disputes in the many disciplines of the hospitality industry.

Arbitration

Arbitration is a well-established form of dispute resolution that provides the parties with a final and legally binding decision. The decision is enforceable by a court of law typically after only a very limited review and may not be appealed except under very limited circumstances. Occasionally, the parties may agree to a nonbinding arbitration, but this is the exception rather than the rule.

For years, arbitration was viewed as an effective alternative to litigation and trial through the court system only in certain types of disputes, including construction and design, labor and employment, disagreements over the purchase and sale of residential real property, consumer stock brokerage, and medical care. Early on, arbitration was pushed primarily by such parties as stockbrokers, architects, construction professionals, labor unions and hospitals. They perceived arbitration as an effective alternative to trial for a variety of reasons: they had a large number of lawsuits involving repetitive, cookie-cutter issues, they wanted to achieve some uniformity of result, they wanted confidentiality to the extent possible, and they wanted their disputes to be heard by an arbitrator with industry savvy, if not industry expertise.

These industries recognized early on that the risks they were hoping to avoid could be contained more effectively in an environment in which disputes could be aired with greater confidentiality and speed than was possible in the court system. Additionally, due to the repetitive nature of the disputes facing those industries, they found that certain economies and greater predictability could be achieved with an arbitrator knowledgeable in their particular industry. They also found that the arbitration environment allowed the process to be tailored and customized in a way that the one-size-fits-all environment of the court system would not allow.

Despite the demonstrable benefits of arbitration to address industry-specific disputes, it took years to catch on as a legitimate alternative to court litigation in business and real estate disputes of any complexity. First, lawyers had to become convinced of the efficacy of arbitration so that they would recommend it to their clients, both at the transactional stage and at the post-dispute stage. For years, there was a predominant idea that a jury of twelve was the universally superior method of dispute resolution. This continues to be true in disputes where punitive damages are possible or where one party's best hope of winning lies in fanning the flames of emotion and passion. Over the course of time, however, most lawyers have gained enough experience in arbitration to learn that with the right arbitrator and efficient rules, their clients are at least as satisfied with arbitration when efficiency, cost, and speed are factored in with the ultimate judgment.

Most commercial arbitration is provided for in a contract where the parties have agreed that if they do have a dispute, rather than pursuing their remedies within the public court system, they will have it resolved in a private, less formal way. Most arbitrations are indeed private—the deliberations, materials used, and testimony of experts and advocates are retained on a strictly confidential basis. Arbitration language in a contract may provide for conditions under which the arbitration can be initiated and set limitations in terms of time, amount of discovery, etc. Others may call for arbitration to be preceded by such preliminary steps as good faith negotiation or mediation.

In the absence of contractual language, the parties to a dispute may nevertheless jointly initiate the process by executing an arbitration agreement that will define the rules and procedures and may deal with such other details as the provider or discovery process.

The arbitrator is chosen by the parties to the contract and is viewed as being neutral and independent. In some instances, a panel of the three arbitrators will be called for in the agreement, in which one party selects one arbitrator, the other party selects a second, and the two party-appointed arbitrators go on to select a third neutral. The parties in more complex matters generally use attorneys, but may represent themselves in simpler arbitrations. Unlike litigation, the rules of evidence in arbitration proceedings are not restrictive and the arbitrators have great flexibility as to what evidence to consider.

The arbitrator will rule on discovery requests and disputes, read briefs submitted by the parties, review documentary evidence, hear testimony during a hearing, and render an opinion on liability and damages, as appropriate. This opinion will be rendered as an "award" after the hearing has been completed, and may be presented with or without the reasoning that supports it. The award may then be confirmed by a court in the appropriate jurisdiction and subsequently entered as a judgment, thus becoming legally binding on the parties involved.

The Federal Arbitration Act, read in conjunction with state arbitration law (where it exists), generally governs the arbitration process. The arbitration provided for in a contract may limit the types of issues to be resolved, the scope of the relief, and a number of the procedures to be used.

If arbitration is provided for in a contractual agreement, the rules to be applied generally are defined in the contract as those of a selected provider of arbitration services. Parties to the arbitration generally will have varying needs for information, which is produced through a process of discovery. This process can range from the informal exchange of information in smaller, less complicated cases to a highly formalized discovery process in larger or more complex cases.

If the parties have retained experts who in turn undertake investigations and have a need for information and access to people, the process of discovery can become extensive and costly. In order to mitigate the costs, some parties will agree to an abbreviated schedule of depositions of key experts and fact witnesses, with rights reserved to continue discovery if a settlement is not reached early in the process. Agreements of this type may be difficult for the parties to consent to, in which case, the process can be mediated by the neutral. There is also a need to consider the appropriate balance between the cost of discovery to the respective parties and the benefit of more complete information.

Occasionally, when the parties have agreed, there may be a provision for a particular form of arbitration. Alternatives include bracketed, baseball, and night baseball arbitration. In bracketed arbitration, the damage awards are limited within a predefined range, where both a floor and a ceiling are agreed upon. Awards that are higher than the maximum are reduced to the ceiling and those that are lower than the floor are increased. In baseball arbitration (also known as final offer arbitration), the arbitrator must select one of two possible damage awards presented respectively by the two parties. In night baseball arbitration, the concept is the same, but the figures are not revealed to the arbitrator. In this latter instance, the parties agree to accept the high or low figure closest to that of the arbitrator's.

The parties to hospitality disputes often want to keep their dispute confidential from hotel employees, lenders, and other third parties who may perceive themselves to be affected by the dispute, but whose involvement is not necessary or would be counterproductive to its resolution.

Arbitration provides much more potential for confidentiality than court proceedings. First, the parties can agree that their proceedings will be kept confidential and all arbitration provider organizations will respect that request. Second, in an arbitration environment, all of the pleadings and other written papers filed in connection with the arbitration and all testimony given at hearings can be provided under the cloak of confidentiality. Contrast that with a court proceeding in which one must first attempt to seal the file during litigation, which is not an easy task because many courts require an extraordinary showing of need. Even if one can seal a court file successfully, it is virtually impossible to keep the actual hearings and trial confidential, except in such very unusual circumstances as high-profile criminal trials, which one can only hope will not involve the hotel industry!

Arbitration by the Rules

The rules for arbitration that are promulgated by organizations that provide arbitration services generally cover much of the same ground, including:

- The jurisdiction and authority of the provider.
- The scope and application of its rules and their amendment.
- The fees for administering the process.
- The limitations of liability.
- The application of waivers.
- The alternative forms of arbitration.
- The agreement of the parties.
- The initiation of arbitration, filing of a claim, and amending the claim.
- Communications.
- Confidentiality.
- Qualifying and appointing the arbitrator or panel of arbitrators.
- Representation of the parties by attorneys.
- Preliminary conferences.
- Disclosure.
- The exchange of information and discovery process.

- The scheduling, notice, and conduct of the hearing.

- The discontinuance and postponement of proceedings.

- Notices and oaths.

- Prehearing submissions.

- Evidence.

- Witnesses.

- Posthearing filings.

- The scope, form, and delivery of the final award.

The rules of all major ADR provider organizations were drafted to accomplish the objectives outlined above: flexibility, selection of the best arbitrator or arbitrators for a particular dispute, confidentiality, expedited resolution, and other efficiencies. At least one provider organization's rules are so loose that they say little more than that the parties are encouraged to fashion their own hearing rules tailored to the unique needs of their individual cases. Most organizations, however, have a set of structured rules that can be found on each provider organization's Web site. Despite this lack of uniformity, most provider organizations' rules cover at least the following four topics.

Selecting the Arbitrator or Arbitrators. It is critical to the integrity of the ADR process that the arbitrator be neutral, which means he or she must not have any financial relationship with any of the parties or counsel, must not have any social relationship with any of the parties or counsel that is not disclosed to and waived by all parties, and must not have any biases or prejudices toward any party, any counsel, or concerning any issue that will be presented at the arbitration. For example, if an arbitrator has for 30 years represented only labor unions and has written extensively about the inherent correctness of labor positions and the inherent fallacy of management positions, it is hard to see how such a person could possibly be a nonpartisan neutral in an arbitration concerning employment issues affecting an individual or a class of hotel workers.

The rules of all major provider organizations provide a mechanism by which such prejudices can be revealed and vetted and they also provide the parties with the ability to challenge arbitrators and to strike them. The rules to challenge and strike an arbitrator are significantly looser than the challenge process in court litigation. It is much easier to strike potential arbitrators than it is to strike potential judges.

While these rules may have been drafted primarily to ensure the integrity of the ADR process and the impartiality of arbitrators, they also make it easier for parties in industry disputes to select an arbitrator with industry expertise. As mentioned above, there is no promise (and often no hope) that the parties to civil court litigation will be assigned a trial judge with any industry expertise. Do the parties to a complicated management contract dispute really want their judge's sole experience in the hospitality industry to be as a consumer while on business or vacation?

Focusing the Issues and Restricting Discovery. Many states' procedural codes provide that in arbitration there is little or no discovery allowed, unless the parties' contract or the ADR provider organization's rules allow for discovery, in which case discovery will be limited in accordance with such rules or contract provisions. The radical curtailment or elimination of discovery probably is acceptable in such cookie-cutter disputes as most construction and employment matters or matters involving guest dissatisfaction.

The more complex the dispute, however, the greater the need for discovery. This is especially true because in many disputes the documents and witnesses are largely controlled by one side, and thus a no-discovery rule puts the other party at a significant comparative disadvantage. That is not to say, however, that the almost limitless discovery allowed in civil court litigation is necessary or appropriate for the vast majority of disputes, and certainly for most disputes affecting the hospitality industry. The rules of most ADR provider organizations attempt to reconcile the need for discovery in complex disputes to the goals of speed and efficiency.

Administering the Dispute. Most ADR provider rules contain procedures for the things that in the court process would take place between filing the complaint and the trial. In addition to discovery, these matters include rules for compelling attendance of witnesses, service of briefs and other papers, presentation of motions and other hearings, and such things as cost allocation, location, changes to claims and counter-claims, replacement of an arbitrator, representation by counsel, and ex parte (one-sided) communication with the ADR neutral. Although the rules of various ADR providers are by no means uniform on these matters, they all have the goal of providing the parties and their counsel with predictable guidelines to make the process fair, fast, and economical.

Conducting the Arbitration Trial and Post-Trial Matters. The provider rules also cover what can (or must) take place at the arbitration trial. In many jurisdictions, there is no right to appeal an arbitrator's award or the right to appeal is limited. Nevertheless, some ADR providers' rules set forth how a party may seek clarification of an award, or even challenge the award in the context of the arbitration, prior to any challenge a party might attempt through the courts after the arbitrator issues the award.

After the trial, the arbitrator (or panel of arbitrators) will issue a written award. Many of the ADR providers' rules set forth detailed procedures and time requirements that the arbitrator must follow with respect to the award. The arbitrator's issuance of the final award typically marks the end of the arbitration.

Examples of Arbitration

Every time the owner of a resort asked for information, the operator forced the requested information to pass through their attorneys before being released to the owner. As performance declined, the owner lost trust in the operator, whom he thought was hiding something. As the market slumped, this situation deteriorated to the point where the owner filed a demand for arbitration, seeking to void the management agreement based on breach of fiduciary duties.

The case went to a panel of three arbitrators, all of whom had experience in the industry. The three panelists had skills in the disciplines of hotel operations, law, and finance. A two-day hearing was held, evidence was submitted and reviewed, and the panel was able to distill the various claims down to the real problem, which was a dysfunctional relationship that stemmed from the owner's lack of fair access to books and records. As part of the order, the arbitrators wrote a procedure for such access that prevented the requested data from passing through the operator's attorneys before reaching the owner. The order also created an IRB, whose chair was empowered to sit on the hotel's executive board and act as a liaison between the owner and the operator on future issues, resolving them before they grew into full-fledged disputes.

Another hospitality industry veteran was asked to arbitrate a dispute between a ground lessor and his lessee, who was obligated to develop a mixed-use resort (hotel, golf and residential) on the lessor's property. The economics of building a luxury hotel, however, were not favorable, so the lessor proceeded to build the residential and golf components first. The lessor sued to force the lessee into building the hotel as well, claiming breach of contract, even though the contract was quite vague as to phasing and timing of the components of development.

The arbitrator held a hearing, reviewed the contract, and was able to run an economic and financial feasibility model to illustrate to both parties that the economics of the resort development would allow the hotel to be built, but only after the homes were sold and the golf course was stabilized. He was able to set up a schedule for resort development to which both parties could agree, in a manner that would optimize the return to the lessee and still achieve the ultimate build-out desired by the lessor.

Mediation

Like arbitration, mediation is conducted in private, but involves a neutral who helps the parties to a dispute to reach their own settlement. While mediation generally is a voluntary process, it can be mandated by a court of law or provided for in a written contract between the parties. It is a relatively straightforward process in which the parties may represent themselves or use advocates. In mediation, the dispute may involve two or more parties. The neutral may either facilitate the process of the parties reaching their own agreement or be called upon to evaluate the arguments and evidence and advise on a resolution.

A skilled mediator, while not having authority to impose a settlement, may have an important impact on the outcome by setting the ground rules, the ways in which the parties understand and analyze their respective positions, and the demeanor and dynamic of the process. The mediator's task is to improve communication between the parties, ensuring an effective exchange of information, and to assist in the development of alternative solutions. The mediator's evolving understanding of the parties' respective interests is also helpful in placing focus on the issues at hand.

As the mediation process progresses, the mediator should attempt to determine the level of resolution that both parties will be willing to accept. This may range from the simple halting of animosity between the parties, to a resolution of the underlying basis for the dispute, to a repair and reconciliation of the relationship. The end result may fall anywhere along this spectrum and may constitute success from the perspective of the parties themselves.

The process typically involves the mediator convening the parties, meeting separately with each side, and listening carefully to their stories. This enables the identification and ranking of the key issues, shuttling between the parties, maintaining confidences when called for, facilitating a solution, and bringing the mediation to closure, preferably with a written agreement prepared and executed by the parties. It is important to have individuals representing the parties who have the authority to negotiate and execute a settlement agreement actually in attendance at the mediation or available by phone.

Mediation is less formal than arbitration, has no rules of evidence, and has little structure in terms of how the facts and positions are presented. Mediation can be designed in whichever way appears appropriate to the parties and to their mediator, with a view to moving the process forward, while producing the optimum exchange of facts, opinions, and interests that will support negotiation and resolution.

The challenge for the mediator is to avoid becoming evaluative when the role calls for mere facilitation. The time for evaluation is when the mediator is asked by the parties to provide it and when such assistance is needed. It is more frequently used in larger, more complex matters, where the gap between the parties is very wide. On such occasions, the mediator may provide an assessment of the case, evaluating its strengths and weaknesses, its value, and the likely outcome if the process were to move to arbitration or litigation. Unlike arbitration, however, this evaluation and the conclusions that may be drawn from it do not produce a binding outcome unless the parties agree to make it so.

A successful mediator needs to bring some important qualities to the task to be effective. They include, among other traits, sincerity, trustworthiness, honesty, integrity, maturity, tact, the ability to appear and behave in an independent and neutral way, open-mindedness, a positive and optimistic attitude, the ability to ask relevant questions, and the ability to listen carefully. It clearly helps if the individual has the ability to quickly grasp complex business matters that may involve strategic, marketing, organizational, process, technology, financial, or economic issues. It is especially beneficial if the person has experience with the particular type of business involved and understands the industry context within which it operates.

Mediation tends to have a high success rate because the parties are involved in the process, have more control over the outcome, and are more inclined to follow through and comply with the settlement agreement. In addition to whatever economic or financial considerations are at stake, the preservation of valuable relationships often is just as important.

Because of the time-consuming and costly nature of litigation, mediation offers the parties a potentially appealing alternative even when litigation already is underway. Summary judgment motions, for example, while designed to bring a matter to prompt closure in court, often take some time and if the outcome is in doubt, it may be prudent to attempt settlement and use mediation to bring a mutually acceptable resolution to the dispute.

As with arbitration, the mediation process may be subject to a provider's rules and procedures. These rules tend to be less extensive than those of arbitration, but provide an appropriate framework within which the process can be directed and managed.

Examples of Mediation

A group canceled its reservation at a hotel shortly after September 11 because many of its out-of-town members did not want to travel to the company's annual conference. The hotel operator allowed the group to reschedule the meeting for a few months later without penalty, maintaining the same room rate and size of room block, and asking for a second deposit of 25 percent of the total expected amount of charges. The problem arose when the group canceled a second time, indicating that many of its members were still reluctant to travel. The hotel owner decided to enforce its cancellation policy, and sued the group for the lost revenue for the two events. The group disputed the damage claims and insisted it was really only one event and the two parties went into pre-trial mediation.

As a hospitality industry veteran, the mediator understood the issues and was able to objectively asses the damages claimed by the hotel owner. He was able to reduce the claim to a more supportable level of incremental lost profit and facilitated an agreement between the parties, in which the group committed to holding two additional events over the next three years at the subject hotel. The hotel owner would hold the deposits and apply them to the rescheduled event costs. Both sides agreed and the litigation was dropped.

Another dispute that was resolved using an experienced hospitality industry mediator involved a partnership comprising a group of unsophisticated limited partnership (LP) investors ("owners") and a hotel management company ("operator"). The operator, acting as a general partner (GP), developed the hotel and presented projections of anticipated operating revenues and profit distribution to the owners. Several years after the hotel was built and operational, however, the projected distributions to the owners did not materialize as presented, and the income and return to the GP was significantly in excess of those of the owners. Predictably, the owners had lost trust in the operator and sued for misrepresentation, breach of fiduciary duty, etc. Both sides agreed to a pre-trial mediation.

The mediator was able to apply hospitality industry financial expertise and duplicate the model originally used by the operator when "selling" the deal to the LPs. He evaluated the relative cases of both parties, indicating where their claims or defenses were weak, and brought both sides toward the middle in terms of a settlement amount. Finally, he was able to show the operator, based on its own projections of future performance, how it could achieve a decent internal rate of return by buying out the LPs' interests for close to their original investment. By regaining control of the real estate, the operator could then flip it to a third-party REIT. The LPs agreed to accept the settlement and exit the partnership. The operator lined up a new owner, whose investment in the real estate paid off the LPs.

Issue Review Boards

An IRB is ideally suited to those ongoing business relationships where there is a need to quickly resolve issues before they become disputes. Used historically in the construction industry, where time-sensitive projects must move forward promptly and where delays for dispute resolution can have significant economic impacts, the IRB also has application in operational environments. Within the hospitality industry, these may be used, for example, not only for development projects, but also with owner/operator issues that might arise out of a management agreement.

Promulgated by ICM, IRB procedures may be amended by the parties to a relationship to suit their particular needs. The intent is that any party may refer an issue to the board that is within its purview. The IRB is designed to function quite independently of the parties' interests and render a nonbinding recommendation for resolution of the issue. While the recommendation is nonbinding per se, it may be admissible as evidence in the event the parties subsequently take the issue further into the dispute resolution process. This gives the recommendation some teeth.

The IRB itself typically comprises a panel of three members, whose two party-appointed members, like an arbitration panel, are selected first by each of the parties. These two members then select a "neutral" third member who generally will serve as chairperson. Since the IRB serves at the pleasure of the parties, it may be dissolved by mutual consent of the parties, generally upon completion of the project in a development context or at the end of the contract in an operational context.

Meetings of the IRB can occur with as much frequency as the parties deem appropriate, but generally will involve a monthly or bimonthly sequence for a project in development, and a quarterly sequence for operational groups. Within an operational context, an IRB is especially useful for large projects in which the asset management function representing an owner's interests is interfacing with an operational team from the management company. While such relationships tend to bring very knowledgeable people together to deal with operational issues, there are nevertheless frequent occasions when an issue requires resolution in an independently organized forum like an IRB.

The formation of an IRB ideally is conceived during contract negotiation stages so the process for referring issues for resolution is institutionalized from the very outset. Contract language would, among other elements, provide for the selection of the board's members, the nature of the agreement between the board and the parties involved, the process for referring issues to the board, the application of a defined set of rules and procedures, the frequency of meetings, the treatment of fees and expenses, notice and communications, immunity, the basis for board member substitution or replacement, and finally, the board's dissolution.

Examples of Issue Review Boards

The owner and operator of a full-service, first-class resort were unable to agree on items in the annual budgets and capital expenditure (CapEx) programs. Instead of involving the general counsel of both organizations, the parties used the IRB process to resolve these disputes.

Whenever the parties could not agree on cap ex issues, each party prepared a short brief outlining its position on the disputed item and submitted it to the chair of the IRB. The chair reviewed the briefs, conducted a limited investigation into the matter, and ruled as to whether the item should be included and, if so, to what level and at what point in the cycle. Both parties agreed to abide by the decision for the current budget year.

Another issue that an IRB chair decided upon was the composition of a competitive set. The operator's performance test involved comparing its RevPAR performance at the subject hotel to a predetermined competitive set. After five years of operation, both parties agreed that the original competitive set was no longer valid, but could not agree on which properties should be included in the updated set. The parties each submitted a list of five properties to the IRB chair, who visited all of them and selected a competitive set from the ten properties included on the two lists. Both parties agreed to use that competitive set for the following five years, as it pertained to the performance test.

The ISHC Panel

In responding to the need for ADR in the hospitality industry, ISHC has formed a panel of arbitrators, mediators, and IRB members to serve the industry in a neutral and independent manner to help resolve disputes that arise within the industry. The ISHC panel today comprises approximately 30 members, all of whom have been trained in dispute resolution and are certified to serve in this capacity. ISHC plans to add additional members to this panel of individuals with deep hospitality industry knowledge and experience, who bring to the dispute resolution process an understanding of the context of the business arrangements within the sector and how they function.

Cornell University's Survey on the Use of ADR

In a comprehensive study of the use of ADR in American industry, Lipsky and Seeber surveyed the corporate counsel of the 1,000 largest U.S. corporations and found that the vast majority of corporations had used one or more ADR procedures in recent years.[2] A total of 88 percent of the 606 respondents had used mediation and 79 percent had used arbitration. Most respondents indicated that they believed that use of ADR would grow significantly in the future. More than 84 percent said they are likely or very likely to use mediation in the future, while 69 percent said the same about their future use of arbitration. The survey did not ask about the use of IRBs.

Corporate policy appeared to vary, but most respondents indicated that they either litigate first and then move to ADR or litigate only in cases where it seems appropriate to do so, and use ADR for all others. Smaller companies appeared to be more litigious, while larger ones were more pro-ADR. Aside from the economic motivation to use ADR, respondents in the Cornell survey suggested a desire to gain greater control over the process and the outcomes, especially given their general concerns about the risk and uncertainty of litigation. High levels of respondent satisfaction with the results achieved through ADR also support the study's conclusion concerning future growth as ADR increasingly is adopted as an alternative to litigation.

Of particular interest in the Cornell study was the concern respondents expressed related to the qualifications of mediators and arbitrators. A majority believed that they were "somewhat qualified" and almost half stated that they lacked confidence in the arbitrators in particular. Nearly 30 percent reported that there was a shortage of qualified arbitrators. There did not appear to be a shortage of ADR neutrals, but rather a shortage of *qualified* neutrals—individuals with expertise in both the process and the topic.

In preparing for the development of its panel of ADR neutrals, ISHC conducted an informal survey of the general counsels of a number of hospitality companies. The survey confirmed what was already apparent from Cornell University's more general survey of U.S. companies at large—that there was a favorable attitude toward ADR as a process, but concern about the lack of qualified arbitrators and mediators. It is believed that the ISHC program will provide the necessary framework for more utilization of this process in the hospitality industry in the future.

Endnotes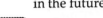

1. Issue Review Board® and IRB® are registered trademarks of the Institute for Conflict Management, LLC.

2. David B. Lipsky and Ronald L. Seeber, "The Appropriate Resolution of Corporate Disputes: A Report on the Growing Use of ADR by U.S. Corporations" (Ithaca, N.Y.: Cornell University, 1998).

Appendix A: Dispute Resolution Matrix

The selection and confirmation of a dispute resolution process should be completed as soon as possible, and ideally before a project begins. The time sensitivity of a project will determine how quickly the dispute needs to be resolved. Evaluating the type and timing of the relationship will help the parties determine which process best fits the situation when an issue or dispute arises.

No single dispute resolution process fits all issue or dispute scenarios. The matrix in Exhibit 1, which was designed by Dave Armstrong of ICM, provides a guideline for suggested dispute resolution processes to use when writing the dispute resolution clause of a contract. Following these steps with the matrix will allow the best process to be designed for each unique situation:

1. Locate a relationship in the left side column that is similar to or the same as the subject relationship.

2. Determine at what stage/time frame the relationship is currently or will be operating.

3. Follow that row across from left to right to determine what dispute resolution processes and sequence of use are appropriate for a given situation.

Exhibit 1   Dispute Resolution Matrix

Relationship	Time Frame	PRO-ACTIVE		RE-ACTIVE		Discovery Limits
		Conciliation	IRB®	Mediation	Arbitration	
General Partner & Several Limited Partners						
	Negotiating Partnership	X		X*	X*	
	During Partnership	X		X	X*	
	Dissolution of Partnership through Post-Partnership	X		X	X	Full Discovery
Equal Partnership						
	Negotiating Partnership	X		X*	X*	
	During Partnership	X		X	X*	
	Dissolution of Partnership through Post-Partnership	X		X	X	Full Discovery
Managing Partner & Shareholders						
	Negotiating Partnership	X		X*	X*	
	During Partnership	X		X	X	
	Dissolution of Partnership through Post-Partnership	X		X	X	Full Discovery
Buyer & Seller						
	Offer	X		X*	X*	
	Acceptance	X		X*	X*	
	Closing	X		X*	X*	
	After Closing	X		X	X	Full Discovery

Exhibit 1 *(continued)*

Relationship	Time Frame	PRO-ACTIVE		RE-ACTIVE		Discovery Limits
		Conciliation	IRB®	Mediation	Arbitration	
Buyer & Consultants						
	Offer	X			X*	
	Acceptance	X			X*	
	Closing	X			X*	
	After Closing	X			X	Full Discovery
Buyer & Franchisor						
	Offer	X		X*	X*	
	Acceptance	X		X*	X*	
	Closing	X		X*	X*	
	After Closing	X		X	X	Full Discovery
Franchise & Hotel Owner						
	Franchise Development	X		X*	X*	
	During Operation	X		X*	X*	
	Post-Franchise Agreement	X		X	X	Full Discovery
General Contractor & Client						
	Preconstruction	X		X*	X*	
	During Construction	X	X	X*	X*	
	After Construction	X	X	X	X	Limited to brief interrogatories, production of documents, intrusive testing by experts, and estimates to correct defective design

(continued)

Exhibit 1 *(continued)*

Relationship	Time Frame	PRO-ACTIVE		RE-ACTIVE		
		Conciliation	IRB®	Mediation	Arbitration	Discovery Limits
General Contractor & Subcontractor						
	Preconstruction	X	X	X*	X*	
	During Construction	X	X	X*	X*	
General Contractor & Vendor						
	Preconstruction	X			X*	
	During Construction	X			X*	
	After Construction	X			X*	
Employer & Employee						
	During Employment	X		X*	X*	
Employer & Independent Contractor						
	Employment Offer Phase	X		X*	X*	
	During Employment	X		X*	X*	
	Post-Employment	X		X*	X	
Employer & Union Employee						
	During Employment	X		X*	X*	
Hotel Owners & Operators						
	Negotiations and Pre-Operations	X		X*	X*	
	In Operation	X	X	X*	X*	
	Post-Operations	X		X	X	

Exhibit 1 *(continued)*

Relationship	Time Frame	PRO-ACTIVE		RE-ACTIVE		
		Conciliation	IRB®	Mediation	Arbitration	Discovery Limits
Hotel Owners & Vendors						
	Negotiations and Pre-Operations	X			X*	
	In Operation	X	X	X*	X*	
Hotel Owners & Service Providers						
	Negotiations and Pre-Operations	X			X*	
	In Operation	X			X*	
	Post-Operations	X			X	
Hotel Owner & Guest						
	Reservation Stage			X*	X*	
	During Hotel Stay			X*	X*	
	After Hotel Stay	X		X*	X*	

* An expedited process using ICM's Rules and Procedures

4. Write the dispute resolution clause for the contract according to the suggested processes.

Components of the various processes listed in the chart are as follows.

Conciliation

Conciliation is an informal dispute resolution process in which a third-party neutral is selected by the parties to review issues that arise during the course of a project or relationship and make a nonbinding recommendation for immediate resolution. This process can be implemented by the parties even after a project is already underway. The conciliation process includes the following steps:

- The provider submits names of potential conciliators and the parties agree on one.

- The conciliator shall have experience in the industry in which the issues occurred.

- The conciliator is on call as needed during the project/relationship.

- The process includes on-site visits and meetings.

- The conciliator can make recommendations the same day—even during the meeting—if requested by the parties.

- No formal documentation is required.

- The cost of resolution is split equally by all parties.

Issue Review Board

The IRB is a proactive issue resolution process in which a panel of three neutrals with extensive knowledge and expertise in a particular industry is selected to serve as resolutionists when an issue arises during the project/relationship. One of the three experts acts as the chair of the panel and together they render nonbinding recommendations, which are admissible as evidence in any future court or arbitration proceedings, regarding the issues. By addressing issues as they arise, the parties can avoid major disputes. The IRB process includes the following steps:

- An IRB is established before the project begins (during contract development).

- The provider submits names of potential IRB panelists.

- The panelists shall be experts from the industry.

- The IRB panel is organized before the project/relationship begins.

- Copies of pertinent contracts and documents are kept on file with the provider.

- IRB panelists are on call as needed during the project/relationship.

- The process includes on-site visits and meetings.

- The cost of resolution is split equally by both parties.

For smaller projects, a single-member IRB can be established before the start of the project.

Mediation

Mediation is a dispute resolution process in which a third-party neutral facilitates discussion between parties to help the parties design their own solution. The mediator makes no decisions or rulings. The mediation process includes the following steps:

- The provider selects the mediator unless the parties have already agreed upon another mediator.
- The mediator shall have extensive experience in the industry.
- Discovery is limited to the production of documents unless otherwise noted.
- Parties can predetermine the length of the process.
- Mediation can be used at any time during the life of the project.

An expedited version of the mediation process can be adopted in which parties agree that the mediation will be held within a preset number of days after the initial filing.

Arbitration

Arbitration is a dispute resolution process in which a third-party neutral listens to statements made by various parties and renders a binding award enforceable by courts. The arbitration process includes the following steps:

- The provider proposes names of prospective arbitrators and the parties agree on one or the provider selects one—whichever the contract designates.
- The arbitrator shall have extensive experience in the industry.
- Discovery is limited to the production of documents unless otherwise noted.
- The parties can predetermine the length of the process.
- Arbitration can be used anytime during the life of the project.

An expedited version of the arbitration process also is available. This process stipulates that the arbitration shall be held within a preset number of days of the initial filing, and that the arbitrator's decision will be submitted to the parties within a preset number of days after the initial filing.

Appendix 2: Frequently Asked Questions

What is the distinction between arbitration and mediation? An arbitration is a process that generally produces a binding resolution to a dispute, decided by an arbitrator or panel of arbitrators based upon examination of evidence and hearing of testimony. By contrast, mediation may or may not produce a tangible result and involves the facilitation of a dialogue to bring the disputing parties to a mutually acceptable resolution.

What is an Issue Review Board? An IRB comprises a panel of independent experts brought together as needed to produce nonbinding recommendations concerning issues between parties to an agreement before they rise to the level of a dispute.

How are arbitration and mediation proceedings initiated? Arbitration and mediation proceedings may be promulgated by contract, in which case one party to an agreement has the right to call for a proceeding to help resolve a dispute. In cases where there is no such contractual right, the parties may agree between themselves to go to arbitration or mediation. In either circumstance, the parties will follow an agreed-upon process of arbitrator and mediator selection and the appointment, if necessary, of an organization (provider) to manage the process.

What are the key advantages of arbitration and mediation? The principal advantage of both arbitration and mediation is the avoidance of a time-consuming and expensive litigation process through the judicial system. Generally faster and less expensive than litigation, the results of arbitration are for the most part binding and recognized by the judicial system as such. Mediation is a less complex and therefore less expensive process than arbitration and is to be favored when the parties have faith in the process and the mediator involved, as well as some sense that such a process might produce a satisfactory result.

What are the discovery rules in the typical arbitration? There generally are no explicit discovery rules in an arbitration, although some arbitrators will look to the rules of civil procedure for guidance. Arbitrators may rule on discovery disputes between the parties as part of the process.

How are IRBs useful in development and operations within the hospitality sector? IRBs are of value to hotel development by dealing with issues as they arise, preserving critical relationships, avoiding lengthier dispute resolution, and mitigating the risk of delays in a project's completion. Within operating agreements between management entities and owners, for example, such boards assist in the preservation of the relationships and provide a venue for dealing with issues that should not be left unresolved and may not be significant enough (yet) to trigger a more formal dispute-resolution process.

What is the role of an ADR provider organization? An ADR provider is an organization designed to administer an arbitration or mediation process. Such an organization generally will provide rules by which the parties agree to abide, will assist in the appointment of the arbitrator(s) or mediator, and will communicate with the parties on such administrative matters as arrangements for hearings, billing for services, and the issuance of rulings and findings.

How is independence assured in an arbitration or mediation process? In an arbitration, the parties generally will have decided upon either a single arbitrator or a panel of arbitrators (typically three). In the latter instance, the parties appoint their respective arbitrators, and these two party-appointed arbitrators will select a third neutral. The panel will then function using majority rule. Arbitrators and mediators who are members of such professional organizations as ISHC or are affiliated with such ADR provider organizations as ICM, AAA, and JAMS have been selected for membership through a rigorous process. Such arbitrators have agreed to abide by strict standards of professional conduct and are required to disclose to the parties any real or perceived conflicts of interest that might be seen as impairing their independence. Users of arbitration and mediation services clearly are obligated to ensure that they understand their appointees' background and independence of standing regarding the parties and the dispute in question. If an appearance of bias is present in a neutral, the parties can replace him or her immediately.

Why should arbitration clauses be incorporated into hospitality industry agreements and what should they cover? Investors, lenders, developers, management companies, and franchisors, among others, are well-advised to incorporate standard arbitration clauses into their agreements, because of the significant advantages of arbitration over litigation. Since the stakes generally are high and the relationships are so critical, providing for ADR processes makes very sound business sense. Although counsel should be consulted in drafting and negotiating such provisions, among the most important provisions to include are (1) naming the provider organization of your choice, (2) specifying the rules for conduct of the arbitration if no provider is to be identified, (3) determining how much discovery will be allowed, and the limits on such discovery, (4) whether costs and fees are to be allocated to the prevailing party, and (5) whether there is any right to appeal.

Do arbitrators and mediators require a professional certificate or designation to practice? There are no formal requirements for arbitrators and mediators to be licensed, either at the state or federal level. However, the imprimatur of such organizations as ISHC ensures that such individuals have (1) undergone training in the process of dispute resolution, (2) continue to take professional education coursework to remain current in the field, (3) have valuable industry experience, and (4) are committed to abiding by strict standards of professional performance.

How are arbitrators appointed? There are several ways that arbitrators may be appointed. In cases where the parties have agreed to use a provider organization to handle the arbitration process, this organization will present candidates or provide access to a list of such candidates. A formal selection process will follow that often provides a timetable for completion. In the absence of a designated provider organization, the parties may nevertheless have agreed to appoint a panel of three members. In this case, each party will appoint its respective arbitrator, and these two party-appointed arbitrators select a neutral third member. In the absence of a preexisting agreement regarding arbitration, the parties will need to appoint either a single arbitrator that they can agree upon, or a panel in the manner described previously.

What laws govern the practice of arbitration and mediation? The laws of each state govern the arbitration of claims that would have been brought in a state court absent an arbitration clause. Similarly, if a claim would have been brought in federal court absent an arbitration clause, the Federal Arbitration Act (FAA) generally will govern. The U.S. Supreme Court ruled in 2003 that to be covered by the FAA, an agreement must be a "contract evidencing a transaction involving commerce," a definition that undoubtedly includes most disputes in the hospitality industry.

What is the role of ISHC in the ADR process? A group of ISHC members have been certified as arbitrators and mediators and are certified to serve on IRBs. These ISHC members have taken the requisite training and continuing education, are well versed in ADR processes, have extensive hospitality industry experience and knowledge, and are committed to ADR and its growth and development in the industry. ISHC is therefore well-equipped as an organization to serve this important need and is ready to provide its roster of competent, certified ADR practitioners to third parties in need of such service. ISHC provides background information and knowledge on the practice of ADR and can assist third parties in identifying the available resources to complete a successful arbitration or mediation or organize an IRB.

If my arbitration clause designates a provider that I don't have confidence in, what should I do? If all parties to the arbitration clause agree to do so, they may designate whatever provider they like, or they can dispense with the provider entirely and designate whatever arbitrator(s) they want to. A provider organization like AAA, ICM, or JAMS is not necessary. Only the arbitrator(s) and a set of agreed-upon rules for conducting the arbitration are required. If, however, a contract designates a provider and all parties do not agree to an alternative to the contractual terms, the contract will govern.

Are the decisions final and binding? This depends on the language of the ADR clause and the prior agreement of the parties. That said, decisions reached by arbitrators typically are final and binding. Arbitration orders usually are confirmed by the parties with the local courts, so they can be enforced by local laws. By contrast, agreements reached by mediation typically are nonbinding and voluntary. IRB recommendations also usually are nonbinding, but tend to have more force behind them because they are admissible in any subsequent litigation and a noncooperating party would be at a disadvantage to show why it did not follow the panel's recommendations.

Where will the arbitration or mediation occur? The location of the venue should be identified in the ADR clause of the contract. Typically the ADR process occurs in the county where the property is located, although both sides could agree to hold it at a more convenient place.

Why is it important to have someone knowledgeable in the hotel industry arbitrate or mediate these disputes? Historically, both parties are better off having a neutral who is both knowledgeable about the hospitality industry and trained in dispute resolution processes. This eliminates the need to educate the neutral about the industry, takes advantage of the neutral's many years of experience in industry-related disputes, and avoids the problem of one party attempting to hide information or confuse the neutral about the key issues. Most retired judges are extremely knowledgeable about the law, for example, but have little or no working knowledge of hospitality industry economics, and their direct hotel experience may be limited to simply having been a guest at a related facility.

Appendix 3: Sample Standard ADR Clauses

To help interested parties develop workable ADR processes, we have written and offer the following standard ADR clauses to be used in most agreements, including management contracts, franchise agreements, employment contracts, development agreements, partnership agreements, construction contracts, and other related agreements.

Issue Review Board

The parties hereby agree to establish an Issue Review Board® ("IRB®") in accordance with the Issue Review Board Rules and Procedures of the Institute for Conflict Management, LLC ("ICM") ("the Rules"), which are incorporated herein by reference. The IRB shall have [one/three] member[s] appointed pursuant to the Rules set forth by ICM.

All disputes arising out of or in connection with the present Contract shall be submitted, in the first instance, to the IRB in accordance with ICM's Rules. For any given dispute, the IRB shall issue a Recommendation in accordance with ICM's Rules. If any party fails to comply with a Recommendation when required to do so pursuant to the Rules, the other party may refer the failure itself to arbitration under the Arbitration Rules and Procedures of ICM by one or more arbitrators appointed in accordance with ICM's Rules of Arbitration.

If any party sends a written notice to the other party and the IRB expressing its dissatisfaction with a Recommendation, as provided in ICM's Rules, or if the IRB does not issue the Recommendation within the time limit provided by ICM's Rules, or if the IRB is disbanded pursuant to ICM's Rules, the dispute shall be finally settled under the Arbitration Rules and Procedures by one or more arbitrators appointed in accordance with the Arbitration clause presented below.

Mediation

In the event of any controversy or claim between the parties to this Agreement arising out of or relating to this Agreement [expressly excluding any claim for_____], and including without limitation any legal or equitable claim, and if the parties are unable to agree to a settlement of such disputes by direct negotiations, the parties shall promptly mediate any such disagreement or dispute in (*City/State*) under the rules of (*the International Society of Hospitality Consultants or its designee/other ADR provider organization*) ("ADR Provider"), with a mediator selected from a list of mediators with experience in the hospitality industry proposed by the ADR Provider.

Arbitration

If the parties are unable to resolve any such disagreement or dispute through mediation, then such disagreement or dispute shall be submitted to binding arbitration in (*City/State*) under the ADR Provider's rules. The ADR Provider or its designee shall administer the arbitration proceedings.

A panel of (*one/three*) neutral arbitrator(s) shall be appointed pursuant to ADR Provider rules, (*each of whom/who*) shall be qualified as (*an*) arbitrator(s) through training programs approved by the ADR Provider, and have extensive experience in the hospitality industry. From the date the panel has been appointed and has agreed to serve, a preliminary hearing date shall be set within thirty days. Time is of the essence in the resolution of any dispute, and the panel shall be mindful of that in setting all dates related to the arbitration, unless all parties to the Agreement agree to a more relaxed schedule for the conduct of the arbitration hearings and discovery.

At the preliminary hearing, the arbitrator(s) and the parties shall establish an expedited schedule for any discovery that may be provided pursuant to the ADR Provider's rules or by stipulation of the parties. At that time, the arbitrator(s) shall also establish an arbitration hearing date following at least twenty days after the cutoff of discovery.

Ten days before the arbitration hearing date, each party shall exchange briefs and any reports prepared by expert witnesses upon whom such party intends to rely at the arbitration hearing. Ten days before the arbitration hearing date, each party will also exchange copies of all documentary evidence upon which such party will rely at the arbitration hearing, and a list of the witnesses such party intends to call to testify at the hearing.

In addition, the parties shall exchange, on the date set by the arbitrator(s), but at least five days in advance of the arbitration hearing, any documents that the arbitrator(s) determine(s) to be relevant to the issues to be arbitrated. Each party shall also make its respective experts available for deposition by the other party prior to the hearing date, according to a schedule to be ordered by the arbitrator(s).

The parties' intention is that for most disputes under this Agreement, the arbitration hearing shall be concluded no later than one hundred twenty days after the preliminary hearing date. The arbitrator(s) shall make (*his/their*) award within thirty days after the conclusion of the arbitration hearing and the final submission of any post-hearing briefs. (In the event of a three-member panel, the decision in which two of the members of the arbitration panel concur shall be the award of the arbitrators.)

In the event the hearing cannot be concluded within the specified one hundred twenty days after the preliminary hearing date, and the parties cannot mutually agree on an extension of the date for the conclusion of the hearing, the arbitrator (*chair of the arbitrator panel*) may prepare a declaration setting forth the reasons why an extension of time which shall not exceed sixty days is required for any deadline for concluding hearings or issuing an award. Either party may then present the declaration and an application to a court of competent jurisdiction requesting an extension of the date by which the hearing is to be completed for good cause shown, and which motion may be brought on five days notice or on an order shortening time, if necessary. The parties to this Agreement expressly authorize a court of competent jurisdiction to extend the time limits provided for this arbitration proceeding for good cause shown, and to do so on shortened time, if necessary.

Except as otherwise specified herein, there shall be no discovery except such limited discovery as may be permitted by the arbitrator(s), who shall authorize only such discovery as is shown to be necessary to ensure a fair hearing, and no such discovery shall in any way conflict with the time limits contained herein unless otherwise agreed by the parties in writing or extended by a court.

The arbitrator(s) shall not be bound by the rules of evidence or civil procedure, but rather may consider such writings and oral presentations as reasonable businessmen would use in the conduct of their day-to-day affairs, and may in (*his/their*) discretion preclude the presentation of redundant or cumulative evidence of material. It is the intention of the parties to limit live testimony and cross-examination to the extent necessary to ensure a fair hearing to the parties on the significant matters submitted to arbitration. The parties have included the foregoing provisions limiting the scope and extent of the arbitration with the intention of providing for prompt, economic and fair resolution of any dispute submitted to arbitration.

The arbitrator(s) (*is/are*) authorized to consider and to dispose of issues by motions for summary judgment or for summary adjudication provided the party opposing any such motion has received reasonable notice and a fair opportunity to conduct discovery of facts relevant to the motion and a fair opportunity to respond to any such motion, or where the matter can be disposed of purely as a matter of law without determination of any facts. With respect to a motion for summary judgment or summary adjudication, the parties shall comply with the applicable procedural rules and/or statutes for making and opposing such motions of the state in which the arbitration is taking place, except that the arbitrator(s) may shorten the time limits specified in such rules and/or statutes, and notwithstanding any other provision herein to the contrary, the rules of evidence shall apply with respect to the disposition of any such motion.

The arbitrator(s) shall have the discretion to allocate in (*his/their*) award the costs of arbitration, arbitrator fees and the respective attorneys' fees and costs, including expert witness and consultant fees and costs, of each party between the parties as (*he/they*) believe(s) is appropriate under the circumstances.

Judgment upon the award entered by the arbitrator(s) may be entered in any court having jurisdiction thereof.

Notwithstanding the parties' agreement to mediate or arbitrate their disputes as provided in this Agreement, any party may seek emergency relief or provisional remedies in a court of law without waiving the right to arbitrate or mediate the merits of the dispute provided no arbitration panel has yet been convened, or if it is not practicable for such application to be considered and determined by the arbitration panel. If the arbitration panel has been appointed and is available to consider and rule on the application in a timely fashion, any such application for provisional or emergency relief shall be made to the arbitration panel and the panel shall be vested with the same power as a court to award such provisional relief.

The arbitrator(s) (*is/are*) hereby specifically authorized to hear, consider and rule on motions to dispose of issues if there are no material disputed issues of fact, and/or if an award is appropriate as a matter of law without the necessity of an arbitration hearing and hearing live witness testimony.

The arbitrator(s) shall make (*his/their*) award based upon the applicable legal principles and based on the documents and testimony presented by the parties, and at the request of any party prior to conclusion of the hearing, shall provide a reasoned award and shall include in (*his/their*) award findings of fact and conclusions of law supporting such award. Statutes of limitation under the applicable state law shall be applied by the arbitrator(s).

The arbitrator(s) may not by (*his/their*) award change any terms of the underlying business agreement in which this arbitration clause is embedded.

15

Lodging Industry Exit Strategies

By *Paul Beals, Ph.D.,* and *John V. Arabia, CPA*

Paul Beals *is currently Visiting Professor at France's IMHI-ESSEC Business School, where he is responsible for MBA courses in finance and hotel real estate. For more than 25 years, his academic research and consulting have been concentrated in hotel-industry development and financing, asset management, and management contracts. He is the editor, along with Greg Denton, of* Hotel Asset Management: Principles and Practices. *In addition to two other books, he has written more than 50 book chapters and articles, primarily in the area of hotel finance and investments, that have appeared in* The Cornell Quarterly, Journal of Real Estate Finance, Real Estate Review, Journal of Hospitality Financial Management, Journal of Retail and Leisure Property, L'Hôtel Revue, *and* Le Monde. *A member of Phi Beta Kappa, the Hospitality Asset Managers Association (HAMA), and the Cornell Hotel Society, he earned his master's and doctorate degrees from Cornell University.*

John V. Arabia *is a Principal with Green Street Advisors, an independent research firm concentrating exclusively on the securities of publicly traded real estate companies, including lodging owners and operators. Mr. Arabia, who oversees Green Street's lodging research, has authored numerous research reports on individual companies as well as industry trends and topics. He has been a speaker at various industry-related events, and his comments on the lodging industry often appear in publications such as* Barron's, The Wall Street Journal, Forbes, Business Week, Crain's Business, *and* Realty Stock Review. *Mr. Arabia is a member of the Hotel Development Council or the Urban Land Institute. Before joining Green Street in 1997, he was a Hospitality Consulting Manager at EY Kenneth Leventhal. He received a master's degree in Business Administration form the University of Southern California and an undergraduate degree in Hotel Administration from Cornell University.*

Rᴇᴄᴇɴᴛ ᴅᴇᴠᴇʟᴏᴘᴍᴇɴᴛs ɪɴ ᴛʜᴇ ɪɴᴠᴇsᴛᴍᴇɴᴛ and capital markets have led to record prices for the sale of both operating businesses and real estate assets. As noted in the journal *Mergers & Acquisitions,* the liquidity driving 2005's sales activity had multiple, interrelated origins.[1] Following the stellar stock-market returns of the 1990s, the tepid yields of most of the first decade of the new millennium have driven many investors to hedge funds, with their exotic strategies for trading various financial instruments. At approximately mid-2005, it was estimated that the coffers of the 9,000 extant domestic and international hedge funds held $1 trillion in assets.[2] On the private side, some 3,000 opportunity funds were struggling to deploy $711 billion committed by investors seeking premium returns.[3] Many mature corporations, after selling off noncore assets and generally reorganizing in response to the 2001–03 downturn, came into 2005 with cash hoards that allowed them to spurn banks and other financial intermediaries that traditionally have provided liquidity to big business. The lenders' competitive response was to open the credit spigot wider, offering borrowers ever more accommodating terms, including—despite the Federal Reserve's precautionary belt-tightening—interest rates that remain attractive by historical standards as foreign investment flows prop up U.S. credit markets.

For the hotel industry, the ready availability of capital, the low-interest-rate environment, and dramatically improved operating fundamentals have resulted in low cap rates and high valuation multiples not seen for many years. What appears to be aggressive pricing has led many owners to conclude there is no better time to sell. Jones Lang LaSalle estimates that 2005 transaction volume in the domestic hotel industry will total $15 billion, surpassing the already impressive $12.9 billion rung up during 2004.[4] In such an environment, there is much interest in surveying the various exit strategies available to hotel investors. In the following pages, we will discuss some of the most commonly practiced exit strategies.

Our discussion will focus on the broad strategic implications of each exit strategy, the likely impact of the choice of exit strategy on valuation, and each strategy's tax ramifications. We will devote only limited space to a consideration of the process and cost for each exit strategy. As experienced hotel investors will attest, each deal is unique, featuring untold wrinkles and complexities peculiar to the circumstances of the seller and the buyer. Recognizing that attempting to model all the nuances of a deal is impossible, we will offer only broad outlines for each of six exit strategies, emphasizing the comparative merits of each of the deal structures. We will, however, offer illustrative mini-cases describing past lodging-industry transactions employing selected exit strategies.

The Scenario

Let us assume that the sellers are two individuals, each a 40 percent shareholder in a limited liability company (LLC) that holds 15 hotels. The remaining 20 percent of the shares are held by longstanding employees who are members of the small executive team responsible for the day-to-day asset management functions of the LLC. The principals, who are veteran hotel investors, find the current situation in the transactions and capital markets optimal. They have therefore decided to monetize the value of their holdings.

The portfolio of hotels, which represents the LLC's only significant asset, consists of full-service, nationally branded properties in major urban and resort markets. All hotels in the portfolio are considered investment grade. Property management for the portfolio is assumed by a third-party management company. The management contracts for the 15 hotels are terminable according to buyout provisions spelled out in each agreement.

Take Public as a REIT

As the number of hotel equity real estate investment trusts (REITs) coming to market over the last two years suggests, the structure has gained acceptance as the most appropriate ownership entity in which to hold hotels subject to third-party management agreements. The most salient advantage of REITs is their tax-favored status, but it is worth noting their other advantages, as well as the constraints that develop from their special status.

REITs are a creation of the Internal Revenue Code (IRC). A corporation may elect REIT status while maintaining all the benefits of a conventional corporation, including limited liability, ready transferability of ownership interests, and continuity of existence. Unlike the owners of traditional corporations, however, REIT shareholders are not subject to double taxation. Instead, if a REIT pays out substantially all of its taxable operating income and capital gains to its shareholders in cash, the dividends are tax deductible, leaving the entity tax-free. From the perspective of the shareholder, the REIT acts as a pass-through entity, or conduit, with two especially attractive features: realized income is accompanied by a cash flow and capital gains are taxed at the preferential rate available to individual taxpayers.[5]

REITs were approved by Congress to provide investors with the same benefits they enjoyed through mutual funds, including above all the ability to invest in a diverse portfolio of professionally managed real estate assets. In keeping with this intent, equity REITs are constrained by rules that limit their investments to real estate and require that substantially all of their income be derived from real-estate sources. Originally, REITs, like mutual funds, were constrained to acting as passive investors, holding investments in real estate operated by third parties. While this restriction has been relaxed considerably, especially by the passage in 1999 of the REIT Modernization Act (RMA), the essential construction of the REIT as a passive investor has not changed. Thus, unlike other conduits familiar to real estate investors (e.g., limited partnerships or limited liability companies), REITs cannot pass losses to their shareholders and distributions must be pro rata within each class of REIT stock.

Strategic Considerations

Going public as an equity REIT will establish the value of the principals' holdings because the offering will be scrutinized by analysts and professional money managers before the portfolio is marked to market. In the initial public offering (IPO), the principals or sponsors of the REIT can take cash (i.e., liquidate), take shares or equivalent ownership units (i.e., carry an interest in the public entity), or take a combination of the two. However, using the IPO to liquidate the principals' positions would be greeted with suspicion by the buy-side analyst community and prospective investors. Notwithstanding this initial limitation on the principals' flexibility, the liquidity of publicly traded REIT shares is vastly superior to ownership interests in a closely held LLC over a longer term. Marking to market the value of their portfolio and converting it to a tradable currency are useful tactics for various aspects of the principals' wealth-management efforts, including tax planning, credit management, estate planning, and philanthropy.

Going public also will provide the principals surcease from constant efforts to raise capital. In addition to using the IPO to increase the firm's equity, the principals will enjoy access to capital through secondary, or follow-up, offerings. As their structure has evolved in North America and as the securitization of myriad real estate interests has become commonplace, REITs have gained acceptance among investment bankers, institutional money managers, and retail investors. As a result, it is possible for a publicly traded REIT to raise significant sums virtually overnight, permitting management to take timely advantage of value-creation opportunities that may not be available to capital-constrained private firms.

The REIT roll-up also provides the principals an opportunity to maintain and reward their executive team through stock-based compensation. Like the principals, the LLC's minority shareholders establish a value for their interests and convert them to a liquid currency—though if they continue as the publicly traded entity's management in the near term they, too, are constrained to hold their shares due to lock-up provisions of the IPO or vesting limitations on employee stock-based compensation. If, however, a member of the executive team needs to achieve liquidity—say, by pledging his or her shares as security for a loan—possession of a tradable interest in a public company offers more flexibility than ownership of an illiquid stake of indeterminate value in a private company.

The Price. As any entrepreneur who has taken an enterprise public will attest, there are multiple offsetting constraints and costs. Going public has always come at the expense of much disclosure, as well as increased general and administrative costs. The advent of the Sarbanes-Oxley Act (SOX), however, has added a new, much deeper layer of costs that begin accumulating during the process of going public and continue as the compliance requirements are implemented throughout the firm's life as a publicly-traded entity.

For some entrepreneurs taking their firms public, accountability under SOX, while costly, seems a mild form of torment in comparison to their accountability to the investment community. The travails of disclosure begin with "road shows," the orchestrated sales pitches the firm's management and investment bankers make to analysts and money managers during the IPO process. More daunting than road shows—which end, after all, when the offering is brought to market—is management's continuous accountability to the investment community once the firm has gone public. The pressure culminates with quarterly earnings reports, but is most tellingly evoked by management's complaint that the investment community relentlessly asks, "What have you done for me lately?"

For the principals in our example, the decision to go public as a REIT entails rewards, but it also entails attendant risks. By sponsoring a publicly traded REIT and retaining their stakes in the entity, the principals mark their holdings to market while also positioning themselves to share in the REIT's upside potential. But maintaining "skin in the game," while pleasing to the market, also continues the principals' exposure to the firm's fundamental business risk. Perhaps more important, the principals shoulder the additional risk of market fluctuations in the value of their holdings. If, for example, the principals need to gain liquidity at a juncture when lodging REITs are out of favor, their shares may well be trading at a discount to their net asset value (the private-market value of the portfolio minus outstanding liabilities).

Other risks come with the decision to operate as a REIT. The requirement that a REIT disburse its earnings as dividends means management continually must return to the market to raise capital.[6] Although this has become a streamlined process for the modern publicly traded REIT, there are transaction costs. Investment-banking fees and costs for an IPO, for example, can run past 6 percent of the gross proceeds raised, while secondary offerings typically require discounts of 5 percent from the nominal share price to move blocks of stock. In contrast, other hotel companies, including especially those that derive a large percentage of their earnings from franchise and management fees, can retain substantial earnings because they are not obligated to pay dividends, yielding less costly internally generated cash to fund growth. And of course, when growth opportunities are in short supply, fee-based hotel companies can improve shareholder value by using their cash to buy back shares.

A further disadvantage of lodging REITs in comparison to hotel companies structured as conventional corporations derives from their status as passive investment vehicles. Under the RMA, a REIT may form a taxable REIT subsidiary (TRS) that leases the parent's assets, but neither the REIT nor the TRS may manage or franchise hotels. Thus REITs do not enjoy the flexibility of lodging C corps, including the domestic big three (Marriott International, Hilton Hotels, and Starwood Hotels and Resorts), each of which has set a course favoring brand expansion over hotel ownership. The big three are deploying their cash hoards to grow via less risky lines of business, including franchising, third-party management, and the creation of new brands. The same companies also have turned to timeshare, a cash-intensive business that allows branded operators to increase the number of rooms in their systems, albeit with greater risk than purely fee-based activities.

Entrepreneurs taking their companies public often chafe under a final constraint that typically runs counter to their long experience as private investors. To be considered an institutional-grade investment, the capital structure of a publicly traded hotel entity should consist of no more than 50–60 percent debt. For private hotel investors, long accustomed to transforming 11–14 percent unlevered returns into total returns of more than 20–25 percent, eschewing debt seems counter to all economic logic. They likely will protest to their investment bankers that they can't possibly buy hotels at competitive prices if the firm's overall cost of capital is not reduced by large doses of cheaper debt capital.[7] Although the entrepreneur's investment banker has nearly 50 years of financial theory at his disposal to demonstrate that, except in extreme cases, capital structure has no impact on asset value or cost of capital, he will probably respond more pertinently, warning the entrepreneur that too much debt will drive down multiples (and likely reminding him that the plan is to *pay down* debt as one of the first uses of the cash raised in the coming IPO).

Valuation Issues

Because REITs are treated under the IRC as conduits, their earnings are not reduced by entity-level taxes, which results in greater shareholder wealth. An entity taxed at the 35 percent corporate tax rate, for example, must earn $1.54 pre-tax to increase its shareholders' wealth by $1.00, while a REIT need only earn $1.00 to match the taxable company's performance. Since the return required by the shareholder is a cost to the entity, REITs should enjoy a lower cost of equity capital and trade at higher valuations than entities taxed at the corporate level.[8]

Moreover, in a low-yield investment climate, cash dividends have taken on new importance. As a result, REIT shares have been bid up by income investors, both institutional and retail.

Clearly, when an arbitrage exists between the private-market, or "Main Street," value of an entrepreneur's holdings and the value ascribed by Wall Street (i.e., when public REITs trade at a premium to net asset value), it is an opportune time to go public. In 2004, for example, the premium to net asset value of all equity REIT shares ranged from 3 percent to 22 percent, with the largest premium of Wall Street over Main Street value recorded in the period of February and March of that year. For lodging REITs during the same period, the discrepancy was slightly less favorable, with hotel REIT shares typically trading at a 5 percent to 10 percent premium to net asset value.[9] Not surprisingly, during the 2004–05 period, four hotel REITs came to market through IPOs.[10]

Tax Implications

Under the IRC, if the principals contribute their assets to the REIT in exchange for shares in the newly formed entity, a sale is deemed to have occurred. Because shareholders in LLCs are subject to partnership taxation rules, the taxable event would trigger capital gains and possibly depreciation recapture for each principal, depending on his basis in the assets. Although the principals, as individual taxpayers, enjoy a preferential capital gains tax rate (and depreciation recapture is capped at 25 percent), an immediate tax liability that probably would need to be met by liquidating a portion of their REIT shares would be a strong deterrent to doing the transaction.

Happily, a structure has existed since 1992 to address the principals' dilemma—the umbrella partnership REIT, or UPREIT. The structure was developed to facilitate the exit of owners from distressed assets. Although they were selling their holdings at deep discounts, legions of real estate owners in the early 1990s had bases in their properties inferior to their market values. For these owners, a sale of their assets and the assumption of debt by the purchaser would have triggered a devastating tax bill, especially as there was no preferential capital gains tax rate in effect until 1997.

Enter the UPREIT, a structure devised by shopping center magnate William Taubman. When an UPREIT sells shares to the public, the cash received is contributed to a limited partnership, called the "operating partnership," in exchange for operating partnership units (OP units). At the same time, the UPREIT's sponsors contribute their properties to the partnership in exchange for OP units. Since the UPREIT serves as the general partner of the operating partnership, the REIT sponsors maintain control of their contributed assets, as well as the cash paid in by the IPO purchasers. OP units, which typically are convertible to the UPREIT's shares on a one-for-one basis, also can be used as a currency to pay owners other than the

REIT sponsors who contribute assets to the partnership, both at the IPO and subsequently.

The key to the effectiveness of the UPREIT structure is that the contribution of properties to the operating partnership in exchange for OP units is not a taxable event. Under the IRC, the transaction is not recognized as a taxable event because it meets two criteria. First, since the UPREIT's sponsors and other contributors of assets typically hold their properties in partnerships, the *form* of their interests has not changed; they merely have traded their original partnership units for OP units. Second, the IRC provides for the non-recognition of certain transactions as taxable events under the concept of wherewithal to pay, which acknowledges the difficulty a taxpayer would have acquitting a tax liability resulting from certain transactions that yield no liquidity. Since rolling their properties up into a REIT in exchange for OP units provides no liquidity to investors, the transaction also meets the wherewithal-to-pay test and qualifies for non-recognition.

Of course, the use of the UPREIT structure permits only the deferral of the recognition of a gain. When the entity's investors convert their OP units to shares, it is a taxable event that generates a tax liability for each investor to the extent that the value of the shares received exceeds his basis in the operating partnership. However, the ability to defer the tax consequences yet consummate transactions when market conditions are favorable is a powerful strategic and wealth-management tool. As a result, virtually all REITs coming to market since the early 1990s have in fact been UPREITs.

Exhibit 1 provides a brief summary of a REIT transaction parallel to the one contemplated for the principals in our example. The structure of the Sunstone Hotel Investors' roll-up addresses many of the considerations involved in forming a REIT.

Take Public as a C Corporation

Under select circumstances, the principals in our example might decide to bring their holdings to market as a publicly traded corporation taxed under Subchapter C of the IRC and hence widely known simply as a "C corp." Since the two transactions are parallel means to access public capital, both through the IPO and follow-up offerings, there are more similarities than differences between the two options. Both alternatives, for example, offer the principals the opportunity to mark their holdings to market, but in both cases, the equity markets will prefer that the principals maintain skin in the game and continue as shareholders in the public entity. Whether the IPO is for REIT or C-corp shares, the principals maintain their same exposure to the entity's fundamental business risk while shouldering the risks of price fluctuations in the often fickle equities market. Similarly, the disclosure requirements, SOX compliance costs, road show travails, accountability to the investment community, and limitations on leverage are features of both options. Finally, going public by either route provides an opportunity to reward and maintain the principals' executive team using stock-based compensation.

Although the differences between the two options are fewer than the similarities, they are significant across all three dimensions: strategic, valuation, and taxation.

Exhibit 1   Private Company to REIT in an IPO

Sunstone Hotel Investors, LLC, Rolled Up Into a REIT

In 2004, Sunstone Hotel Investors, a private company, owned 54 upscale and upper-upscale hotels with over 13,000 rooms. Sunstone internally managed most of its hotels, which were subject to franchise agreements with such nationally recognized brands as Marriott and Hilton. Sunstone's majority owner, Westbrook Real Estate Partners, desired to liquidate partially or fully its ownership stake in the hotel company.

In October 2004, Westbrook chose to take the company public as a REIT through a $400 million IPO in which Westbrook partially liquidated its position and retained shares and operating partnership units in the new entity. Sunstone's management team, including CEO Robert Alter and CFO Jon Kline, continued as executives of the publicly traded REIT. However, Sunstone's property-management operation was sold to Interstate Hotels and Resorts just prior to the IPO because of the prohibition against REITs managing their hotels internally. To reduce property-level operating disruption through the transition and maximize Sunstone's input into property operations, the property-management group became a separate division of Interstate but maintained its offices in Sunstone's corporate headquarters in southern California.

Through its exit strategy, Westbrook was able to liquidate a substantial portion of its interest in Sunstone while increasing the liquidity of the remainder of its holdings in the company. In the first year as a public company, Sunstone increased its total assets by roughly 50 percent through the acquisition of approximately $700 million worth of hotels.

Strategic Considerations

Going public as a C corp provides dividend flexibility and operating flexibility for the principals. The ability to retain earnings and capital gains is a major advantage of a C corp because it permits the entity to grow using internally generated capital. In contrast, a publicly traded REIT must distribute its earnings to maintain its tax-free status, which forces it to seek capital for expansion through secondary offerings and debt financing or joint venturing—all options that have a cost associated with raising the requisite capital. Similarly, the requirement to distribute capital gains limits a REIT's flexibility to reconfigure its portfolio. If a REIT sells a noncore asset at a capital gain, the original capital returned to the REIT can be recycled by investing it in an asset more appropriate to the REIT's strategy, but the capital gain must be distributed to shareholders or it is subject to tax (at corporate tax rates, since only individual taxpayers enjoy a preferential capital gains tax rate).

C corps also enjoy full operating flexibility. Thus a C corp is permitted to operate its owned hotels, manage hotels for third-party owners, and create (or buy) a branded franchise system—all of which are forbidden for REITs. If our principals' strategic analysis led them to the conclusion that the best avenue of growth for their company was to use its real estate holdings and hotel experience as a base to develop a publicly traded operating company, going public as a C corp is a more practical option than going public as a REIT.

Exhibit 2 Private Real Estate Owner to a C Corp in an IPO

Capstar Hotel Company Goes Public

In the mid-'90s, Capstar Hotel Company, a private entity controlled by Oak Hill Capital Partners, owned 12 hotels and operated roughly 70 more properties across the United States. In 1996, Oak Hill sought liquidity and evaluated several exit strategies, including a public offering, outright sale of the company to another lodging concern, and individual asset sales. In a somewhat unconventional move for a property owner at the time, Oak Hill chose to take Capstar public as a C corp rather than a REIT, for multiple reasons.

First, because REITs are precluded from managing and franchising hotels, Capstar's management business would not fit into the REIT structure. Second, the company wanted to continue to manage the twelve hotels it owned to avoid the conflicts that often arise between owners and third-party managers. Third, Capstar sought to avoid the complicated and cumbersome lease structures that were required for hotels owned by REITs prior to the RMA. Fourth, the company was not expected to generate significant taxable income in the near future; therefore, the primary advantage of the REIT structure (tax savings at the corporate level) was not a material consideration.

Follow-Up

In 1998, Capstar merged with American General Hospitality to form Meristar Hospitality, a publicly traded REIT. Because of the REIT limitations on property operations, Capstar's property-management business was spun off as a separate public company, Meristar Hotels and Resorts. Meristar Hotels and Resorts subsequently merged with Interstate Hotels and Resorts, one of the largest independent hotel operators in the country.

C Corp or REIT? Despite its flexibility, a C corp is not the unalloyed best choice as a public market vehicle for hotel ownership. It has required a great deal of education (and patience) to focus investors on after-tax cash flow, the fundamental determinant of real estate value. But the REIT industry has succeeded. A structure once viewed as arcane by most investors has become a mainstream asset class, and is better understood as a real-estate ownership entity than a C corp. If the principals take their holdings public as a C corp with the intent of using the entity as a base to grow an operating company, they run the risk of confusing institutional investors, particularly dedicated REIT money managers.

Let us assume, however, that the offering, after some discounting by the market, is successful and the company grows as intended (i.e., by adding rooms operated on behalf of third-party owners). At some point in the evolution of the C corp, the principals probably would find themselves contemplating moving the firm's real estate holdings into a tax-advantaged REIT, leaving the C corp as a "pure play" operating company. The experience of Capstar Hotel Company, whose management followed a parallel strategy, is described in Exhibit 2.

C Corp Roll-Up: Valuation and Tax Issues

Under the conduit concept of the IRC, partnerships, LLCs, and REITs can exist as legal entities, but they are extensions of their owners and thus taxed only at the ownership level where individual tax rates, including a preferential rate on capital gains, apply. C corps, on the other hand, are subject to the entity concept, with the result that, from an investor's perspective, returns are subject to double taxation, first at the entity level and then at the shareholder level. The negative implications of double taxation for the principals in our example are several.

Finance theory holds that an investor, observing that the cash flow from a share of stock in a C corp is diminished by two tax bites, will discount the price she is willing to pay to boost her risk-adjusted after-tax return to an acceptable level. The practical import of this application of finance theory is that the principals can expect the valuation attained by taking their holdings public in a C corp will be less than the price that would have been set if their interests were rolled up into a conduit.

Perhaps of more immediate concern to the principals is the tax liability incurred by contributing their properties to a C corp in exchange for its shares. Although the IRC permits non-recognition in limited circumstances, a transfer of property to a C corp in exchange for stock generally is a taxable event. Unlike the treatment an UPREIT is accorded under the IRC, there is no structure available to defer the recognition of a gain; the principals will be taxed on the difference between the market value of the stock received and their respective tax bases in the property transferred. Finally, to the extent the firm produces taxable income and capital gains, the returns from all shares in the newly formed C corp will be diminished by the amount of the entity-level taxes. Although there are means to reduce the C corp's taxable income while passing economic benefits to the principals (i.e., salary and interest payments), such devices have their own tax consequences to shareholders, and the amounts that can be disbursed through such arrangements are subject to a reasonableness test. At the end of the day, in choosing the C-corp structure the principals accept to increase the effective tax rate on returns derived from their holdings by the applicable corporate tax rate.

Sale for Cash

As suggested in the preceding sections, a public offering would not permit the principals a definitive exit from the ownership of their assets, although it provides flexibility on many other fronts. In the paragraphs to follow, we will consider the risks and rewards of a sale for cash—a transaction that might be termed the "take-the-money-and-retire-to-a-tropical-isle" exit strategy. Since private equity funds are so abundant in the current environment and their pursuit of all real estate asset classes so ardent, we will assume the principals in our example are selling to private equity. Most of the observations to follow, however, apply to any sale for cash, regardless of the acquiring firm's structure.

Strategic Considerations

Although a doubt will always linger in a seller's mind regarding the appropriateness of the price he receives for his holdings, the value of the consideration tendered is categorical when cash is the currency. Thus, assuming the principals are reasonably assured the selling price negotiated is a fair one, they probably will derive more satisfaction from selling their holdings for cash than for, say, shares in an acquiring enterprise. In addition, of course, they achieve immediate liquidity, permitting them maximum flexibility to pursue other interests and, if necessary, meet tax liabilities and estate-planning objectives.

While a sale for cash fixes definitively the value of their holdings, the principals forego any upside they might have achieved by taking their holdings public and retaining interests in the new entity. The tradeoff for the opportunity foregone is that the principals shed the business risk of their holdings and escape any exposure to fluctuations in the value of their interests in a publicly traded entity. If the sale for cash is to private equity, however, the principals are not likely to have occasion to debate the merits of retaining a carried interest in their acquirer. Since private equity funds are structured to reward their organizers through fees—commonly a maintenance fee of 2 percent of invested assets, plus a premium of 20 percent of profits after a priority return to investors—there is a strong motivation to put as much capital to work as possible in any single transaction by buying out a seller's entire position.

Like the principals, the LLC's executive team will mark to market the value of their minority stakes and gain liquidity. But since the principals retain no measure of control over their assets or their management after a sale for cash, there is a potential loss of jobs for the executive team. Continuation of the executive team will depend on the individual circumstances of the deal, but key factors in the team's employment future include the members' interest in following the assets to another employer, the principals' willingness to advocate for their employees in the negotiations leading up to the execution of the purchase-and-sale agreement, and the private equity fund's plan for absorbing the portfolio into its holdings.

In Exhibit 3, the sale of KSL Recreation Corporation's portfolio of six luxury resorts to CNL Hotels & Resorts for cash is discussed. Although CNL works with multiple branded and independent third-party operators, KSL retained the management of a few of the properties sold pending CNL's identification of new operators.

Valuation Issues

Despite the pressure on the organizers of funds to invest cash, there is no firm evidence to suggest that private equity underwrites investments differently from other participants in the lodging-transactions market or that they regularly overpay in the market. However, the pressure to invest cash may lead private equity to do the occasional marginal deal at a higher price than might be achieved by selling to other prospective purchasers. This potential upward bias in valuation might lead the principals to favor sale to private equity.

Regardless of the principals' preferences for sale to private equity or another type of investor, they are well advised to engage an investment advisor to help them achieve the maximum value from the sale of their holdings. Although the cost of investment advisory services inevitably reduces their net sale proceeds, the principals cannot be assured they have secured the best price unless their assets are fully shopped to the market, bidders are prequalified, and a competitive auction ensues. Notwithstanding their hotel-investment experience, it would be

Exhibit 3   Sale of a Portfolio for Cash

KSL Sells Portfolio to CNL for $2.2 Billion

KSL Recreation Corporation, a private hotel investor backed by the experienced private equity firm Kohlberg Kravis Roberts & Co. (KKR), began investing in upscale and luxury resorts in the early 1990s. KSL internally managed its six unbranded destination resorts, including the Grand Wailea on Maui, the La Quinta Resort in the Palm Springs area of California, and Phoenix's Arizona Biltmore.

In 2004, KSL's investors, having garnered significant appreciation in the value of the portfolio as a result of smart acquisitions and aggressive asset management, sought liquidity to fund nonlodging investment opportunities. KSL hired a financial advisor that widely marketed the portfolio of six resorts (3,531 rooms) and several golf courses. Because the hotels were unencumbered by long-term management contracts or franchise agreements, would-be buyers had the opportunity to assume management and brand the hotels, if so desired. Given the opportunity to add these high-quality properties to a national brand's hotel offerings, the KSL portfolio drew attention from nationally branded operators as well as public and private financial investors.

CNL Hotels & Resorts, an Orlando-based private REIT, was the high bidder for KSL's portfolio. In mid-2004, CNL acquired KSL for $2.24 billion in cash, which equaled roughly $500,000 per guestroom after an allocation for KSL's golf membership business. The transaction was one of the largest hotel portfolio transactions witnessed in years.

---

imprudent for the principals to market their portfolio without engaging an investment advisory service to bring its contacts, experience, and process-management skills to the effort.

Tax Implications

The sale of the portfolio for cash is a taxable event, creating an immediate tax liability if the sale proceeds exceed the principals' bases. Although the principals have the liquidity to acquit their obligations, there are some near term tax-avoidance alternatives they may seek to employ in an effort to reduce their tax liability.

A shareholder in an LLC, who is subject to partnership taxation under the IRC, typically prefers to sell his or her interest in the LLC because the sale of the interest is a less complex transaction and because the entire gain will be taxed at the preferential capital gains tax rate. In contrast, if the assets controlled by the partnership are sold, each partner may be liable for taxes—at ordinary income-tax rates—on losses included in the calculation of his or her taxable income over the preceding five years.[11] This occurs because, under a so-called "look-back" recapture rule of the tax code, the losses are recovered from profits on the sale before capital gains are realized.

To some extent, any strategizing by the principals to convey their interests instead of assets is moot because it is likely to be resisted strongly by the acquirer. Buyers will insist on a sale of assets so that their basis in the assets is stepped up, maximizing their depreciation tax-shield, and because they seek to avoid assuming any of the partnership's contingent liabilities. Because acquirers are unlikely to agree to a purchase of the sellers' interests, sellers are well advised to understand their potential tax liability in a sale of assets so that they can attempt to negotiate price concessions to provide a measure of compensation for the diminished after-tax proceeds they will receive.

Other Standard Approaches. Two other common tax-deferral alternatives deserve consideration by the principals. Structuring the transaction as an installment sale would permit the principals to spread their tax liability over several years. This would be an especially appropriate tactic if the partners expected to have capital losses from other activities in upcoming years. However, installment sales usually are a feature of smaller transactions, in which the seller's tax-planning needs are accommodated and the purchaser can husband cash more effectively by paying in installments. For the reasons cited previously, a private equity purchaser would have little interest in preserving cash, so this option probably would not be available to the principals.

A second means of deferring a part of the principals' tax liability would be to allocate a portion of the sale proceeds to a non-compete covenant. This allocation of the sale price probably would be acceptable to the private equity fund because it would provide a deduction from operating income over a shorter period (15 years) than the cost-recovery period allowed for real property. The principals, on the other hand, would delay the payment of taxes on a portion of the gain but trade this advantage for a higher tax rate because the payments received under a non-compete agreement would be taxed as ordinary income.

Sale to a Publicly Traded Entity with a Carried Interest

If the principals find features of each of the three preceding exit strategies attractive, they might be led to contemplate a mixed option whereby they sold their holdings for a combination of cash and shares in a publicly traded REIT or C corp. As the following discussion will demonstrate, some of the risks and rewards of this exit strategy parallel those of going public and a cash sale, but new considerations also surface in evaluating the option of sale to a publicly traded entity with a carried interest.

Strategic Considerations

Regardless of the precise mix of cash and shares paid as consideration, the principals' holdings in the private LLC are marked to market. Of equal importance, the principals can influence the degree of liquidity achieved through the sale by negotiating the proportion of the consideration to be paid in cash. When going public, either as a REIT or a C corp, the principals have very little flexibility to liquidate immediately more than a modest portion of their shares without being penalized by the market. In contrast, in a cash sale to private equity, the principals must accept the opposite outcome, receiving only cash as consideration. Lastly, if the acquirer is a large public company, the principals' carried interest provides diversification beyond that available from the private company's holdings of 15 assets.

Exhibit 4   Sale for Cash and a Carried Interest in a Publicly Traded Entity

Blackstone Sells Portfolio to Host Marriott

In the late '90s, The Blackstone Group, a private-equity investment firm, owned a portfolio of 13 upper-upscale and luxury hotels with an unlevered asset value of approximately $1.8 billion. The portfolio included two Ritz-Carlton hotels, two Four Seasons properties, and several Hyatt hotels. In January 1999, Blackstone sold the hotel portfolio to Host Marriott Corporation (HMT), a hotel REIT that owned at the time approximately 100 high-end hotels. Total consideration included a combination of $940 million of HMT's operating partnership (OP) units, which were convertible into HMT's common shares, and $835 million in cash and assumed debt.

By taking OP units, Blackstone became HMT's largest shareholder and diversified its holdings while maintaining a significant investment in the lodging sector. Blackstone was able to maintain some control over its investment because the firm was accorded one of HMT's board seats. Despite share-sale, or "lock-up," limitations that ranged from six months to one year, Blackstone's units and shares in HMT were considerably more liquid than its real estate holdings. The sale also marked to market the value of Blackstone's portfolio.

Prudence on Both Sides. Although the preceding advantages are appealing, they come with cautions. For example, if the value of the shares pledged by the acquirer falls significantly before the deal closes, the transaction could be scuttled. A prudent acquirer will stipulate in the purchase-and-sale agreement a minimum market price per share that represents a floor under the deal. By doing so, the acquirer avoids a situation in which the firm must issue an excessive number of shares to consummate the transaction. If the acquirer's management did not negotiate this escape clause, the firm could find its share price in a downward spiral as each additional share issued further diluted shareholders' interests in the firm. In addition, to the extent that the principals accept shares in the acquirer as consideration for their holdings, they are subject to market fluctuations in the value of their securities and the continued business risk of the underlying holdings, which are now in the hands of another management team.

Further, the principals' part ownership of a larger portfolio of assets does not necessarily ensure that they have reduced their risk. The acquirer may, for example, have a large concentration of hotels in a single state, such as Florida or Texas, where a catastrophic hurricane season or a downturn in the oil market would severely depress earnings and share prices. A seller accepting a carried interest in an entity acquiring his holdings must scrutinize the assets and business risks of the acquirer to determine if the apparent diversification offered by more numerous holdings represents a real reduction in risk.

In Exhibit 4, we present a thumbnail sketch of a large transaction, Blackstone Group's sale of a $1.8 billion portfolio to Host Marriott in exchange for cash and a carried interest. An important objective Blackstone achieved in the transaction was the diversification of its hotel holdings—in this case, by about eightfold.

In tendering their stakes in the private LLC, the executive team's members share the same risks and rewards as the principals. However, they also bear the risk of a potential loss of employment, as they would in an all-cash sale. Their potential for continuance depends on the same factors as in a sale for cash.

Valuation Issues

Their stake in the acquirer allows the principals to share in the acquirer's upside, thus providing a partial hedge of the sale price. If the assets contributed to the acquiring firm's holdings outperform the principals' expectations, the excess value should be reflected in the acquirer's share price, effectively yielding additional proceeds from the transaction for the principals (although their increase in wealth is shared with the acquirer's other stockholders).

Realization of this upside potential is not ironclad because it depends on two assumptions. The most important assumption is that the underlying value of the shares tendered when the transaction closes is reflected in their market price. For example, what is the true longer term value of the shares tendered if they currently are trading at a significant unwarranted premium to net asset value? Similarly, is $50 million worth of Company X's shares at today's price the same value as $50 million worth of Company Y's shares at today's price? Achieving the appropriate valuation for their holdings requires that the principals and their investment advisors understand the acquirer and its business prospects.

The second assumption is that the acquirer's management will maximize the value of the firm's holdings. Before the transaction, the principals and their executive team control the value-creation opportunities of the LLC's holdings, but control of the future value of their investment passes into the hands of the acquirer's management upon sale. The principals likely will be daunted by the prospect of ceding control over a significant portion of their personal wealth—as they should be. Ideally, however, they will analyze, with the help of their investment advisors, the expertise and previous performance of the acquirer's managers, yielding an understanding of the value they bring to the transaction.

The mix of flags represented in the principals' portfolio may affect the valuation achieved on exit. Publicly traded branded hotel companies may not have an interest in the portfolio unless it contains a significant number of properties carrying its brand(s). Similarly, a number of private investors and REITs prefer to align themselves with specific brands, which may not be represented adequately in the portfolio to draw their interest. If important players in the market are sidelined because of the properties' branding, the competitive bidding may be less intense, with the result that the valuation achieved may be less than commensurate with the underlying quality of the assets.

Tax Implications

As suggested above, the ability to negotiate the mix of cash and shares received as consideration provides liquidity, which may be an important consideration to the principals in acquitting their tax liability. A REIT may prefer making acquisitions with cash if its shares are trading at a discount to net asset value and the firm has available borrowing capacity, but the principals likely would have reasonable latitude to negotiate for a proportion of the consideration to be tendered in OP units, permitting them to control the timing of the recognition of gains.

The amount of the potential tax liability will be affected by the principals' bases in the assets as well as the acquirer's tax status. If the acquiring firm is a C corp, the principals will owe taxes on any gain, calculated as the difference between their individual bases in the assets and the total consideration received, regardless of mix of cash and shares paid. If the acquirer is a REIT, the principals can defer recognition of the gain on the proportion of the assets exchanged for OP units, but have an immediate tax liability for the gain on the portion of the assets purchased with cash.

Whether C-corp or REIT shares are received in the transaction, the principals have the same philanthropic opportunity as they do with an IPO: the option to donate appreciated shares to a qualified charity and take a tax deduction for their market value instead of their cost basis, thus avoiding taxes on their capital gains.

Sale of Partial Interest (Equity Leveraging)

The sale of a partial interest, sometimes termed equity leveraging, provides some of the advantages of a sale for cash with the oversight features of an IPO. Depending on the level of continued involvement in their portfolio's direction sought by the principals, they might choose to sell a 49–90 percent interest in their LLC. Although equity leveraging ostensibly is a cautious exit strategy, it creates risks that the principals need to weigh.

Strategic Considerations

The principals' sale of an interest in their LLC marks to market a portion of their holdings and suggests a fair market value (FMV) for the whole of the enterprise. Since it is a cash transaction, the principals will have the wherewithal to meet tax obligations. Moreover, they can calibrate the proportion sold according to the degree of control they wish to retain over the restructured enterprise and the liquidity needed to meet such personal objectives as pursuing other interests, estate planning, and philanthropy.

Above all, the transaction permits the principals to "take some chips off the table" and reduce their risk by realizing the value of a portion of their holdings in cash. At the same time, however, the principals maintain a position in their enterprise and can participate in the eventual appreciation of its assets. Moreover, the new shareholder(s) may bring expertise and contacts to the endeavor, creating value unavailable to the principals before the business combination was formed.

Happily Ever After? There are three tradeoffs the principals must accept in exchange for the advantages of equity leveraging. Above all, they must share the direction of the firm with the new partner(s). The principals' relationship with their new investor(s) can be as complementary and harmonious as suggested in the preceding paragraph or it can be difficult, mirroring the accounts of troubled mergers seen periodically in *The Wall Street Journal*. Second, unlike exit strategies that leave the principals with publicly traded shares that can be liquidated, their retained stake in the LLC is not liquid—and, in fact, may be more difficult to trade because of the presence of the additional shareholder(s). Finally, the principals' stake in the LLC does not offer the same potential for diversification as a carried interest in a large, publicly traded entity.

Valuation Issues

Because it is the sale of only a partial interest—and because prospective investors, like the principals, perceive the risk of taking on partners—there is likely to be less interest in the offering than in an outright sale. With restrained competitive bidding and incremental risk that is difficult to quantify, the valuation of a partial interest will be affected. In fact, joint venture opportunities in general typically are discounted in the marketplace. Exceptions to this generalization may occur, however, when a partial interest is sold to an insider, who obviously is in a better position to analyze the risks and determine an appropriate value.

Equity leveraging is a specialized exit strategy with particular risks, yet it is a transaction that is more likely than any other exit strategy to be accomplished without the participation of an investment advisor. Although the cost of investment advisory services will reduce the principals' proceeds, matching the opportunity with the appropriate investor(s) probably is the most important factor in achieving full value from the sale. If the principals weigh fully the strategic and valuation implications of equity leveraging, the risk reduction available from investment advisory services should be apparent.

Exhibit 5 describes the sale of a partial interest for cash by a Goldman Sachs opportunity fund to publicly traded Kerzner International, an owner and operator of casinos and upscale resorts. In this example of equity leveraging, the opportunity fund returned profits to investors while also gaining the operational and marketing expertise of its joint venture partner.

Tax Implications

The most tax-efficient means of conveying a partial interest in the principals' LLC is not to sell the individual shareholders' stakes, but to issue enough new shares to dilute the existing owners' stakes to the level at which the joint venture partner's interest equals the negotiated level of ownership. Thus, in a simplified example, if the existing equity interest of the principals and their executive team consisted of 100 shares outstanding and the principals wished to sell a 50 percent interest to their joint venture partner, the LLC would issue 100 new shares in exchange for the new investor's payment of the negotiated price. Structuring the deal in this fashion effectively conveys a 50 percent interest to the principals' joint venture partner but provides two tax-avoidance possibilities to the current shareholders.

Since the LLC's shareholders are subject to partnership accounting, from a tax perspective, each has an individual capital account representing his or her cost basis in the pass-through entity. If a partner sells half of his partnership interest, the cost basis deducted in calculating any gain or loss is one-half of his capital account. If the transaction results in a gain, tax is due immediately. In contrast, if the cash contributed by the joint venture partner is distributed incrementally from the partnership, the principals and their executive team can "time" the recognition of their gains. More important, any distribution received can yield a realized gain only to the extent that it exceeds the partner's entire cost basis.

Exhibit 5   Sale of a Partial Interest for Cash

Sale of a 50 Percent Interest in the Palmilla Resort to Kerzner International

In 2002, an emerging-markets opportunity fund sponsored by Goldman Sachs wished to sell or reduce its interest in the exclusive Palmilla Resort & Golf Club, located at the tip of Mexico's Baja peninsula. The fund's managers sought a transaction to return capital to investors and because they felt the property was not being managed to its potential, heightening the fund's risk.

The offering drew five firm bids, including two all-cash offers and a proposal to purchase a 50 percent interest. Ultimately, Goldman chose to enter the joint venture proposed by Kerzner International. The offer was made attractive by a number of considerations, including the promise of a speedy close; the purchaser's willingness to serve as the developer and finance nearly two-thirds of the $60 million investment needed to expand and upgrade the property; and the "fit" of the resort with Kerzner's efforts to build a worldwide luxury brand.

By accepting to do a joint venture with Kerzner, the fund achieved several positive outcomes: it reduced its risk in the project, both because the transaction took chips off the table and because it brought Kerzner's commitment and expertise to the project, allowing both to share in the property's upside; it provided profits to the fund's investors (the deal valued the property at $650,000 per key versus a cost of $235,000 per key); Goldman retained consent rights over major decisions; and through a put-and-call mechanism, Goldman could sell its remaining interest to Kerzner or market the property if the joint venture foundered.

Source: Dana Michael Ciraldo, MAI, Hodges Ward Elliott.

Section 1031 Tax-Deferred Exchanges

Although like-kind exchanges did not gain widespread notice until the 1990s, they have been permitted under the IRC since 1921. Like the taxpayer contributing property to a partnership in exchange for a partnership interest, a taxpayer who exchanges a property for a similar property is merely continuing the investment. Moreover, if the FMV of the property received exceeds the owner's adjusted basis in the property given up in the exchange, he or she has realized a gain on the transaction but has no immediate liquidity to pay taxes. Thus under Section 1031 of the IRC, gain (or loss) realized on an exchange is not immediately recognized, but instead deferred.[12]

It is important to note that the non-recognition of gain applies only to the amounts exchanged in the form of qualifying like-kind property. Other consideration that may be part of an exchange—including cash and assumed debt—is termed "boot" and its receipt is a taxable event. An example will illustrate the deferral mechanism of a 1031 exchange and the treatment of boot.

Simultaneous Exchanges

Let us assume the scenario sketched in Exhibit 6, in which the owner (Owner A) of an asset with a FMV of $18 million wishes to exchange her hotel (Property A) for Property B, which has a FMV of $15 million. Owner A's adjusted basis in her asset

Exhibit 6   Simultaneous 1031 Exchange Illustrated

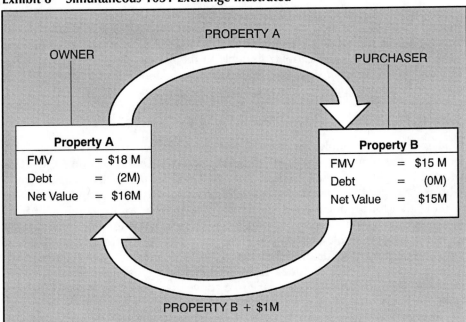

is $7 million and the property's outstanding debt is $2 million. The purchaser (Owner B) will assume the $2 million debt on Property A, while Property B is being conveyed to Owner A free of debt. Since the net value of Owner A's property is $16 million ($18 million FMV minus the assumed debt of $2 million), Owner B will not only convey his property to Owner A in the exchange; he also will pay boot of $1 million in cash. From a tax perspective, on conclusion of the reciprocal trade, Owner A will have received $18 million of value in exchange for conveying Property A, calculated as follows:

Fair market value of Property B:	$ 15 million
Cash received:	1 million
Debt transferred to purchaser:	2 million
Total consideration received:	$ 18 million

The key to the tax-deferral mechanism of the 1031 exchange is that the owner-taxpayer must carry Property A's adjusted basis ($7 million) forward as the *substituted basis* in her newly acquired Property B. Thus, on conclusion of the exchange, Owner A has a potential tax liability for $11 million of gain ($18 million of consideration received less the substituted basis of $7 million).

The $3 million portion of the gain that represents boot ($1 million cash + $2 million of debt assumed by the purchaser) is immediately taxable. However, because Owner A pays tax on the $3 million of boot, this portion of the gain is added to her basis (to avoid further taxation on the sum when the property is sold), yielding an adjusted basis in Property B of $10 million ($7 million + $3 million). The end result of applying the Section 1031 rules is that Owner A's tax basis in Property B is $8 million *less* than the economic value of the property relinquished in the exchange. Thus the gain attributable to the like-kind property received is "built in" to the reduced basis and its recognition is deferred until Property B is conveyed in a subsequent taxable event.

Gaining Flexibility: Delayed Multi-Party Exchanges

In our preceding example, Property B, conveyed to Owner A in exchange for a hotel, might be any number of real estate asset classes. Under Section 1031, a tax-deferred exchange takes place when "property held for productive use in a trade or business or for investment...is exchanged for property of like kind which is to be held either for productive use in a trade or business or for investment."[13] Subsequent paragraphs of Section 1031 make the IRS's intent even more patent: only the exchange of tangible income-producing or investment property qualifies for non-recognition. Thus, such instruments as stocks, bonds, notes, and partnership interests are specifically excluded from Section 1031 exchange treatment, as are properties held for sale (e.g., by dealers or developers) and assets held for personal use.

However, because income-producing and investment properties are considered "like kind" under Section 1031, business property may be exchanged for business property or investment property, while investment property may similarly be exchanged for investment property or business property. This provides significant flexibility in the exchange of an owner's real property—permitting, for example, a "land-poor" farmer to convey $2 million of unproductive land to a shopping-center developer in exchange for the ownership of multi-family housing producing regular cash flows.[14] Similarly, an investor seeking a lifestyle change might use a 1031 exchange to trade a hotel in the Northeast for real estate parcels in south Florida as different as unimproved land or an operating orange grove.

Despite the ability to exchange disparate real estate asset classes under Section 1031, negotiating one-for-one exchanges of property potentially is cumbersome. Differences in the value of properties exchanged can be adjusted through the payment of (taxable) boot, as in the preceding example, but identifying appropriate properties and engineering a simultaneous conveyance of both sides of the exchange makes for a complex transaction, especially for the small individual investor. Thus, over time—and despite numerous challenges from the IRS—taxpayers won the right to enter into delayed exchanges. In 1984, definitive rules governing the timing required to qualify as an acceptable nonsimultaneous exchange were added to Section 1031 by Congress. In 1991, Section 1031 was further modified to define the role of a qualified intermediary and create several safe harbors, thus significantly streamlining multi-party delayed exchanges and spawning the development of today's 1031 exchange industry. An example will illustrate the incremental flexibility of delayed multi-party exchanges and the role played by the qualified intermediary (also known as an exchangor, facilitator, or accommodator).

Exhibit 7   Delayed Multi-Party Exchanges

Relinquished Property	
Sale price of hotel:	$ 15 million
Less adjusted basis:	7 million
Potential gain:	**$ 8 million**
Cost of Replacement Property: $18 million	
Purchased Using:	
Cash released from exchange trust account:	$ 15 million
Additional cash from owner:	3 million
Total consideration paid:	**$18 million**
Owner's Basis in Replacement Property:	
Substituted basis (adjusted basis of relinquished asset):	$ 7 million
Boot paid:	3 million
Adjusted basis in replacement property:	**$10 million**

Source: Karen Jonas, CBIZ Accounting, Tax & Advisory Services.

Example. Assume a hotel owner wishes to realize the appreciation of his hotel, which has a FMV of $15 million, to reinvest his equity in a hotel of greater value. The hotel's original cost basis was $10 million, its current adjusted basis is $7 million, and there is no outstanding debt on the property. As shown in Exhibit 7, if the owner sells the hotel, he will have a taxable gain on sale of $8 million—and payment of the tax liability on his profit, even at the preferential capital gains tax rate, will reduce the proceeds available for reinvestment. If, however, the owner works through a 1031 facilitator, he can structure the transaction to qualify as a like-kind exchange and defer recognition of the $8 million gain.

Assume our owner has found a purchaser willing to acquire the hotel for $15 million in cash. If the owner wishes to avoid immediate payment of the tax due on his transaction, he must enter into an exchange agreement with a qualified intermediary before the sale of the relinquished property closes. In this "downleg" component of the exchange, the owner assigns his purchase-and-sale agreement to the qualified intermediary, who closes the transaction with the purchaser, confirms receipt of the $15 million, and instructs the owner to pass title to the purchaser. Under one of the safe harbor rules established by the IRS, the owner is deemed not to have constructive receipt of the proceeds—and no sale has occurred—if the $15 million is held by the qualified intermediary in a separate exchange trust account.

Under Section 1031 rules, two clocks are set running when the relinquished property closes. Within 45 calendar days the owner must identify and formally communicate to the qualified intermediary the specifics of a limited number—typically three—of possible replacement properties. Within the earlier of 180 calendar days or the due date (including extensions) of the owner's tax return, the purchase of the replacement property must close. Both deadlines are hard and fast. For example, if the 45th or the 180th day falls on a weekend or legal holiday, no surcease is accorded; the exchange fails, resulting in recognition of the sale of the relinquished property and the resultant tax liability.

If the owner has planned carefully for the exchange, either by identifying a suitable replacement in advance or by working with brokers referred to him by the qualified intermediary, closing on a replacement property in the required 180 days should not be a Herculean task (although the most common reason for an aborted exchange is failure to close the replacement-purchase transaction). When the owner has identified a suitable replacement property and negotiated an acceptable price, the "upleg" portion of the exchange is effected. The owner assigns the purchase-and-sale agreement to the qualified intermediary and authorizes the release of the funds in the exchange trust account. The qualified intermediary closes the purchase of the replacement property and instructs the seller to convey title to the owner. If title to the replacement property is conveyed to the owner within the required 180-day timeframe, and all the applicable IRS rules are followed, the owner is construed to have entered into a reciprocal trade with the qualified intermediary, thus conforming to the essential structure of a straightforward exchange, as described in Exhibit 6.

Tax Implications. To examine the tax consequences of the exchange, let us assume that the hotel acquired in the exchange has a FMV of $18 million. As shown in Exhibit 7, to meet the $18 million acquisition price, the exchanger must pay $3 million of cash boot in addition to the $15 million released from the exchange trust account.

The $15 million of consideration paid from the proceeds of the sale of the relinquished asset consists of $7 million of cost recovery, plus $8 million of gain. Recognition of the $8 million gain is deferred, however, by requiring the owner to carry over his basis in the relinquished asset as the basis of the replacement property. Thus, the owner's basis in the replacement property is his substituted basis ($7 million) plus the cash boot paid ($3 million), or $10 million. The $8 million of value purchased with the gain from the sale of the relinquished asset will be taxed when the replacement asset is subsequently sold. At that time, the taxable gain will be calculated as the difference between the net sale proceeds and the replacement asset's adjusted basis. But the starting point for the calculation of the subsequent adjusted basis is $10 million, not the $18 million cash cost of the replacement asset.

1031 Exchange Services. As the above description of a multi-party delayed exchange suggests, the qualified intermediary has a rigorous fiduciary role in the execution of a complex transaction. The taxpayer-owner is vulnerable on numerous fronts, not the least of which is that the proceeds of the conveyance of the relinquished property are held by the facilitator. The taxpayer-owner also relies on the qualified intermediary to observe the complex requirements established by the IRS for the execution of a valid exchange, while of course consummating the purchase of the replacement property(ies) within the prescribed 180-day time frame.

Although some of the most active 1031 facilitators are subsidiaries of large, well-known financial services firms, to date the industry is largely unregulated. A taxpayer contemplating the use of an exchange service is therefore well advised to exercise appropriate due diligence and verify the service's track record, capitalization, and levels of insurance coverage, including fidelity bonding and errors-and-omissions policies.

Finally, a recent development further enhancing the utility of 1031 exchange services deserves mention. A revenue procedure issued by the IRS in 2002 clarified the circumstances under which the ownership of an undivided fractional interest in real property would be considered a tenancy in common, avoiding partnership treatment of the investment. The practical import of the IRS pronouncement is that ownership of income-producing real property may be subdivided into as many as 35 tenancy-in-common interests available for purchase as replacement properties in 1031 exchanges. For real estate owners seeking flexibility through an exchange, the possibilities are diverse: ownership of pieces of larger, professionally managed properties with high quality tenants, geographic diversification, portfolio diversification, trading up by leveraging the equity extracted from relinquished property, and relief from the active management of real estate holdings.

Strategic Considerations and Valuation Issues

Multiple assets may be relinquished and multiple properties may serve as replacement assets in Section 1031 exchanges. However, it is unlikely that the principals stipulated in our scenario would employ a Section 1031 exchange to dispose of all the properties comprising their portfolio. Although such a transaction would mark to market the principals' holdings, it merely would substitute one portfolio of real property for another—hardly an exit strategy—and would be a difficult series of exchanges to consummate under the constraints imposed by Section 1031.

There are several strategic objectives the principals might achieve, however, by using a Section 1031 exchange to convey one or two of their properties in conjunction with a separate exit strategy for the remainder of the portfolio. If the principals, jointly or individually, desired to remain active in the ownership of lodging investments, a 1031 exchange could prove an effective way of reinvesting equity in a hotel (or hotels) situated in a desirable locale and likely demanding less of the principals' attention than ownership of a 15-hotel portfolio.[15] Or the principals could use a 1031 exchange to gain significant geographic, asset-class, and performance diversification, perhaps reinvesting the proceeds of the "downleg" of a 1031 exchange in a variety of tenancy-in-common interests spread across multiple commercial real estate sectors featuring different risk, capital-appreciation, income, and leverage characteristics.

Perhaps of equal appeal are the wealth-management opportunities provided by 1031 exchanges. At their option, the principals may put the property(ies) enjoying the greatest equity build-up into a 1031 exchange, redeploying their equity while maximizing the wealth sheltered from current taxation. Similarly, the principals may choose when to recognize the gain deferred in a 1031 exchange, timing the recognition to offset capital losses or to meet other tax-planning needs. Finally, deferred gain from a 1031 exchange ultimately may escape income taxation if the replacement property eventually is passed to legatees, who inherit the asset at its stepped-up basis (i.e., FMV at the time of the inheritance), although there may be estate-tax implications.

Overly cautious—or perhaps cynical—observers sometimes conclude that there are valuation implications if the seller in the "upleg" segment of a 1031 exchange perceives that the owner is under pressure to close a transaction to meet the deadline imposed by the IRC. But the threat of "retrading" exists in all real estate transactions—and is very real in IPOs as well, where the founding shareholders cannot be sure the price "pegged" by investment bankers will be achieved (and eleventh-hour withdrawals of IPOs occur). There need not be valuation implications merely because a transaction is structured as a 1031 exchange. An owner-exchangor who plans prudently, is transparent with the purchaser of the relinquished property and the seller of the replacement property, identifies replacement properties early, and works with competent investment advisors and qualified intermediaries should achieve the market price for both legs of a 1031 exchange.

Conclusion

Real estate investors constantly ask, "Is it better to be a buyer now or a seller?" The question has significant practical importance, but it is difficult to answer. Accordingly, we resort to finance's all-purpose answer: it depends.

The choice of the best time to "pull the trigger" and the best exit strategy depends on a confluence of factors. The lodging industry is at a point in its cycle where there appears to be another two to three years of upside. Of equal importance, capital is readily available and investor attitudes toward the hotel industry are positive. Finally, deal structuring is facilitated by the availability of efficient investment vehicles and a relatively investor-friendly tax environment. There are abundant signs indicating a generally favorable climate, but the individual seller must weigh his or her risks and rewards in deciding to sell and structuring the exit. We hope that this chapter has provided some useful insights to assist in the process.

The authors express their appreciation to Karen Jonas, J.D., CPA, of CBIZ Accounting, Tax & Advisory Services for her counsel on many of the tax issues treated in the chapter.

Endnotes

1. Martin Sikora and Joan Harrison, "Gusher on the Sell Side," *Mergers & Acquisitions* 40, no. 5 (May 2005): pp. 28–31.

2. Sikora and Harrison, p. 30.

3. Erin E. Arvedlund, "Private-Equity Funds Lower the Bar," *Wall Street Journal*, August 2, 2005, p. D2.

4. Amy Yee, "Value of US Hotel Sales Set to Hit Record High," *Financial Times*, August 8, 2005, p. 16.

5. Although capital gains paid to shareholders are taxed at preferential capital gains tax rates, REIT dividends—like current income from partnerships—are ordinary income, taxed at the investor's applicable ordinary income tax rate.

6. Commentators on REITs as investments frequently note that a portion of the dividend paid to REIT shareholders may be a nontaxable return of capital. Rarely, however, do they explain why this return of capital occurs. Like most corporations, a REIT may use accelerated depreciation schedules to determine its taxable income. However, when calculating income available for distribution, straight-line depreciation is deducted, yielding accounting income that exceeds taxable income. From a tax perspective, the accounting income distributed includes a return of capital (the excess of accelerated depreciation over straight-line). Capital returned to REIT shareholders is reported separately on Form 1099 and reduces their basis in their shares.

7. In the mid-1990s, when several private hotel entities were rolling their holdings up into REITs, a veteran hotel investor, describing his firm's IPO at a national investment conference, observed, "When our investment banker told me we had too much debt to go public, I couldn't believe it. Here I'd spent my whole professional life finding ways to leverage up, and now he was telling me I was wrong!" That market pressures have periodically obliged the investor's REIT to delever suggests he was not entirely convinced by his investment banker's arguments.

8. It should be noted, however, that on an after-tax basis, the return to C-corp shareholders may be improved from what is suggested in our simplified example. This is because qualified dividends paid by C corps are taxed at the preferential dividend rate, whereas REIT dividends, as explained in note 5 above, are taxed as ordinary income. Moreover, since C corps can retain their earnings and reinvest them to increase shareholders' wealth, there is greater opportunity to achieve share-price appreciation, which is taxed at the preferential capital gains tax rate.

9. Source: Green Street Advisors.

10. We count here the following REIT IPOs: Strategic Hotel Capital, Sunstone Hotel Investors, DiamondRock Hospitality, and Eagle Hospitality.

11. The principals also may be taxed, at ordinary tax rates (capped at 25 percent), on recaptured depreciation of personal property (i.e., furniture, fixtures, and equipment), but these amounts usually can be reduced by allocating most of the sale proceeds to real property.

12. The application of Section 1031 is not a taxpayer election, but a requirement and a loss realized in a 1031 exchange would, like a gain, be deferred. Therefore, a taxpayer holding a property with a FMV less than its adjusted basis would find it more advantageous to sell the property in a taxable event, recognize the loss, and reinvest the proceeds in the exchange property sought.

13. Internal Revenue Code, Sec. 1031(a) (1).

14. Property defined under the IRC as personal property, or personalty, also qualifies for 1031 exchanges, but the definition of like-kind property is far more restrictive, disqualifying, for example, the exchange of automobiles for light trucks.

15. If the principals' desired locale is outside the United States, a 1031 exchange is not available to them. The IRS has long held that foreign property is not like-kind property.

Asset Management's Impact on Value

By *Chad Crandell, ISHC,* and *Kristie Dickinson*

Chad Crandell is a co-founder of Capital Hotel Management (CHM), where he serves as President and operations leader of hotel investment advisory and asset management services. Since its inception, CHM has provided asset management services to investors and developers holding hotels and resorts valued at more than $3 billion. Before forming CHM, Mr. Crandell held a senior-level position at a major consulting company firm. His 20 years of hospitality industry experience includes hotel management and franchise selection and contract negotiation, operational reviews focusing on market positioning and financial performance, and development of hotel acquisition and disposition strategies. He has held numerous operations and development management positions with InterContinental Hotels, Chalet Suisse International, and Koala Inns of America. He currently serves as an active member of the International Society of Hospitality Consultants, Counselors in Real Estate and Cornell Hotel Society, as well as a member of the board of directors of the Hospitality Asset Managers Association.

Kristie Dickinson, Vice President of Portfolio Management for Capital Hotel Management, has more than a decade of experience in hotel operations, development, and related advisory services. At CHM, she is responsible for overseeing portfolio projects, including implementing revenue enhancement programs, conducting pricing analyses, monitoring labor productivity and market trends, and identifying profit improvement opportunities. She also coordinates the marketing and public relations efforts for the company. Prior to joining CHM, Ms. Dickinson held various positions at two leading hospitality consulting firms, and was a member of the development and franchise team at Doubletree Hotels Corporation. Ms. Dickinson has consulted on numerous development, operations, market positioning, management, disposition, and strategic planning projects for a variety of hospitality-related land uses, including resort, golf, and vacation ownership, and has advised on various support facilities for the United States Air Force at bases in the United States, Korea, Japan, and Germany.

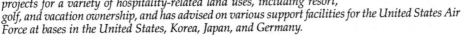

THE ROLE OF THE ASSET MANAGER has evolved considerably over the years from its former association largely with distressed properties and short-term financial workouts to today's asset managers, representing fiduciaries on a higher level who often have investment advisory and asset oversight. Historically, the relationship between hotel owner and asset manager was linked solely to an individual asset, but today it is long-term and investment based. While there are several factors that contribute to the evolution and elevation of the asset management role, the two driving forces are the wide range of hotel owners with varying levels of experience and available resources and the increasing domination of brand operators in the market. Asset managers bring investment and operations expertise to owners that may not have the necessary experience or resources to effectively manage their hotel holdings, while providing an essential balance to brand/operator objectives to protect owner/investor goals. They are in a position to understand the goals and objectives of the owner and are close enough to the operation to help sift through management/brand requests to determine what is financially permissible/affordable and what is operationally necessary. From this vantage point, asset managers have the ability to act as a liaison, filter and analyze information, plan, and implement recommendations for the betterment of the hotel. Asset managers also have the added benefit of thinking on a strategic level for multiple assets and can share best practices. In short, asset managers are in a position to enhance revenues, contain cost, and maximize owner returns. Simply put, they *add value* to the hotel investment.

Asset managers enhance value, but how is the value of a hotel determined? Hotel valuation in the open market is predicated largely on operating cash flow, as well as such factors as how much capital has been reinvested in the property, the market in which the hotel operates, the degree of difficulty of entering the market, comparable property sales, and speculation of operating potential. The value of an asset typically is determined for the purposes of selling, buying, and refinancing.

If value is largely predicated on operating cash flow, then is it logical to say that enhancing cash flow will translate into higher value? Yes and no. Increased cash flow must be sustainable and cannot be detrimental to the hotel. For example, one cannot simply cut back on repairs and maintenance or marketing to enhance cash flow in a singular effort to improve value. Neither of these activities could be sustained without hurting the long-term potential of the asset. As such, improving cash flow to enhance value requires efforts beyond simply cost cutting. Value enhancement comes from an asset manager who is creative and looks for ways to enhance revenue while improving the guest experience; who cuts costs through technological advancements, streamlining operations, and value engineering; and who maximizes asset value by selectively approving projects that can improve productivity, enhance the guest experience, and preserve the asset. Because the industry is constantly moving and changing, there are always opportunities to enhance value throughout the life of the asset. An overview of the value enhancement process is shown in Exhibit 1.

Buying and selling are how money is realized, but what owners do in the meantime is how the money is earned and how value is created. Value enhancement can be achieved through many means and on several levels. The most obvious means of value enhancement is the improvement of operating performance, but it doesn't stop there. As illustrated in Exhibit 2, asset value can be influenced by internal factors, as well as such external factors as market conditions, competition, the economy, and travel industry and world events. Value creation comes from managing those factors over which owners have control and from constantly monitoring and reacting to external factors to mitigate potential negative impact, as well as identifing opportunities for value enhancement.

This case study is intended to assist hotel owners, asset managers, and operators alike to think outside the box in the continual pursuit of value preservation

Exhibit 1   The Value Enhancement Process

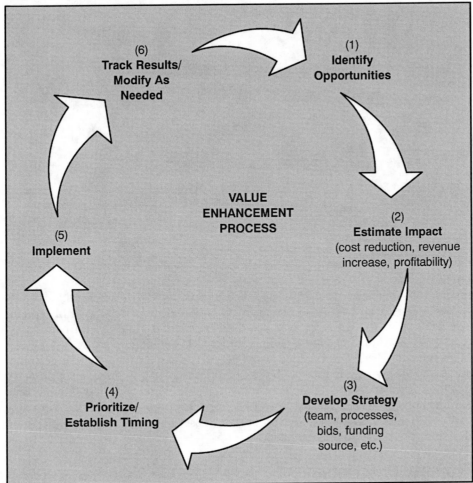

and enhancement. We have selected the Frenchman's Reef & Morning Star Marriott Beach Resort—a property we have worked with for nearly five years—as our subject. It has weathered storms (literally), endured global events and an economic downturn, and still improved its overall value considerably, confirming that regardless of size, positioning, market, economic conditions, or investment strategy, value enhancement can be achieved through effective asset management.

Ownership History

Frenchman's Reef & Morning Star Marriott Beach Resort was originally developed in the early 1970s, and independently operated as a Holiday Inn. Years later, the property was purchased, converted to a Marriott, and operated as a franchise by

Exhibit 2   Copnents of Asset Value

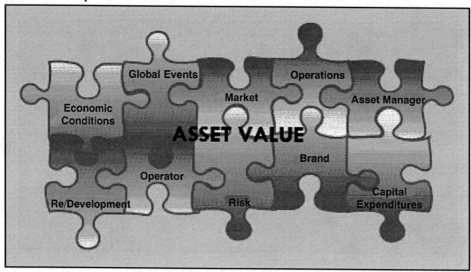

several subsequent ownership groups. In March 2000, Marriott International purchased the resort and assumed management and interim ownership until September 2000, when the property was acquired by Capital Hotel Investments, LLC (CHI). Marriott remained the operator under CHI ownership, and Capital Hotel Management (CHM) was retained as the property's asset manager and investment advisor to the ownership group. The resort was purchased as part of a six-property portfolio acquisition and, while viewed overall as a higher risk, Frenchman's Reef & Morning Star Marriott Beach Resort had significant upside potential. With new ownership and professional and progressive asset managers, it was anticipated that this potential would be realized.

Property Description

Frenchman's Reef & Morning Star Marriott Beach Resort occupies a prime location on the island of St. Thomas in the U.S. Virgin Islands, approximately three miles east of downtown Charlotte Amalie, the island's capital city. The area around the site is known as Estate Bakkeroe, which is situated at the point of Frenchman's Bay and Frenchman's Reef. The resort is sprawling, encompassing approximately 17 acres, and is surrounded by water on three sides (Charlotte Amalie Bay and the Caribbean Sea) with residential housing toward the north. Even with its secluded location, it is very convenient to town, where a major Caribbean cruise ship port is located.

The resort was developed in two phases with the main building (Frenchman's Reef), including 408 rooms contained in an eight-story tower atop a sea-view cliff and several low-rise wings, opening in 1973. The Morning Star section of the resort contains 96 units and was constructed in 1984. Morning Star units are contained in

Exhibit 3   Frenchman's Reef Facility Description

Location	U.S. Virgin Islands
Year Opened/Renovated	1973/1985/1995
Guestrooms	477
Suites	27
Total	504
# of Meeting Rooms	14
Total Meeting Space	60,000
Ballroom	14,112
Restaurants/Lounges	6
Labor	USWA, LU 8249

two- and three-story cottage-style buildings located along the beach and a considerable distance from the main tower.

The resort represents the largest conference facility in the Virgin Islands, featuring 14 meeting rooms with a total of 60,000 square feet of indoor function space. Recreational and guest amenities include two freshwater pools, four tennis courts, a health club and spa, a salon, retail shops, beach and water sports, a business center, five restaurants, and a gourmet convenience store. The resort's property profile can be seen in Exhibit 3.

Frenchman's Reef comprises the main resort, housing the meeting space, spa, salon, retail outlets, and recreation desk. While guests have access to all areas of the resort, given the distance between Frenchman's Reef and Morning Star, each area is designed to operate on a relatively independent basis, with its own guest check-in area, swimming pool, food and beverage outlets, and back-of-the-house facilities, including kitchens and laundry. Guest transportation is provided by van shuttle between the two areas of the resort, as well as to in-town locations.

Reportedly $52 million was spent between 1996 and 1997 on rebuilding significant portions of the resort in the aftermath of Hurricane Marilyn, which nearly devastated portions of the U.S. Virgin Islands, including St. Thomas. Since then, an estimated $60 million has been spent on capital improvements to maintain the resort's standing as the premiere resort within the Caribbean. A $6 million guestroom renovation is currently underway and slated for completion in 2006.

Unique Operating Environment: Guest Paradise, Owner Paradox

Frenchman's Reef is an irreplaceable asset—the largest property and premiere resort operating on St. Thomas, as well as one of the most popular destinations in the Caribbean. While certainly a remarkable asset, the acquisition of Frenchman's Reef posed as many challenges as it did opportunities. In addition to the challenges specific to the property, there were several factors inherent in its island location that added to the complexity of owning and operating this asset. The following challenges were identified and considered when developing the strategic asset management plan for Frenchman's Reef and provide a snapshot of the unique context in which the asset operates.

Island Economy

Tourism is the primary economic activity in the U.S Virgin Islands, accounting for 80 percent of GDP and employment.[1] The balance of the Islands' economy is supported by the manufacturing sector concentrated in petroleum refining, textiles, electronics, pharmaceuticals, and watch assembly. International business and financial services are growing components of the economy, but remain small contributors to the Island's overall economic base, as does the agricultural sector. With limited on-island resources, the majority of goods must be imported. This adds considerably to the cost of operations, requires storage facilities, and slows the speed with which supplies are delivered. In some cases, delivery speed can impact product quality, particularly with perishable items. To help offset expenses and promote the growth of economic activity, the U.S. Virgin Islands Industrial Development Commission (IDC) offers various tax incentives. Certain businesses, including hotels and light manufacturing companies, can receive an exemption from 90 percent of local income taxes and 100 percent of gross receipt taxes, property taxes, and excise taxes. Additionally, eligible companies pay only a 1 percent custom duty (instead of 6 percent) and can reduce certain withholding taxes from 10 percent to 4 percent. In return, companies must invest a minimum of $100,000 in an eligible business and employ at least 10 local residents on a full-time basis. In addition, there are strict rules governing the procurement process that require businesses to include local firms in any formal bidding in order to receive related benefits. While the resort has been successful in maintaining its eligible status for IDC benefits, there is no guarantee that tax benefits will remain indefinitely, and remains one of the biggest operating risks of owning a resort on St. Thomas. Annual savings attributed to IDC benefits at Frenchman's Reef are estimated in excess of $1 million.

Labor Pool

The labor force in the U.S. Virgin Islands is estimated at approximately 49,000, with the most recent available unemployment statistics in the single digits. Given the heavy reliance on the tourism sector, the majority of the labor force is employed in the service industries, creating an extremely competitive and costly environment in which resorts must find and retain qualified labor. There also is strong union presence and labor agreements between unions, and most resorts typically do not favor the owner. Given the Islands' seasonal fluctuations in tourism and the fact that labor can comprise upward of 60 percent of the hotel's total operating expenses, labor unions and their agreements can be a significant challenge to hotel owners. Lastly, attracting and retaining talented managers and executive key team members is a major challenge, given the remoteness of the location. Significant cost is attributed to recruiting senior staff, premium salaries, relocation expenses, and housing allowances.

Demand

Another challenge of operating on St. Thomas is the small percentage of overall demand generated locally, with the majority of guests originating from off-island locations. Approximately 80 percent of the U.S. Virgin Islands' overnight visitation comes from U.S. markets. This situation makes hotels extremely vulnerable to and highly dependent upon external factors over which resort management has little to no control. Regardless of the facility's quality and service and the effectiveness of sales and marketing efforts to generate business, delivering the guest to a destination ultimately is a function of airlift capacity and cost. Cyril E. King International Airport on St. Thomas is one of only a few Caribbean airports that can accommodate larger jet service; it hosts several major air carriers and select direct flight service (from New York, Chicago, and Miami, with frequent service from San Juan, Puerto Rico), but with only eleven gates, the number of flights is limited. When travel is down, air carriers have the tendency to reduce the number of flights even more, which drives the cost to visit the destination way up and often requires hotels to lower rates to attract guests. Reliance on wholesalers and charter aircraft can become a double-edged sword. While they provide much-needed demand during the off-season period, they often do so at below-market rates. Once they begin generating demand during the off-season, they often require access to the hotel during the peak season months at less than favorable rates for the hotel.

Another factor playing into overnight demand is the cruise ship industry. As a destination, the Caribbean attracts more cruise traffic than any other region and will accommodate 52 percent of the worldwide passenger capacity in 2005.[2] With the growing popularity of cruising in the Caribbean, it is becoming more evident that cruise ships actually compete with hotels in certain market segments. The increase in cruise capacity in the Caribbean, coupled with reduced airlift capacity and escalating fares, suggests additional risk to hotel owners.

Climate

St. Thomas is a true vacationer's paradise, boasting some of the Caribbean's most popular beaches, a subtropical climate, easterly trade winds, relatively low humidity, and little seasonal temperature variation. The island experiences a fairly predictable rainy season between September and November, which is also the period in which hurricanes are most prevalent. While 1995 marks the most recent year in which the island experienced a severe hurricane, the effects of these potential weather conditions are devastating from both a visitation and property standpoint. Simply being located in the Caribbean inhibits demand during hurricane season, whether or not there is, or has been in the recent past, any significant hurricane activity. The island's location in the hurricane belt poses a considerable risk and results in higher insurance premiums and deductibles.

Environmental Issues

The beach area is one of the resort's most valuable commodities. Unfortunately, a common problem facing several Caribbean islands is beach erosion, representing a very real and extremely costly issue. Beach erosion is a natural phenomenon that is worse in areas where significant dredging occurs, which often is the case in major cruise ports that need to be able to accommodate large ships. There are steps that can be taken to help mitigate the effects of beach erosion, but they are very costly and require significant government commitment.

Value Enhancement at Frenchman's Reef

While there are countless examples that could be drawn upon to demonstrate the various challenges that were tackled at Frenchman's Reef, the following key areas were selected to highlight those initiatives that yielded the greatest impact to the resort's value:

- Operating model
- Food and beverage
- Sales and marketing
- Timeshare development
- Building systems
- Risk mitigation

Operating Model

After a careful review of monthly operating statements during the due diligence period, it was clear that an opportunity existed to modify the resort's operating model to improve performance in several areas, particularly during the off season. The property was generating more profit in the first four months of the year than it was on an annual basis, essentially losing a fair portion of peak-season profit over the course of the year—not exactly a successful strategy. While it is not uncommon for destination resorts to generate a disproportionate share of annual cash flow during the peak season, losing $1.5 to $2.0 million during the off season was significantly affecting the resort's annual profitability. Exhibit 4 shows the resort's performance by month. Therefore, one of the asset management and operating teams' immediate tasks was to examine the resort's operating model and formulate a strategy to minimize operating costs and improve overall performance, particularly during the off-season. The key challenges in this area included:

- Minimizing off-season losses, which historically have ranged from $1.5 to $2.0 million.
- Identifying ways to lower the high fixed costs associated with operating a 504-room property with multiple buildings, outlets, kitchens, and laundry facilities at low occupancy levels.
- Devising an action plan with management buy-in and implementing cost savings initiatives.

Based on forecasted occupancy for each month over the shoulder and off-season period, we determined required room inventory levels and devised a closure schedule for certain guestroom areas of the resort.

Exhibit 4   Fisherman's Reef Historical Performance

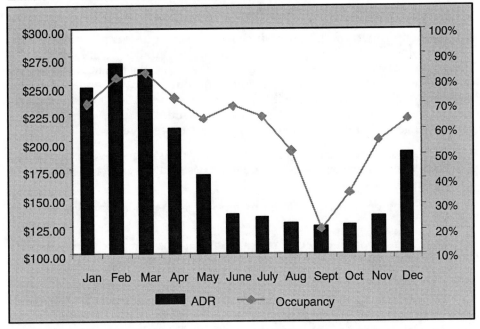

By consolidating operations, we were able to "shrink" the hotel to approximately one-third its size, close the laundry operation at Morning Star, and reduce the operating hours of several food and beverage outlets. This allowed the resort to increase revenue through rate compression while minimizing operating costs significantly between July and November, all with little to no impact on overall guest satisfaction and without compromising brand standards.

Implementation of the off-season resort closure plan has resulted in an average savings of $800,000 each year over the course of the ownership period. Residual benefits of the off-season strategy were realized in the shoulder season, in which incremental profits were generated through implementation of some of the same cost savings measures identified during the off-season.

Food and Beverage

In 2000, the resort was operating six restaurants, room service, two lounges, a nightclub, and a quick-grab market, all of which were fully staffed on a year-round basis. Three of the five restaurants, along with two kitchens, the nightclub, and retail market, were located within the main Frenchman's Reef building, while the other outlets, including two more kitchens, were operated on the Morning Star side of the resort. In total, the resort was carrying the cost of operating *four* separate kitchens (including the banquet kitchen). The fixed costs of the food and beverage operations were so high that they were operating dangerously close to breakeven in the aggregate, with several individual outlets losing money. Further compounding departmental expenses were food costs, which were extraordinarily high due to the cost of importing food.

While having several dining options can generate incremental sales as guests will dine on property more often during their stay, guest capture rates were extremely low, particularly for dinner, due to the number of fine restaurants located downtown. For those guests dining at the resort, the business was spread too thin, creating internal competition among the outlets. Lastly, while the restaurants were well located, several with open-air concepts and direct ocean frontage, the concepts themselves were lackluster and the facilities and décor were tired. The key challenges with regard to food and beverage service were:

- Creating an operating model that lowers fixed costs so improved profits could be realized while continuing to provide guests with a sufficient selection of on-site dining options.

- Identifying opportunities to improve revenue on a significantly lower cost base.

- Revamping food and beverage operations at this complex resort property with a food and beverage director who lacked the necessary experience to do so.

The asset management team worked closely with management to isolate profitability by outlet, for the purpose of identifying areas in which costs could be cut, operating hours adjusted, and menus redesigned. This initiative was particularly challenging, as the financial reporting system did not allocate various kitchen expenses to the outlets. As a result, we developed a series of assumptions by which expenses could be estimated and allocated.

A food and beverage department action plan was developed that included significant meal period and menu adjustment, outlet closures (one permanently), and staffing modifications. Through this process and staff attrition, we were able to further modify the organization. A director of operations who possessed the skills and expertise necessary to execute the food and beverage plan was hired and other operational strategies were implemented. Notable changes included:

- Closing the Bakkaroe nightclub and shifting the evening entertainment venue to an unused space at Morning Star. The result was CoCo Joe's, a casual and funky open-air lounge overlooking the ocean, offering a light-fare menu and featuring live entertainment. The cost of the conversion was minimal and the popularity of this beach bar was so great that it developed a reputation with locals and has expanded into the downstairs space, formerly Caesar's Italian Restaurant.

- Closing Caesar's Italian Restaurant at Morning Star so all dinner volume could be focused at the Tavern Restaurant next door, which featured a superior setting and commanded a higher check average due to its fine-dining positioning.

- Opening a quick-grab coffee shop and market called Star Market at Morning Star, expanding the inventory offering at Presto's (the "grab and go" market located at Frenchman's) to include such higher profit items as gourmet snacks and alcohol, and offering a delivery service to guests.

- Adjusting the operating hours and menu offerings at Window's, the three-meal restaurant, so as not to compete with the adjacent Captain's, Sunset Grille, or room service, all of which also underwent significant adjustments to menu, pricing, and hours of operation.

- Consolidating the resort's four kitchens into three.

Revamping the entire food and beverage department resulted in an increase of more than 50 percent in combined restaurant and lounge profit between 2001 and 2004. The resort was able to flow more than 20 percent of the $1.8 million in incremental restaurant and lounge revenue to the bottom line, marking a considerable flow-through improvement over the same time period. In addition, at the end of 2004, the Tavern Restaurant was leased to a local restaurateur, and is now operating as Havana Blue. The lease enabled the resort to eliminate yet another kitchen, allowed the restaurant to generate more cash flow than it generated as a self-operated outlet, and increased exposure of the resort by capturing patrons from the local market and guests from other area resorts.

Sales and Marketing

Frenchman's Reef is one of the, if not the, largest conference facility in the Virgin Islands. From a facilities standpoint, it is well positioned to capture group business given the room count, meeting space, and available support amenities. Although historically operated under the Marriott franchise (up until the purchase by Marriott in March 2000), the resort lacked the support of a national sales force, and as such was operating well below its estimated potential for group business. Significant financial upside was projected for generating greater volumes and higher-rated group business resulting from the combined Marriott-branded management. When Marriott assumed management of Frenchman's Reef in early 2000, the resort was not fully integrated into the Offshore Resort Network (OSRN)—Marriott's national sales and marketing organization for offshore resorts, until almost June. With an average group booking window of 12 to 18 months, the opportunity to have a material impact on the first full year under new ownership was lost. The resort entered 2001 with approximately 20,000 group room nights on the books—a far cry from achieving its goal of 38,000. Key sales and marketing challenges included:

- Increasing group rooms and revenue.

- Assessing the effectiveness of OSRN's selling strategies.

- Ensuring national sales support from Marriott targeted to the Frenchman's Reef selling effort.

We conducted a thorough review and analysis of the organizational structure selling practices of the OSRN and determined that the group-selling approach, in which all staff had the responsibility to sell all properties, was not effectively generating group business for Frenchman's. Additionally, the cost of participation in the OSRN was close to double that of any other hotel—including resort proper-ties—within CHM's asset management portfolio. As such, representatives from both the asset management and operating teams met with the OSRN to initiate changes to the marketing approach of Frenchman's Reef, all of which were insti-tuted by the fourth quarter of 2001. These changes included the following:

- Adding an on-site director of sales.

- Adding several dedicated sales managers, both on property and at the OSRN, in addition to employing various commissioned sales managers.

- Establishing routine detailed reporting requirements from the OSRN for the purposes of monitoring ongoing production.

- Developing a secondary Web site and hiring an external marketing firm.

- Enhancing group sales contracts to provide for greater resort protection in the event of cancellation.

- Improving relationships with wholesalers by changing room type offerings and pricing structure to improve marketability within this segment.

It is difficult to measure the true impact of all of the changes made with respect to the sales and marketing efforts at Frenchman's Reef during that first year, as the events of September 11 and the war with Iraq had a significant impact on all travel outside the United States. In the face of unanticipated world events and a declining economy that spanned the ownership period, group room nights and revenue increased approximately 17 percent and 11 percent, respectively, resulting in a more than $600,000 increase in sales between 2001 and 2005 (fore-cast). By gaining a better understanding of wholesaler needs and selling strategies, the resort was able to enhance visibility while increasing control over inventory and pricing, ultimately yielding more than a 50 percent increase—approximately $2 million in incremental wholesale revenue—over the same period.

Timeshare Development

Before CHI's acquisition, Marriott Vacation Club International (MVCI) proposed the development of 182 two-bedroom timeshare villas, to be constructed in seven phases on a site adjacent to the Frenchman's Reef. Phase one is scheduled to be available for occupancy in March 2006. Project amenities will include a kids' activ-ity area, central facilities building (Marketplace Express), activities building (with a fitness center and outdoor pool bar), and two swimming pools/spas. While CHI will not actively participate in development, the asset management team immedi-ately began negotiations with MVCI on potential areas of revenue generation and cost savings that could occur with the two properties working together. The key challenge presented here was deriving maximum value from opportunities result-ing from MCVI's timeshare development.

We negotiated the use of guestrooms, the Bakkoroe Nightclub, and a market-ing desk in the lobby for their use as a sales center. In addition, the integration agreement calls for integration of services, costs, and benefits related to the opera-tion of the hotel and timeshare properties. Primary benefits to the resort include:

- Generation of sales center rent for non-revenue-generating space. At the end of the lease, this space will be converted back to its original use at no cost to the resort.

- Increased resort visibility given the volume of tours and guests to be generated in connection with timeshare sales.

- Operational integration/cost savings of select key executive staff.

- Shared systems upgrade and maintenance expenses (private branch exchange, point-of-sale, etc.).

- Shared expenses for shared hotel amenities (i.e., pool, tennis, beach).

- Shared marketing and sales commissions.

- Preview room night revenue over the life of the project, as well as incremental spending from tour incentive certificates.

- Incremental spending by vacation ownership guests at Frenchman's restaurants, retail outlets, and recreational amenities over the life of the project.

In total, there is an estimated $12 to $15 million in additional value attributed to the successful timeshare project and integration agreement.

Building Systems

Converting to Island Power. When purchased, Frenchman's Reef was operating its own power plant to provide electric power to the resort. While the power plant provided an efficient and cost-effective means of delivering electricity, safety and environmental issues, as well as mounting maintenance and eventual replacement costs associated with the aging plant, were identified as considerable risks to the new owners. Therefore, it was decided that the resort would undergo a conversion project to connect to the power grid of the Virgin Islands Water & Power Authority (WAPA). Key challenges related to this conversion included:

- Effectively managing through the project, which was scheduled to occur during the peak operating season, including working collaboratively with the property team to minimize business interruption and potential impact to guests.

- Limiting potential risk exposure attributed to the project, including ensuring good standing with the Environmental Protection Agency and making sure no existing environmental issues or operating violations existed.

- Negotiating with island authorities to obtain favorable utility usage rates.

- Closely monitoring project costs to ensure proper accounting for expenses.

The original WAPA conversion project schedule reflected a "going-live" date of January 15, 2001, which was later pushed back to mid-February because of a delay in the switch-gear delivery and permit issues. The date was then delayed to mid-April, although the resort went live on WAPA power on March 21. As a result of this delay, rental generators were returned later than anticipated and plant staff was employed for longer than originally budgeted, but no business was lost or other operating difficulties experienced.

The magnitude and technicality of this conversion process, the use of resort staff and resources to perform various WAPA-related services, and various project delays associated with working on an island (delivery, weather, permitting, etc.) all added to the complexity of managing the accounting for this project. The asset management team conducted a post-project accounting review and identified approximately $300,000 in savings to the owner. As a result of this exercise, all appropriate funds were reimbursed to the hotel.

Utilities. Utility expenses at Frenchman's Reef were extremely high, and while utility rates are largely beyond the resort's control, consumption can often be controlled to reduce expenses. Energy management systems were researched and identified as a long-term capital project toward a goal of better managing utility costs, particularly electricity. In the interim, we focused on reducing water costs because the resort was purchasing all of its water from WAPA and paying a premium. The key challenge was identifying a way to reduce overall water expenses.

The asset management team identified an opportunity to segregate the source of water by usage. Water would continue to be purchased for all consumable needs (drinking, cooking, bathing, etc.) and supplemented with a small desalination system with which seawater could be reconditioned for landscaping and other work-related uses.

The team also researched development and operating costs and ultimately selected a professional third-party firm to design, build, operate, and maintain a new seawater reverse osmosis (RO) desalination system at the resort by which potable water would be delivered back to the resort for a negotiated fixed fee based on usage estimates. The RO plant was developed proximate to the existing waste-water treatment plant, which afforded the resort the ability to expand to handle excess capacity should additional portions of the site be developed in the future (timeshares, condominiums, etc.).

The total project had a one-year payback, and savings were estimated at approximately $500,000 per year.

Wastewater Treatment Plant. In addition to a power plant, the new owners also inherited a wastewater treatment facility, representing a significant biological liability. Historically, the wastewater treatment plant was resort-operated. Key challenges here included:

- Minimizing owner risk exposure.

- Operating within mandated environmental standards.

- Reducing operating costs.

The asset management team performed an analysis that showed outsourcing the operation to be the most cost-effective and least risky option. CHM worked with the management team to reduce owner risk by employing a specialist and to free up staff resources for other maintenance and related tasks.

Risk Mitigation

Mitigating owner exposure to risk is a critical function of asset management. While risk-related initiatives typically do not translate into asset value from a cash flow standpoint, value is derived in the form of protecting owner interests by preventing payouts under various circumstances, such as hurricane damage, guest or employee accidents, environmental issues, or anything else that could potentially cost the operation money. Essentially, risk mitigation in asset management terms is trying to foresee the unforeseen.

Over the ownership period, the cost to insure Frenchman's Reef nearly doubled—a significant increase to an already high fixed cost of operations. As such, the asset management and operating teams continually pursued opportunities to reduce insurance costs, seeking both premium and deductible reductions. The key challenge was identifying these opportunities.

The resort was insured through a group coverage policy that covered all of the hotels in the six-hotel portfolio to which Frenchman's belonged. On an annual basis, the asset management team obtained bids for insuring Frenchman's independent of the group, but found that it was actually more costly to isolate.

The team succeeded in reducing the insurance deductible from $7.5 million to $5.0 million and lowered premium costs by approximately $600,000 to $800,000 dollars on an annual basis by installing wind shutters. The wind shutter project was funded partially out of reserve funds, which served to lower the amount of owner-invested capital required. The project had a one-year payback based on savings achieved through reduced premium costs.

Conclusion

In a relatively short period of time—less than five years—and in the face of significant world events, including September 11, war, and economic turmoil, significant value was created through effective asset management and collaboration with the operating team at Frenchman's Reef. As demonstrated, effective asset management can yield significant results, but it is not a function that can be performed by a single individual. It requires the support of a team of professionals with experience and expertise in a wide range of areas to achieve desired results.

How much value was created at Frenchman's Reef through asset management? Based on the examples described in this case study alone, incremental value was estimated at more than $5.5 million, averaging more than $1.3 million per year over the ownership period, *not* including additional value derived from the timeshare project. Considering all efforts in total, the significance is staggering. It is relatively easy to quantify cost savings and incremental revenue initiatives, but it begs the question of what would have happened if the asset management team hadn't done these things. What would the opportunity cost of not making some of these decisions have been? How much value could potentially have been at risk, whether through declines in operating performance or otherwise? Whatever that number may be is the total value equation that asset management brings to hotels and owners.

Frenchman's Reef yielded a positive financial transaction for its owner (our client) the very night the draft of this case study was completed. Just as the lodging industry is ever evolving and dynamic, more value enhancement opportunities await the next owner, including such areas as legalization of video gaming on St. Thomas, re-concepting of select restaurants, implementation of an energy management system, condominium development at Morning Star, and expansion of the spa. The point is that through asset management, owners can look to enhance the value of their hotel assets at any stage of the investment cycle, regardless of the hold period.

Endnotes

1. CIA World Factbook, available online at http://www.cia.gov/cia/publications/factbook/index.html.

2. "Caribbean Cruise Capacity," *Cruise Industry News*, March 15, 2005.

Indoor Waterparks and Hotels

By *David L Sangree, ISHC*

David J. Sangree, MAI, CPA, ISHC, is President of Hotel & Leisure Advisors, a national hospitality consulting firm. He performs appraisals, feasibility studies, impact studies, and other consulting reports for hotels, resorts, waterparks, golf courses, amusement parks, conference centers, and other leisure properties. He has performed more than 1,000 hotel studies and more than 100 indoor waterpark resort market feasibility and/or appraisal studies across the United States and Canada. He received his Bachelor of Science degree from Cornell University's School of Hotel Administration in 1984 and is a certified public accountant, an MAI member of the Appraisal Institute, and a member of the International Society of Hospitality Consultants. He has been previously employed with Westin Hotels and Resorts, Pannell Kerr Forster, and US Realty Consultants. He has spoken on various hospitality and waterpark issues at seminars throughout the United States and has written numerous articles for, and is frequently quoted in, magazines and newspapers covering the hospitality field.

T HE INDOOR WATERPARK RESORT and the addition of indoor waterparks to existing hotels have become more widespread phenomena in the hotel industry in the United States and Canada since 2000. The growth of indoor waterparks is due to their popularity with children and to their parents' and grandparents' interest in selecting lodging locations that will be fun for children. In addition, indoor water-park resort properties are increasingly popular for short weekends and two- or three-day getaways for families that may not have time for longer vacations. The indoor waterpark resort has established itself as a viable segment of the hotel industry and expanded well beyond its original Wisconsin base. Across the United States and Canada, new indoor waterparks are being added to existing hotels and new indoor waterpark destination resorts are being constructed. The primary growth of indoor waterparks is in what were historically summer resort locations, although they also are increasingly being developed in suburban and urban locations.

I define an indoor waterpark resort as a lodging establishment containing an aquatic facility with a minimum of 10,000 square feet of indoor waterpark space and inclusive of such amenities as slides, tubes, and a variety of indoor water-play features. Although many hotels bill their indoor pools as waterparks, those with less than 10,000 square feet should be categorized as properties with water features rather than as waterparks. I further divide indoor waterpark resorts into two categories. A hotel with an indoor waterpark has an attached waterpark with between 10,000 and 30,000 square feet of indoor waterpark space where the waterpark serves as a hotel amenity rather than a destination itself. An indoor waterpark destination resort is a resort with a minimum of 30,000 square feet of indoor waterpark

Exhibit 1   Types of Indoor Waterparks in Lodging Establishments

	Hotel with Water Features	Hotel with Indoor Waterpark	Indoor Waterpark Destination Resort
Size of aquatic area	1,000 to less than 10,000 square feet	10,000 to less than 30,000 square feet	30,000+ square feet
Possible amenities	Swimming pool, slide, toddler area with mushroom, spray gun	Multiple slides, tree house with slides, spray guns, tipping buckets, Jacuzzi, various pools, lazy river	Multiple slides, tree house with slides, spray guns, tipping buckets, Jacuzzi, various pools, lazy river, wave pool, water coaster, surfing, outdoor waterpark features
Capacity	up to 250 people	250 to 750 people	750 to 5,000 people
Minimum number of lifeguards	1	3	10
Arcade size	0 to 1,000 square feet	1,000 to 3,000 square feet	3,000 to 10,000 square feet

Source: Hotel & Leisure Advisors.

space that is considered a true destination resort that families visit year-round, primarily to visit the waterpark and secondarily to visit other attractions or events in the area. Using these definitions, Exhibit 1 describes the three types of indoor waterparks that currently exist and are being developed in the United States and Canada.

This case study discusses the following aspects of indoor waterparks:

- Indoor waterpark history
- Current market for indoor waterparks
- Reasons for indoor waterpark success
- Financial impact of indoor waterparks
- Indoor waterpark design and costs
- The future

Indoor Waterpark History

The first large indoor waterpark in North America was the World Waterpark inside Alberta, Canada's West Edmonton Mall. This indoor waterpark, which opened in 1985 and contains over 200,000 square feet of waterpark space, was an immediate hit and helped the West Edmonton Mall to become an international retail and entertainment destination. The Fantasyland Hotel, which has achieved some of the highest occupancy levels in Alberta, is attached to the mall and offers packages with the waterpark.

The first indoor waterparks in the United States were developed in Wisconsin Dells, Wisconsin. For generations, Wisconsin Dells has been a popular summer tourist destination, providing vacationers with a wide variety of family-oriented outdoor activities such as shopping, dining, scenic boat tours, amusement parks, miniature golf, outdoor waterparks, and similar attractions. Traditionally, "the Dells" ran at very high capacity between Memorial Day and Labor Day, but many of the attractions and hotels closed down for most of the rest of the year. Beginning in 1994 and especially in the late 1990s, the resort city became nationally known for its new indoor waterparks and activities.

The Polynesian Resort was the first large hotel in the Dells to add an indoor waterpark to its existing structure in 1994. The Polynesian differentiated itself from other hotels with its large indoor pool, modest water slides, and other attractions. The project was an instant success, achieving well-above-market room rates and occupancy. The project also did strong business during the off season when many other area hotels were closed. Families that had long come to the Dells during the summer started to return to enjoy the indoor waterpark and a brief getaway any time of year.

Over the ensuing years, The Polynesian, which now has 232 rooms and 38,000 square feet of indoor waterpark space, added amenities and more guestrooms and continued to perform well. Because of this, several more waterpark destination resorts were developed. These include Wilderness Hotel & Golf Resort, Treasure Island Water & Theme Park Resort, Great Wolf Lodge (formerly Black Wolf Lodge), Chula Vista Resort, and, most recently, Kalahari Resort. Each of these properties features an adventure theme and extensive indoor waterpark activities. Each has been very successful as demand has outgrown the size of the projects. All six of these pioneering water activity resorts have added guestrooms to meet their high demand. In addition, there are ten other hotels in the Dells with smaller indoor waterparks that have achieved lesser degrees of success because they have been overshadowed by the six larger destination properties.

Hotels with indoor waterparks and indoor waterpark destination resorts can justify substantially higher room rates than hotels without indoor waterparks during the off season, since the rate includes admission to the indoor waterpark (a $15–$40 value per person per day).

The resort hotels of Wisconsin Dells have created a year-round family resort community, which is generating strong room rates and higher year-round occupancy in what had once been a strictly seasonal market. Particularly on weekends, in the winter, and during school vacations, resorts in the Dells attract strong family demand.

Between 1983 and 2004, 63 indoor waterpark resorts opened or expanded their properties in the United States and Canada, totaling approximately 1,840,400 square feet and offering over 15,000 hotel rooms (see Exhibit 2). The size of indoor waterparks has grown significantly since their inception in the mid-1980s, and the average number of hotel rooms attached to these waterparks has also increased substantially over the years.

For example, in 1994, there were five indoor waterpark resorts operating in the United States and Canada with a total of 1,159 guestrooms and 297,800 square

Exhibit 2   U.S. and Canadian Indoor Waterpark Growth, 1983–2004

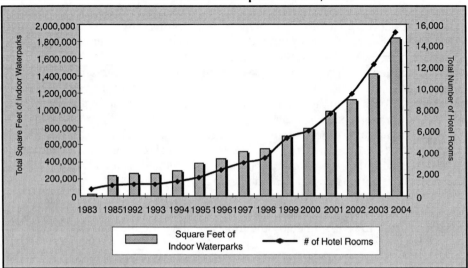

feet of indoor waterpark space. This equaled approximately one guestroom per 257 square feet of indoor waterpark space offered. By the end of 2004, 63 indoor waterpark resorts were operating with a total of 15,095 guestrooms and 1,840,400 square feet of indoor waterpark space. This represented approximately one guestroom per 122 square feet of indoor waterpark space. The increase in the number of guestrooms constructed has kept pace with increases in demand for indoor waterparks, which has also grown steadily.

Current Market for Indoor Waterparks

The number of indoor waterparks within resorts and connected to hotels continues to grow. The Midwest has attracted the most attention for indoor waterparks, followed by the Northeast. Exhibit 3 indicates that there were 52 indoor waterparks in hotels and resorts located in the United States with 42 percent located in Wisconsin. In addition, there were 11 indoor waterpark resorts operating in Canada, although there are many other hotels in Canada offering smaller indoor water features with less than 10,000 square feet.

Exhibit 4 indicates indoor waterparks that opened and hotels that added indoor waterparks in 2004 in the United States and Canada. Fourteen waterparks opened in new resorts or as expansions of existing hotels and resorts in 2004. Approximately half of the properties that opened in 2004 added or expanded waterpark facilities in existing hotels. Castaway Bay operated as a Radisson hotel until November 2004, when ownership added a 38,000-square-foot indoor waterpark, renovated the property, and dropped the franchise. In the case of the Kalahari, the developers added 360 condominium sleeping units to the 378-room, 125,000-square-foot indoor waterpark resort, bringing the total number of available guestrooms to 738.

Exhibit 3   Indoor Waterpark Resort Supply Analysis as of Year-End 2005

State or Province	Number of Resorts	Average Room Count	Indoor Waterpark Size in Square Feet			Percent Franchised
			Average	High	Low	
Idaho	1	98	25,000	25,000	25,000	100%
Illinois	1	100	24,000	24,000	24,000	0%
Indiana	1	344	30,000	30,000	30,000	100%
Iowa	2	174	18,000	25,000	11,000	50%
Kansas	2	250	33,000	38,000	28,000	0%
Kentucky	1	80	10,000	10,000	10,000	100%
Massachusetts	1	260	10,000	10,000	10,000	0%
Michigan	7	198	29,714	58,000	10,000	43%
Minnesota	9	162	26,444	40,000	13,000	56%
Missouri	2	617	20,000	20,000	20,000	0%
North Dakota	4	186	13,250	21,000	10,000	100%
Ohio	3	368	50,333	80,000	33,000	0%
Pennsylvania	2	385	64,750	78,000	51,500	50%
South Dakota	1	150	30,000	30,000	30,000	100%
Virginia	2	301	48,500	55,000	42,000	0%
Washington	2	111	10,000	10,000	10,000	100%
Wisconsin	30	216	30,303	160,000	10,000	20%
United States	**71**	**223**	**29,248**			**36%**
Alberta	3	260	80,600	217,800	12,000	67%
Manitoba	2	148	10,000	10,000	10,000	100%
Ontario	4	303	18,750	25,000	15,000	75%
Quebec	1	222	10,000	10,000	10,000	100%
Saskatchewan	1	157	10,000	10,000	10,000	100%
Canada	**11**	**242**	**32,436**			**82%**

Note: Properties have a minimum of 10,000 square feet of indoor waterpark space.

Source: Hotel & Leisure Advisors, December 2005.

Indoor waterparks at hotels and resorts range in size from 10,000 square feet at numerous smaller properties to 160,000 square feet at Wilderness (which was developed over a number of years). Properties in Wisconsin Dells have been expanding the sizes of their waterparks in the past three years, with three of the properties adding substantial new indoor waterparks. Kalahari opened a $12 million, 58,000-square-foot addition to its waterpark in December 2002. The Wilderness Resort constructed a 70,000-square-foot indoor waterpark called the Wild West Waterpark, which opened in late February 2003 within the resort. In addition, in 2003 it opened a 15,000-square-foot indoor waterpark on Lake Delton connected to its 108-unit condominium development.

My research shows that, during 2005, 23 indoor waterpark resorts opened or expanded their properties in the United States and Canada, totaling 644,000 square feet of additional waterpark space and 2,908 additional rooms. Approximately 23 new indoor waterpark resorts or indoor waterpark additions to existing properties will open in 2006, offering a total of 3,041 guestrooms and 978,000 square feet of

Exhibit 4   Indoor Waterparks Opened in Hotels and Resorts in 2004

Property	Location	New Rooms	Sq. Ft. of Waterpark
Holiday Inn Amana Colonies	Amana Colonies, IA	0	11,000
Holiday Inn Select Indianapolis North	Indianapolis, IN	0	30,000
Grand Prairie Hotel & Convention Center	Hutchinson, KS	218	28,000
Holiday Inn Express Hotel & Suites	Grand Rapids, MI	79	10,000
Grand Rios Resort	Brooklyn Park, MN	0	35,000
Courtyard/Residence Inn Downtown	Minneapolis, MN	357	15,000
Sleep Inn & Suites	Minot, ND	126	21,000
Castaway Bay at Cedar Point	Sandusky, OH	0	38,000
Ramada Inn & Suites Airport	Sioux Falls, SD	150	30,000
Blue Harbor Resort	Sheboygan, WI	247	40,000
Lodge at Cedar Creek	Wausau, WI	140	50,000
Kalahari Resort Condominium Expansion	Wisconsin Dells, WI	360	10,000
Copa Cabana Resort Hotel & Suites	Wisconsin Dells, WI	0	10,000
Americana Conference Resort and Spa	Niagara Falls, ON	0	25,000

Note: Resorts have a minimum of 10,000 square feet of indoor waterpark space.

Source: Hotel & Leisure Advisors.

indoor waterpark space. In addition, a number of indoor waterpark resorts are in the planning or development stages in a variety of locations throughout the United States and Canada. Exhibit 5 presents information about the 157 projects I was tracking as of December 2005. These projects have an average of 47,355 square feet of indoor waterpark space and include expansions of existing hotels and development of new resorts. If all of these facilities were constructed, this would result in approximately 6,784,740 square feet of new indoor waterpark space. The largest developer of new projects is Great Wolf Resorts, Inc., out of Madison, Wisconsin, with its branded Great Wolf Lodge resorts. The majority of the planned indoor waterpark resorts are located in northern states. In such southern states as Florida, hotels are beginning to add outdoor waterpark areas. For example, Holiday Inn's Nickelodeon Family Suites opened a large outdoor waterpark area in 2005.

Hotel companies, investors, and developers in the United States are only beginning to explore the potential benefits of affiliating indoor waterpark resorts with a national hotel franchise; franchised indoor waterpark resorts are more common in Canada. Exhibit 3 shows that only 36 percent of U.S. indoor waterpark

Exhibit 5   Indoor Waterparks Proposed or in Progress as of December 2005: United States and Canada

Region	Number of Properties	Number of Rooms	Average Room Count	Waterpark Area	
				Total (Sq. ft.)	Average Sq. Ft.
Northeastern United States	35	6,998	219	1,518,500	46,015
Midwestern United States	79	14,379	192	3,298,240	42,285
Southern United States	12	2,392	299	553,000	50,273
Western United States	26	5,657	236	1,155,000	46,200
United States	152	29,426	236	6,524,740	46,193
Canada	5	910	182	260,000	52,000
Total	157	30,336		6,784,740	
Average			225		47,355

Note: Resorts have a minimum of 10,000 square feet of indoor waterpark space. Updated May 2005.

Source: Hotel & Leisure Advisors, December 2005.

resort rooms are affiliated with a national hotel chain, while 82 percent of indoor waterpark resort rooms in Canada are franchised. Even though the nonfranchised resorts can benefit from offering a wider variety of indoor waterpark amenities, they lack the benefits of a central reservation system and franchise recognition. Holiday Inn is the only national hotel chain currently considering adding an indoor waterpark resort prototype to its offering of hotel types. As of December 2005, there were 11 Holiday Inn properties in operation that are attached to indoor waterparks, as the chain has been very open to the idea of allowing franchisees to add indoor waterparks to their existing properties. Also as of December 2005, there were 19 additional Holiday Inn indoor waterpark resorts or additions to existing Holiday Inn properties planned for development in the United States.

Reasons for Indoor Waterpark Success

The reason for the strong growth in indoor waterparks is the customer's willingness to pay higher room rates for the waterpark amenity. In addition, the indoor waterpark substantially increases demand during weekends and school vacations. By increasing the number of potential days on which a hotel can achieve higher occupancy levels, the hotel's overall occupancy will increase. Indoor waterpark resorts are outperforming non-waterpark hotels in all markets in terms of their occupancy and average daily rate. Typically, the average daily rate includes use of the indoor waterpark. There appear to be several reasons for this premium performance, including:

- Seasonal resorts gain year-round appeal
- Elimination of weather-related vacation risks
- Wide appeal of water-based recreation

- Increasing demand for short drive-to getaway vacations
- Themes with varying levels of appeal
- Location proximate to customer base and within established family vacation market

The popularity of indoor waterparks is due to the increase in water recreation. Waterpark attendance was between 72 and 73 million people in 2003, according to the World Waterpark Association, which is an increase from the attendance of 42 million people in 1991. The waterpark segment of the amusement industry is growing at a faster rate in both new facilities and attendance than any other segment, including amusement parks and family entertainment centers.

Twenty-four percent of trips (134.9 million) in the United States included children under the age of 18, according to the Travel Industry Association of America's (TIA) *Domestic Travel Market Report, 2003 Edition.* Eighty-seven percent of trips with children are for leisure reasons, with nearly half taken to visit friends or relatives. The strong travel levels recorded by the families with children is generating interest in indoor waterpark resorts as they are very popular with children. These activity resorts provide fun activities for children and their parents. Indoor waterpark resorts also appeal to the increasing numbers of families taking weekend trips for various leisure- and sports-related events.

TIA reports that people are taking more trips, with the number of person-trips increasing from 941 million in 1994 to 1.114 billion in 2003. Travel volume is forecasted to reach 1,230,000,000 person-trips in 2006. The average trip duration has dropped from 7.1 nights in 1977 to 4.1 nights in 2001. Between 1994 and 2003, leisure person-trips have increased more than 16 percent, while business/convention travel volume fell by more than 15 percent. Of the 1.114 billion domestic U.S. trips in 2003, 82 percent were leisure trips.

These trends are positive for indoor waterpark resorts as they indicate that people are visiting for shorter durations and looking for activities that children will enjoy. The indoor waterpark resort is very popular for two- to three-night stays and most children enjoy the indoor waterpark area extensively. The typical family will spend three to five hours a day at the indoor waterpark and utilize the remaining time for such activities as shopping, amusement parks, miniature golf, or other attractions, either within the resort or in the surrounding area.

Financial Impact of Indoor Waterparks

The financial impact of an indoor waterpark on a hotel property generally is that the property should achieve a higher occupancy and average daily rate level while also recording higher expenses. My experience reveals levels of performance between five and 30 occupancy points above hotels without indoor waterparks within the same market. Additionally, hotels with indoor waterparks can achieve an average daily rate from $20 to $150 per room higher than a hotel in the same market without an indoor waterpark.

The six largest indoor waterpark resorts located in Wisconsin Dells outperformed the chain-affiliated, non-resort hotels in overall average occupancy by 15

Exhibit 6   Great Wolf Lodge Performance Statistics

Great Wolf Lodge Indoor Waterpark Resorts
Statistical Data for 12 Months Ending December 31, 2004

Location	Month Opened	Rooms	Indoor Entertainment Area[1] (approx. sq. ft.)	Occu- pancy (%)	Average Daily Rate ($)	RevPAR ($)	Total Revenue per Occupied Room ($)	Total Revenue per Available Room ($)
Wisconsin Dells, WI	May 1997	309	65,000	62.2	188.76	117.47	267.20	166.29
Sandusky, OH[2]	March 2001	271	42,000	68.0	231.45	157.50	325.78	221.68
Traverse City, MI	March 2003	281	53,000	69.4	223.43	155.04	320.68	222.52
Kansas City, KS[3]	May 2003	281	50,000	64.4	196.18	126.31	285.85	184.05
Sheboygan, WI[4]	July 2004	183	50,000	58.3	190.35	110.93	351.61	204.91
Average		**265**	**52,000**	**64.5**	**206.03**	**132.81**	**310.22**	**199.89**

Notes:

1. The indoor entertainment areas generally include the indoor waterpark, game arcade, children's activity room, fitness room, Aveda concept spa, 3-D virtual reality theater, Wiley's Woods, and party room in resorts that have such amenities.

2. Prior to May 2004, this resort was operated as Great Bear Lodge.

3. The company currently leases the property on which the Kansas City Resort is located pursuant to a ten-year ground lease with a local governmental authority. It intends to convert this leasehold interest into a fee simple interest.

4. The Sheboygan resort is known as the Blue Harbor Resort.

Source: Great Wolf Resorts SEC Filing, February 2005.

occupancy points and in average daily rate by $112 in 2003. According to their recent Securities and Exchange Commission (SEC) filings, the five Great Wolf Lodge properties open in 2004 averaged an occupancy level of 65 percent with an average daily rate of $206. Exhibit 6 presents 2004 year-end performance figures for five Great Wolf Resorts indoor waterpark destination resorts. The figures shown for Sheboygan represent seven months of performance, while the other properties include figures for 12 months of performance. The strong performance of these and other large indoor waterpark destination resorts is due primarily to the stronger off-season demand and a much higher quality level of property. The addition of an indoor waterpark extends the season and length of stay for a resort hotel.

Operating statistics indicate that indoor waterpark resorts located close to higher population densities in traditional summer vacation destinations are achieving higher levels of performance than those properties located in areas with lower population density or without such traditional summer vacation destination attractions as amusement parks, beaches, or other family-friendly destination activities.

The addition of an indoor waterpark dramatically increases various expense ratios, especially in the area of salaries for lifeguards and waterpark staff, utility costs, and repairs and maintenance. Indoor waterparks require multiple lifeguards on duty at all times when the park is open. The typical indoor waterpark is open from 9:00 A.M. until 10:00 P.M. and will require a minimum of between two and 15 lifeguards. These are fixed costs for these properties. On busy Saturdays, when

Exhibit 7   Financial Data for Resorts With and Without Indoor Waterparks

Comparison of Indoor Waterpark Destination Resort's Financial Performance with Host Operating Statistics

	Indoor Waterpark Destination Resorts	Host Study–Resorts
Year of Data	2004	2003
Occupancy %	65.4%	64.8%
ADR	$191.88	$165.80
Average Room Count	305	394

	Ratio to Sales	Per Available Room	Per Occupied Room Night	Ratio to Sales	Per Available Room	Per Occupied Room Night
Total Revenue	100%	$69,043	$288.43	100%	$74,699	$315.92
Total Expenses	67.2%	$46,256	$193.63	76.6%	$57,175	$241.83
Income before Reserve for Replacement	32.8%	$22,787	$94.80	23.4%	$17,524	$74.09

Source: Hotel & Leisure Advisors and Smith Travel Research.

most indoor waterparks achieve their highest usage level, the staffing may be two to four times that of a slow period. Utility costs also increase, due to the fact that the indoor waterpark is kept at 85 degrees Fahrenheit on a year-round basis. Our review of a variety of indoor waterparks indicates that overall utility costs for an indoor waterpark resort are similar to a typical full-service hotel, running between 4 and 6 percent of revenue. The dollar amount, however, increases because of the addition of the indoor waterpark.

Exhibit 7 compares the average performance of six indoor waterpark destination resorts located throughout the United States with the performance of the Resort Hotel category from Smith Travel Research's 2004 *HOST Study*, which is a compilation of resort hotel financial statements from across the United States. The statistics indicate that the indoor waterpark destination resorts included in our analysis achieved a similar level of occupancy but a substantially higher average daily rate as compared to the general resort category, primarily because admission to the indoor waterpark is included in the average daily rate. In many resort hotels, there are additional fees for performing different activities.

The analysis indicates that the total revenue per occupied room night is lower in the indoor waterpark destination resorts than the general resort category, due to the fact that most resorts have more revenue producing activities (including golf, larger spas, higher-priced restaurants and lounges, and larger retail outlets) than the indoor waterpark destination resorts. Total expenses were lower in the indoor waterpark destination resort and the net income before reserve for replacement was higher, primarily due to the focus on the indoor waterpark while many other resort hotels have a wider range of amenities with their related expenses.

Indoor Waterpark Design and Costs

Indoor waterpark design has improved in recent years as increasing numbers of architects and designers have entered the field and resorts achieve more user-friendly waterpark features. There has been an increase in the entertainment value of the indoor waterparks when one looks at an older facility versus a newer facility. There is increased use of high-speed water slides, wave pools, and indoor water coasters to enhance the entertainment value of the indoor waterpark for older children and adults. The typical smaller slides, tree houses, and spray guns have always been popular with younger children. Particularly in larger indoor waterparks, designers increasingly are trying to include features that will be popular for a variety of ages. Most indoor waterparks will have a separate toddler area, a section appealing to elementary school children, and higher-speed rides or activities for middle school and high school children. An indoor waterpark has definite capacity issues due to its size and its relationship with the hotel's size.

A typical indoor waterpark resort property has an average of 125 square feet of net indoor waterpark space (including waterpark area play areas, but excluding arcades, gift shops, mechanical rooms, and offices) per guestroom. This correlates with research that indicates an indoor waterpark should have approximately 35 to 40 square feet of space per person. As a typical hotel room will house between three and four people, this implies between 105 and 160 square feet of indoor waterpark space per guestroom. For example, a 200-room resort should have between 21,000 and 32,000 square feet of indoor waterpark space to accommodate guests.

Indoor waterpark resorts have grown in size as well as popularity since their inception in the 1980s. The average size of the indoor waterpark component has swelled to accommodate more amenities such as wave pools, additional activity pools, "toddler-friendly" play areas, dry activity components, and more intricate tubes and slides. For example, Great Wolf Resorts, Inc. has increased the size of its indoor waterparks as demand for more intricate water-play features has increased. The company's Great Wolf Lodge property in Sandusky, Ohio (which opened in 2001), was constructed with a 33,000 square foot indoor waterpark area. Great Wolf Lodges in Kansas City, Kansas, and Traverse City, Michigan, both opened in 2003 with 38,000 square foot indoor waterpark areas. In 2005, the Great Wolf Resorts will open three new resorts in the Pocono Mountains, Pennsylvania; Williamsburg, Virginia; and Niagara Falls, Ontario. The indoor waterpark components at these three resorts will average 57,000 square feet.

Many indoor waterpark destination resort properties also have some kind of outdoor waterpark. Currently, the destination resort properties in Wisconsin Dells have the most elaborate outdoor waterparks. Resort properties' outdoor waterpark components may range from an outdoor pool with slides to a large 35-acre outdoor waterpark like the one at Treasure Island in Wisconsin Dells.

Other components of an indoor waterpark destination resort include meeting space, birthday party rooms, food and beverage facilities, attractive lobbies, fitness centers, business centers, gift shops, arcades, children's activity centers, and other resort- and hotel-style amenities. The difference between an indoor waterpark resort and a typical resort is that the amenities should be more focused upon children and families instead of strictly adults. Some indoor waterparks have conference centers attached, while many do not. Conference guests may not use the indoor waterpark, but will still appreciate an upscale conference facility that offers the indoor waterpark for any conference guests bringing their families.

The Future

The future for the indoor waterpark appears very bright, as families and children will continue to enjoy water activities in these facilities. An indoor waterpark offers an entertainment venue for overnight guests that a typical hotel does not have. There currently are many markets that do not have indoor waterpark facilities for families to use when traveling. The concern for the future is the potential for oversupply of indoor waterparks in certain markets as they may become as common as the Holidome became 20 years ago. At the time this case study was written, only Wisconsin was facing this issue. In Wisconsin, hotels with smaller indoor waterparks receive more limited benefits from the waterpark due to extreme competition from the larger resort facilities. The indoor waterpark will become a necessary amenity for hotels wanting to attract leisure demand and/or establish themselves as a resort destination. Indoor waterparks will become a necessary amenity, particularly in seasonal resort communities, for properties wanting to attract year-round demand. In the author's opinion, families will choose to stay at hotels with indoor waterpark components when they are traveling with children. However, when people are traveling alone for business, the waterpark will be an unnecessary amenity.

A number of indoor waterpark resorts in the Midwestern states have used the sale of condominium hotel units in raising funds to construct indoor waterpark additions. Prices for condominium units, which are then rented out by the management company, range from $200,000 to $500,000 for a two- to three-bedroom unit. Condominium buyers typically use the unit only one to two weeks per year. They hire the hotel management company to rent the unit out on a nightly basis and the management company receives between 40 and 50 percent of the room revenue.

As with the amusement park industry, owners and operators of indoor waterpark resorts have discovered that in order to attract new families to their facilities and keep their repeat guests coming back for more, they need to continually add new components and keep the concept fresh. I predict that the average size of indoor waterparks constructed will continue to increase as resorts add attractions that are larger in scope, including wave pools, areas specially designed for younger resort guests, and faster, taller, steeper, and more intricate waterslides and tubes. As more and more indoor waterpark resorts are constructed throughout the United States and Canada, developers will need to focus on individualizing the offerings of their resorts, maintaining customer service levels as attendance increases, and adding new components whenever possible.

Resort Spas

By *Patty Monteson, ISHC, and Judy Singer, Ed.D., ISHC*

Patty Monteson is co-owner of Health Fitness Dynamics, Inc. (HFD), an internationally recognized firm specializing in planning and management support of health spas for fine hotels, resorts, and mixed-use developments. She is a recognized author; has been featured and interviewed by international publications and media; and has presented spa seminars to international conferences. Recently, she was on the committee for the Leading Hotels of the World to develop standards for their Leading Spas. Ms. Monteson is an associate member of the Urban Land Institute (ULI) and is Secretary of the Board of Directors for the International Society of Hospitality Consultants (ISHC). She received both her Bachelor and Master of Science degrees from Slippery Rock University in Pennsylvania and currently serves on the school's President's Advisory Council.

Judy Singer is co-owner of Health Fitness Dynamics, Inc. (HFD). Since 1983, HFD has been the spa consultant to more than $650 million of spa development. In addition to her consulting, Ms. Singer has also overseen several HFD economic spa research studies such as HFD's 2003–2004 Spa Financial Benchmark Study. She has published in prominent trade publications and speaks regularly at international spa, hospitality, and tourism conferences. She is a member of the International SPA Association, where she served on the committee to develop the Uniform System of Financial Reporting for Spas, and ISHC, of which she is a former Chair. She received her Bachelor degree from the University of Massachusetts and her Master's and Doctorate degrees from Boston University.

THE DEVELOPMENT OF RESORT-BASED SPAS has increased in the past 10–15 years to the point that today spas have become an important component for most four- and five-star resorts and upscale hotels. Once considered marketing tools for resorts, many of today's spas have become viable businesses in and of themselves. As the popularity of resort spas continues to grow, it is important to understand the economic realities of developing and operating a spa. Resort spas should be profitable businesses and assets to the core business of selling rooms and/or real estate.

The International SPA Association (ISPA) estimates that in 2003, spas were a $11.2 billion industry. Day spas contributed $5.4 billion to this total. Day spas usually are located in an urban or suburban setting and do not have a lodging component. With 8,734 establishments in the United States (out of an estimated 12,100 total spa establishments), day spas comprise 72 percent of all spas. Resort/hotel spas were the second largest segment, with $4.5 billion in revenue. Destination spas placed a distant third with revenue of $400 million.[1]

The two types of lodging-based spas are the *destination spa* and the *resort spa*. At a destination spa, everyone is at the property for the spa program and guests usually have physical, emotional, or behavioral goals they want to accomplish. The primary components of the destination spa program are exercise, nutrition, wellness, and spa services. The lodging accommodations range from spartan to luxurious. In the United States, examples of destination spas are Canyon Ranch (Tucson, Arizona, and Lenox, Massachusetts) and The Golden Door (Escondido, California). There are 191 destination spas in the United States, making this the smallest segment of the spa industry.[2]

At a resort spa, guests may "spa" by taking massage, facial, body, bath, nail, and hair services or by relaxing in the steam, sauna, whirlpool, lounge, or pool, but they also can participate in other recreational and social activities typically available at a resort. Examples of resort spas in the United States would be those found at Four Seasons, Marriott, Fairmont, and Ritz-Carlton resorts and at such properties as Pinehurst, The Homestead, and Montage Resort & Spa. There are 1,662 resort/hotel spas in the United States, representing 14 percent of the spa industry.[3]

Many resorts have an opportunity to capture the best features of the destination spa and the resort spa in what we term the *hybrid* resort spa. During the peak season or prime times during the week, the spa is a vacation and/or conference enhancer. During the shoulder or off season or during the midweek period, it may attract people interested in special, multi-day themed wellness and lifestyle programs.

This chapter will focus on resort spas. The case study will detail the process of adding a spa to an existing resort. For our purposes, the word *resort* also can refer to a hotel or any other type of lodging establishment.

Step-by-Step Process for a Turnkey Resort Spa

In order for a resort spa to be a tangible as well as intangible asset to the property, it must be properly conceptualized, programmed, designed, themed, marketed, and managed. It is important to follow a logical, step-by-step process.

Analyze the Market

Define and analyze each market segment (e.g., social guests, incentive travelers, group guests, families, couples, and so on). Defining the market means looking not only at the property's existing resort market and perhaps at ways to increase it, but also at potential new markets. The spa certainly can act as a day spa to attract and accommodate day guests from the local community, but most spas are built because they are important must-haves for their resorts. The market analysis also should identify and analyze the competition, including other resort spas, day spas, salons, and health clubs.

Define the Objectives

When a resort is planning to add a spa, some objectives might include:

- Maintaining or enhancing its competitive position.
- Generating additional room nights, especially in the off and shoulder seasons.
- Expanding the peak and shoulder seasons.

Exhibit 1   2003 Spa-Related Revenue Per Occupied Room

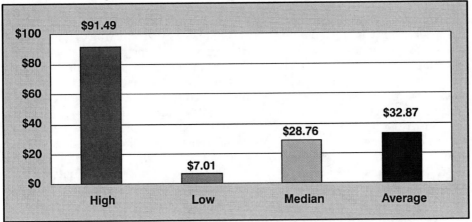

Source: Health Fitness Dynamics, Inc., *2003 Resort Spa Economic Research*. (N = 36 resort spas)

- Meeting the demands and expectations of guests.
- Expanding the resort's market appeal.
- Generating additional revenue per occupied room (see Exhibit 1).
- Enhancing perceived value for room rate.
- Having an additional profit center.
- Providing an indoor activity during inclement weather.

Most resorts want to have a spa that not only will be a profit center, but also will help to improve the marketability and profitability of their core business and, in some cases, will help sell real estate. A mixed-use resort with a residential component, a condo hotel, or a timeshare/vacation club/fractional ownership facility is selling a lifestyle and the spa has become an important part of that lifestyle. Spa-enhanced "lifestyle real estate" is a trend that will attract people who seek balance, stress-reduction, pleasure, purposeful leisure, and ways to look and feel good.

Develop the Concept

One of the first, and perhaps most important, steps when contemplating a spa is to determine what type of spa will meet market expectations and accomplish a resort's objectives. The concept is the foundation upon which everything is created, built, and marketed. Some spas will offer a sense of place and the spa reflects the geographical or historical aspects of the area. Others may take a theme (Asian, for example) and plan the spa services and facility around it. Still others create such signature themes as age management, medical aesthetics, mindfulness, fitness, wellness, luxury, or others. Recently, many resorts have positioned their spas as signatures for the property and some have even become notable because of their spas. Some hotel companies have even developed concepts and created spa brands within a hotel brand, such as The Willow Stream Spa for Fairmont Hotels & Resorts.

No matter what its concept, a spa should create an *experience* for all guests. The spa's identity is created with the concept and it must stay true to that concept in terms of spa treatments, facility features, professional and retail products, collateral material, and service standards. The spa must touch all the guests' senses, evoke their feelings, and create memories. A series of signature touch points and pleasant surprises must be created through facility features, unique treatments, exceptional delivery, and connecting with guests on an emotional level.

Most resorts want to create and maintain control of the guest experience as well as extend the resort brands' value and integrity, so they choose to manage their spas in-house. According to the *2004 Spa Industry Study*, 94 percent of resort/hotel spas manage their own operations and do not have an outside franchise affiliation.[4] The small percentage of resorts/developers who have chosen to enter into a franchise or license agreement with an outside spa management company typically must adopt that brand's concept.

There are four primary approaches taken by companies that offer outsourcing:

- A branded product company offers the resort a brand name, branded products, and a branded spa. The resort offers a distribution channel for these products. Examples of this are Elizabeth Arden and Givenchy.

- A company provides consulting and/or management services and has a product line that the spa must use. The company may or may not invest capital. An example is Steiner Leisure Limited with its Steiner and Mandara brands.

- A spa operator seeks to expand its brand awareness and name via additional management contracts and possibly with real estate development initiatives. The spa's identity and guest experience are based on the spa company's brand standards. Examples of this are Canyon Ranch's SpaClub and Canyon Ranch Living.

- A local or nonbranded company manages the spa.

A property needs to determine if one of these choices is truly beneficial or merely convenient. There are many issues to consider when making this decision, but the two largest ones often are money and marketing during the development phase.

Plan the Facility

The key in planning a marketable and profitable spa is to make sure it is market-driven and operationally efficient. The components and flow are critical to both the guests and the staff. No matter how small the spa is, it should create an experience for your guests.

The spa should be conveniently located for resort guests. If it is open to day guests from the local community or to members, it should be easily accessible to them without infringing on the security and privacy of hotel guests.

The size of the spa is based on the market demographics, market mix, hours of operation, concept, objectives, budget, etc. Bigger does not necessarily mean more profitable, but some spas may need size to create their theme or feel.

Providing a sense of place is important and whenever possible, this ambience should combine indoor and outdoor space. It is imperative to have enough profit centers, guest comfort zones, and back-of-the-house support areas for administration, staff, and storage. If there is a chance for future expansion of the spa, plan for it during this stage.

Design meetings need to address practical operational topics. For example, if drinking water will be readily available to guests in a spa, will it be in logo bottles? Will it come from a water bubbler with five-gallon water bottles? Will it be filtered water from a drinking fountain or water dispenser? Each scenario has different storage, plumbing, and refrigeration requirements to address during planning.

Be aware of the spa's impact on such resort departments as laundry, housekeeping, and maintenance. Determine the spa's laundry/linen requirements with the number and par of each item (based on projected spa occupancy and the number of items used in each treatment, in locker rooms, and in fitness areas) in order to see if the current laundry can handle the increase in load. The resort's housekeeping department may be assigned to do the night cleaning of the spa. The department manager and cleaning crew should be given clear written directions for each area to be cleaned and should be given several tours of the spa, so they can become familiar with the facility. The maintenance/engineering department should be present during installation of and training for such special equipment as the steam and sauna rooms, whirlpool, and pool. Once the spa opens, it might be advantageous to assign a part-time person from this department to the spa for a couple of months.

Determine Start-Up Costs

An accurate start-up budget should be created during the due diligence and feasibility analysis. It should include such items as construction costs, professional fees, furniture, fixtures, and equipment (FF&E), operating supplies and equipment (OS&E), marketing, pre-opening training and payroll, and miscellaneous expenses.

It is not uncommon for a four-star quality spa to have a turnkey cost of $425–$475 per square foot. A five-star quality spa can cost $475–$550 per square foot and more, in some cases. Having a realistic budget is critical in the planning stages. If the budget must be reduced, do so in areas that will not adversely affect the guest experience or compromise the operational efficiency needed for the spa to be profitable.

Prepare the Pro Forma

Most resort-based spas are not independent business units (IBUs). They receive some subsidy from the resort and very few, if any, pay rent. We recommend using a zero-based budget when developing a pro forma. Data to collect and analyze includes, but is not limited to, number of hotel rooms, number of guests per room, length of stay, occupancy by season and average occupancy for a five-year period, market mix by social/leisure, group, and business, future plans for the resort,

Exhibit 2 Resort Spa Pro Forma Guidelines

	Full IBU[1]	Semi-IBU[2]	Department[3]
Payroll Before Benefits	35%–45%	35%–45%	35%–45%
Payroll and Related	45%–55%	45%–55%	45%–55%
Operating Expenses	25%–30%	20%–25%	15%–20%
Net Operating Income	10%–20%	20%–30%	30%–40%

1. Spa is almost a stand-alone business.
2. Spa is responsible for all direct operating expenses and most administrative and general expenses.
3. Spa is responsible for all direct operating expenses and limited or prorated administrative expenses.

Note: The spa does not pay rent (square foot fee or percentage of revenues), nor is it responsible for land value or the amortization of building expenses.

Source: Health Fitness Dynamics, Inc.

demographic profiles of existing and future markets, lifestyle residential programs, and competitive market research. Exhibit 2 lists spa pro forma guidelines.

Spa gross revenue comes primarily from à la carte spa services. The remainder comes from spa packages (services only), facility fees, retail, and membership, if applicable. It is important to look at how the spa can make money beyond its four walls and when the guests are not on property. Include spin-off opportunities with signature products and logo items that not only can be sold in the spa, but also can be used for in-room amenities (and sold there too), incentive gifts for groups, and on-line shopping.

Labor is the most expensive operating cost. Planning less labor-intensive facilities and creating a realistic (for both the employee and employer) salary and incentive package for the spa staff are of critical importance if the spa is to be profitable.

Operating expenses can vary based on whether the spa is a department, semi-IBU, or full IBU. Very few resorts position their spa as a full IBU with responsibility for rent and debt service. Exhibit 3 shows payroll and operating expenses and net operating profit for spas in 2003.

Develop the Marketing/PR/Advertising Plan

Spas must be proactive before opening and go after their target markets. The fact that a resort has a spa does not mean that guests will use it. Resorts need to market their spas externally as well as internally on an ongoing basis. Managers should monitor and measure marketing strategies and adjust them as necessary.

Exhibit 4 shows treatment room utilization. Treatment rooms typically are underutilized, which means the spa is not maximizing its revenue potential. In order to increase treatment room utilization and revenue, spas need to have a

Exhibit 3   2003 Spa Payroll, Expenses, and Operating Profit as Percentages of Gross Revenue

	Payroll and Benefits	Operating Expenses	Net Operating Profit
High	112.60%	90.00%	64.00%
Low	20.71%	2.80%	−39.40%
Median	55.00%	12.54%	28.00%
Average	54.92%	23.96%	23.96%

Source: Health Fitness Dynamics, Inc., *2003 Resort Spa Economic Research.* (N=36 resort spas)

Exhibit 4   Treatment Room Utilization

	Utilization*
High	75.92%
Low	17.37%
Median	32.00%
Average	35.33%

*Based on available treatment rooms (number of treatment rooms or stations multiplied by hours of operation).

Source: Health Fitness Dynamics, Inc., *2003 Resort Spa Economic Research.* (N = 36 resort spas)

strong, cohesive marketing strategy that responds quickly to forecasts, and reception staff members need to upsell, link-sell, and monitor their wait list.

As part of an overall plan, spas should identify the target markets; develop the collateral information (brochure, press kit, public relation pieces, video/DVD); create the Web site; determine the sources for advertising/media placement and best times for each resource; develop the public relations program, including press releases, stories, and advertorials; create direct mail and e-mail awareness programs; develop internal and external marketing strategies; train spa and resort staff to be spa ambassadors; create a grand opening party; and conduct familiarization tours for meeting planners, travel agents, and writers.

During this phase, it is important to create brand identity. This includes, among other things, developing a logo with memorable and identifiable fonts and colors that appeal to men and women. Spas also should consider how this logo will look on printed collateral materials, private label bottles, and on logo clothing and accessories.

All collateral information should be inviting and simple to understand and convey an enticing image as well as factual information. Readers need to see the features as well as the benefits. Avoid complexity in the spa brochure. While it is important to have variety, avoid being trendy or overwhelming when designing your spa treatment menu. The most popular services continue to be massages and facials. In some situations, it might be better to have a simple menu where all treatments are personalized and customized and guests buy time, where the price of time does not vary with the treatments performed or the products used.

A spa should create a marketing plan for its members and day guest markets if they exist. Local advertising for special packages and gift certificates are a must. Form strategic alliances with such complementary businesses as flower shops, photographers, candy stores, wine shops, bridal stores, wedding planners, and so forth to reach the local market.

Regardless of a spa's market, it is essential to create an awareness of who it is, what it offers, what makes it different, where it is located, and why guests should visit. Never take anything for granted. Getting a message out and making sure it is clear and market-specific is an ongoing process that requires constant communication and commitment.

Plan for Opening

A carefully orchestrated pre-opening plan is essential in order to make sure that everything envisioned will actually happen. It is important that the spa be fully integrated into the resort so the spa enhances the overall guest experience and brand identity.

It is also important, after spending a great deal of time and money planning the spa, to do the same when selecting and training the spa staff. These people are the spa's heart and soul and often are the reason guests will return. The spa team needs to be compensated fairly and trained for both technical and hospitality skills.

The hiring and training time frame will depend on the size of the spa, but here are some general guidelines. The spa director can be hired six to eighteen months out, depending on whether there is a start-up team to assist with all pre-opening responsibilities. This start-up team could be the corporate spa department that may exist within the resort chain and/or the spa consultants. The spa salesperson, if applicable, should start six to eight months before opening. Supervisors can be brought on board two to four months out and receptionists should start shortly afterward. Technical and hospitality training of the rest of the team is likely to take two to four weeks. In addition to training the spa team, it is imperative to orient and train the resort staff.

The soft opening should be three to five days before the actual opening, again depending on the size of the spa. This is when a spa simulates operations by first having the spa team rotate being "guests" and "employees." Next, key resort staff, and later, friends and family would be the "guests." Have comment cards during this phase so you can fine-tune the experience before the spa opens to outside guests.

Monitor and Measure Spa Operations

Once the spa is open, keep monitoring and training the staff. Exhibit 5 suggests key metrics to measure. Refine the guest experience as necessary. Make market-driven adjustments—speak with guests, look at comment cards, and follow up with guests after their visits. Make sure the seamless integration of the spa and hotel continues, pay attention to trends, and continue training, educating, and motivating the team.

Exhibit 5   Sample Spa Metrics

Baseline metrics	Market segments, capture rate by market segment, treatments per guest, treatment room utilization
Revenue metrics	Revenue by guest type, revenue by treatment, revenue by department, revenue per occupied treatment room, revenue per available treatment room, revenue per visit
Payroll metrics	Payroll as percent of gross revenue, payroll as percent of treatment revenue, payroll cost per treatment, productivity per employee, revenue generated per employee
Expense metrics	Operating expenses as percent of gross revenue, product/supply cost per treatment, operating cost per guest, laundry usage and cost per guest

Source: Health Fitness Dynamics, Inc.

Case Study: The Spa at Sawgrass

Located in Ponte Vedra Beach, Florida, between Jacksonville and St. Augustine, the Sawgrass Marriott Resort & Spa is situated on 6,300 acres of lush landscaping, nature, and golf courses. The resort is synonymous with golf and is the second largest golf resort in America, with 99 holes of world-renowned championship golf on five courses, including the famous Tournament Players Club Stadium Course. The resort also has access to 2.5 miles of pristine Florida beach nearby, which is home to its private membership club and also is available to resort guests.

The resort opened in 1986 and has 508 guestrooms, suites, and villas. It is owned by Interconn Ponte Vedra Company, LLC, which is comprised of Cigna Realty Investors (90 percent) and Interstate Hotels & Resorts (10 percent). Interstate also manages the property as a Marriott franchise.

The resort had a health club with fitness equipment, small locker rooms, and two treatment rooms in the main hotel building. It did not serve the spa needs of resort guests, especially groups. Once the spa opened, the health club was converted to a fitness room with free access for resort guests. Guests who use the new spa fitness studio pay a facility fee that entitles them to use the locker room, steam room, sauna, whirlpool, and outdoor pool for the day.

The owners and management knew they needed a spa, not only because other properties in their competitive set either had or were adding spas, but also to give the resort another profit center, increase additional revenue per occupied room, generate additional room nights, offer an activity for non-golfers and companions of group guests, provide an indoor activity during inclement weather, and position the property as a full-service resort. There was a plan to expand the conference facilities, and the owners knew a spa was needed to complement this expansion because it was difficult to get group business without a spa.

Competitive Analysis

As part of due diligence, a competitive spa analysis was performed in early 2003. There were seven regionally competitive resorts and no day spas of comparable quality. We examined what each offered in terms of concept, guest experience, treatment types and fees, facility fees, membership programs, facilities, and plans to build a new spa or expand an existing spa.

Market Analysis

The spa experience and facilities were based on the resort market, so we primarily analyzed the mix of business, potential new target markets, profile of the existing markets, length of stay, and occupancy. Two key factors needed to be considered. This is a strong conference resort (70 percent group business), so there is a limited window of opportunity in which conference guests can use the spa, and golf is the number one recreational activity for them when not in meetings. This information told us we needed to find additional markets to use the spa when guests were in meetings, provide services/activities that were attractive to golfers, and create something for non-golfers.

Since the resort has a private membership, it seemed reasonable to consider a spa membership that could be an add-on to this or sold on its own without adding too much additional space to the facility. Knowing there would still be some slow periods during the day, especially Monday to Thursday, the spa would manage its yield with day guests from the local community.

Concept and Program

The original concept was to create a hybrid spa primarily for the group and leisure resort guests that also would be attractive to spa members and local day guests. The spa experience was intended to help guests feel good, be pampered, indulge themselves, unwind, recharge, and gain a sense of balance.

The spa would have signature products and treatments and a brand identity, but we did not want to limit it to one signature theme or specific market. It would not be everything to everyone, but as a full-service spa in a full-service resort, it needed to provide many venues and doors of opportunity to attract the various markets.

The spa needed to have a "club spa" feel with a strong fitness and personal training program to appeal to its major guest base of mostly male golf and fitness enthusiasts. The environment and experience needed a sense of energy balanced with serenity. We called this "Zen with a zest." The spa needed to capture the feel and authenticity of old Florida under the oaks and Southern hospitality in a stress-free environment. It was to be an oasis of tranquility—an adult enclave to provide an experience that engages the guests and touches their senses. Every decision made from this point forward needed to be consistent with and complementary to this conceptual vision.

Location

We examined numerous locations that ranged from renovating existing space in the hotel, building an addition to the hotel, or creating a freestanding building near the hotel. The freestanding building was chosen as the best option. The team then looked at several parcels of land that had character, accessibility, and privacy. The site that finally was selected was at the entrance of the resort where the tennis courts and event tent were located. Tennis players would have playing privileges at the nearby ATP (Association of Tennis Professionals) Tour facilities. The event tent would not be needed once the proposed new conference center opened. This site, with its quiet setting under mature oak trees, was accessible to all resort guests by a nice three- to five-minute walk along the lagoon and over one of the bridges (a new bridge was part of the construction budget). Furthermore, it provided easy access for the community to drive up and self-park or to use the hotel's valet service. Its prime location and setting make a statement that the spa is an important part of the resort.

Feasibility Analysis

As part of the feasibility analysis, we prepared a zero-based pre-opening budget and a five-year pro forma. The pre-opening budget, with a 10 percent contingency, was $2.3 million dollars and included:

- Insurance.
- Pre-opening and training payroll.
- Relocation expenses.
- Conferences.
- Spa-specific FF&E.
- OS&E.
- Specialty systems (music and emergency call, for example).
- Marketing/advertising/public relations.
- Retail products and displays.
- Fees and reimbursable expenses for spa consultants and special trainers.

The project manager incorporated this information into his budget.

The five-year pro forma was based on a detailed set of assumptions for each line item so that there would be benchmarks to monitor and measure during operations. This included:

- Revenue line items and capture rates for each market.
- Treatment prices, utilization, and membership programs.
- Payroll, with staffing forecasts and compensation schedules for core and non-core staff.
- Operating expenses, including all direct spa expenses (decorations, equipment rental, purchasing and cleaning linens and towels, guest, professional, office, and cleaning supplies, licenses and permits, telecommunications, uniform purchasing and cleaning, VIP amenities, printing and stationery, postage, spa-specific marketing and advertising, business promotion, training, and miscellaneous).

- Most indirect administrative and general expenses.

The pro forma was developed so that the spa would operate as a semi-IBU based on the above allocation of expenses.

During the design/development and pre-opening operations meetings, the budget and pro forma were reviewed and reconciled with all design and operational decisions on a monthly basis.

Design/Development

Based on the market and concept, the spa facility program and conceptual space plan were created with the proper components and flow. Marriott brand standards were followed because the resort wanted to use the word "spa" in its name. The resort's original name was the Sawgrass Marriott Resort & Beach Club and would be changed to the Sawgrass Marriott Resort & Spa.

The seven-month design process began in September 2003. On a monthly basis, the project manager met with the design team and consultants to review plans, signage, interior design, budgets, etc. This type of close communication was in addition to ongoing communication and was essential if the spa was to be built on time and on budget.

We prepared the *Construction- and Spa-Specific FF&E Book,* which included the functional and performance criteria for such areas as millwork, electrical, plumbing, lighting, music, telephones, computers, etc. This reference book for the design and construction teams included the cut sheets, vendor contact information, and technical and installation instructions for all spa equipment. Everything in the book and on the floor plans needed to match so that the spa would be functional as well as aesthetically pleasing. The equipment sheets were later used in the development of the *Spa-Specific Construction-Related Equipment Purchasing Book* that was given to the contractor for built-in or special installation equipment and the *Spa-Specific FF&E Purchasing Book* of movable equipment that was given to the purchasing company.

The initial facility program was about 26,300 square feet but, as a cost reduction measure, was reduced to 19,600 square feet with a provision to allow for future expansion. The spa team reduced the number of treatment rooms from 23 to 19, eliminated the spa treatment suites, indoor spa pool, and co-ed relaxation lounge, made the fitness areas a bit smaller, and created a nail care studio rather than a full-service salon with hair and makeup (eliminating four stations, plus support areas). In anticipation of later growth, we included a future expansion plan for the areas that were reduced or eliminated.

The spa facility consists of:

- A reception lobby with a three-station reception desk.

- A spa shop, including a gift area and point-of-sale system for busy times.

- A nail studio with five manicure stations, five pedicure stations, and a prep room.

- A fitness studio with cardio and strength equipment for personal workouts, circuit training, and golf fitness.

- An exercise/spinning studio for supervised classes as well as private and small group workouts.

- Men's and women's locker rooms, each with steam, sauna, whirlpool, and private wet and dry lounges.

- A treatment area with 19 treatment rooms.

- Soothies, a spa food and beverage serving area.

- An outdoor pool area with heated lap pool, relaxation deck, and whirlpool.

- Outdoor massage teahouses under the grand oak trees near the lagoon.

- An administration area with spa director/assistant spa director offices and space for a future reservations office. Two additional offices were eliminated in order to increase the retail area.

- Back-of-house area with retail and professional product storage, laundry storage, a staff break room, a spa supervisors' office, and a treatment prep room.

It took ten months to build the spa. Ground was broken in April 2004 and the spa opened January 29, 2005. During the summer of 2004, four different hurricanes were forecasted for the Jacksonville/Ponte Vedra area. Each time, construction had to stop and the site was secured. After the hurricanes, there was a shortage of building materials and time delays in getting what was needed. Approximately six weeks were lost, but the spa had to open in late January 2005. This opening date was critical because Super Bowl XXXIX was going to be played in Jacksonville on February 6, 2005, and the resort was selected to host the NFC team.

Turnkey Costs to Build the Spa

The turnkey cost for the spa was $8,423,000, or $430 per square foot, excluding the cost of the land. The actual final numbers, including freight, shipping, installation, warehousing, and purchasing fees, were as follows:

- FF&E, special equipment, and spa supplies: $1,482,000, or $76 per square foot; 18 percent of project costs

- Consultants' professional fees and reimbursable expenses: $705,000, or $36 per square foot; 8 percent of project costs

- Construction company and construction-related fees: $5,263,000, or $269 per square foot; 62 percent of project costs

- Miscellaneous: $973,000, or $50 per square foot; 12 percent of project costs

The development process was managed by Continental Design & Supply Company, LLC (a wholly owned subsidiary of Interstate Hotels & Resorts), and was financed by Cigna as part of its real estate investment.

Pre-Opening

Although operational issues were always part of the design and construction meetings, the operational phase of the project started in February 2004. The search for a spa director began immediately. The resort's retail manager was offered the position of assistant spa director and was involved in the operational phase from the onset.

In early April 2004, the spa ops team began monthly meetings, in addition to conference calls and other methods of regular communication. Spa ops consisted of the resort's executive committee (general manager, hotel manager, director of sales and marketing, controller, director of engineering, director of human resources), the assistant spa director, and the spa consultants. The spa director joined the group as soon as she was on board. The resort's public relations, marketing, and advertising agency was also involved in pertinent communication and meetings. The agenda for these meetings was written and circulated to the team for edits about a week before the meeting and included not only critical path and to-do list items, but also issues that came up during informal conversations since the previous meeting and construction updates. The critical path included 170 major items and every meeting included reviews of the pre-opening budget and five-year pro forma.

In April 2004, the following took place:

- The spa concept statement was fine-tuned.

- The agency began creating the materials and script for the advertising/public relations campaign.

- The team started analyzing companies and products for the primary product line and signature private-label products and explored companies that provided gift cards that would be compatible with the spa software.

- The executive committee began interviewing candidates for spa director.

- The engineering department began constructing a Japanese teahouse in the resort that symbolized the spa's Zen-inspired design.

Key objectives for the May 2004 spa ops meeting were getting a marketing/public relations update, reviewing the proposed membership program, identifying locations in the community to sell gift certificates, selecting the primary skin-care company, and identifying a spa director to start in June.

During the early June 2004 meeting, the agency presented initial ideas for the marketing/public relations/advertising campaign and corresponding budget for "The Spa at Sawgrass," introduced the spa's tag line (*"touch. mind. body. soul."*), and presented the spa's signature color, a shade of orange. Other agenda items included:

- Presentation of the pre-opening spa fact sheet.

- A Web site status report (the spa has its own Web site that is linked to the resort's).

- Presentation of the marketing strategies for each market segment.

- The spa's utilization policy for resort associates.

- Staff uniforms and guest robes and rubber scuffs.

- Selection of a music system vendor.

- Laundry transport procedures.

- Flow chart and procedures for group sales.

With regard to Web site development, the primary skincare company and the exercise equipment company supplied photos for the site and this helped significantly to contain the initial cost. On-line shopping was going to be an important component for the site, so the team began exploring the options.

The main topics of the late June meeting pertained to ordering the computers, phones, and spa software, organizing the upcoming "ground-breaking event" for key people in the local community, and setting staff compensation.

Instead of a July meeting, the team focused on introducing the spa to select people in the community. This took place at an outdoor brunch and coincided with public relations directed to print and broadcast media. The primary skin care company provided travel kits with products for each guest at no charge and there was a drawing for a day at the spa. Spa renderings, marketing posters, membership information, and the spa fact sheet were available. The teahouse was a prominent feature and chair massages were given there. The spa was featured not only on targeted local radio stations that morning, but also on television in the evening and in subsequent newspaper articles.

August 2004's meeting pertained to:

- The spa's opening date and training schedule, including training room requirements.

- Purchasing spa products and supplies.

- Finalizing the creative materials and media plan.

- Finalizing the membership letter.

- Initiating immediate marketing strategies for the resort, including a workshop for the resort sales team.

- Selecting the company to manufacture the spa's signature products.

The focus for the remainder of the month was the signature products. These products included the shampoo, conditioner, bath gel, and body lotion for the locker rooms and treatment rooms and select products that would be used in the spa's signature treatments. After weeks of testing various samples for smell, texture, ease of application, and color (variations of the signature color), the samples were narrowed down. Next, the general manager, spa director, assistant spa director, and spa consultants spent a day in the product company's laboratory and experimented with the targeted colors and scents until the final color and two final scents were chosen. These product samples were tested and evaluated by several resort associates in order to come up with the final signature color and scent. The next step was to finalize the style of bottles, jars, tops, and packaging. The product company did not charge a research and development fee, nor did it limit the number of samples it made for the team to test. It also did not require any minimum professional and retail orders. All of this significantly reduced the start-up cost for signature products.

In September 2004, the spa brochure draft was finalized to reflect the spa products. The monthly meeting focused on staffing guidelines, wages, and recruiting, the preliminary menu for the spa café (Soothies), and spa retail. The general manager began working with the product company to create a presentation of select signature products for resort in-room sales.

October's spa meeting took place via conference call and focused on staff recruiting and the upcoming job fair. Spa "mini-facts" were presented to the resort team via payroll stuffers and during departmental meetings. In-house marketing expanded to include:

- Bottled water with the spa logo label served during group meetings.

- The teahouse being prominently displayed in the conference center, themed as a massage area, accompanied by the spa fact sheet and a pre-opening information packet.

- An "opening soon" campaign, which included a sign at the resort entrance, guestroom key cards, posters throughout the resort, lapel ribbons worn by resort staff, signage on resort vehicles used for guest transportation, the telephone hold message, and the resort Web site.

The main topics for the November 2004 meeting included:

- A construction update.

- Determining where to store the products and supplies that would be arriving in a few weeks.

- Recruiting, chart of accounts, licenses, and gift certificate sales status reports.

- Staff uniforms.

- Web site update.

- Examining business on the books.

The supervisors (massage, fitness, skin/nail care) started working at the end of November and they soon began interviewing candidates that had been screened by human resources. The reception/retail supervisor started earlier because her team needed to be hired by the middle of November to train on the spa software, begin keying information into the software, and start calling groups that were on the books beginning February 2005 to reserve their spa appointments.

The last spa ops meeting was in December 2004, two weeks before the beginning of the training program. The main topics were:

- A construction update and verification of the spa "move in" date.

- A facility walk-through.

- The status of the new massage teahouses (these were designed for outdoor massage use, unlike the original temporary marketing structure).

- Hiring spa associates.

- OS&E delivery.

- Licenses.

- Retail.

- Staff uniforms.

- Pre-opening payroll.

- Presentation and tasting of the spa food and beverage menu items.

- Confirmation of the training schedule and finalization of the training manual.

At this time, the resort was in the process of implementing Marriott's new program of upgrading its beds and the general manager wanted a spa pillow and a relaxing spa logo CD to complement this upgrade that helped create awareness for the spa. The team found a company that could make the pillow in the signature color with the spa logo and tag line and another that could private label the CD.

On December 30, 2004, training began and after two days of general and hospitality training, departmental training began. This was in addition to the training conducted by human resources.

January 2005 was dedicated to training, deep cleaning, final equipment set-up, moving into the spa, setting up treatment rooms, ribbon cutting, spa tours for the community, dress rehearsals, and pre-opening simulations with spa and resort team members as "guests." Throughout January, the general manager took small groups of resort associates on spa tours. This orientation and overview helped to educate them on how to explain the spa to resort guests. Resort departments with direct guest contact were also given a spa fact book with general information to help them answer frequently asked questions.

The spa opened on January 29, 2005, and was immediately busy because of high resort occupancy due to the upcoming Super Bowl. The spa figured prominently in the daily activities for Philadelphia Eagles players and Fox Sports personnel, who used the fitness studio, steam room, sauna, and whirlpool and took spa services during the week.

Post-Opening

The spa, coupled with the new conference center, has enabled the resort to attract higher-end groups and increase the resort's average daily rate. As of June 1, 2005, the spa has shown a net operating profit (income before depreciation, amortization, interest, income taxes, or debt service) every month. Revenue per occupied room has increased steadily and was $15.21 for the first four months of 2005. The spa's operating profit for the same time period was 17.2 percent. In May, in-room sales of the spa's signature products amounted to $5,300. Membership sales have been lower than projected, but a proactive campaign to reach the local day spa business and resort groups is intended to replace some of the unrealized membership revenue.

It is unusual for a spa to show such positive numbers, especially when it first opens. Part of the success may be due to the fact that the operating expenses are low, since the spa is still using some of the professional supplies, retail items, and collateral material from the pre-opening budget. The spa's current and ongoing success can be attributed to the clear direction, defined expectations, and goals that are jointly established by the general manager, controller, and spa director. The spa is expected to be profitable, and each resort department has been trained on how it can contribute to the spa's success. Although this requires constant and ongoing training, it is one of the most effective and inexpensive ways to market the spa. On a monthly basis, the resort controller meets with the spa director to review the profit and loss statement. They also talk on an ongoing basis during the month. The general manager formally meets with the spa director, assistant spa director, and spa sales manager on a weekly basis to discuss spa operations, financial goals, and so forth. The general manager also visits the spa three to four times a week. The spa director reports directly to the general manager, but is not on the executive committee.

The spa has been well received by the resort guests, and its GSS rating (a score based on a survey by an outside company after a guest's visit) is a perfect 100 percent. As for personnel, turnover has been 30.9 percent (excluding on-call and seasonal personnel and interns). Understanding that the spa team is critical to the success of the spa, the spa supervisors and management team continue the training program established in pre-opening, set goals and monitor the results, and motivate and coach the spa team on a regular basis.

The spa awareness campaign continues throughout the resort and, since the opening, spa golf umbrellas and a golf cart for the sales team, both in the spa signature color, have been purchased. As for on-line shopping, the team identified a company that is in the process of creating the online catalog of spa, golf shop, and bedding products. This company will also take care of inventory and shipping for all online sales.

In mid-June, the spa consultants met with the spa management team as well as the hotel executive committee during two days of post-opening review to examine what is working and what is not, fine-tune marketing strategies, examine financial statements, review metrics, and set goals for the next three months.

Lessons Learned

It is important to have a kick-off session to make sure everyone (owner, operator, design team, marketing team, etc.) understands the spa concept and is focused on how to take the vision and make it a reality within their disciplines.

It is difficult to open a spa in January. A lot of potential staff did not want to leave their current place of employment until after the holidays (due to holiday gifts and year-end bonuses) and the contractors typically had vacation time.

Communicating and making key decisions in a timely manner are essential.

Facility Planning. It is important for all members of the design/construction/operations/ownership team to be involved in value-engineering decisions in order to create a functional, marketable, profitable, and aesthetically pleasing spa.

Sales and Marketing. The resort had 50,000 room nights on the books a year before the spa opened. A "spa closing" room where meeting planners could meet with the spa group sales manager may have helped to better sell the spa to groups on a pre-arrival basis. It was critical for the spa group sales manager to immediately contact groups that were already confirmed, introduce them to the spa, and make pre-arrival spa appointments. The spa membership and local sales coordinator should be hired six months prior to opening. Public relations was better than advertising.

We would like to thank the following people for their assistance with this case study: Colin Dunkley, Senior Vice President, and Dave Smith, Project Manager, from Continental Design & Supplies, LLC (a wholly owned subsidiary of Interstate Hotels & Resorts); Debi Bishop, General Manager, and Michael Wigg, Controller, from the Sawgrass Marriott Resort & Spa.

Endnotes

1. International SPA Association, 2004 *Spa Industry Study.*

2. *Ibid.*

3. *Ibid.*

4. *Ibid.*

Post-Hurricane Asset Restoration and Business Recovery

By *Elaine M. McLaughlin* and *John M. McCarthy*

Elaine M. McLaughlin, MPA, CDME, *is currently an instructor at Florida Gulf Coast University. She is a member of the faculty of the newly established Resort & Hospitality Management program. For over 12 years, she served as executive director of the Lee Island Coast Visitor and Convention Bureau. Twice named one of the leading women in tourism by* Travel Agent Magazine, *McLaughlin led the Bureau in innovative programs that fully integrated the tourism industry with the overall goals of county government. She led the development of the first comprehensive tourism destination recovery program after witnessing the economic damage created by Hurricane Hugo to South Carolina communities. In 1995, she represented Florida at the White House Conference on Tourism, and for over six years she served on the Florida Commission on Tourism and the board of VISIT FLORIDA, Inc. The first person in Florida to achieve the prestigious Certified Destination Management Executive designation, she also served two terms as the President of the Florida Association of Convention and Visitors Bureaus.*

John M. McCarthy is President of Liberty Hospitality Group, which he joined in 1989. During his tenure with Liberty, he has managed Liberty's hotel investments, including a world-class hotel in Florida and a large portfolio of Residence Inn by Marriott (RIBM) hotels. He also has participated in numerous real estate transactions, including the acquisition of a substantial portfolio of Resolution Trust Corporation assets. Currently, he oversees all aspects of Liberty's investment in Sanibel Harbour Resort & Spa, a four-diamond destination resort in southwest Florida. Mr. McCarthy completed Marriott's Management Training Program in 1984 and has held various management positions at hotels throughout the United States. He is a former Chairman of RIBM's National System Marketing Fund Committee and a former member of the Residence Inn Association's Board of Directors. From 1998 to 2001, he served on the board of directors of the Hospitality Asset Managers Association (HAMA) and continues to be an active member. He has co-authored several chapters in conjunction with the Educational Institute of the American Hotel & Lodging Association, HAMA, Florida Gulf Coast University (FGCU), and the University of Denver and his work has been published on numerous occasions. He is a frequent guest lecturer at colleges and universities, including University of Denver and FGCU, and has been invited to speak at numerous industry conferences, including the Americas Lodging Investment Summit, Hospitality Design Expo, and Hotel Investment Conference. Mr. McCarthy is a graduate of Ithaca College and currently serves on the FGCU Resort and Hospitality Management Advisory Board.

IN *RESTORING TOURISM DESTINATIONS IN CRISIS,* David Beirman defines a crisis as "a situation requiring radical management action in response to events beyond the internal control of the organization necessitating urgent adaptation of marketing and operational practices to restore the confidence of employees, associated enterprises and consumers in the viability of the destination."[1] On August 13, 2004, the Sanibel Harbour Resort & Spa (SHRS) experienced an event that fit this definition and required a new level of urgent and radical action. The wrath of Hurricane Charley moved ashore and within several hours, lives and livelihoods were dramatically altered.[*]

Several managers remained on-property and served as the critical incident storm team. They now refer to the period leading up to, during, and immediately following the storm as "hours of anguish and intense prayer."

As Hurricane Charley intensified, the building began to breach as the roof peeled, windows shattered, and rain entered from every direction. The sound of large objects hitting the hotel tower contributed to the terror felt by those hiding within. They realized that it would be impossible to adequately describe the basic fear for life shared by everyone who experiences a category 4 or 5 hurricane directly.

Many resorts have recovered successfully from natural disasters, but we know of no other example in which front-line employees have been engaged emotionally in the day-to-day challenges of the recovery process—in this case, a process that led to reopening a higher quality resort experience in record time.

In this case study, we will examine a unique approach to inspiring a workforce during a crisis and focus on team member engagement as a seldom recognized dimension in the "art" of asset management. We will share lessons learned that may help others identify and develop a best-practice plan for managing externally driven crises.

Background

On August 12, 2004, the day before Hurricane Charley came ashore, SHRS was operating as a 400-room destination resort positioned as an independent luxury property competing in the upscale southwest Florida market segment. After operating without a major brand or national operating company for more than a decade, SHRS was in its first year as a member of Preferred Hotels & Resorts.

SHRS opened as a contemporary destination resort in 1989 and expanded with the addition of a marina during the early 1990s and subsequent acquisition of several large watercraft vessels, including a 92-foot, 149-passenger yacht. In 1999, it expanded again with the addition of a 30,000-square-foot conference center located adjacent to the primary resort complex and an additional 107-room hotel building on adjacent waterfront land.

---

[*] *The analysis, conclusions, and opinions expressed in this case study are the authors' own and do not necessarily reflect the position of Sanibel Harbour Resort & Spa, Liberty Mutual Group, or its policyholders.*

SHRS was operated by Liberty Hospitality Group, a subsidiary of Liberty Mutual Group, and had a healthy presence in the group meetings market, frequently receiving awards of distinction. The property also benefited from a consistent flow of vacation travelers, contributing to an annual capture of between 35,000 and 40,000 leisure room nights. Additional business activity was attributed to being located in the eco-rich Gulf Coast area of Lee County along the shore of the San Carlos Bay where the Caloosahatchee River opens to the Gulf of Mexico.

The resort, situated on more than 85 acres of environmentally protected land, consisted of seven buildings that played host to a wide array of resort facilities and services. Liberty Mutual owned five of the seven buildings and the remaining two buildings were independently operated by two associations of condominium owners. Despite the condominiums' separate and distinct ownership structures, many individual owners maintained their units in the resort's rental program. The condo rental program allowed the resort to supplement the 347 rooms and suites with approximately 50 vacation condo units, bringing the total lodging inventory to nearly 400 units.

From a real estate perspective, the seven buildings were strategic assets within the resort complex. Each building component was somewhat analogous to an instrument in an orchestra and was an integral part of the resort's operational theatre. The asset was balanced with a dedicated spa building, a freestanding restaurant and tennis building adjacent to a series of clay tennis courts, and a freestanding 107-room lodging facility near the resort entrance. The other two buildings, connected by a sky bridge, housed a modern conference center and a multifaceted 240-room central building. All real estate components were designed to operate in concert with one another to enhance the destination resort's value proposition.

Before Hurricane Charley, SHRS offered guests:

- A 40,000-square-foot destination spa, salon, fitness, and tennis center.

- A marina featuring the Sanibel Harbour Princess, a 149-passenger yacht, extending guests the opportunity to enjoy various food and beverage functions on the water. The marina also featured a pontoon boat for fishing and shelling excursions.

- 40,000 square feet of meeting space, featuring a 10,000-square-foot ballroom, a 7,000-square-foot ballroom, and many waterfront breakout rooms with terraces.

- Multiple food and beverage outlets, including three restaurants, a poolside snack bar and lounge operation, a waterfront lounge, a deli, room service for each building, and a fully integrated banquet and catering services operation.

- A walking trail to encourage guests to enjoy the rich ecosystem and wildlife, including mangrove forests, giant ficus trees, osprey nests, fishing and observation piers, several thousand linear feet of natural coastline, and an estuary with a wide variety of bird species.

- An award-winning children's program called Kids' Klub.

- Three retail shops including a spa boutique, ship's store, and general gift shop.

- Two primary pool decks, supplemented by three smaller pool decks at the condo towers and the 107-room inn.

The traditional mix of business at SHRS was about 60 percent group meetings and 40 percent leisure clientele. The resort employed more than 500 team members, the majority of whom were employed on a full-time basis. Managers adhered to a well-established mission statement and team members were core to the unique business culture that existed at SHRS before August 13, 2004.

In the days, months, and years before the hurricane-forced closing, the SHRS staff maintained healthy guest satisfaction scores and the overall team member satisfaction index was also above industry average.

Mission Statement

As stated by Christopher K. Bart, "There is a relationship between the words and concepts of a mission statement and that firm's success as a business."[2] Part of SHRS's mission statement is as follows:

> Sanibel Harbour Resort & Spa is a Resort whose most compelling features are timeless The team members of the Resort are committed to exceeding the expectations of the guests, owners, and each other. We will provide guests with a sense of well being through the consistent delivery of personal service in a clean, safe, and environmentally friendly setting. We will offer a rewarding work experience and encourage the professional growth of our team members through training and individual development. We will be active in our community and remain a positive part of its growth. We will respect the owner's investment through constant improvement of facilities and property, focusing on best practices. By embracing these principles, the team members of Sanibel Harbour Resort & Spa will remain true to our core values while ensuring the legacy of the Resort.

In accordance with its mission statement, SHRS's ownership representatives and senior management historically have embraced the promotion of best practices. Hurricane preparation was one of many disciplines in which ownership and management were dedicated to promoting what is best for guests, team members, and owners.

Preparation

In order to evaluate the efficacy of the SHRS hurricane plan, we first will examine the issues and challenges associated with hurricane preparation. Later, we will examine what was learned and what improvements could be made during a post-hurricane recovery.

Unlike other natural disasters that strike without advance warning, hurricane activity is seasonal and most storms are tracked many days in advance. As a major storm approaches, senior management is responsible for ensuring that the business is prepared for the event. As with most southwest Florida residents, the 2004 hurricane season was not the first time that SHRS team members had to prepare for a potential hurricane. Many were involved in the preparation activities for Hurricane Andrew in 1992 and Hurricane Georges in 1998. In fact, many tenured team members were involved in the creation and implementation of the official SHRS hurricane preparation plan.

Most hotels and resorts have certified emergency plans that have been reviewed thoroughly by due diligence officers, lenders, insurance adjusters, local officials, corporate officers, and asset managers, just to name a few. Hurricane preparation planning, including an evacuation policy, is standard operating procedure for businesses operating within the state. When it comes to hurricane preparation, there are many valuable resources available to owners and operators, including:

- VISIT FLORIDA's media kit and information on recovery issues by state region at www.visitflorida.org.

- Lee County Visitor & Convention Bureau's (www.leevcb.com) model plan for hotel hurricane preparation and initial recovery.

- The Lee County Economic Development Office site for hurricane preparation registration located at www.leecountybusiness.com.

- The Lee County Emergency Management Web site, with weather updates, storm preparation tips, listings of upcoming seminars, links to the National Hurricane Center, and updated shelter information at www.leeeoc.com.

- The National Oceanic & Atmospheric Administration at www.noaa.com.

At SHRS, preparation for Hurricane Charley began on August 11, 2004. Instructions were delivered to each guestroom, alerting guests that the region had been placed under a hurricane watch and that if the county's Emergency Management Agency issued a hurricane warning, they would be encouraged to leave the resort. All team members were given specific instructions by department, some of which are listed in Exhibit 1.

A hurricane warning was issued on August 12, 2004. Jim Cantore of The Weather Channel made an appearance at the resort, requesting permission to do live coverage from the coastline of the SHRS property. Senior management declined the opportunity, intuitively sensing that this type of coverage was not necessarily beneficial to the resort's business interests. Mr. Cantore was, however, influential in prompting senior management's decision to begin evacuating on the afternoon of August 12—24 hours before Hurricane Charley would potentially arrive. A well-known storm tracker, Mr. Cantore was generous in sharing his experience and wisdom and advised that with the ever-increasing probability of severe weather, an immediate evacuation made the most sense.

Team members helped with guest evacuation and all guests were asked to leave the premises by 6 P.M. All team members with the exception of a six-person storm team (two executives, two engineers, and two security personnel) were then excused to allow them time to adequately prepare their own homes for the threatening weather event.

Exhibit 1   Hurricane Preparation Instructions for SHRS Team Members

Executive Office

- Assemble department heads and discuss preparedness and emergency inventories.
- Prepare advisory letters for hotel guests.
- Contact nearby resorts for occupancy levels and placement of possible evacuated guests.
- Identify emergency shelter locations and capacities in the event that evacuation becomes necessary.
- Place hurricane maps with shelter location detail in rooms and other common areas.
- Decide who will stay on-resort in the event suspension of operations becomes apparent.
- Place all salaried managers on standby status.

Reservations/Sales/Conference Planning

- Prepare lists and contact phone numbers of all incoming groups for the next seven days each day during the hurricane watch and warning.

Engineering

- Check resort grounds for loose objects such as dead branches, loose coconuts, etc.
- Recheck emergency supplies.
- Check grounds for possible drainage problems.
- Top off fuel/diesel tanks.
- Check generators.
- Prepare sandbags for low lying access points.

Purchasing

- Check fresh water supplies and food stores.
- Supply fresh water for the six-person storm team for a week if an evacuation is required.

Audiovisual

- Make available a video camera for insurance inventory.

Security

- Check such emergency supplies as batteries, flashlights, and other items recommended for a hurricane kit.

Sunsports/Princess Captain

- Make a decision about stowage of the boats at a safe harbor marina. Contact identified marinas each day for hours of operation and available capacity.

Many hurricanes form strong outer bands and most develop a diameter spanning more than 100 miles. Most, if not all, team members lived within 40 miles of the resort. Hence, any severe storm system or major hurricane that potentially could threaten SHRS real estate would pose a threat to the homes of SHRS team members. This threat was realized by senior management and helped validate the decision to evacuate in sufficient advance of the storm.

Throughout this case study, we will share many of the lessons learned by the managers, team members, and owners of SHRS. One of the many lessons learned by senior management was to act decisively and not wait until the very last minute to execute an evacuation plan. When faced with the challenges associated with an approaching hurricane, leadership must rely on a comprehensive hurricane plan. It is critical for senior management to take ownership and ensure that the plan is dynamic and constantly evolving to the next level of best practices. Hotel operators have many binders filled with emergency plans and they must make sure that such valuable information does not merely sit on shelves and collect dust.

Preparation should include a thorough review of insurance coverage well in advance of the storm threat. While it is important to understand the adequacy of coverage and various sub-limits within the policy, it is equally vital to procure coverage that protects team members. It is inconceivable that a resort could resume operations, restore the real estate, and ensure successful business recovery without team member engagement.

At approximately 3:45 P.M. on August 13, 2004, Hurricane Charley came ashore within a mile of SHRS. The storm team sheltered itself on the mezzanine level of the main hotel, an area that was constructed of concrete block with few windows. The primary risk on the mezzanine level was the laundry hatch, which flew open during the storm. When the hurricane cleared, the storm team emerged to do an initial evaluation of damage.

Recovery

In some instances, a storm can pass through an area and cause little or no damage to the real estate and/or business operations. Unfortunately, it is difficult to forecast the impact or potential physical damage that a storm can cause to a coastal property with seven buildings spread out over 85 acres of mangrove forest. During preparation, each building was treated like an independent asset and the step-by-step hurricane emergency plan was administered to all areas. As the storm team surveyed the damage, it was evident that preparing for the worst had been wise. The main entry road was blocked by downed ficus trees that once had provided an elegant and stately canopy over the entry boulevard. Power lines were down and debris from building destruction was everywhere.

Management immediately engaged a landscape company and assigned it to remove debris. A crew arrived with chain saws to clear the drive into the resort. An early lesson learned was the importance of ready access to chain saws and generators, especially when sited on a beautiful and densely treed property that is susceptible to downed branches, trunks, and power lines. Many properties use electric golf carts to move goods, service staff, and even guests around resorts. Another lesson learned was the need to have gas-powered golf carts and/or other utility vehicles when electricity is not available or in short supply.

Although SHRS had developed a detailed hurricane plan that assisted in evacuating guests and securing property, it became apparent that post-storm recovery had been addressed in a way that did not envision such serious destruction. The lesson learned is that the recovery process requires in-depth planning and should draw on the knowledge of people who have firsthand experience with severe hurricane damage.

In the aftermath of Hurricane Charley, the resort's mission statement continued to be a galvanizing force. More than ever before, the words of the mission statement would require strong action and a renewed commitment to core values. Resort management was motivated to achieve a higher form of leadership in response to the crisis. The management team faced a series of challenges that was unlike anything it had experienced before the loss.

The goal for the management team was to find a meaningful solution to each problem. The extensive hurricane damage created a new set of challenges that required a different way of thinking. One of the initial decisions was to carefully evaluate the value proposition of the resort, ensuring that the SHRS brand of service and quality would be restored to pre-storm standards. Since all of the facilities had been compromised, the August 12 version of SHRS no longer existed and there were many discussions about how best to reopen with all amenities restored and operational. To protect the brand, it was important that all elements of the value proposition be well orchestrated. It became obvious that the effort required resources and skills beyond the scope of a normal resort operation.

Although some of the marina assets, like the Sanibel Princess, were not damaged directly, the dock structures that provided yacht access had to be totally restored. While the spa building sustained less damage, it was located at the far end of the property and access was difficult, resulting in a substandard sense of arrival. Therefore, the business strategy was to accelerate the restoration work while SHRS remained closed and to reopen the resort as a total offering rather than as a piecemeal set of services and products.

SHRS had many real estate components that were critical to the value proposition of the resort, most of which were damaged significantly by Hurricane Charley. The once-beautiful grounds were nearly decimated and most of the buildings were badly damaged. Throughout the property, the roofing systems and many of the glass sliders and windows were destroyed, which compromised the building envelope during the storm. Essentially, the buildings had been breached and had become vulnerable to extensive water damage.

The contents, also referred to as personal property, of the buildings were destroyed, badly damaged, or compromised. Anything worth salvaging still required much attention, especially to restore it to pre-loss condition. Many of the interior design elements throughout the property represented a collection of many years worth of improvements and few would be easily duplicated.

During the most recent refurbishment of 240 guestrooms in 2003, a very popular tropical/botanical scheme had been implemented, but only in the primary tower units. The design process for the 2003 refurbishment had taken more than five months, beginning with initial design in February 2002 through the completion of the model room in July 2002. Given a best-case scenario of 20 weeks to get comparable furniture, it was quickly determined that using a ready-made design scheme for the rest of the resort was the most economical approach. The economic rewards for acting decisively in order to reopen by high season outweighed the risk of spending months figuring out how to replicate years' worth of design that was in place before the hurricane.

The forced changes to the real estate components precipitated changes to the SHRS value proposition. The physical changes required SHRS sales and marketing executives to recreate alignment between the real estate, the business recovery, and the value proposition to the customer. After senior management determined that it was possible to restore the real estate and related business operation by February 1, 2005, a new marketing vision was needed. This new vision had to encompass a resilient recovery campaign and promote the promise that SHRS would come back better than ever.

Working with Vendors

Approximately 50 of the resort's condominium units, though damaged, remained usable for emergency personnel. This allowed the resort to house vendors and key leadership on-site and contributed to rebuilding in record time. The food and beverage team set up a commissary in a conference room that had been stripped down to concrete floors and walls. The team fed as many as 1,000 people each day, including the resort's own team members and outside contractors. There were approximately 200 painters from Texas, 75 contractors from Tampa, and hundreds of others, including designers, architects, landscapers, insurance administrators and adjusters, safety and security officers, and project managers.

Accelerating the restoration in order to resume revenue generation became the primary objective for resort leadership. Therefore, qualified vendors with a proven track record were contracted immediately rather than after a lengthy traditional bid process. In radical times, it may be necessary for finance, accounting and purchasing managers to move away from traditional thinking. In any business crisis situation, the costs of remaining closed for a longer period need to be weighed against the reward of opening as soon as possible.

It is important to remember that Charley was the first of four hurricanes to strike Florida within six weeks. Had the leadership of SHRS not acted quickly to secure contract resources, they would have been competing with many other businesses throughout the state requiring the same construction workers and materials. Because SHRS contracted services and supplies within two to three weeks, they were able to move the restoration ahead much more quickly than competing properties. Acting swiftly and decisively helped mitigate the risks associated with scarcity of resources.

The Role of Mutual Aid

Early in the recovery process, the resort drew on resources provided by the parent company, Liberty Mutual. Liberty Mutual provided a qualified corporate emergency response team (CERT). A CERT is responsible for business continuity and guidance during emergency situations.

People who are not drained from their personal devastation as well as the destruction on-property are better able to step into the fray knowing their families are safe and comfortable in a distant setting. A lesson learned was the importance of injecting positive energy into a crisis situation. Few would argue about the difficulty of staying positive when returning home to an unstable environment without potable water, electricity, air-conditioning, or refrigeration in a sweltering environment. While the arrival of support resources can provide reassurance to residents that help is on the way, seeing the National Guard patrolling the streets is not an indication that all is well.

Mutual aid is defined by the Florida Division of Emergency Management as "a written agreement between agencies and/or jurisdictions that they assist one another on request, by furnishing personnel, equipment, and/or expertise in a specific matter." While mutual-aid agreements typically are used by the public sector, resort hotels would be wise to develop the same kind of assistance agreements. There are several areas within resort operations where mutual-aid agreements could prove beneficial, particularly human resources, media relations, and marketing. In the aftermath of a serious disaster, these departments could use expert assistance, especially while their team members see to their own personal situations. Even if employee homes are not damaged, it is wise to provide an opportunity for team members to leave the area of destruction temporarily and return with renewed energy.

The mutual aid provided by Liberty Mutual included critical supplies like radios, additional cellular phones, and hard hats for all team members needing access to restricted areas. Knowledge and experience with disaster recovery, particularly construction management resources, contributed greatly to the local effort. SHRS's mission to take care of people was in clear evidence. As the entire community was adversely affected by the storm, some team members had an added incentive to come back to work. Because the resort had been equipped with emergency power, water, and limited air-conditioning, it would offer more basic physical comforts than their own homes for many weeks to come.

Through Liberty Mutual, leaders were able to locate and supply the resort with additional generators and diesel fuel, both essential as the recovery moved forward in the first few weeks. Liberty Mutual also procured the services of a professional security firm and several highly trained security officers were immediately deployed to assist in disaster recovery and safety issues. Members of Liberty Mutual's CERT team had extensive experience in matters relating to disasters and insurance coverage and were able to provide clarity on recovery related issues.

Changing Team Member Roles

Fortunately, the SHRS insurance policy included ordinary payroll coverage for the period of business interruption. Procuring insurance coverage to protect the employees helped to avert what otherwise would have been an enormous problem. Instead of losing valuable team members due to the suspension of operations, the resort was able to keep employees working during the time required for the physical recovery.

With so many problems to address, engaging all team members in the restoration process became the most critical component of the business recovery effort. With the team members on board, management identified three major initiatives:

1. Thoroughly assess the damage and set forth a realistic target date for the resort to be restored. The phrase "stake in the ground" became the common mantra and the target date for resuming operations became February 1, 2005.

2. Identify what additional value-added projects could be completed by February 1, 2005, especially while the resort was closed, to ensure that the resort could be promoted as "better than ever" upon resumption of operations.

3. Create and execute a comprehensive business recovery plan with initiatives that would ensure that the resort team could enjoy an accelerated return to stabilized occupancy once the real estate restoration campaign was completed.

The recovery component of the resort's hurricane plan required the executive team to assess damage and risk with an emphasis on safety issues for the team members. The executives and a select group of team members conducted room-by-room assessments and completed a thorough damage analysis. Team members were selected to assess damage according to their familiarity with the resort area and their specific expertise. They were equipped with clipboards and cameras and their assigned task was to communicate the level of damage by providing a detailed list and photographs for executive management.

Within three days, resort management began to bring back many hourly team members as the employees' personal situations allowed. These people were asked to assist in both the damage assessment and initial cleanup. In the immediate aftermath of the storm, many team members returned to work despite some enormous personal challenges associated with damage to their own property.

With operations suspended for at least five months, it was a challenge to strategically engage and involve front-line team members in tasks that would add value to the recovery. With no guests to serve, many positions became temporarily obsolete. What does a bellperson, concierge, boat captain, or massage therapist do during suspension of regular operations at a world-class resort that is now a disaster area?

Fortunately, some team members' core responsibilities continued. Exhibits 2 and 3 show SHRS's organization charts before and after Hurricane Charley. Such internal support services such as human resources, payroll, accounting, security and engineering resumed almost immediately. While the restaurants were now closed, many food and beverage team members were still needed to support the recovery. The difference was that guests now wore hard hats and steel-toed boots rather than spa robes, bathing suits, or golf shoes.

Front-desk personnel found themselves cleaning landscape debris or tearing down water-soaked walls in the early days of the recovery. The marketing staff inventoried and moved all of the salvageable artwork. The executive team moved furniture, linen, and several thousand pillows from temporary storage in a meeting room to an off-site warehouse. For more than five months, team members found themselves without guests to serve or routines to follow.

Exhibit 2   SHRS Pre-Hurricane Organization Chart

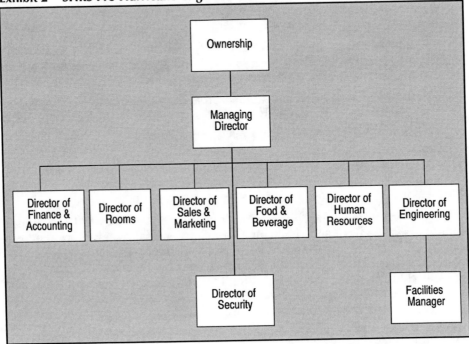

Every day created a new challenge and a change in responsibility. Keeping team members involved in the physical, emotional, and intellectual recovery process became a daily challenge. The role of leadership was to identify meaningful tasks that would enhance the recovery effort and engage staff in the importance of their ever-changing roles. One lesson learned was that the most versatile people were also the most valuable to the recovery process.

Establishing Storm Compensation and Related Benefits. An innovative action initiated by the SHRS human resource team was the development of an equitable compensation plan for those workers who reported gratuities. Management took the average of reported gratuities from the previous 12 months and incorporated that amount in the computation of employee's "storm rate" of pay. Normal vacation and other benefits also continued to accrue for employees during the time the resort was under repair. These actions continued to reinforce the organization's mission of taking care of its team.

Respect for the team member role in the future of the resort was clearly demonstrated when the next storm struck Haiti. Several team members had family who perished in the hurricane. The resort management worked with Liberty Mutual's corporate travel office to provide plane tickets so these employees could return to assist their loved ones, now suffering an even more serious catastrophe. A humbling lesson learned was that no matter how difficult and stressful the resort's recovery appeared, it paled in contrast to the suffering being experienced

Exhibit 3   SHRS Post-Hurricane Organization Chart

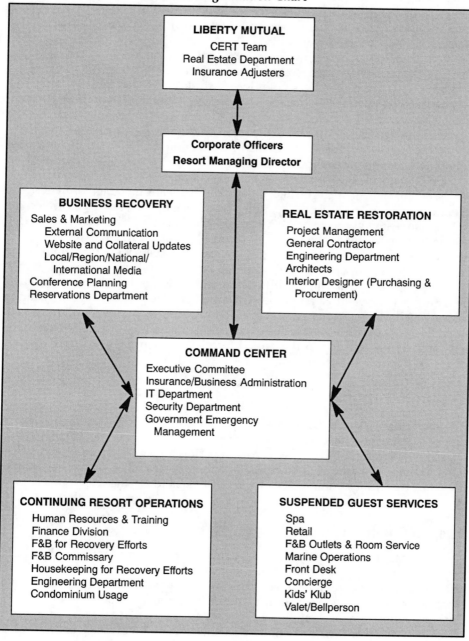

in Haiti as a result of Hurricane Jeanne and then the devastating tsunami that killed more than 200,000 people in Southeast Asia. Resort employees collectively contributed to the recovery effort in both instances.

Celebrating the Recovery. As the holidays approached in 2004, senior management wrestled with how to continue the tradition of hosting a holiday party for the team members. After evaluating the costs and logistics of holding the event elsewhere, it was determined that SHRS could still host this event for more than 500 people. Absent plush carpet, wall covering, artwork, landscaping, and anything else that typifies an upscale resort, the team relied on human spirit to inspire the holiday event. Team members volunteered to decorate the ballroom that had become the commissary for the recovery workers, looking beyond the concrete floors and construction elements to capture the spirit of the season. Much like the characters in "A Charlie Brown Christmas," team members managed less-than-optimal resources and turned a disaster/construction site into a venue for a most joyous and memorable event.

On January 31, 2005, still without a ballroom due to last-minute construction issues, senior management hosted a pep rally for team members of SHRS. The event was held in the basement parking area. Together, everyone celebrated the historic reopening of the resort. With guests scheduled to arrive on the following day, most team members had worked feverishly in the days and weeks prior to ensure a successful reopening. Most of the team members were tired but excited about the prospect of opening and resuming their former jobs.

The pep rally was filled with cheers and ovations for every contributor, including outside vendors and resort departments. There was a ragtime band to set the tone throughout the event. Great food, ice cream, and entertainment captured the spirit of the recovery. The event culminated with a special tribute to the men and women serving in the armed forces and team members and vendors joined to sing the national anthem.

Communications

Communication is perhaps the most critical dimension of organizational behavior during a crisis. One core element for preparation, survival, and recovery success is effective communication. The seed for preparing a comprehensive communications response must be planted in the planning process. The plan must include how the organization communicates with *all* stakeholders since communication is vital to recovery.

Internal Communications

Communication with employees must begin long before a crisis affects a hotel. The organization must have a culture of communication in place that promotes trust and security among team members. This trust begins with the organization's mission statement. In the case of SHRS, the mission statement includes language about the hotel's commitment to employees. The statement speaks to the responsibility of all employees to exceed one another's expectations. Identifying employees as stakeholders provides a foundation for building trust, which is fundamental in ensuring employee loyalty following a natural disaster.

SHRS had in place a comprehensive communications plan to prepare for a storm event. This plan included a system for communicating with executive, management, and hourly employees in the post-storm period. The resort had established an emergency toll-free number call-in system that was provided through Liberty Mutual headquarters in Boston. One of the lessons learned was that it is important to have multiple modes of communication in place. In the immediate aftermath of the storm, only one cellular service remained operational. That single connection now provided the resort's only line to civilization. Had the resort not had multiple cellular phone contracts, there would have been no reliable mode of communication to the toll-free service, the home office, or the employees who soon would be needed. Handheld mobile radio devices and laptop computers were additional communication technology that soon became essential.

SHRS human resources attempted to contact all 550 employees to determine possible injury and assess their personal situations. Many employees had to face significant damage to their homes, but none were injured. They were now concerned for their jobs and their livelihoods. They were asked to remain on standby and told they would be called in as needed.

During early communication, resort leaders assessed damage and worked with internal and external resources to understand the insurance coverage in place. Shortly thereafter, they were able to confirm that ordinary payroll coverage would pay employee wages during the suspension of operations. One of the difficult lessons learned was the need to communicate job security as quickly as possible. The success of the recovery depends on team members' physical and emotional engagement. Therefore, the sooner a corporation can reassure its workforce regarding continued employment and related income, the better.

Developing and Communicating the New Vision. Successful crisis leadership requires that management move the team beyond the daily mission of the organization. When catastrophic damage faces returning employees, leaders must engage team members in a new vision for the resort hotel. SHRS moved quickly to establish this vision. Because resort ownership had invested in business interruption insurance and coverage for ordinary payroll, it was well positioned to retain its loyal and hard-working team members. By emotionally engaging employees and assigning roles for improving and reopening the resort, leadership was able to use the human resource asset so readily available and so seldom used. The leadership team developed a new tag line for both internal and external marketing purposes. Team members now wore shirts emblazoned with the action-oriented phrase "Restoring Legends, Creating Memories." All team members were now engaged in the recovery process. This rapid shift kept a psychology of hopelessness from taking root among the employee group. By focusing on the human aspect of disaster recovery, SHRS was able to capitalize on this asset and assign employees to temporary and new responsibilities in an altered work environment.

Communications Training. One of the most innovative and visionary decisions made by the resort was to make an investment to increase productivity, ensuring a successful recovery once the restoration was complete. English language classes were provided for many of the Spanish and Creole speaking employees, while management learned basic skills in both languages to enable better communication with line employees. All team members spent time focusing on customer relationship development and service education, a true recognition of the value of the human resource asset of a resort property. Research in strategic management has demonstrated that investment in an employee's integrated knowledge of the organization's services and products can produce sustained competitive advantage.[3] The leadership team at SHRS supported this concept and recognized that, in order to return the resort to a competitive market position, both the physical and human infrastructures must be restored.

External Communications

The marketing team at SHRS also learned the importance of consistently communicating with key stakeholders outside the organization.

Meeting Planners. Marketing team members had worked diligently over the months before the storm to book business for the resort. They now had the heartbreaking task of calling other resorts to find a suitable alternate location for their clients. Although emotionally difficult, this care for the client's needs translated into solid long-term relationships with a core group of meeting planners. Where possible, the sales team tried to defer the meeting to a post-recovery date. Through coordination with The Beaches of Fort Myers & Sanibel Visitor and Convention Bureau, an effort was made to try to keep groups in the resort, the county, or at least in the southwest Florida region.

Dealing with the Media. In order to showcase the recovery successfully, sales and marketing executives needed new photography and new print and electronic collateral. Marketing personnel also had to update the various Web sites that served as SHRS distribution channels. Media and travel intermediaries typically require dated photography to demonstrate that the "story" that marketing personnel tells about the real estate represents reality. In the aftermath of a catastrophic event, public perception naturally is negative until there is conclusive evidence to the contrary. One of the best ways to reverse the negative perception caused by Hurricane Charley was to showcase a bold vision for restoration and recovery, supported with verifiable results in the form of pictures, collateral, and timely updates to the various Web sites serving SHRS distribution channels. All of these marketing initiatives were critical to the business recovery campaign, particularly to support the communication with media and travel intermediaries.

The director of sales and marketing was assigned to be the sole contact for local, state, and national media. This decision was consistent with the prestorm planning policy and served the resort well. Although the media was reasonably sympathetic with the plight of the resort and its valued employees, some journalists pushed to obtain contradictory responses to questions like "When do you think you will reopen?" A lesson learned was the value of allowing only one spokesperson to respond to media queries during the entire recovery. Management also invested time in keeping travel journalists apprised of the recovery process. It was important to recognize that these professionals would be helpful in influencing the leisure and convention market decision-makers once the resort was open for business.

Unplanned Opportunities

After determining the extent of damage and setting the course for restoring the damaged property to pre-loss condition, senior management tried to identify value-added business and/or real estate initiatives that could be undertaken during the suspension of operations. On the real estate front, an assessment of the five-year capital plan was examined to identify future projects that could be advanced while the resort was closed. With vast resources already mobilized and deployed on-site, there would be no better time to tackle the following:

- Repositioning the food and beverage operation by modifying the fit and finish of the floor and wall treatments and adding custom millwork to create more dynamic and more contemporary outlets.

- Upgrading the lobby areas by enhancing thousands of square feet of floor tile, installing a lobby fountain, and changing highly visible millwork surfaces, as well as artwork and lighting.

- Improving the sense of arrival by upgrading the porte cochere with custom millwork, new tile with impressive mosaic features, and improved lighting and furniture to offset what was lost because of landscape damage and ensure that the guest experience would remain first rate.

These initiatives, while not directly a part of the insurance claim, helped reduce the loss by improving marketing efforts dramatically.

On the business front, senior management discussed strategic initiatives that could build business value for SHRS, particularly by creating ways to improve team member productivity during the restoration period. Keeping the team members engaged in the real estate restoration and business recovery efforts would ensure success. The following are a few of the many initiatives that were implemented during the restoration period.

Retail Kiosks at Local Malls

Team members decided that the resort should offer spa products and other merchandise in these two high-visibility local malls. This also gave SHRS team members the opportunity to be out in the community in a highly visible location to let people know that SHRS would soon be back in business. Selling merchandise that otherwise would be in a warehouse also created cash flow.

Massage Therapy

Since the spa team members were not serving guests, they were engaged in providing five- to ten-minute shoulder massages to restoration workers in the commissary during lunch breaks. Leadership determined that this deployment supported the mission statement's commitment to helping others and served to maintain the engagement of the spa team members during the resort restoration period.

Training

Training has always been a central component of the SHRS mission statement. Resort leaders recognized an opportunity to supplement their existing programs to ensure a crisp return to operations on February 1, 2005. Establishing training as a top priority is always a challenge when guests are present. Programs typically include English language, wine knowledge, and progressive management development in upscale resort operations. Since there were no guests, training programs were well attended and well executed. Focusing on training helped solidify and fully engage all team members in preparation for reopening the resort.

Community Recognition

Community leaders were elated with SHRS's foresight and commitment to covering ordinary payroll, investing in training, and including team members in the recovery effort. High-level political and business leaders recognized the value of ensuring jobs for 550 local citizens. SHRS has been nominated for the prestigious Horizon Council Business of the Year Award. Further, *Gulfshore Life Magazine* recognized the resort's Managing Director, Brian Holly, as a nominee for person of the year for 2004. The property also was recognized publicly during the Lee County Visitor & Convention Bureau's 2004 "E" Awards that recognize front-line customer service employees in the hospitality industry. The countywide hospitality industry rose to its feet to pay tribute to the commitment of SHRS to its team members and to the community as a whole. Many large resort properties work hard to maintain community goodwill. Staying true to its mission by taking care of its team members has earned SHRS the respect of the community and its leaders.

Florida Gulf Coast University

A crisis of any kind provides a learning laboratory for higher education. The professors in the Resort & Hospitality Management (RHM) program at Florida Gulf Coast University recognized this opportunity and scheduled visits to SHRS so students were able to see the damage firsthand and follow the restoration's progress. The leaders of the resort were generous with their time and with their knowledge. RHM students were able to learn about the challenges involved in bringing a resort to full operation after a damaging hurricane. They met restoration team members and attended sessions outlining the complexity of the process.

Students gained firsthand experience in the restoration process and enjoyed the benefit of guest lecturers who presented the marketing strategy for reopening the resort and protecting the client base. This will serve the industry and these managers well in future crisis events.

Future Considerations

The Condo-Hotel Model

According to Robert MacLellan, Managing Director of MacLellan & Associates, "New hotel construction in the Eastern Caribbean is now clearly being driven by condo hotel type development with few conventional properties currently in planning. Regional banks are getting comfortable with this kind of business model."[4]

Throughout Florida, the Caribbean, and many other hurricane-vulnerable regions, we see this pattern evolving. It is apparent, based on a lesson learned with the SHRS experience, that serious research and consideration needs to focus on the structure of the agreements between condo-unit ownership associations and the managing hotel company. When it comes to authority to restore a building following hurricane damage, delineation of responsibility and accountability must be clear. The five hotel-controlled buildings on the SHRS site were restored and operational in less than six months. The repairs to the two association-controlled buildings are not yet complete a year after the hurricane incident. If, in fact, the condo hotel investment model is a popular vehicle for development of new properties, investors and hotel company partners need to have assurance that their operating and contractual documents address clear authority for decision-making regarding restoration. Waiting for low bids or scarce resources after a serious storm event could jeopardize the long-term viability of a condo hotel.

Planning for Employees in Suspended Operational Units

A lesson learned was the need to plan training that could be implemented during the suspension of regular operations to take full advantage of the opportunities at hand. SHRS used innovative thinking to train front-line employees who would play a role in rapid business recovery. In hindsight, it might have been possible for team members to use their time more productively. The spa team potentially could learn a whole new, more competitive area of spa technology, key food and beverage employees could audit cuisine management courses offered in local universities, or IT team members could similarly update their certifications and skills. Resorts that have secured business interruption and ordinary payroll insurance coverage have an opportunity to maximize the utility of these paid employees by implementing training programs and other educational opportunities during the closure period. This helps to improve the quality of the workforce upon reopening, and also helps to mitigate the overall insurance claim by restoring operations more quickly. Consideration should be given to a recovery training plan that addresses how employees who typically work directly with guests will be used during the restoration phase.

Mutual-Aid Agreements

This case demonstrates the value of mutual aid received by SHRS from its parent company, Liberty Mutual. Many resorts and hotels do not have such resources available. It would be wise for resorts and hotels with limited corporate resources to include in their crisis preparation programs potential partners who could be engaged in a mutual-aid agreement.

Most large resort hotels have a public relations unit, a marketing team, IT support personnel and other skilled professionals who have expertise in their specific areas. In a crisis, team members often face months of life in an area of destruction, both at home and at work. Leadership would be wise to consider a planned arrangement that would exchange staff with a sister property. Such an exchange potentially could offer relief and temporary escape to the team members of the damaged property and also provide a unique learning experience for employees coming from unaffected properties. The lesson learned is that mutual aid deserves further discussion, research, and planning on the part of affiliated resort properties and their leaders.

Conclusion

An investment usually is characterized as an outlay of some form of currency in order for investors to realize income or profit. There is little doubt that the real estate in this case study required enormous investment, both financial and human.

In cases where real estate assets are badly damaged, insurance proceeds serve as the reinvestment and generally provide the fuel for the real estate restoration. In the case of SHRS, the injured business component required more than money. It required the dedication of an inspired workforce—an investment of a different kind. It also required the leadership vision that led to the successful and rapid restoration and excited both guests and team members. The resort's attention to the well-being of its team members has won accolades from the local community.

The demonstrated value of business interruption insurance and the business interruption subset known as ordinary payroll coverage should be recognized. Other major resorts in the area face many months of closure and lost revenue and have lost all of their valued front-line employees as a result of Charley's damage. SHRS is the *only* major resort that has successfully completed restoration following the storm at the time this book goes to press.

The overall lesson learned is the importance of decisive action and doing the right things for the right reasons. Evacuating early rather than later upheld the SHRS mission as energy was focused on protecting both guests and team members. Recognition and understanding of the lifetime value of the customer as an asset helped clarify this decision for the resort's leadership. Valuing team members as important corporate assets made early evacuation essential.

The decision was made to fully restore the resort and to reopen as quickly as possible by securing all available and necessary resources. Since reopening, the resort has enjoyed a record booking pace by securing group market business that would have been greatly compromised without the decisive action of leadership and the dedication of all concerned.

Endnotes

1. David Beirman, *Restoring Tourism Destinations in Crisis: A Strategic Marketing Approach* (Cambridge, Mass.: CABI Publishing, 2003), p. 4.

2. Christopher K. Bart, "Mission Matters," *CAmagazine*, March 1998, p. 31, available online at www.camagazine.com/multimedia/camagazine/Library/EN/1998/Mar//e_d2.pdf.

3. Jeffrey Harrison and Cathy Enz, *Hospitality Strategic Management* (Hoboken, N.J.: Wiley, 2005), p. 77.

4. "New Approach for Condo-Style Hotels," *e-hotelier.com*, May 24, 2005, available online at http://ehotelier.com/browse/news_more.php?id=A5182_0_11_0_M.